A Social History of Leisure
Since 1600

A Social History of Leisure Since 1600

Gary Cross
The Pennsylvania State University

VENTURE PUBLISHING, INC.
STATE COLLEGE, PA 16803

Cover Photo: "The Croquet Craze," Mr. Bush, Harper's Weekly, 1866

Chapter Opening Photographs:
1. "Coasting Party at Coney Island," Frank Leslie's Illustrated, 1886.
2. "Festival Scene,"Daniel Hopfer, 1500s.
3. "Cockpit Fight," William Hogarth, 1759.
4. "The Ducking Stool," A. Earl, 1896.
5. "The Gin Shop," George Cruickshank, 1839.
6. "Poster of British Gas Workers," by permission from Her Majesty's Stationary Office, 1890s.
7. "The Drunkard's Progress," Currier and Ives, 1846.
8. "A Victorian Christmas," Allison-Shelley Collection, courtesy of The Pennsylvania State University.
9. "Chicago Poolroom," Harper's Weekly, 1882.
10. "Yale vs. Princeton Thanksgiving Day Football Game," Harper's Weekly, 1879.
11. "The Darling Cartoon," J. N. Darling, courtesy of The University of Iowa Libraries, 1933.
12. "The Father and Daughter Listening to the Radio," J. Delano, with permission from Farm Security Administration Collection, 1942.
13. "The Jitterbuggers," Washington, DC Elks Club, 1942.
14. "The Pensioners at the Trailer Court in Florida," with permission from Farm Security Administration, 1941.

Copyright © 1990
Venture Publishing, Inc.
1640 Oxford Circle
State College, PA 16803
All rights reserved

Cover Design by Janice Gardner
Production Supervisor Bonnie Godbey
Design by Susan McDade
Library of Congress Catalogue Number 90-70208
ISBN 0-910251-35-5

Gary Cross is a comparative historian at The Pennsylvania State University and in recent years has written extensively on the modern history of leisure and work. He is author of *A Quest for Time: The Reduction of Work in Britain and France* (University of California Press, 1989) and is editor of *Worktime and Industrialization: An International History* (Temple University Press, 1988) and *Worktowners at Blackpool: Mass-Observation and Popular Leisure in the 1930s* (Routledge, 1990). He is currently preparing a comparative study presently titled "Dilemmas of Free Time: 'Democratic Leisure' in the First Half of the Twentieth Century."

Table of Contents

FRANK LESLIE'S
ILLUSTRATED
NEWSPAPER

No. 1,606.—Vol. LXII.]　　　NEW YORK—FOR THE WEEK ENDING JULY 24, 1886.　　　[Price, 10 Cents.

SUMMER DIVERSIONS AT THE SEASIDE.—A COASTING PARTY AT CONEY ISLAND—"MORE SCARED THAN HURT."
FROM A SKETCH BY A STAFF ARTIST.—SEE PAGE 378.

1

Introduction: Why a Social History of Leisure?

Among the ironies of contemporary life is the ambiguity many feel about leisure. Modern people congratulate themselves for creating an economy that has freed the masses from the drudgery of endless hours of work, and many are proud of the varied choices that leisure time has brought.[1] Yet others lament that increased free time has undermined a commitment to competitive work and has led to an untrained, even unrestrained, pursuit of pleasure. An unintended consequence of industrialization, according to this view, is a mass hedonism that threatens western economic and cultural influence in the world. Still others express disappointment that the masses have failed to utilize their free time for personal and social growth and instead have become enslaved to a new tyrant: no longer is that master the parasitical feudal lord or slave-driving factory owner, but the manipulators of mindless consumption. And, if many intellectuals have been frustrated by the use of free time, many too have questioned the practical extent of that liberation from care and work. Contemporary people are a "harried leisure class," burdened by endless demands placed on their free time and, because of commuting, family and other responsibilities, deprived of choice in many hours liberated from the job. In numerous ways, leisure has become work.[2]

It is no surprise then that leisure, like work, is among the most value-laden of concepts. Some refuse its use to those who merely "recreate"—rest and engage in activities which compensate for work. These modern thinkers, following Aristotle, insist that the term leisure be reserved to the disinterested cultivation of personality. Others argue that leisure is no more than a product of economic/cultural power. Social class largely determines leisure choices and economic systems control the range and distribution of recreational activities. A more optimistic outlook is that modern leisure is a concrete form of individualism, valued because it is activity freed from the control of church (or other authority) and natural necessity.[3]

In the midst of so much disagreement about contemporary leisure, what can the historian contribute to the discussion? First and foremost, history can try to set the past record straight. Much of the ambiguity felt toward leisure concerns thinking about how play has changed: about what has been lost and gained. And, ideology naturally colors the glasses from which we see the past. My task is not so much to provide a "value free" history (for I too have biases); rather it is to offer a reasonably concrete picture of how leisure has changed. It is important to know when and why people stopped watching cock fights or started listening to radio. It is also worthwhile to understand when and why leisure behavior took major changes of course. I argue that these transformations have mostly taken place since the 16th century. Whatever your assessment of contemporary leisure may be, it can only be understood in the context of the stream of history.

Perhaps the greatest problem is that historians have seldom shown much interest in the question of explaining people's use of free time. Until recently, most historians have studied the deeds of politicians, generals, intellectuals, and perhaps businessmen. The scope of people's free time was "private" and cordoned off from serious historical inquiry. To be sure, leisure has had a place in the study of everyday life and popular culture. But scholars have usually undertaken these topics for ulterior purposes—like the study of class, gender, or political change. As a result, historians have neglected the story of the modern emergence of free time and the changing meaning of leisure as an activity of intrinsic value.

So what use is history? One answer is that the subdiscipline of *social* history has frequently filled the gap left by more traditional approaches. In recent years, social historians have explored those private sides of history, family, community, and work that had been so long neglected; and they have increasingly linked these social spheres to popular culture, much of which is leisure. People at play are obviously part of a wider society of work, family, religion, and even political power. These broad relationships are surely central to an understanding of the changing meanings of leisure.

This is not to suggest that leisure is merely a function of the prevailing economic/political system. Play may well have been a means of "social control" or a part of the social construction of gender and class roles.[4] Leisure was doubtless often a vehicle for one group to protest the dominance of another. How else do we explain the popularity of traditional festivals that mocked authority? Play was also a reflection of technology and the physical environment, of how necessity determined the time and character of leisure. However, the history of leisure was also created by people and is not merely the effect of social or economic forces. Play was often an agent of social change, not only a consequence. And, in order to understand the varieties of leisure, it is perhaps most important that we understand that specific people *enjoyed* leisure activities—cock fights as well as theater.

We can understand the play of people of vastly different societies because it has something in common with our own pleasures—desire for variety, intimacy, and freedom from anxiety, for example. Yet historical societies shaped that play in ways that make it seem strange to us precisely because it came from a very foreign social context. Rural festivals make sense to us; but we are not tempted to revive them precisely because our social lives are so different from that of peasants.

How do we begin to understand the influence of these social/historical factors upon the scope and meaning of play? Most modern social historians agree that the industrialization of Western economies is the critical factor. Commonly, if crudely, modern social history is divided into preindustrial, industrializing, and consumer phases. The same categorizations may be applied to the closely linked phenomenon of leisure. Thus we speak of the modernization of play.

This approach poses three potential problems: first, our understanding of preindustrial and industrializing societies is far more complete than is the history of consumer society—in large part because the latter is still emerging.

Second, modernization theory implies the very sort of determinism that I have just rejected. It suggests that countries inevitably move through these phases like an organism and that change is simply the effect of technology or economic "rationalization." This book will try to present a more balanced picture: it will stress the role of movements and, occasionally, of individuals in the shaping of modern leisure. It will show the debates, doubts, and conflicts that accompanied this history.

The third problem of modernization theory is that it tends to gloss over national differences; no one can deny that Americans played differently in their preindustrial phase than did Europeans or that regional culture and environment shaped the quantity and quality of free time. Most modern historians analyze the evolution of nations. There are many reasons for doing this. The difficulty comes, of course, when American or European historians mistake a characteristic common to most preindustrial societies as a "national trait." For example, the proclivity of colonial Americans to gamble or drink heavily might be attributed to American character, when, with variations, this behavior was common throughout the peasant societies of Europe. The opposite error is just as important, finding a universal truth in the "accidents" of colonial America or Edwardian England.

The work of sorting out the national from the general pattern can be done only when leisure is studied comparatively. I have chosen two countries— the United States and Great Britain—for my comparison. Given the fact that their histories frequently touched, it is no surprise that their leisure histories had much in common. Yet many factors made them different: physical environment, immigration (and emigration), and contrasting economic histories, for example.

I picked these two countries for several reasons. Naturally, English-speaking readers are most interested in their own leisure history. I regret that I cannot give much space to the unique character of other English-speaking areas.

Moreover, there is a relatively rich historic literature dealing with these two countries from which to draw. At times, I will be obliged to emphasize the experience of one country over the other because of the uneven character of this research. I will stress English leisure rather more in the earlier periods and American play patterns slightly more in the later years. If the 18th and much of the 19th centuries were the years of British economic and cultural dominance, much of the 20th was the American century. Finally, I selected these two countries because they both played such an innovative role in the history of modern leisure. Spectator sports and the Boy Scouts as well as the amusement park and the television sit-com were mostly inventions of Anglo-Americans. The study of the play of these two countries is hardly a substitute for a general history of modern leisure, yet it is a practical surrogate.

This will be an integrative, not a descriptive history of play, isolated from the rest of social experience. As sociologists of leisure frequently point out, play cannot be understood apart from work, family, community, and technology.[5] Political pressures also shaped the modern formation of pleasure. At times, the reader may wonder what a passage has to do with leisure. But I hope that the connection will soon become clear. Some may have a greater personal interest in either the American or British experience. I hope, however, that a look at both sides may give you insights into your own leisure patterns as well as broaden your perspective on other cultures. This book has packed much history into relatively few pages. It must gloss over a great deal of fascinating detail. Notes provide a guide for further reading.

This book may not resolve the ambiguity that many feel about contemporary leisure, but I hope that it will clarify some of the issues.

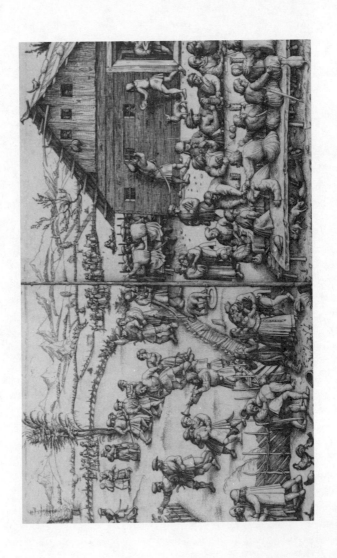

2

Traditional Society and the Place of Leisure

Telling the story of how people played in the past may seem to be a relatively straightforward task. Yet, to get beneath bare description and the distortions of common assumptions about the past, we must consider two problems.

First, there is no consensus about the "world we have lost" of our ancestors. Many share the view of the 17th century philosopher, Thomas Hobbes, who believed the life of the past was "nasty, mean, brutish and short." To this group the "bad old days" were filled with war, early and unpredictable death, oppression, and most of all, unstinted work. According to this view there was scarcely any time for leisure. The sociologist of recreation, Joffre Dumazedier, paints a picture of "traditional" leisure as throttled by religious and family controls, with no room for individual expression. A recent historian agrees: the social demands of elders and clergy and the unpredictability of life produced a "siege mentality" and a "general psychological atmosphere of distance, manipulation, and deference...."[1]

Yet others have argued the opposite. In the 19th-century, British labor leaders told factory workers that before industrialization, Englishmen worked no more than eight hours per day; the medieval King Alfred had established the right of "freeborn" Englishmen to the three-eights division of the day into work, rest, and leisure. Some contemporary historians also lean toward this point of view. One scholar writes of 17th century England as a time "when the whole of life went forward in the family in a circle of loved, familiar faces, known and fondled objects, all of human size."[2]

This conflict over the reality of traditional life is, at least, as old as the modern discipline of history. Since the 18th century, thinkers have disputed the gains and losses of modernity. If the Enlightenment believed that the world was inevitably improving over the "Dark Ages" of the past, the Romantics of the early 19th century were less certain of the benefits of individualism, science, and industry. In many ways this debate is still going on. It reflects as much our ambiguity towards our own world as our uncertainty about how our ancestors really lived.

There is a second problem to be confronted before we consider premodern leisure. There is much confusion about what is *traditional*. When most of us think of the traditional world, we really picture a relatively modern experience, often customs and attitudes that are less than two hundred years old. The traditional Sunday family get-togethers and the circus under the big top are quite new, even if they are now passing from the scene. In the perspective of historians, these leisure forms are really modern, not only because of their comparative youth but because of their links to the rapid change that is so characteristic of 19th-century America and England. We, who live in the late 20th century, have far more in common with these traditional ways of life than with what preceded it.

Yet, even historians, who ought to have a firm grasp on the concept of the traditional, find it hard to pin down this notion. After all, its opposite, the *modern*, we are told, already appeared in the 1500s with the Protestant Reformation and still more in the late 1600s and 1700s with the Scientific, French, and Industrial Revolutions. Yet, outside of the urban centers, life had scarcely changed in 1800, or even much later, from how it was in the Middle Ages.

One striking example of this survival of the traditional is the case of the Cow's Head festival still celebrated in 1937 in West Houghton, a village in the Midlands of England. Like the festivals of the past, it was a four-day celebration, held the last week of August. The event was held in remembrance of a farmer, who finding a neighbor's cow caught in his fence, cut off the animal's head. By the 1930s, the tradition of parading a cow's head on a pole throughout town (with its undertones of a fertility rite) had disappeared and the custom of eating a cow's head was restricted to a few bars. Yet this village, which was only a few miles from the factory towns of Bolton and Wigan, continued to use the occasion for drinking and consuming pasties. What is also intriguing about this apparent holdover of rural myth in an industrial society is the fact that this seemingly archaic rural tradition dates only from 1815, well into the so-called modern age of industrialism when we should assume that leisure was being modernized. Tradition can, in fact, be "invented."[3] Obviously, premodern leisure cannot easily be fixed in chronological time.

How then do we get beyond our feelings about the present in our view of the past? And how do we divide the modern from the old world? There is no easy solution to these problems. There is no value-free history nor is there a sharp line that separates the two worlds. Perhaps the simplest way of approaching these problems is to begin by defining a series of economic, social, and cultural patterns which we will call "traditional." We apply this label because these patterns prevailed before the revolutions which, for many reasons, historians believe shaped the contemporary world. Yet we must keep in mind that these premodern ways of life often survived the radical transformations in religion, science, politics, and economics, which ultimately produced modern leisure forms.

Many historians argue that the "modern world" really begins only about 1800.[4] This is true especially if one focuses on the life of ordinary family. The dramatic struggles for empire and world exploration as well as the intellectual life of the elite, which take such a prominent place in the history of Europe between 1450 and 1800, played only an episodic role in lives of most the villagers. Far more important were the relatively unchanging facts of technology, family, and local society.

The Primacy of Technology

Key to an understanding of traditional life is the snail-pace of technological and economic change. To be sure, the 12th and 13th centuries brought water-and wind-powered grain mills and the vertical loom; the 14th century saw an hour clock; and the 15th century introduced printing and iron blast furnaces. Still, such innovations scarcely affected the 75 percent or more of the population whose lives were tied to hand tools and draught animals which had dominated agricultural life for centuries.[5] Farmers relied primarily on grain crops, the productivity of which had scarcely improved since their domestication in ancient times. Standards of living rose slowly and were repeatedly set back by famine and disease.[6]

Obviously, the lack of labor-saving devices meant that the hours of work often stretched from 5:00 AM to 8:00 PM or even 9:00 or 10:00 PM. Twelve or more hours of work per day was common; meal and rest breaks were pauses, not modern leisure. Iron founders and glass makers usually labored in 12 hours of continuous work seven days per week. And, of course, in most out-of-door occupations, work extended from sunup to sundown.[7] Artisans or craftsmen spent a majority of their income on food, in hard times up to 90 percent. There was little chance of saving for retirement or allowing the young the luxury of a work-free childhood. And, if few adults survived their sixtieth birthday, there was always an excess of youthful mouths to feed. In the 16th century, over 40 percent of the population of Italian towns was under 16 years old and, as late as 1820, 48 percent of the population in Britain was under the age of 20. Small wonder that child's play was sacrificed to labor. For the poor, work often began at scarcely six years and apprenticeships regularly started at ten.[8]

Yet there was another side to technological backwardness. The pace of life was clearly not dictated by the speed of the machine or the demands of the market as it is today. Rather, nature's seasons organized the peasant's time. Plowing, seeding, and harvesting alternated with periods of relative inactivity. Working longer and harder than one's neighbor or parent hardly guaranteed one a better life. Dependence on the luck of weather and the soil's fertility made peasants fatalistic.

In the premodern world, a work ethic made little sense. Long days of work were often punctuated by moments of refreshment (often accompanied with beer or wine), games, or other play. From the 16th century, English merchants tried to tap this underutilized rural labor. They put farmers to work in the winter spinning yarn or weaving cloth. This so-called putting-out system, however, frequently frustrated merchants. For, if rural labor was cheaper than urban workers, the episodic and slow pace of agricultural work made these part-time peasant artisans undisciplined and unreliable producers. They not only freely abandoned craft work to tend to farm animals or crops, but found the regular pace of industrial work psychologically unacceptable. This preindustrial work culture of peasants still plagues those manufacturers who attempt to utilize cheap rural labor throughout the world.

To be sure, the seasonal character of farm labor meant long working hours in Spring and especially from late June until the end of September. During the harvest in England, even the village blacksmith and landowning gentry would join in the work, so important was the wheat, barley, and hay produced in this relatively unfavorable climate.

Yet there is another side of this story, the frequent holidays celebrated in the off-season. In France in 1700, there were about 84 holidays per year, not including (for those working out-of-doors) about the same number of days of idleness because of inclement weather. In 17th-century Paris, there were 103 holidays and in parts of northern Italy in the 16th-century the figure was about 95 (including Sundays). In 1552, The English Parliament attempted to restrict holidays (excluding Sunday) to 27 per year but met with much resistance in rural areas.[9]

Most of these work-free days were tied to the religious calender. But they were also spaced in the relative ebbs of the rural work year: All Soul's Day (or Halloween) and Guy Fawkes Day (November 5), Christmas to Shrove Tuesday (or Mardi Gras), and Easter to Whitsuntide (or Pentecost). Each of these featured specific customs: decorating churches with sprigs of birch trees and dressing up on Whit Sunday, for example. But during the days following a religious holiday there were also sometimes "horse parades, processions of trades' and benefit clubs; fairs, menageries, circuses and traveling shows; sports meetings for running, wrestling, cudgelling, boxing, cricket, and ....the climbing of a greased pole having a leg of mutton or other trophy on the top....." Shrove Tuesday (just before the onset of Lent) was the day of giving pancakes to children. Youths banged stones against the doors of villagers, while shouting.

English parish festivals or *wakes weeks* often occurred in the early or late summer. They celebrated the founding of the parish church. But, by the 17th century, they had largely lost their religious meaning except, perhaps, in the procession of children carrying rushes through the village to lay on the floor of the church. Wakes weeks were, in reality, a period of largely secular diversion—of sport, drinking, and dancing. They occurred mostly during lulls in the agricultural work cycle. Midsummer or St. John's Eve (June 23-24) largely served the same function with the added spectacle of midnight bonfires and dances.[10]

Holidays were also related to annual fairs, the traditional marketing of goods. Fairs sometimes specialized in livestock, cheese, hardware, or general goods. These annual gatherings of migratory merchants were essential in a rural

society, which lacked adequate retail shops or wholesale facilities to market
agricultural products. Other fairs were primarily for the annual hiring of young
farm servants. They often coincided with All-Soul's Day or Midsummer's Eve.

In the 18th century, at the English Stourbridge Fair, there were stalls
not only for the sale of practical goods but:

> Coffee-Houses, Taverns, Eating Houses, Music Shops, Buildings
> for the Exhibition of Drolls, Puppet Shews, Legerdemain,
> Mountebanks, Wild Beasts, Monsters, Giants, Rope Dancers,
> etc.... Besides the Booths, there are six or seven brick houses... and
> in any of which the Country People are accommodated with hot or
> cold Goose, roast or boiled Pork.

The oddities we associate with the traveling carnival or stalls at Blackpool and
other inexpensive seaside resorts were long customary in rural English fairs.
Wax figures of the famous and infamous, painted panoramas of historic events,
curiosities such as dwarfs, a thin man, pig-faced ladies, and people from exotic
places were all commonplace in fairs in the 17th century and much earlier. So
too were clowns, puppet shows, and gingerbread stalls. Hiring fairs especially
were noted for bringing together young men and women. Farm hands, complained one 18th century observer, "consider themselves as liberated from
servitude on this day; and, whether they be already hired, or really want masters," they rushed to the fairs. Men displayed their bravado in matches of
singlesticks and backswords as well as a variety of races; evenings would be
filled with dancing. The young coupled during such fairs: and if we note
village records, disproportionate numbers of babies were born nine months
following these festive periods.[11]

The character of the agricultural work year made for seasonal leisure
and the blending of work and play. Yet the constraints of nature or technology
also shaped the use of time by merchants and urban craftsmen. The speed of the
ox cart or sailing ship controlled the pace of business for the merchant and
producer. So slow were communications and so costly was the transportation
of goods and raw materials that few craftsmen or merchants had markets beyond
their own limited surroundings. The price of goods could easily double with a
50 mile overland journey to market. Thus craftsmen usually worked for
individual or custom order. Wealth was too scarce to be tied up or risked in
accumulating an inventory of manufactured goods. This meant that even the
industrial and commercial population worked on a seasonal basis when customers wanted shoes or clothing—and often at a pace that we moderns would find
downright lazy.

For merchant-manufacturers (who supplied raw materials to craftsmen
and marketed finished goods), profit came less from lowered production costs
and efficient hard work than from successful risk-taking and high markups in

relatively small luxury goods markets. Success or failure sometimes turned on the fate of a relatively fragile cargo ship sailing the high seas. Life was more of a gamble and less the reaping of the fruits of hard work. Small wonder that Virginia tobacco planters in the 17th century would wager half of their harvest on a horse race. Ordinary business might well be just as risky. This was even true of 17th century Puritan merchants in New England, whose business dealings in sugar, slaves, and naval stores were strung out over months of waiting between the coming and going of ships. This left hundreds of empty hours, not only for religion but also for conversation and personal pleasures, for these presumably hard-working Yankees.[12]

The slow pace of technological change meant that leisure customs could long survive and be passed on from one generation to another by example and word of mouth. Urban workers, for example, celebrated not only the usual Christian holidays, but suspended work on special days in honor of the patron saint of their trade. It was customary in Medieval Europe for masters to grant workers a half-day off in order to prepare for each holiday. In many trades, masters were expected to pay workers for these days. Sometimes this meant that holidays were piled on holidays over the generations. For example, after many centuries, the tradition-bound Romans of the fourth century AD celebrated 175 annual holidays! And, despite the rigors of the night work, some French bakers in the 17th century still were at leisure for the equivalent of 141 days.[13]

In periods of relative prosperity (like the 16th or 18th century), crafts-men reduced the hours of labor sometimes by two hours per day. This was possible because "employers" (often little more than suppliers of raw materials and marketers of finished products) had little direct control over the pace or methods of work. The actual production process was usually controlled by a father in a household of workers; laborers were often members of his family. The employer seldom entered this cottage and certainly had no direct means of forcing weavers or spinners to work rapidly or regularly.

Low prices for the family's output of yarn or cloth might force the head of the household to insist on longer working hours. Indeed, in the early 18th century, economists advocated that merchants collude to lower prices. This, they believed, was the only effective means of forcing cottage producers to work steadily every day. However, higher prices often meant that work discipline was relaxed. The pace and length of the workday, especially in the early part of the week, was reduced. Both rural and urban artisans seem to have had a fixed notion of an appropriate standard of living. If prices were raised, instead of working steadily for increased income, these craftsmen seem to have reduced their time at work in order simply to earn their accustomed wage. Apparently they possessed a stronger leisure ethic than work ethic.[14]

Yet, even when a craftsman worked for himself and presumably would be interested in accumulating wealth, he seldom had any incentive to increase his hours of work. There was little advantage in building up an inventory of goods. A blacksmith, for example, generally lacked the funds necessary to stock up in pig iron or charcoal much less to tie up his scarce resources in ready-made horse shoes. As a result, his work was paced by demand. And this meant a rather leisurely tempo, frequently interrupted by informal conversation and other forms of play.

An English law of 1495 attempted to impose a 12-hour day upon producers in a work schedule of 5:00 AM to 7:00 PM. But a 10 1/2 hour workday was far more common in the 16th century. While 18th-century British ship builders were "bound over" to work 12 hours per day, they often quit work at 11:30 AM (not noon) and returned at 3:00 PM (rather than at 1:00 as proscribed in their contracts). In effect, the ten-hour workday prevailed in such trades.

Many skilled trades long celebrated an informal holiday at the beginning of the week in what, somewhat mockingly, was called St. Monday. This custom epitomized an often-noted characteristic of preindustrial labor: its preference for leisure over increased income. When prices for their products rose or when costs of living decreased, they often responded with working less and playing more rather than attempting to accumulate wealth. What marked off the privileged trades from the lowly occupations was less a higher material standard of living than greater time free from work. In the face of social solidarity or inertia (depending on your point of view), reformers had much difficulty in uprooting this leisure ethic. Only the revolutionary impact of economic and technological change would seriously threaten this customary leisure and break up the communities that perpetuated and defended it.[15]

The Impact of Family and Community

Sociologists have long distinguished traditional from modern society by the role that kin and neighbor played in the shaping of the individual's life. In the old world, almost no one lived alone or even within the strict confines of the nuclear family. Few had privacy. The humble lived in rural cottages or quarters above or behind a shop. These lodgings seldom consisted of more than one or two rooms. And, while the size of the household, especially in Western Europe, was seldom more than five, close quarters had an immense impact on the individual. It necessarily produced a collective outlook on work and leisure. In an environment where the same space was used to work, eat, sleep, and play, these functions were bound to be mixed. Where no one had a room of one's own, individualized or age-specific leisure had no space to develop—at least at home.

Historian Philippe Ariés argues that before the 18th century both the young and the old played the same games and shared in the same leisure. From about four years of age, children joined in the dancing and card games of ale houses. They were even allowed to gamble. Both rough outdoor sports like bull baiting, which to us are suitable only to adults, and seemingly childish activities like swinging, teeter-totter, or parlour games were played by both child and adult. This promiscuous mixing of the young and old in leisure ended only as graded schools deliberately separated the child from adult society. These schools emerged only in the 17th and 18th centuries (and then only for the elite).[16]

Moreover, because of the lack of private living space, the community, rather than the home, dominated leisure moments. Even more than today, recreational periods were organized in sex-segregated activities away from the home rather than in family units. Since the Middle Ages, in the relatively warm climate of southern France, the village square and town well formed the foci of male leisure. In the colder and damper regions of England, the alehouse performed a similar role.

For example, in the 14th-century French village of Montaillou, seven or eight villagers regularly met at one of their houses to play dice and chess. Others joined over the dinner table or fire to sing or play the flute. Indeed, a shepherd considered himself a failure if he could not afford a flute. More significant, however, were the neighborhood meetings of men under the elm tree on Sundays. There the men would talk about both women and religion. The 17th century British ale house was often little more than a room in the cottage of a villager, who was licensed to serve beer. The owner was usually a farmer aided in his second calling by his wife, who often served as brewer. Small groups, mostly of men, gathered, especially on damp and cold days, for cards, conversation, and drink.[17]

Women usually lacked these public and carefree opportunities for leisure. Their social pleasures were confined to church and to conversations at the market, well, or mill. Also important were the get-togethers when women worked. The 18th century has left witnesses of French *veillées*. These were gatherings of country people on Saturday evenings, most often held in winter months in barns. Women knitted or crocheted while talking, sharing information, and even singing. Each participant would contribute to the costs of the lantern and would share the warmth of a fire and animal heat. These *veillées* were similar to the sewing bees of American pioneer women a century later.[18]

Poverty may have dictated these collective pleasures. Yet even for the rich there was no privacy. The intimacy of the dining room or the drawing room was unknown in the 17th century, even for royalty. For the French King Louis XIV, the pleasures of conversation or eating were open to an army of courtiers and distant relatives in multipurpose halls at his palace of Versailles. Even the privacy of the bed was inhibited by the nearly constant presence of servants; aristocratic women in 17th-century France were oblivious to the presence of male servants while taking baths. Individualism and the ideal of the intimacy of family had yet to be invented.[19]

The primacy of the community over the family or individual was also a product of inadequate medicine and food. Both the individual and the family were most precarious entities. Up to half of children were dead by age four; a 20 to 30 percent mortality rate among babies less than one year of age was common. In 17th century England, death rates for youth in their 20s was as high as mortality for people today in their 60s. As a result, parents might well have to rely on relatives or neighbors to raise children. Put differently, families were often "invaded" by the casualties of biological catastrophe, the widows or orphans of relatives.

Moreover, because of the economic costs of large families, the young often married relatively late. In 17th century England, except for the very rich, men seldom married before age 27 and the mean for women was only a year or two younger. Thus, women and men remained in the homes of their parents often until their elders died or were incapacitated. Marriage was reserved for those capable of supporting a household. There were few who worked at jobs in offices or factories. This was because almost all production was done in the house. As a result, a couple married only when they could establish such a house. They not only had to have a skill and employment, but land, tools, and a cottage in order to support a family.

Especially in Western Europe, the young hired themselves out as servants. They usually lived in the homes of their masters and shared social as well as work lives with their superiors. Thus, the master tradesman, rather than the parent and family, often initiated the young into the world of work and leisure. A 17th-century English apprentice agreed to follow the master's commandments both on and off the job:

> Taverns and alehouses he shall not haunt; dice, cards or any
> other unlawful games he shall not use; fornication with any
> women he shall not commit; matrimony with any woman he shall
> not contract. He shall not absent himself by night or by day with-
> out his master's leave but be a true and faithful servant.

Masters would sometimes be legally accountable for the morality of their apprentices and servants.[20]

Yet the older journeymen (workers who had completed their training but were still not masters) were often as influential on the young apprentice. In France, for example, organizations of journeymen dominated the leisure life of young male workers. They initiated youths into an often rich tradition of secret initiation rites, brawls with other trades, and annual festivals celebrating patron saints. These recreations, so reminiscent of the activities of modern college fraternities, colored artisans' attitudes toward work and leisure for the rest of their lives. The artisan "works to live and have a good time; he does not live to work." Even masters were patrons of journeymen celebrations. On specific occasions, bosses were expected to finance the parties of their journeymen. This free and easy way with money often meant that the master's wife took charge of business finances. Because she lacked these "hallowed traditions" of the journeyman's organizations, the wife "is a good manager essential to the success of the shop, for it is she who runs it."[21]

There were some who resisted these collective pressures for pleasure. In his *Autobiography*, Benjamin Franklin notes how the journeyman at an London printing shop, "drank every day a pint [of beer] before breakfast, a pint at breakfast with his bread and cheese, a pint between breakfast and dinner, a pint at dinner, a pint in the afternoon about six o'clock, and another when he had done his day's work." This was a custom which was reinforced by rules requiring newcomers to provide the others with "Foot ales." The tee-totaling Franklin reluctantly gave in to this ritual, but he was thankful that it did not exist in America.[22]

Despite individualists like Franklin, peer pressure on leisure and work customs prevailed. Communal controls on leisure cemented group loyalties, regulated courtship, and chastised those who violated group expectations. For example, the sewing bee was as much a place for the supervision of unmarried couples and of the selection of appropriate matches as it was of diversion and sociability.[23] Sporting contests were often waged between villages (or their champions) rather than between individuals. The purpose was less the display of personal athletic skill than the building of loyalty to the group. The community rather than the individual controlled the content and purpose of leisure life.

Elite Culture and Popular Culture

Traditional society was characterized by a basic division between the elite and the common people, a split that fostered a unique contrast between elite and popular cultures. The relative absence of a class in the middle created a cultural world quite different from our own.

The ideals of a leisure class were expressed by Aristotle as early as the 4th century BC. For this Greek philosopher, leisure was "freedom from the necessity of labor"; it was self-cultivating activity without any utilitarian purpose. As Sebastian De Grazia argues, the Greek aristocratic ideal was "the hearing of noble music and noble poetry, intercourse with friends chosen for their own worth, and above all the exercise, alone or in company, of the speculative faculty."[24]

Yet, the class that was free from the necessity of labor seldom reached these standards. In the Middle Ages, the aristocratic leisure class was materially based on ownership of land and control of peasant labor. The institutions of serfdom and (especially after 1400) rents, dues, monopolies, and royal posts provided the necessary income. Both the upper clergy and the warrior class participated in this way of life and often came from the same families. Of course, freedom from regular toil guaranteed time for diversion and self-cultivation.

But in the early Middle Ages (10th to 12th centuries), elite male leisure was dominated by physical training for combat and hunting. The tournaments, in which young knights competed for prizes in mock combat, were a central part of the recreational calender. Still, the English crown encouraged the lesser ranks to practice and compete in the use of the longbow from the time of the Hundred Years War in 1338. Until the French Revolution in 1789, hunting was the exclusive right of the aristocracy. In any case, only the aristocracy possessed the vast stretches of land and horses that were required for the full enjoyment of this sport. The domestication of hawks was another upper-class recreation—of women as well as men—in the Middle Ages. In many ways, the medieval aristocracy set the stage for later ideas of leisure, especially in physical activity. The nobility also supported the traditions of the strolling singer or minstrel who performed in the great halls of the nobles at dinner. More important, the after-dinner entertainment was often devoted to dice and chess, both known to the ancient Greeks, as well as to other board games like backgammon and draughts, and to card games, from the 14th century.[25]

As the warring classes were pacified and court life emerged in the 12th century, the leisure culture of chivalry began to compete with these physical and gaming traditions. A new stress on music, poetry, and even romantic love emerged in the court of Eleanor of Acquitaine. Yet it is important to note that chivalric leisure had little impact beyond the courtiers, a small group of retainers with little social or political influence outside the most urban parts of Europe, i.e. Southern France and Italy. The ideas of romantic love hardly penetrated the common classes and were weak even among the elite.

The emergence of an urban society in northern France and Italy in the 14th and 15th centuries played a far more influential role in transforming the leisure society of the European aristocracy. The so-called Renaissance, so well known for its contribution to the recovery of ancient artistic and philosophic ideals, was at least as important for its innovation in the arts of leisure. The Italian and French aristocracy of the 15th century no longer lived in the isolation of the manor or castle. Instead, they congregated in the bustling life of urban centers like Florence, Milan, Lyons, and Paris. There, they began to develop unique urban cultures.

These societies were characterized by their quest for individual expression and their openness to, even obsession with, change or fashion. The invention of fashion in the Renaissance is one of the key changes that made the European elite unique in the world. It sparked the development of clothing industries in Italy and the Low Lands, later stimulated the fur trade in North America, and led to a virtual revolution in home furnishings. This meant the development of upholstered chairs, wallpaper, and carpets. It created new standards of comfort. Fashion became a key element in the filling of hours of leisure.[26] Even more important was the development and partial rediscovery of the ideals of self-cultivation. This had little to do with Aristotle's call for contemplation. Rather self-training was to provide the elite with appropriate etiquette and skills necessary for social success in new status-conscious aristocratic halls. The warrior had become the gentleman.

Baldesar Castiglione's *The Book of the Courtier* (1516), one of the first self-help books, outlines the steps for the making of the gentleman. The perfect courtier can come only from the man of noble birth "since this luster of nobility does not shine forth in the deeds of the lowly born." His principle "occupation" must still be "arms and that he be known among the others as bold, energetic, and faithful to whomever he serves." But he must have also "that certain grace which we call an 'air,' which shall make him at first sight pleasing and lovable to all who see him." He must "make whatever is done or said appear to be without effort and almost without any thought about it." He must be athletic and a good horseman. But he must also be "versed in the poets, as well as the orators and historians" and be able to play musical instruments and to paint. He should "honor his lady....and love in her the beauty of her mind no less than that of her body." He should dance but with dignity; and he ought to dress appropriately. Castiglione advocated a degree of reserve in sharing leisure time with the humble: in "horseback vaulting, in wrestling, in running and jumping, I should be very glad to have him shun the vulgar herd or at most put in a rare appearance with them." The playing of cards and dice is acceptable unless the gentleman cheats or diverts time from other noble pursuits. In all manners of pleasure, he should follow a "certain decorous mean." The women courtier must learn to cultivate a "certain affability" and be beautiful. She too should "have a knowledge of letters, of music, of panting, and know how to dance," although with modesty.[27]

These ideas greatly influenced modern notions of social perfection. The air of effortlessness still is our ideal of the man with "class." Castiglione also provided models for "polite society" in an age when the military prowess of the nobility was growing irrelevant. Still, the popularity of the joust and other medieval entertainments also increased at just the time when the emergence of standing armies and the new gunpowder weapons made such sport irrelevant in warfare. They became instead displays of wealth and status.[28] Many modern diversions were aristocratic in origin or expression.

Yet we owe as much to the customs of the common people. Popular culture is, of course, much more evasive than that of the elite. Much less was written about their leisure lives. What literary or pictorial evidence survives the centuries is often distorted by the prejudice of reforming clergy or the hostility of the aristocracy or merchant. However, recent historians have succeeded in recovering the dynamics of popular culture before industrialization.

Popular culture was predominantly rural, relatively unchanging, and characterized by numerous regional variations. Traditions were transmitted from one generation to the other orally and through example. Self-cultivation literature, of course, played little role. The people's pleasures were almost always more conservative, in the sense of being resistant to change. Commoners retained their communal pleasures and resisted the individualist far longer; their games remained rougher and less constrained by rules; and these pleasures were expressed in the traditional episodic festival or in small single-sex groups rather than in the regularized form of individual and family moments of fun. The upper classes, not the popular classes, would invent the weekend and the summer vacation.

The preindustrial European enjoyed lengthy breaks from the daily drudgery of manual work. Perhaps the most unique feature of popular leisure culture was its principle of *saturnalia,* which derives its name from the ancient Roman custom of a week of drinking in early December. At base it was a "binge"—the unrestrained indulgence in food and drink, so often noted by anthropologists studying primitive village culture, was common in medieval European rural society. Saturnalia served as a psychological release for people who knew scarcity all too well. Finally, in annual festivals like Mardi Gras and May Day, the common people indulged in a variety of games, plays, and songs that expressed many subtle forms of protest against the rich and powerful. The May Pole was long a symbol of dissent from authority, a major reason for its occasional suppression in troubled periods of English history.[29]

Still, the elite—whether the clergy, local lord, or king—seldom attempted to repress these popular enjoyments. Even though popular leisure activities were often chaotic and crude, even violent and critical of the status quo, the powerful often patronized them. Sometimes they contributed land for games or food and drink. Quite often, an aristocrat, even one trained in the new arts of the gentleman (despite Castiglione's admonition), would wrestle with his peasants or join them in a dance or song. At least until the 17th century, popular leisure was enjoyed by both the rich and the poor. There was always an interpenetration of the two cultures. Chivalric tales (like Tristan and Isolde) reached down into popular folklore. They became the major themes of cheap "blue" or "chap" books which were widely available to the laboring classes by the 17th and 18th centuries. At the same time, traditional popular dances, like the waltz, percolated up to the upper classes in the 18th century.

Moreover, the powerful felt that these periodic outbreaks of playful disorder were essential for the stability of society. Even the mocking of authority by the election of a boy or madman to the title of bishop or sheriff in a "feast of fools" was viewed as an effective way of releasing hostility.

This point of view was expressed in the *Book of Sport* published by the English kings in 1618 and 1633. These declarations, to be read in church, encouraged the traditional sports and pleasures of dancing, archery, jumping, or "any other such harmless recreation." They also approved of "May-games, Whitsun-ales, and Morris dances; and the setting up of May-poles." These activities would reinforce loyalty to the king and the passive acceptance of the status quo.[30]

The same sort of pleasures were tolerated, even encouraged, in slaves on the southern American plantations in the 1850s during a traditional work break between Christmas and New Year's Day. The ex-slave, Frederick Douglass, reported "that it was deemed a disgrace not to get drunk at Christmas.... These holidays serve as conductors, or safety-values, to carry off the rebellious spirit of enslaved humanity.... The slaveholders like to have their slaves spend those day in such a manner [of drunkenness] as to make them as glad of their ending as of their beginning."[31] Elite and popular leisure in preindustrial society coexisted and sometimes interpenetrated each other.

Leisure and the Traditional Meaning of Time

Leisure in preindustrial societies played radically different roles in the social routine than it plays in the modern world. Recreation was closely tied to the agricultural cycle and was far more irregular than in our rationalized industrial society. It also served social functions that differ sharply from our more individualized leisure activities. And, leisure often provided a necessary release of tensions borne of the rigidities of societies where class and status required constant subordination and social control. The following discussion of Saint Monday, charivari, and carnival will illustrate these distinctive qualities of traditional leisure, especially among the common people.

One of the clearest expressions of the irregular character of the work and leisure lives of the preindustrial artisan is the custom of Saint Monday, absenteeism on Monday morning if not the whole day. St. Monday was usually practiced by the traditional urban crafts. For example, as late as the 1860s, it was common among skilled tradesmen, such as tailors and mechanics, in the capitals of Paris and London and in major cities like Lyons and Birmingham. Women's trades (lace, laundry, etc.) did not provide the income nor the organizations necessary to impose these extra days of leisure upon reluctant employers.

There were a number of reasons why this custom emerged: necessary materials for the week's work often did not arrive until Monday afternoon or Tuesday. Orders did not have to be filled until Saturday morning; thus work early in the week was less pressing. Saturday pay burned holes in the pockets of working people on Mondays. Male workers celebrated Sunday with family but then spent Mondays with comrades in ale houses—while money was still available. Often this custom was organized by the journeyman's organizations. Among early 19th-century Parisian machinists, workers regularly participated in organized drinking parties twice a week on the edge of town where the wine was cheaper. Especially in good times, St. Monday was often extended to St. Tuesday. Porcelain makers in Limoges, France seldom worked more than 15 days a month in the 1850s. And, as late as the 1860s, some skilled iron workers in Birmingham, England worked no more than a three- or four-day work week. This behavior was justified as the ancient right of members of skilled trades.

From the 1820s, employers' attempts to eliminate St. Monday were not always successful. Because entry into the skilled trade was controlled by craftsmen, these artisans were able to ignore the admonitions of their bosses. Only the erosion of the power of the skilled trades and their organizations gradually eliminated this custom.[32]

The same behavior frustrated the managers of the American government armory at Harper's Ferry in the early 19th century. Frequently, each month gunmakers completed a pile of work (which they deemed appropriate) and then spent the rest of the month hunting, fishing, farming, and generally doing as they chose. Moreover, there were a vast number of trades where work was not regular, for example on the docks or construction sites. There laborers did not develop "work discipline," the willingness to apply themselves consistently to any one job, because they never experienced regular work. These laborers lived an unstable existence, alternating work and play in irregular patterns. And, even when presented with the opportunity for regular work, they found it hard to accept.[33]

Recreation also served as opportunities for the coupling of the young. Yet these occasions for alliances between the sexes were radically different from the modern notion of dating. Unlike the modern concept, courtship in traditional society was socially regulated and ritualized. Matches deemed by the community to be inappropriate would be clearly ostracized in the practices of charivari. Perhaps most important, courtship was concentrated in the annual cycle of festivals.

The week preceding the onset of Lent, the 40 days of solemnity before Easter, was called Carnival (or Strovetide). It culminated in Mardi Gras (Strove Tuesday in Britain.) These seven days offered repeated opportunities for coupling in village dances and other festivities—yet, well within the watchful eye of relatives and neighbors. On the continent, one week following Mardi Gras, a ritual, called in France "donnage," took place in the village square. At this time, after the community had ample opportunity to make opinions about the coupling of the previous week, young adults would make matches. One of their number would announce the "giving of" males to females. The young, but with the subtle involvement of the old, not only confirmed the affection between two people but stated the village's view of the appropriate match.

More negatively, festivals were the occasion for social pressure to be brought to bear on those who violated community norms. On Mardi Gras, men who did household work or (worse) were cuckolded (or cheated on by their wives), were mocked or charivaried: villagers gathered around their houses, banged pots, and blew horns. Sometimes the offending party would be seized and paraded through town seated backwards on a donkey. Mismatched couples (of grossly unequal ages or of greatly different economic backgrounds) would also suffer the charivari. The same fate befell the young woman who broke off an engagement or deprived the village males of her presence in the marriage pool by taking a husband from another town. Variations on these customs, (called schurren, skimmingtons, or shivarees) were known from Germany to colonial New England. They survive today in the taunting of newlywed couples.[34] Thus, festivals served to place the stamp of approval or disapproval on the individual's conduct.

Clearly, festivals were central to the leisure of premodern people. In fact, they reckoned time by reference to festivals. They lived "in remembrance of one festival and in expectation of the next." Cottage walls were decorated with souvenirs of pilgrimages and symbols of the current festival season. In 17th-century Sweden, the common type of house had two main rooms, one for ordinary use and the other for guests and for festivals. Festivals were certainly expressions of regeneration and renewal. Midsummer's Eve was a celebration of the birth of St. John the Baptist. The custom of jumping over bonfires and bathing in rivers were rites of purification and of fertility, as if to assuage anxieties about the fate of the upcoming harvest.

Perhaps the most characteristic festival was Carnival. In southern Europe, this festival season began as early as late December and activities increased with the approach of Lent. As the historian Peter Burke describes it, "carnival may be seen as a huge play in which the main streets and squares became stages. The city became a theatre without walls and the inhabitants, the actors and spectators, observing the scene from their balconies." Carnival usually included three elements: food, sex, and violence. The last week was characterized by the massive eating of meat (thus carnival, derived from the latin root, *carne*) and pancakes. But more than this indulgence, *carne* also meant the flesh or sex. Weddings often took place at carnival and so did pre-marital pregnancies. Students of the carnival have been quick to point out the presence of phallic symbols in the long-nosed or horned masks of revellers. The normal constraints of hierarchical life were also removed. "People threw flour at one another, or sugar-plums, or apples, or oranges, or stones, or eggs..." Moreover, roles were reversed as men wore women's clothes and women dressed as men. And, in plays and songs, the authorities were frequently mocked. "Carnival was, in short, a time of institutionalized disorder, a set of rituals of reversal."[35]

The British tradition of mumming on All-Soul's Day and Strove Tuesday and the Christmas holiday custom of the Lord of Misrule were quite similar to Carnival. Mumming consisted of groups of youth going from door to door singing or dancing for food and drink from the householders. Sometimes these mummers at least feigned threats of damage to the owner (usually the well-to-do) if rewards were not forthcoming. This custom (like so many) survives among children in the relatively placid form of American Trick or Treating on Halloween. The custom of appointing a young man at the court to be Lord or Abbot of Misrule was a common medieval English practice. Sometimes he had license to organize mumming and to make an appearance in front of the homes of the nobility where he and his followers sang loudly and played tricks. In parish churches a Lord of misrule was elected by the "wild heads of the parish flocking together..." He would appoint a guard who would dress themselves in loud green or yellow clothes and "then they would bedeck themselves with scarves, ribbons, and laces... This done, they tie about either leg twenty or forty bells, with rich handkerchiefs in their hands..." These revellers then marched with pipes and drums toward the church and "though the minister be at prayer or preaching," they danced and sang "like devils incarnate." After disrupting the service, they went into the church yard where they feasted and danced all day. This occurred not only with the population's compliance but often with their financial assistance—if only in fear of retaliation if they did not give freely. The May Day custom of people dressing like Robin Hood (dating from the 16th century) was a similar expression of anarchy in an otherwise hierarchical and self-controlled society.[36]

These expressions of licence only occasionally took the form of overt protest against the status quo. Instead, they gave vent to built-up frustrations. Festive leisure thus both expressed feelings of anger among the common people and pacified them with relatively harmless and temporary forms of symbolic aggression and emotion.

Compared to the often ephemeral character of modern leisure, these traditional forms of play had an amazing staying power. It was only the emergence of new social elements—a middle class of merchants, businessmen-farmers, and later of industrialists, social reformers, and trade unionists—that would change these patterns. The first systematic efforts to reform leisure, however, were undertaken by the religiously motivated. The origins, character, and fate of this enterprise will be our next topic.

3

Leisure and Reform: 1500-1700

Between 1500 and 1660, many Europeans and (later in this period) American colonists began to question the traditional balance of work and play in daily life. Long before industrialization, some farmers, craftsmen, and merchants rejected old community recreations, the festival calender, and even the love of sport, gaming, and drink that had so long linked the peoples of Europe. In England and America these reformers, who embraced a work ethic, were usually radical Protestants or Puritans. Their gospel of labor was not merely a way of earning time and money for pleasure; for them, work was an end in itself, almost a form of worship. Labor was also transformed from the episodic exertions of medieval society to a methodical, self-disciplined, purposive activity. As New England Puritans were reminded, "God sent you not into this world as into a Play-house, but a Work-house."[1]

An emerging middle class embraced this new attitude toward work and defined itself against the presumed sloth, inconstancy, and indulgence of both the masses and the elite. It rejected the attitude common among the "unregenerate poor" that work was merely the means to pleasure; nor did they see labor as did the "leisure class," as a degrading activity suitable only for servants or slaves. Rather, methodical work was the mark of an improving humanity, its own reward but also a promise of future benefits, both spiritual and material. These values became the bedrock of the modern notions of rationality, accumulation of wealth, and even progress.

Ironically, these reformers also produced new forms of leisure and new relationships between work and recreation. Even if they never succeeded in imposing their values on the majority of humanity, they shaped the course of Western society in many ways.

For many readers, the first question will be: why did anyone adopt such a dreary doctrine, much less practice it? One theory claims that this ideology was a product of religious change; another explanation is that the ideology resulted from economic crisis. I will consider both arguments.

Religious and Economic Roots of Leisure Reform

When the German monk, Martin Luther, broke from the Roman Catholic church in 1517, he set in motion, not only over a century of religious ferment, but a cultural revolution. The Protestant doctrine, especially as developed by that second-generation reformer John Calvin in Geneva, Switzerland, went beyond the rejection of the authority of the Catholic church and its sacraments. It established a new way of life. A powerful combination of ideas greatly affected Western culture—especially in the English-speaking world where Calvinist Protestantism spread from the 1550s. These doctrines dominated the 17th century and were associated with Puritanism both in the British Isles and the North American colonies.

The key idea was that God "elects" or chooses those who will be saved. This means that the individual's participation in the rites of the church and confession has no bearing upon his own salvation. This doctrine freed the person from the anxiety of not knowing whether he had done enough "good works" to be saved: salvation was a "free gift." On the other hand, it often left the believer uncertain whether he was one of "God's elect." Protestant faith (especially in Calvinism) also meant that the Christian was able to grow in godliness and "to cultivate blamelessness and purity of life." This process of "sanctification" meant that the believer was to be God's instrument on earth to "glorify" the deity. This did not involve withdrawal from the world into the Catholic monastery or in contemplation, but in serving God in everyday "callings" or jobs. As William Penn insisted, "True Godliness don't turn men out of the world (into) a *lazy, rusty, unprofitable self-denial*."[2] Rather, the Elect were to grow in sanctity by their diligence in their ordinary work.

These religious concepts affected ideas about work and leisure in many subtle ways. As the sociologist, Max Weber, noted, the notions of election and sanctification created a "Protestant Ethic," a new more methodical attitude toward work. Anxiety over whether one was one of God's elect made believers behave as if they were godly or sanctified in their everyday callings. This meant that the Protestant had to follow God's will *constantly*.

It would not do to continue in the traditional culture of Carnival and Lent—indulgence in the flesh to be offset by repentance and austerity. The popular Catholicism of the Middle Ages tolerated a degree of license because, in the confession and in the sacraments, these sins could be blotted out and the offender forgiven. For the Calvinist, there was no such opportunity. Either you were damned and nothing could be done for you or you were saved and God expected growth toward perfection. The ancient Greek ethic of moderation in all things was no more satisfactory. Just a "little sin" was but an opening to debauchery. And the old comforts of community leisure were but a snare in dragging the individual believer down from his isolated path of following Christ.

Finally, the Protestant could not isolate his piety in the church on Sundays. Rather, he had to act religiously all the time because, according to this belief, God values all "callings" or vocations. This meant that work became a holy task—akin to prayer. And, if the ordinary day's activities belonged to God, then "God's time" should not be wasted in trivial pursuits. As the Massachusetts divine, Increase Mather, warned, " Every man's Eternity ....will be according to his improvement of time here."[3]

The Protestant work ethic drove pleasure out of the lives of believers; leisure was feared both as a lure to sin and a threat to godliness. The mere desire to play made Puritans doubt their status as being among the elect. Leisure also threatened to "profane" (give offense to) God and His mission of creating His Kingdom on earth. As one of God's chosen people, the Puritan believed that he not only had to avoid pleasures in his own life but to struggle against them in the community. He had to discipline the retrograde so that there would be no "dishonor of God" and that the "Lord's Supper may not be profaned by being administered indiscriminately." Puritans believed that God's mission was not only to sanctify the believer, but also to use the elect to make the world holy. Thus, the Puritan could not remain content in his own piety. He had to reform the world.[4]

Why, we might ask, was the Puritan so certain that God disapproved of traditional leisure? This conviction came partly from a belief that customary pleasures were opportunities for sin—dancing and drinking led to sexual promiscuity. The ale house competed with the church for the loyalty of the villager. And, many traditional recreations, such as church ales, profaned the church and diverted the parish from its godly purpose. Gambling also "prostituted divine providence to unworthy ends" because "God determines the cast of the dice or the shuffle of the cards, and we are not to implicate His providence in frivolity."[5] Perhaps most generally, to the Puritan, customary leisure was the opposite of self-control and serious pursuit of purpose. Drinking and rough community sports reduced one's rational facilities.

To be sure, leading 16th-century Protestants did not oppose exercise: Luther claimed it was a Christian duty and Calvin even played bowls on Sunday afternoons. However, Protestants in England took a firm stance against violence-prone group sports. Oxford University banned football in 1555. A game which "withdraws us from godliness, either upon the Sabbath or any other day, is wicked." Football was one of the worst because it was a "friendly kind of fight" rather than a "fellowly sport," noted an English Puritan in 1581.[6] Physical activity was fine if it profited a man's calling. However, if it had no moral or social purpose and, if it led to pride in one's athletic prowess, sport not only diverted the believer from work but encouraged the sin of vanity.[7]

The Catholic Church was hardly immune from similar ideas. The Catholic Reformation of the mid-16th century reaffirmed traditional doctrine and sacramental religion, but it also attempted to purge Catholic culture of the profanation of the sacred. Like their Protestant competitors, Popes and Jesuits endeavored to instill a new respect for the Church by driving out the irreverent from feast days. The anarchy of Carnival was increasingly seen as a mockery of

Lent and as essentially pagan. Reforming Catholics in France and Germany also preached a constancy to labor and the threat of leisure. In the 17th century, French and German Catholic leaders reduced the numbers of feast and saint's days and insisted on a less profane celebration of those that remained. Priests were no longer allowed to join in Carnival and the church ceased to finance drunken processions. Reforming Popes drove prostitutes out of Rome and insisted that the clergy tend their Christian flocks rather than live like a leisure class. The Council of Trent, which reaffirmed traditional Catholicism in 1562, also denounced the use of saint's days for "boisterous festivities and drunkenness, as if the festivals in honor of the saints are to be celebrated with revelry and with no sense of decency." By the mid-17th century, "this-worldly asceticism," as Weber called this ethic, was almost as common in Catholic Munich and Milan as in Protestant London and Boston.[8]

This common obsession with leisure reform suggests that factors other than religion were shaping this new attitude toward traditional leisure. Social historians have argued that these puritanical ideas were products of an economic crisis during the 17th century. War, bad harvests, disease, and increased economic competition forced elites to pressure the people into working harder just to maintain production. Thus, the Puritan's admonition to Godly work was reinforced in 1495 by the English king's insistence on a twelve-hour workday and harsh treatment of vagrants.[9]

Yet the work ethic was not shared by all classes or even all the elite. And, while an austere ethic was common in 17th-century Europe, it was held most thoroughly by English-speaking Puritans. A key to explaining this fact is that a new middle class in England had emerged in the 1600s which embraced Puritanism as a "natural ideology" that fit its economic and social aspirations. In response, Puritanism was resisted both by the landed or court aristocracy and by the "improvident" poor. As Michael Walzer puts it, Puritanism was the "religion of the sociologically competent," those who found in Puritan religion a rationale for their quest for order in a world in crisis. They "discovered in work the primary and elemental form of social discipline." Moreover, the godly "were distinguished from the disorderly mob of worldlings by their industry and diligence: their industry *revealed* their saintliness—to themselves as well as to their fellows." The Puritans represented the new social forces that would emerge from the decline of the medieval manor and the community traditions of the rural village. They emerged among the artisan, the merchant, and the individualistic farmer.[10] These groups, armed with Puritan convictions (dare we say self-righteousness), had the self-control and purpose to create societies in their image of God's kingdom.

These new classes were concentrated in southern England where industry and commerce were more developed. By 1650, they were able to prevail over the Stuart monarchy and to impose their culture upon more backward regions to the north. And, at the same time, these people were able to create a new colony in the wilderness of New England. With their methodical devotion to work, they inevitably became economically dominant. "Tempered by self-examination, self-discipline, self-control, [the Puritan was] the practical ascetic, whose victories were won not in the cloister, but on the battlefield, in the counting-house, and in the market."[11]

Puritans and the Sabbath

Let us focus, then, upon the Puritans of England and the colonies. Puritans represented a broad movement of Protestants that emerged relatively clearly within the Church of England in the 1590s. Their objectives were both to purify worship (eliminating remnants of Catholicism from church doctrine and practice) and to purge society of godlessness. Perhaps the most important of these efforts was the Sabbatarian movement.

The idea of "keeping the Sabbath," of course, was Biblical and not unique to the Puritans. Yet these radical Protestants developed this doctrine far further than the Christians before them and even more so than the Calvinists in Europe. The Puritan's obsession with the sanctity of Sunday went far deeper than a desire to make the Bible (or their interpretation of it) the foundation of civic law. It symbolized much of the Puritan attitude toward work and leisure. Essential to Sabbatarianism was a rejection of saints' days and other traditional holidays. Unlike the Sabbath, they believed, these holidays were not Biblical but invented by men for pleasure. As Luther said, "We increase the wrath of God more on holy days than on others." Their God—who valued work and discipline so highly—was most happy when his people were productive. During emergencies, Protestants in the 16th century even worked on Sundays.[12]

Yet most Puritans recognized that, if the saints' days were to be abolished, it was essential that Sunday be preserved to assure a "comfortable relaxation to beasts and men." A day of weekly rest was required to guarantee a new kind of balance between work and relaxation. This regular pattern—one day in seven—coincided with a new industrial and commercial rhythm of work. Unlike the rural cycle of seasonal labor and rest, the newer industrial pace was more steady and unwavering. Their model was the Genesis story of God's six days of work and one day of rest. This model meant both a more uniform and more full work year (with the elimination of saint's holidays). Sabbatarians also recognized the need for regular rest. Some Puritans were modern enough to warn employers that if weekly rest were not granted, then servants would work less steadily during the work week to the detriment of business.[13]

This idea, of course, marked the Puritans against the hierarchy of the Church of England (or Anglicans). While the official English Church had broken from Papal control in the 1530s, it was reluctant to accept Protestant (especially radical Calvinist or Puritan) doctrine. From the 1590s, English bishops prosecuted those Puritans who worked on feast days. Sabbatarianism was a key element in the half-century of revolution in England. In the view of one Puritan, "England was at rest till they troubled God's Sabbath."[14]

The idea of Sunday rest went beyond a restructuring of the work calender or the struggle over control of church and state. Instead, Sunday was to be the day when, as Calvin wrote, "believers were to cease from their own works, and allow God to work in them."[15] This means that Sabbatarianism was not only a critique of work on Sundays but also of traditional leisure. To follow attendance at services with an afternoon of games and drinking was to profane the serious intent of religion. As the historian Christopher Hill put it, "The Sabbath was not a day of leisure, on which it was lawful to waste time; it was a day for a different kind of labour, for wrestling with God."[16]

The believer was, of course, unable to devote the whole day to church, but he should follow worship with *family* devotions. The father was obliged to control his children and his servants to shelter them from idleness and to lead them to prayers. This was no easy task for, as one English Puritan writer admitted, Sunday was the workman's "revelling day, which is spent in bull-baitings, bear-baitings, bowls, dicing, carding, dancing, drunkenness and whoredom...."[17]

Between 1640 and 1660, the Puritans were in ascendence in England. They led a revolution, executed Charles I in 1649, and began in 1650 a decade of Puritan rule under the Cromwells. They used this power to attempt to control popular recreation not only on Sundays but throughout the week. The Puritans outlawed a whole range of traditional leisure activities from 1555 to 1557. They attacked gambling and animal baiting as well as Maypoles and most theatre. They enforced these prohibitions with military power throughout the island.[18] Even after the Restoration of the monarchy in 1660, the influence of Sabbatarianism continued. In 1663, the Bishop of London outlawed all commercial transportation on Sunday. By 1677, a law that prohibited almost all business on Sunday culminated two generations of Sabbatarian agitation. It solidified an almost unique British tradition: "Preaching and sitting on Sundays [became] the religion of England."[19] The quiet day of family and later Sunday newspaper reading, which dominates England today, has its roots in the 17th-century Puritanism.

However, the Puritans were always a minority and enjoyed power only briefly. From the 1590s, they faced persecution from the crown and the established Church. Some, like the Separatists, fled England to Holland in 1619 because they had abandoned hope of reforming the English church. They were disappointed with the neglect of the Lord's Day in this more tolerant Protestant region. Worrying that their children would fall to the snare of such worldly ways, these Separatists or Pilgrims emigrated to the New World to found the Plymouth Colony.[20]

Between 1620 and 1640, other less radical English Puritans (who rejected total separation from the English Church) also despaired over the possibility of reforming England. After obtaining an official charter from the king, their leader, John Winthrop, established the Massachusetts Bay Colony in 1630. Like the Pilgrims, these Puritans hoped to establish a Christian common-wealth. They felt themselves to be "grains" sifted by God to come to the wilderness. The wilds of New England were to be God's test for them.[21]

True to the ideals of the English Puritan, the New England colonies banned dice, bowls, cards, and even smoking (except at dinner) as time wasters. Even the less religiously committed saw the wisdom of such controls, for survival depended on hard work. This fact led the non-Puritan colony of Virginia also to adopt strict controls on idleness in the first generation. By 1619, the governor there had banned dice and card games.

New England Puritan colonies prohibited any Sunday labor, travel, or even recreation, including in Massachusetts, "all unnecessary and unseasonable walking in the streets and fields." One 17th-century minister from Boston refused to baptize children born on the Sabbath believing that they must have been conceived on that day of the week. Only one in four of the first generation of migrants to Massachusetts were Church members (for most lacked sufficient evidence of conversion); yet all residents were obliged to attend services. All festivities on holidays were condemned as pagan; Puritans associated these celebrations with the boisterous and disrespectful practices of the "Lords of Misrule." The Plymouth colony Governor William Bradford, in fact, demanded that everyone work on Christmas.[22]

This regimen hardly meant that Puritans rejected all recreation and play. Even stern Puritan divines in Boston, like William Sewell, enjoyed good food, black-cherry brandy, and even quiet walks in a friend's orchard. Puritan children enjoyed dolls and toys. Youth played football, stoolball, and cricket. And, although the Puritans attempted to regulate the inn, they never attempted to eradicate alcohol.[23]

More to the point, recreation was tolerated and even embraced if it "joineth pleasure and profit together," as the Englishman Richard Baxter put it. Moderate exercise, especially if it involved individual activities, like walking, riding, or even shooting, was acceptable. Health-giving recreation could "help you in your duty" and was laudable if it was put in "its proper time and place, as you do your meals." The same methodical and individualistic attitude toward work was to be applied to recreation. This attitude shaped the 19th century movement for "rational" or purposive recreation, which contributed much to modern physical fitness movements.[24]

Still, as historian William Brailsford stresses, Puritan views did not lead to a reform of the chaotic games and leisure of the English peasant and lords. Puritans were too inflexible and repressive to really reform leisure or sport. They tended to drive traditional leisure underground in much the same way as the American Prohibitionists created the speakeasy in the 1920s.[25]

Yet, the Puritans introduced new tastes that would have great impact later. If Puritans condemned theatre, they accepted singing (at least of Psalms) and encouraged reading (at first, only of the Bible and devotional works). This venting of emotional needs in song and literature provided the foundation for new pleasures. The popularity of choral societies that embraced Bach and Handel and the massive market for the novel and magazine in the 18th century were indirectly due to the Puritans.

There was an even more important, if subtle, influence. The Puritans helped to create a new locus of leisure by replacing the community or parish with the family as the focus of a more restrained social life. This change meant a withdrawal of leisure from the often boisterous activities of the village and tavern and the creation of a more intimate familial circle. The Puritan encouraged fathers to take charge of the religious education of their household (including servants). They were expected to give the household servants Sundays off. Cotton Mather's well-known detailed monitoring of his children's moral development was only the repressive side of this new familial ethic. Puritan fathers could also share time with their children. Puritans also embraced a new respect for marital togetherness, and they were noted for their serious attachment to their spouses. Adultery was a far more grievous offense to them than it was to the Anglicans and they condemned it both in males and females. Companionship in marriage was highly praised. A French traveler in 18th century London wrote of the impact of this new marital style when he describes an affluent couple:

> It is extremely rare to see one of them without the other. The richest people have only four or six carriage-horses; they have no need for more, because they do all their visiting together. It would be more ridiculous in England to do otherwise than it would be in Paris to go around always with one's wife. They give the impression of the most perfect harmony."[26]

This attitude contributed to the individualized leisure built around family and "improving recreation" of the 19th century.

Limits of Leisure Reform in the Anglo-American World

Puritan reformers (like their Catholic competitors) were a relatively small, if rather successful, pressure group. But they were rowing against the tide of tradition, both in the inertia of the masses and in the power of the aristocratic elite. Their efforts to shape leisure were limited before the English Revolution in 1640 and their unquestioned power hardly lasted more than the decade of the 1650s during Cromwell's dictatorship. In the New England colonies, Puritanism was more firmly rooted in the self-selection of colonists, the ease of the Puritan elite in driving out opponents, and the need for a strong work ethic to subdue the wilderness. Yet, despite the blue laws, in New England too, by the end of the 17th century, religious austerity had succumbed to a more relaxed cultural style.

Puritanism was a middle-class movement. It attempted to influence the poor through the patriarchal hand of the masters of households, and during the Cromwell period, through the power of the law. Still, peasants and journeymen were often loath to give up their Sunday games. They took their cockfights indoors and retreated to the alehouse when the Puritan government banned public rowdiness. Even New England Puritans found that Thursday church meetings were often followed by a day of playing and drinking by the less-than-arduous Christians. Their only practical response was to delay the festivities by holding services in the afternoon rather than in the morning.[27]

The same resistance was evident among the aristocracy. Just as the Puritans were rising in England, James I established the Newmarket racetrack, which soon became a den of aristocratic gambling. James I defended traditional Sunday sports in 1618 with his famous *Book of Sport,* which encouraged games and exercise. Sports, James claimed, were necessary to train the young for military service; repression of these traditional pleasures would only produce discontent and drive the people to the alehouses.[28]

Sometimes the common people and the aristocracy joined forces. For example, in about 1608, a noted royalist and opponent of Puritan austerity, Robert Dover, attempted to counteract the Puritan influence by sponsoring the Cotswolds "Olympick" Games on his estates near Gloucestershire. He turned over his land to contests of cudgeling, leaping, races, pitching the bar and hammer, and wrestling. He even staged chess matches, hare hunts, and horse races in order to attract the aristocracy. In 1637, the Anglican Bishop of Hereford restored church ales, which had previously been banned, arguing that they brought people to church and reduced conflict between the rich and the poor.

Thomas Morton led a similar protest against Puritan controls in New England. A libertine and later a royalist, Morton offended the Pilgrim Fathers in 1627 by setting up his own fur trading company and by trading guns with the Indians. He went too far, however, when he celebrated a traditional English May Day at Mar-re Mount. William Bradford called him a "Lord of Misrule, [who] maintained (as it were) a School of Atheism." Morton and his followers "set up a maypole, drinking and dancing about it many days together, inviting the Indian women for their consorts, dancing and frisking together like so many fairies, or furies rather." The Pilgrim response was predictable. John Endecott led a group to burn Mar-re Mount, cut down the maypole, and drive Morton out of the colony.[29]

Both the Restoration of the monarchy in England in 1660 and, more generally, the dilution of the Puritan spirit in New England by the 1680s meant the decline of austerity. Perhaps even more important was the growing influence of commercial economic forces. As we shall note in the next chapter, growing affluence made possible the mass marketing of cheap versions of aristocratic pleasures. Secularization paralleled these commercial forces. The conviviality of the church ales (partially undermined by Puritan restrictions) was gradually moved to the coffee house and tavern. Sunday Bible reading at home eventually was replaced by the newspaper and novel by the end of the 18th century.[30] Against the appeals of affluence and secularization, the Puritan message was drowned.

The Legacy of the Reformers

So pervasive, however, was the work ethic that it survived the demise of its religious roots. It cropped up in the 19th century in the words of the English essayist, Thomas Carlyle, who wrote lovingly of work: "What is immethodic, waste, thou shalt make methodic, regulated, arable, obedient and productive to thee. Wheresoever thou findest Disorder, there is thy eternal enemy: attack him swiftly, subdue him."[31]

Yet perhaps the most famous exponent of the work ethic was the 18th century businessman-statesman, Benjamin Franklin of Philadelphia. Although a child of Boston Puritans, in adult life he was unchurched and found doctrinal complexities utterly unintelligible. He retained a simple moral belief that "truth, security, and integrity in dealings between man and man were of the utmost in the felicity of life." But he followed the Puritan work ethic: "I spent no time in taverns, games, or frolicks of any kind." He advised, "lose no time; be always employed in something useful; cut off all unnecessary actions." In his *Poor Richard's Almanac*, Franklin extolled the virtues of time thrift: "Sloth like Rust, consumes faster than Labour wears... Do not squander Time, for that's the stuff Life is made of.... The sleeping fox catches no Poultry.... There will be sleeping enough in the Grave."[32]

Yet, this evangelist of the work ethic was not a proponent of unstinted labor. He also had a "leisure ethic." In his autobiography, Franklin lists his ideal scheme for the "natural day": From 5:00 to 7:00 AM after rising, he leisurely planned the day while having breakfast. From 8:00 AM to 12:00 PM he worked. This was followed by a two-hour break for reading and dining. Only at 2:00 did he return to work until 6:00 PM for an eight-hour workday! In the evening he would eat, examine the day's activities, and enjoy "music, or diversion, or conversation" until he retired at 10:00 PM. This was a well-ordered life but hardly one enslaved to work. It was rather a surprisingly modern allocation of work and nonwork time. His prize for his rationality was retiring from business at the age of 42 after which he spent the rest of his 86 years in an amazing variety of self-determined activities that any modern person would surely call leisure.[33]

Franklin was the model of the self-made man: methodical work and "character" were the keys to personal success. Like the famous 19th-century British manual *Self-Help*, by Samuel Smiles, Franklin promoted an individualistic set of values. He rejected the traditional fraternity of the shop and neighborhood in drink, conversation, or play for the self-improving ethic of diligence. Its reward was not only self-mastery but independence. In Franklin's case, it also

meant early retirement. This "leisure ethic" survives today in the dreams of
many an entrepreneur and professional.

Franklin expressed a middle-class vision of self-control and material
(if not spiritual) fulfillment in work. His life also revealed a real anxiety toward
"idleness." Franklin's values were reinforced by the growing availability of
relatively cheap pendulum clocks in the 18th century and by the appearance of
the mass-produced pocket watch in the middle of the 19th century. Time pieces
allowed the industrious to closely monitor their own time.[34] Nevertheless, as
we shall show in Chapter 5, only the mechanization in the new factories would
impose "clock discipline" on the mass of men and women.

Moreover, despite the great secularization of the 18th-century, the
religious roots of the work ethic did not die. The "Great Awakenings" of John
Wesley and Charles Whitefield, both in England and the colonies, revived this
Puritan ideal. These great outpourings of evangelism and reaction to irreligion
were important vehicles for the transmission of the middle-class culture of the
Puritans to large sections of the laboring classes. Methodists, from the mines
of Cornwall to the American frontier, "declared holy war on drink, hurling,
wrestling, bull baiting, cock-fights, and folk superstition." Yet these spirited
evangelists replaced condemned pleasures with the emotional expressions of
revivals and hymn singing. This same impulse would reappear periodically in
the Anglo-American world in waves of evangelical fervor. The most obvious
occurred in the first two decades of the 19th century and then again toward the
end of the century. In each case, these revivals prompted prohibitionism,
sabbatarianism, and other movements against traditional leisure.[35]

Finally, the revolt against popular leisure took still another form. It
appeared in a new movement for social discipline, the French Revolution of
1789-1794. The leaders of this upheaval were, like their distant Puritan cousins,
generally middle-class advocates of increased output. On the eve of the Revolution in 1788, lists of grievances sent to the king were replete with complaints
from the middle class that religious holidays were keeping France uncompetitive
and poor. Once the Old Regime was overthrown in the summer of 1789,
middle-class revolutionaries attacked the tradition of saint's days and festivals.
Although they were attempting to undercut the influence of the church, they also
challenged customary work and leisure patterns. In 1791, when the new
revolutionary government granted employers the right to set working hours,
many masters removed traditional breaks and holidays enjoyed by artisans.

Finally, at the height of the revolution in 1793, the Jacobin government
abolished the seven-day week along with the Christian calender. In its place, the
revolutionaries introduced a ten-day week. This liberated 17 days per year from
the holiday calender and created a new festival of 5 days at the end of the year.
To be sure, its purpose was to destroy the culture of traditional Christianity and
to replace it with a new cult of the nation. Yet it also was designed to decrease
the idleness made possible by the old holiday calender. Napoleon restored the

Christian week in 1806 and King Louis XVIII, when the monarchy was restored in 1814, reinstated the old prohibitions against work on Sunday. However, these laws had only a limited impact: the French never enjoyed the nearly universal leisure on the Sabbath known in England.[36]

Puritan reformers in the 16th and 17th centuries attacked the traditional balance of work and play. Salvation came not from liturgical acts but from a total transformation of life. This meant that the believer must constantly do God's bidding and that as God's full-time agent, the Christian could not waste God's time. Reformers identified godliness with methodical work and sought to purge the "disorder" of leisure from the world. These ideas were embraced by those seeking an alternative to the chaos of the economic crises of their times. The Puritans were or became industrious people—those who prospered in the painful transition from a rural subsistence economy to a new commercial one.

However, by the 18th century, the siege and wilderness mentality that had nurtured this austere religiosity had declined. As a result, this doctrine began to lose its power. Still, its kernel remained in the rationality of enlightened men like Ben Franklin. They represented an industrial urban world-view dominated by the virtues of work discipline and accumulation rather than by present-minded pleasure. The work ethic may have been more deeply rooted in America than in Europe. The payoff of economic success in the New World was a real prospect for many, at least until industrialization emerged in full force after 1850.[37]

These ideas never entirely prevailed over the champions of traditional leisure. Puritans and their more secular descendants found a silent but persistent resistance from the masses, who were generally unwilling to forgo pleasure in the weary world of labor. For them, the secularized "salvation" of economic security and independence through hard work was too faint a hope to stake their lives on. And the common people, in England especially, had an ally in the aristocracy, who likewise embraced sport and games even if for somewhat different reasons. Yet the austere message was threatened from still another quarter, the very commercial success that Puritanism encouraged. As the sociologist Daniel Bell argues, the work ethic inevitably produced a material plenty that ultimately undermined that austerity. Merchants who marketed pleasures were the best propagandists for leisure, towering over the austere admonitions from the pulpit or pen. After about 1660, new generations of merchants traded the meeting house for the counting house and eventually the coffee house.

Still, there was no simple trend. All of these forces would reappear time and time again in the 19th and 20th centuries. Elite and popular leisure, as well as the reformer's alternative, continued to conflict and interact with each other. The characteristics of elite and popular leisure and the relationships between them following this age of the Puritans will be our next topic.

The Ducking-Stool

4

Anglo-American Leisure on the Eve of Industrialization: 1660-1800

England and the United States share far more than a common language and similar political and economic system. They participate in a similar leisure culture. Before industrialization, they shared common patterns of elite and popular play. In both countries, rigid social and economic barriers assured distinct and separate recreational forms. Yet economic change and the emulation of the rich by the poor softened these differences between the privileged classes and the masses. Following the austerity of Puritanism and the economic crises of the 17th century, the full expression and interaction of elite and popular leisure culture became possible.[1] The task of this chapter is to present the various forms of traditional leisure on the eve of modern industrialization.

American Exceptionalism

At the outset, we must consider a major historical debate: to what degree was it true, as the German sociologist Max Weber once argued, that "America was born modern." According to this view, transatlantic migrants were less tradition-bound than those who remained; and, perhaps more important, colonists found a new environment free of the institutions and customs left behind. These facts produced significant differences in American and English leisure cultures. For example, traditions often associated with the journeyman organizations, the village, or the parish church did not always make the Atlantic journey insofar as immigrants intermingled and formed new communities. Thus St. Monday, foot ales, Strove Tuesday cock throwing, and "parish wakes" largely disappeared in the colonies. The selective migration of Puritans to the Northern colonies meant a partial abandonment of the leisure of "Merrie England." The mixing of different ethnic cultures (e.g. the Dutch and German in the middle colonies) added new games and recreations to the English repertory. Moreover, the simple facts of plentiful land and wildlife as well as sparse population shaped leisure. Hunting became far more democratic and frontier social gatherings, such as camp meetings, became imprinted upon the American leisure traditions.

However, the differences between the two areas can be easily over-stated. Colonial settlers on the western shore of the Atlantic attempted to duplicate the English way of life. The founders of Jamestown in 1607 hoped to recreate a class of gentlemen planters and to enjoy the aristocratic way of life of the English nobility and gentry. The custom of educating young male colonists in England reinforced common leisure patterns as did cultural and commercial imports from the mother country long after the Revolution. Migrants from western England and the Scots-Irish brought their customs to the southern and middle colonies. Traditional English leisure ways were at least tolerated by the Anglican church, which dominated the southern colonies, especially after leaders abandoned efforts to repress idleness among the Jamestown colonists. Once the Virginia experiment had surmounted its first thirty years of instability and the planters had become enriched in tobacco farming, a more relaxed leisure culture emerged among the elite and the common European settler.

The practice of seasonal communal leisure did not vanish. In this way, too, America was not born modern. To be sure, colonists created a new festival cycle that was not built around Mardi Gras and Whitsuntide. But when colonists gathered for elections or for training in local militias, they also indulged in many of the same traditional communal games as practiced in England. And, the lengthy festivities of Christmas week or around May Day were not unknown in America. Despite the miseries of black slavery, custom prevented many masters from working slaves on holiday periods, Sundays, and even late Saturday afternoons. Parties were common on Saturday night when slaves reunited families and couples, sometimes from different plantations, for dancing and singing, with or without the master's approval. Finally, the kill-joy image of the Puritan has often been exaggerated, and by the end of the 17th century the emerging mercantilist centers of Philadelphia, New York, and Boston were beginning to adopt a more relaxed attitude toward play. The customs of the English urban elite were eagerly adapted by colonial businessmen.[2]

We find change and contrast but also similarity between the pattern of the Old and New Worlds. American elites imitated their aristocratic cousins in England and old popular customs took new forms. This chapter will offer a series of examples of elite and popular leisure activities that were common on the eve of industrialization—and long before. How, and to what extent, the Americans differed from the English will be stressed.

Popular Pastimes: Rough and Blood Sports

Despite efforts of Puritans to reform popular leisure (Chapter 3), these pastimes remained largely untouched into the late 18th century. Opportunities for leisure among all classes grew from the mid-17th century with the decline of authoritarian religion and the growth of material wealth. In Britain, country squires tolerated and even sponsored popular leisure in their rural districts as a means of winning the loyalty of the people. The governing English oligarchy, unwilling to accept the cost or political threat of an enlarged army or national police, also accepted the disorder inherent in popular leisure customs. There was even more tolerance among the barely-governed peoples of the colonies. The result was a complex and not always gentle leisure culture.

Most characteristic, perhaps, were rough team and blood sports, which differed radically from our modern notions of athletic games. In England, traditional sport was nearly without rules. In Derby England, for example, until the 1830s, Shrove Tuesday afternoon was devoted to a free-for-all between the boys and young men of two large churches. As many as a thousand youths on a side crowded around a ball pushing, kicking, and, in general, fighting to drive the ball toward "goals" a mile out of town (a water wheel in one case and a garden gate in the other). The whole town was the playing area. There was no sense of "out of bounds" or "legal play." Shops closed to avoid the intrusion of the players. And teams would even take the ball into the icy river in the hopes of gaining victory. Some historians have argued that these annual contests were "remembrances" or sublimated forms of war between closely-knit villages. This recreation was certainly a "periodic release necessary in a rigidly hierarchical society."[3]

Sporting contests were often slightly civilized forms of combat. The practice of cudgelling dated from medieval times and consisted of two men fighting with broad sticks or cudgels with the hand protected by a wicker basket attached at the base. The object was to guard oneself and "to fetch blood from the other's head; whether by taking a little skin from his pericranium, or drawing a stream from his nose, or knocking out a few of ...the teeth." Variations on this sport were backsword or singlestick, where the free arm of the combatants was tied. These contests competed with boxing, a no-holds-barred affair, unconstrained by rounds, gloves, or referee. Gouging of eyes as well as punching were allowed. Wrestling was also common in western England (often in informal matches outside the alehouse on summer evenings) but also in scheduled games at rural fairs.[4]

Such events often were the foci of a series of rural contests of physical skill and endurance. "Pedestrianism," or amateur foot races, were closely related to hammer throwing, leaping, and similar contests. Unlike modern track and field sports, pedestrianism lacked both regulation courses and uniform equipment. These games were natural extensions of everyday work lives using ordinary tools and stressing physical endurance (e.g. in races involving the carrying of heavy objects). Finally, a principal attraction of such games was gambling rather than the aesthetic of the sport itself.[5]

Often at the heart of these games was cruelty to animals. Cock throwing—tossing missiles at a rooster tied down with a five-foot rope until it was dead—was a popular, if, by modern standards, rather unsportsmanlike amusement. Another diversion, "ratting," involved a dog placed in a pit with rodents. The object was to wager on the number of rats that this dog could dispatch in a given time. The English *Sporting Magazine* (October 1822) reported one of these matches involving a dog named Billy and 100 rats:

> ... turned out loose at once in a 12-feet square, and the floor whitened, so that the rats might be visible to all. The set-to began, and Billy exerted himself to the utmost.... [The dog] entered the arena, and in vain did the unfortunate victims labour to obtain security by climbing against the sides of the pits, or by crouching beneath the hero. By twos and threes they were caught, and soon their mangled corpses proved the valor of the victory....Billy was decorated with a sliver collar, and a number of ribbon bows, and was led off amidst the applauses of the persons assembled.[6]

Cock fighting was surely the most widespread and popular of these blood sports. It cut across class lines and was even practiced by pupils and their schoolmasters in the courtyard. Here is a well-known account of an English match:

> When it is time to start, the persons appointed to do so bring in the cocks hidden in two sacks, and then everyone begins to shout and wager before the birds are on view. The people, gentle and simple (they sit without distinction of place) act like madmen, and go on raising the odds to twenty guineas and more.... Then the cocks are taken out of the sacks and fitted with silver spurs.... Then it is amazing to see how they peck at each other, and especially how they hack with their spurs. The combs bleed terribly and they often slit each other's crop and abdomen with the spurs. There is nothing more diverting than when... the cock that appeared to be quite done for suddenly recovers and masters the other. When one of the two is dead, the conqueror invariably begins to crow and jump on the other.[7]

One might see in this violent ritual simply a people acclimatized to the slaughter of animals enjoying the thrill of contest. Others might give it a psychological significance and argue that the cock fight was a displacement of the aggression of the multitude: the cocks performed like people with both fear and courage; and many poor peasants surely could identify with the boasting victorious rooster even if their low status prevented them from crowing like a cock on the walk.

Another popular blood sport, bull baiting, should be mentioned. It often took place in front of a village pub because its owner sponsored the event. The bull was fastened to a ring on a leash about 15 feet long. A dog, trained for the event, would be freed to 'bait' the bull. In 1719, a Frenchman described this custom in England:

The Dog turns at the Bull; the Bull, immovable, looks down upon the Dog with an Eye of Scorn, and only turns a Horn to him to hinder him from coming near: The Dog is not daunted at this, he runs around him and tries to get beneath his Belly, in order to seize him by the muzzle, or the Dewlap, or the pendant Glands... The Bull then puts himself into a Posture of Defence; he beats the ground with his Feet; which he joins together as close as possible, and his chief Aim is not to gore the Dog with the point of his Horn, but to slide one of them under the dog's Belly, (who creeps close to the Ground to hinder it) and to throw him so high in the Air that he may break his neck in the Fall. This often happens: When the Dog thinks he is sure of fixing his Teeth, a turn of the Horn, which seems to be done with all the Negligence in the World, gives him a Sprawl thirty Foot high, and puts him in Danger of a damnable Squelch when he comes down. But if the dog succeeds in grasping the bull's underbelly, he sticks to him like a Leech. Then the Bull bellows, and bounds, and kicks about to shake off the Dog; by his Leaping the Dog seems to be no Manner of Weight to him, tho' in all Appearance he puts him to great Pain. In the end, either the Dog tears out the Piece he has laid Hold on, and falls, or else remains fix'd to him, with an Obstinacy that would never end, if they did not pull him off.[8]

This custom (along with its variants like badger or bear baiting) baffles the modern sensibility with its violence. Why did rural people derived pleasure from watching a tethered bull fight a dog trained to attack the underbelly of this mighty animal? There surely was the element of rooting for the "underdog" and perhaps some distant meaning to the dog's attack on this ancient symbol of animal fertility.

Bull running was a less popular festive sport but revealed perhaps even more the disorderliness of traditional group diversions. It was a well-established tradition at Stamford in Lincolnshire and at Tutbury in Staffordshire in the 17th century and long before. At Stamford, it was performed 42 days before Christmas. The local butchers selected the wildest bull in the region. The shops were closed up and then the bull was let loose to be harassed by the townspeople through the town: "Men, women, and children of all sorts and sizes, with all the dogs in the town, promiscuously run...after the [bull] with their bull-clubs, spattering dirt in each other's faces, that one would think them to be so many furies started out of hell...." Once the bull was exhausted, he sometime would be thrown over the bridge into the river or simply slaughtered. This sport, of course, survives in the 20th century as the preliminary to bull fights in Spain.[9] Whatever their significance, these rough, even cruel and anarchistic sports had a tenacious appeal to all classes. Only gradually and with much resistance would the common people abandon these recreations.

To a degree, they even survived the journey across the Atlantic. Bull running was unknown and animal baiting was rare in the American colonies. The communitarian character of the bull run (already severely localized in England in the 17th century) never withstood the migration westward. It was otherwise with cock fighting. There are plenty of examples of this sport in Virginia from 1725. Apparently, in the first century, colonists sated their thirst for blood sports in frequent hunting. Cock fighting was also associated with the mixing of upper and lower classes, something that Virginia gentry, still in an insecure social position in the early years, would not tolerate. Only in the 18th century did cockfighting become widespread in Virginia and other southern colonies, especially among the small farmers around rural taverns and at county fairs. In New England, the Puritan influence largely eradicated this traditional blood sport but not wrestling, cudgeling, backsword, or singlestick, which were played on the Boston Common on "training days" during the colonial period. The age-old sports of boxing and wrestling were also as common in America as in England. Not only were frontiersmen like Abraham Lincoln skilled wrestlers in their youths, but chaotic games such as greased pig contests were common to American fairs and other festive occasions.[10]

Hunting and Racing: Patterns of Elite Play

In contrast to the popular origins of rough ball games or rough fight contests between men or animals, hunting was an elite pastime in England. Long associated with ownership of land and possession of weapons, it was usually the privilege of the European aristocracy. Humbler people seldom had either the right to hunting lands or could afford handcrafted firearms. On the European continent especially, nobles and kings not only reserved lands for hunting but even had exclusive rights to hunt on common lands and even on the farms of the peasants. Although wolves still roamed the streets of Paris and other European capitals as late as the 17th century, wildlife was beginning to get scarce. Laws dating from the reign of James I in the early 17th century protected game in England from indiscriminate killing. These conservation measures, however, were designed primarily to preserve the sport of the aristocracy. They ignored the needs of farmers for protection from predators and sought to punish poachers seeking food or income in game meat. Only those who possessed a specific amount of property (the lordly sum of £100 of income per year in 1671) had the legal right to kill deer, hares, pheasants, partridges, and rabbits. It was illegal to sell game, although the black market for fine game birds in London inns made this aspect of the law a dead letter. Sometimes gamekeepers and gangs of lower-class poachers shot it out and, although juries were reluctant to convict minor poachers, several months in jail was not an uncommon punishment. Only in 1831 were these undemocratic laws repealed, at least for those farmers who wanted to shoot game on their own land.

The use of firearms in hunting came rather slowly. The weight of tradition assured that, until the 18th century, the English method of taking partridges still consisted of stalking the birds with dogs and horses and then netting them. Dogs were also trained to pursue and kill small game. Although matchlock guns had been available since the 1520s, only with the improvement brought by the introduction of the flintlock musket in the late 17th century did the gun become a practical weapon against birds on the wing and other speedy animals.[11]

Hare hunting was an exception to the aristocratic character of European hunting. Middling farmers as well as country gentlemen kept harrier dogs to pursue the rabbit, which was a widespread nuisance. Gradually in the 18th century, however, the gentry adopted the more difficult sport of fox hunting. Only slowly did the gentry abandon the hare hunt because of the scarcity of foxes and the lack of properly trained fox hounds. The sport of the fox hunt was to lead a pack of dogs (bred for their noses and speed) across hedge and field to catch a fleeing fox. This sport commonly led to accidents as man and horse crashed through the numerous fences enclosing farm land. The fox chase appealed to social exclusivity: it required expensive specially-trained horses and dogs kept for the autumn hunts. By the 1840s it had become a complex ritual. The country squire was paid deference as Master of Fox Hounds and prosperous farmers gratefully accepted his nod of recognition and followed his lead on the hunt. Fox hunters took as much pleasure in their hounds as they did in the hunt itself. And, the event was surrounded by an elaborate ritual—the early morning breakfasts, the horn calls, and fox hunting fashion. Deer (like fox) hunting was often a contrived affair with the stag being carted to the field for a chase.[12]

Horse racing was also pursued with a passion by the English aristocracy. In the 17th and 18th centuries, there were private matches held on open field or commons; horse owners usually put up prize money (in effect, betting on their horse). The race was conducted in a series of heats; the winner was the horse that won the most races. Crossing and jostling a competing horse were generally permitted. The English development of the thoroughbred horse increased both the quality of the races and their exclusivity.[13]

Again, American patterns were somewhat different. Hunting was far more democratic in the colonies; it was undertaken as much for utilitarian reasons as for sport and with a far less concern for conservation. Deer were plentiful nearly everywhere, and game attracted both the townsman and farmer from New England to the Carolinas. Not only did flocks of wild turkey and pigeons provide an easy meal, but moose appeared on the outskirts of Connecticut towns in the 17th century. Even buffalo were found in western parts of South Carolina in the early years. Massachusetts farmers joined together to hunt wolves, raccoons, and, of course, squirrels. Even the Puritan divines, Cotton Mather and Samuel Sewall, enjoyed fishing. Throughout the 18th century, New Yorkers utilized the ponds and forests of Long Island for angling and hunting.

Guns were never the preserve of the rich in the colonies. Unadorned flintlock muskets were cheaply made in the log-cabin shops of frontier gun-smiths and blacksmiths in the 18th century. The Pennsylvania rifle was a popular weapon for hunters. Shooting contests, of course, were featured in many fairs.

Frontiersmen often enjoyed mass hunting without any of the refine-ments of the English fox hunt. A group of hunters from Kentucky returned one day in 1797 bragging that it had bagged 7,941 squirrels. Wolf drives and ring hunts were also popular. A crowd of hunters would encircle an area of perhaps forty square miles, gradually closing on all the game they could scare up. "At one such hunt, some sixty bear, twenty-five deer, one hundred turkeys, and even larger numbers of smaller animals and game birds were reported to have fallen before the enthusiastic hunters."[14]

Indeed, wildlife was so plentiful that the colonists were often unre-strained in the slaughter of such birds as wild turkeys, partridges, and especially pigeons, setting a trend that would be reversed only at the end of the 19th century. During their annual migration, carrier pigeons were so numerous in the 18th century that they darkened the sky; hunters not only shot them but struck them down in huge numbers with poles when they landed on trees to rest. The peculiar character of American hunting—its uniquely popular and wasteful form—was the product of an open frontier environment.

Racing, too, was more democratic in America, if only because horses multiplied so quickly in the colonies. Both the wealthy and humble spontane-ously raced their horses in quarter-mile sprints. Virginia gentry attempted to imitate their English aristocratic forefathers by legally excluding poor whites (as well as blacks) from horse racing. For example, in 1674 a Virginia tailor was fined for racing against a planter. It was "contrary to Law for a Labourer to make a race, being a sport only for Gentlemen." By the 18th century, the planters imitated the British with the circular tracks and thoroughbred horses. Still, poor farmers everywhere in the colonies held their own horse races across fields or down country roads.[15]

Urban Pleasures in an Emerging Commercial Age

Of course, traditional leisure was not restricted to the countryside. Indeed, much of the variety and change in preindustrial pastimes occurred in the city, town, and especially pacesetting capitals. As the historian Lewis Mumford notes, the 17th- and 18th-century royal capital was a creation of power and for pleasure, not of trade and industry. The medieval arts and amusements, once controlled by the church, were increasingly dispersed into various quarters of the city. The morality plays (extensions of the liturgy) became the theater patronized by the aristocracy and even by the common people. The choir moved into the concert hall and the sociability of the monastic order eventually reemerged as the male club. The royal court was imitated by the aristocracy and its pleasure emanated throughout the capitals, where the old landed elite increasingly resided.

These leisure forms, borne of the social contact, wealth, and time available to the aristocracy, were founded on exclusivity. They were enjoyed in protected isolation from the people and imparted status to those who participated; they were valued for the fact that only the "well-born" had the resources, training, or time to enjoy them. Nevertheless, the prestige of elite leisure made it an object of imitation by the other classes, who gradually adopted it as their incomes rose and as leisure was commercialized. Growing affluence made possible the mass marketing of cheap versions of aristocratic pleasures.[16]

The royal palaces in Paris, London, and Vienna were imitated in the "Hotels" (or urban mansions) where the aristocracy congregated. In the 1670s, the pressure of urban congestion and fear of the mob persuaded Louis XIV of France to build a suburban palace at Versailles. This flight from the city was not only imitated in the 18th century by other monarchs but copied in the sprouting of chateaux and country mansions of the great lords. These centers of pleasure—both urban and suburban—later would become the modern museum, as princes and lords filled their halls with collections of art and curiosities. Many of the old palaces, such as the Louvre, became museums. Aristocrats and kings also collected wild animals and plants first for the private amusement of the court. These collections, in the late 19th century, were transformed into modern public zoos.

Surely of more immediate impact were the aristocratic pleasure gardens, the expanses of green space, manicured gardens, fountains, and alcoves. The English royal parks at St. James and its Mall provided walkways for promenades. Also important were Kensington Gardens and Hyde Park. These parks formed the background for walks, parties, games, and dances, and even concerts, providing the "gaiety and license of the carnival, offered daily," at least in the summer season. Swings and roundabouts with their thrill of speed originated in the pleasure garden. Even the carrousel was originally a plaza for the display of aristocratic horsemen. The wooden horses on the merry-go-round were the poor person's equivalent.

The spirit of the private gardens of the court were recreated in the ring of commercial pleasure gardens that surrounded London—especially Ranelagh in the 17th century and Vauxhall in the early 18th century. The private gardens of royalty and the lords could be enjoyed in the form of the commercial suburban resort. As Roy Porter noted, "admission fees were great [social] levellers." Some offered evening music or tea gardens. Others were built around spas where businessmen and professionals gathered to drink the "healing" waters (Tunbridge Wells). Most London pleasure gardens had walks, lawns, clipped hedges, a grotto, fountains, and statues. Some had arbors for tea drinking and often were decorated with paintings. The larger spots had large rooms for concerts as well as a bun or cake house. People played variations on lawn bowling or nine pins. Some even had cricket fields. Often, even the common class went out on Sundays for a Sunday Ordinary (a filling meal) for the whole family at or near the pleasure gardens.[17]

The urban aristocrats also invented new leisure spaces in the private dwelling. The 17th century began a process of spatial differentiation in the houses of the rich. Servants were increasingly banned from the common dinner table. Dining rooms became specialized and formal chambers, while the common spaces of the great halls were divided into areas for receiving guests and for bedrooms. Dining dominated private parties; but guests also enjoyed amateur plays and, inevitably, cards—especially 100 and whist. The privacy and heat provided in the bedroom made sexual activity a year-around recreation. The growing desire for privacy created the need for a new meaning to the word "hall"- it was less a large common space than a corridor for public movement throughout a house that was broken up into private chambers. The male had his library (as often for billiards, drinks, and smoking as for reading) and the mistress, her boudoir.[18] Of course, the common people remained in their two-room houses for a far longer period.[19]

The 18th-century city also offered the pleasures of shopping. Partially to accommodate the long hours of craftsmen, many stores kept open until 10:00 PM, or even later on Saturdays. Shopping was also a social experience. It was an opportunity to see friends and to get out of small lodgings. Customers expected tea in London bookshops. When the church was purged of its "ales," drinking and conviviality moved to the coffee houses. London had over 2,000 of them by 1700. The 18th-century coffee house was an important institution in England, where professional men gathered to mix pleasure with business. This was the origin of the Lloyd's of London insurance company, whose principal partners first met in a coffee house by that name. Some became exclusive clubs. Political groups frequently formed in them. In others, such as White's Coffee-house, cards and dice dominated. While artists and the literary elite converged on coffee clubs in Covent Garden, many were simply places for the reading of newspapers. By 1790, there were 14 morning papers in London; by 1799, the first of that great English institution, the Sunday newspaper, had arrived.[20]

The elite, who had the funds and time to travel, also developed a taste for the seaside at Scarborough, or later in the 18th century, at Margate and Weymouth. At these exclusive spots, they indulged in cold-water bathing and drinking of sea water. Modest 18th-century gentry used carriages to enter the water "behind a covering that lets down with hoops, so that people can go down a ladder into the water and not be seen, and those who please may jump in and swim."[21]

More traditional were the inland spas like Bath—where a daily routine of morning bathing and drinking of waters was combined with rounds of socializing. In addition to the medicinal attractions of water, visitors were drawn to the "assembly rooms" for music and dancing as well as gaming rooms, bowling greens, and shops. These clusters of buildings and activities would be imitated in the 19th and 20th centuries in the seaside amusement centers of Blackpool and Coney Island or in the "holiday camp."

So important did these resorts become to the English elite that one historian has called the 18th century "an age of water-places." The training of the young aristocrat would also be incomplete without the European tour, especially to the Renaissance centers of northern Italy. While only the very rich had the time and income necessary for such a major trip, the middle classes emulated their social superiors by traveling to the country in more comfortable commercial carriages. Even the 18th-century English poor could get a holiday to the south in late summer if they were willing to hire themselves as hop pickers.[22]

In the 17th and 18th centuries urban working people's leisure was, of course, more closely tied to the festival cycle rather than to the social season at the resort or spa. Weddings, and even funerals, were occasions for dancing, drinking, and games, and urban festivals, such as St. Bartholemew's Fair in London, attracted a motley crowd with its trained animals, curiosities, and exotic foods.

Still, in the 18th century, the lower classes imitated their superiors in the adaptation of social tea drinking. They followed the rich to the suburban pleasure gardens on Sundays at least, and they played cards and other games developed first by the aristocratic leisure class. Urban living made possible the commercialization of leisure and offered the elite's pleasures to the masses in cheap forms. It produced the very modern notion of the "star." Actors, lion-tamers, and even healers became well-known. There were even sex therapists like James Graham, who promised to relieve impotence at £50 a night with his Celestial Bed.[23]

Lewis Mumford and others have argued that urban aristocratic pleasures of the period after 1650 were products of the boredom of the idle. The property-owning elite had slowly lost control of its destiny to the king or prince; and pleasure had became a substitute for politics. Perhaps we, like the aristocrats of two centuries ago, have substituted passive amusements for participation in the affairs of the world.[24] Yet these leisure traditions were expressions of human longings, including competition, sociability, of variety, and even creativity. These activities were surely gentle and relatively humane alternatives to incessant warfare and religious bigotry, which so long dominated the history of Europe.

Social Leisure Among the American Colonists

Both the mercantile elite of the northern American ports and the Southern colonial gentry imitated the urban enjoyments of the London elite. Still, the American environment created both more rustic variations on the European leisure themes and, on the frontier, some quite different forms of sociability.

New wealth in New York, centered around the English garrison, emulated London society: "The fashionable paraded in the late afternoon around Hanover Square dressed in latest London mode. The gentlemen were resplendent in powdered wigs, varicolored coats, lace, and ruffles, the young dandies wearing silver-hilted small swords and ostentatiously taking snuff from jeweled boxes." The rich had even their version of the suburban pleasure garden. They took excursions by chair or chaise to stylish country taverns for turtle, madeira, and music. By the end of the 18th century, many took the ferry to horse races on Long Island. Others as far away as the West Indies and the southern colonies traveled to Newport, Rhode Island, in the summer for health and the pleasure of racing "frolics" or picnics on Goat Island. Balls, card parties, and especially the theater dominated the winter season. English theatrical troops entertained in New York from about 1700 and the first permanent theater opened in 1767. Northern mercantile elites imitated their London counterparts with exclusive coffee houses and private clubs, which met almost nightly for dinner at taverns. Even in Puritan Boston, dancing instruction was offered to young ladies and gentlemen by 1716 and the elite flocked to them to pick up the latest fashions. Even though the Puritan establishment succeeded in prohibiting theater until the end of the century, public concerts were a regular feature on the social calender in Boston by the 1760s.[25]

Members of the Southern colonial gentry, such as George Washington, supplemented their Sunday afternoon rounds of visits with frequent treks to Annapolis, Williamsburg, or Charleston for balls or plays. And, unimpeded by a hostile clerical eye, they enjoyed the gossip and conviviality of an ongoing social life. The renowned hospitality of the wealthy gentry, like that of Colonel Robert Carter at his estate of Nomini Hall, provided a stage for bowling, boat and horse racing, dancing schools, and even cockfights and fox hunts—as well as a table of wines, liquors, and expensive foods. Nomini Hall even provided guests with concerts of piano, flute, as well as Ben Franklin's invention, the harmonica.[26]

Despite these rather urbane leisure styles in both the north and south, the more traditional work-centered recreations survived the end of the 18th century even among the well-off. A New York mansion was the spot for a "candle-dipping frolic" long after this ancient "bee" had ceased to be a necessary part of winter preparation for the well-to-do. It was, in reality, an opportunity for 32 couples to gather in a huge kitchen to socialize while leisurely indulging in that traditional craft of dipping wicks in a kettle of melted tallow. This was followed by a feast of cold fowl, hot sausages, madeira, and egg-nog, and still later by dancing to amateur fiddles. The final dance, begun at midnight, was called the "fire dance" because the couples alternately swung each other around the huge triangular-shaped fireplace that lay astride several rooms.[27]

Another significant variation in the American leisure pattern is the unusual role played by camp meetings. In the sparsely-populated frontier, the dreary and lonely routine of farming and hunting was relieved in fairs, weddings, and especially religious camp meetings. Around 1800, thousands gathered in forest clearings like Cane Ridge, Kentucky, for up to a week of religious enthusiasm. While the purpose was, of course, spiritual renewal and conversion, the camp meetings became an occasion for massive socializing and emotional catharsis:

> The night meeting was picturesque, with the deep shadows of the primeval forest lighted up by lurid flames... This scene, with its background of the majestic forest, presented an imposing affect... As the night progressed, wilder and wilder became the disorder... [with] shouting, creeping, leaping, jerking, clapping of hands, falling and swooning away... So popular was the movement that everybody came. Young ladies were there to show themselves and their costumes. The young men went to see the girls and frolic in a quiet way... It was an enjoyable social season as the long isolated frontiersmen joined together for a time in the warmth of Christian fellowship. While guards were stationed on the fringes of the camp, there were many 'camp babies.' And the opportunity for both the religious and irreligious to gather (and taunt one another) was unique.[28]

The Universality of Gambling and Drinking

In the 18th century, wagering and imbibing alcohol were the lubricants of most adult male leisure. The social pathologies that emerged from gambling and drink in the 19th and 20th centuries have, of course, contributed to numerous efforts to control these activities. Yet in traditional societies, attitudes toward gaming and alcohol were different.

Of course, gambling has been common in most cultures and, as we have already noticed, was at the heart of plebian blood sports and aristocratic racing. Historians identify a tremendous growth in all forms of wagering from the late 17th century. Betting was the principal reason for the growth of the aristocratic Newmarket race course near London as well as the more popular track at Epsom. The passion of card playing shared the same purpose. The popularity of gaming in the English court and among merchants of London spread to all layers of society and even to women. And betting was the main point of pugilism and cockfights. Even traditional participant games, like the once-plebian sport of cricket, became spectator sports, drawing crowds up to 20,000 by 1772, to the gambling mania which was sweeping England. Gambling also pervaded the gentile atmosphere of the post-Puritan English club and coffeehouse.[29]

How do we explain this passion for gambling? The spread of commercial enterprise from the time of Queen Elizabeth led to a growing legitimacy to speculative endeavor. This positive attitude toward risk-taking complemented the behavior of the gambler. Most authorities did not condemn gaming itself; rather, churchmen and magistrates feared immoderation and the influx of the "ungentlemanly" professional or cheater who undermined the sport. The same commercial spirit, which fueled the taste for risk-taking, also demanded that chance be minimized and deceit eliminated. As in business, luck and competition was inevitable, but there also had to be rules to assure predictability and a fair chance to win. In order to guarantee a rational assessment of risk, games were regularized. Card game rules were codified in manuals; boxers were matched by weight and regulated by referees in order to reduce cheating. As gambling became commercialized in the urban culture of London, club and race-track owners had to guarantee bettors fair play.[30]

Gambling was also at the heart of colonization and the western migration in America. While the Virginia Company sought to outlaw the gambling of Jamestown settlers in order to impose work discipline, the company nevertheless sponsored a lottery in England in 1612 to raise funds for the financially unstable colony. New England Puritans attempted to suppress betting by outlawing cards and horse races and, in less-commercial America, casinos never prospered as they did in London. While individuals in taverns often bet on cards, backgammon, and billiards, truly commercial games like roulette and faro did not appeal to colonial Americans. Still, towns imitated the British with lotteries to finance public improvements.[31]

Gambling should be understood in its social context. In one sense, it was merely another way of accumulating money. The adventurers who settled Virginia scarcely saw any difference between the dangers of settlement and risks of the wager. Gambling debts, like any other unpaid liability, were legally binding as contracts. Anglican clergy sought not to eliminate gaming but to restrain it as a threat to the financial independence and responsibilities of bettors. As the historian John Findlay writes, gambling and the westward movement, so central to American culture, were closely related:

> From the seventeenth century through the twentieth, both gambling and westering thrived on high expectations, risk taking, opportunism, and movement; and both activities helped to shape a distinctive culture. Like bettors, pioneers have repeatedly grasped the chance to get something for nothing—to claim free land, to pick up nuggets of gold, to speculate on western real estate. Like bettors, frontiersmen have cherished risks in order to get ahead and to establish identity.[32]

Gaming was also a means of displaying wealth and bravery. In Britain it was a legal privilege exclusively of the aristocracy, except during the Christmas holiday season. Gambling was not merely a status symbol but a pleasure enjoyed by the masses—as would be proved by the 20th-century Littlewood football pools in England and the illegal industry of the numbers games in American cities. It channeled the excitement of risk-taking and competition into relatively pacific directions; it expressed the value of individuality and the dream of gain. Authorities sought to control gambling in England but only for the poor, just as they conserved wildlife by restricting hunting to the elite. In America, it was more a matter of church pressure. But in most cases, regulation failed. The financial reward to the government of lotteries and the enterprise of gammers proved too alluring.[33]

Alcohol played a no-less-dominant role in creating conviviality among people of all classes and in relaxing the social constraints that were so overpowering in this era of deference and repression. Drink was perhaps even more central to the meal and conversation than it is today. Beer, wine, and spirits were ageless means of conserving fruit and grain in a world without refrigeration and modern food preservation. American corn (i.e. maize) was, of course, cheaply converted into whiskey, and apples, peaches, and cherries were made into brandy in the American south. Beer, fermented cider, or wine at work was long viewed as nourishment. It "strengthened" the laborer and got him through a 10- or 12-hour day. In rural England, beer or wine rations were a part of the pay, offered at the midday meal. In New England, rum was rationed out to artisans and was used in trade with Indians. Drink was an integral part of work and social life.[34]

The emergence of a seafaring class in Boston, Newport, New York, and Philadelphia led to the growth of taverns near the wharfs. Yet in no town in the colonies was there a shortage of alehouses and retail dramshops. By the last decades of the 17th century, New England colonists took advantage of the midweek church meeting to ride from town to town "to drink and revel in ordinaries and taverns" and court records reveal much evidence of drinking on the Sabbath. Frontier gatherings for corn huskings, barn raisings, and weddings were occasions for communal drinking. Cheap home-made whiskey made by the barrel and drunk from a brown jug or "Black Betty" were commonplace in rural Virginia and the Carolinas. Wine was mostly imported from France and Portugal and was more common for the wealthy in both England and the colonies.[35]

Drunkenness was common enough but most people in preindustrial times drank in moderation. Total abstinence was a 19th-century phenomenon. Rather in both the old and new worlds, drink was an integral part of life, at work, meals, and, pleasure, and was viewed as much as a food as an intoxicant. While Puritans and other reformers struggled against its excess, few opposed drink on principle.[36]

The attitude toward leisure, which prevailed in the 18th century, arose from many sources. In great measure, it was a product of rural society—and corresponded with the pace and requirements of work on the land and with the natural environment of forest, field, and stream. Yet preindustrial societies also produced urban leisure, rooted, in part, in the privilege of wealth and the time it gave the elite. The late 17th and 18th centuries saw new forms of leisure, such as the resort and commercial club, and these types of play "trickled down" gradually to the masses. Despite the efforts of the trend-setting courtiers from Castiglione down to the 18th-century dance instructors to infuse traditional leisure with civility, manners, and self-control, there remained an anarchic quality to play. Still dominant were rough and blood sports, gambling and drinking. The element of the carnival would always play a vital role in all people's leisure, but there were many who attempted to purge it from society. We have already seen examples of this in the Puritan movement. Far more effective was the complex reorganization of society known as the Industrial Revolution, our next topic.

THE GIN SHOP

5

Industrialization, Work and Play: 1780-1850

Most of us think of early industrialization in economic terms: miles of machine-produced cotton cloth, newly-enriched factory owners, and impoverished mill hands. Yet this complex process had perhaps a more important effect upon the way people worked and played.

The factory institutionalized the Puritan's work ethic, imposing it on the masses in the lock-step movement of machine and the clock-driven demands of the overseer. A more intense work regimen purged much leisure from life and, for the rich and successful, industrialization substituted an ethic of economic accumulation for leisure. The factory imposed a new division in the lives of ordinary people: work time (for income) became separated from family time when jobs were removed from the household and centralized in the workshop or office. The result was an incalculable change in family and recreational life. Finally, industrialization meant the disruption of traditional village or community culture as rural workers flooded the new industrial towns and their leisure customs often were lost. Old paternalistic ties between the elites and the common people were torn when the wealthy withdrew support from festivals and when the powerful attempted to impose new forms of recreation upon an often reluctant population.

Many observers have described these changes in the negative term "breakdown." Industrial society meant a loss of "natural rhythms" of work and leisure, an erosion of traditional bonds within families and between the classes, and the degradation of industrial workers, who often sought escape in alcohol and immoderate sensuality. Yet, as we shall see, this despairing image is exaggerated, for workers retained much of their traditional leisure ethic and, in the long run, industrialization created the foundation, for better or worse, of our modern notions of work and leisure.

This chapter focuses on the linkages between work and leisure during a slow period of economic change, often somewhat misleadingly referred to as the "industrial revolution." It started in Britain about 1780 and in the U.S. about 1810. Its first phase ended perhaps by 1850. For the sake of clarity, I will stress the similarities between the two countries, leaving for later chapters discussion of the differences.

Industrial Time

The mechanized world of work was impossible without a radical change in
thinking about time. Historians have long noted that the clock was as important
as the steam engine in the industrialization of work. It gave the 18th century
employer the ability to precisely measure time and thus to quantify, control, and
eventually to intensify the pace of work. When the cheap standardized watch
emerged in the middle of the 19th century, the possibility of clock discipline
became fully realized. The nineteenth-century factory clock—often perched
high in its ornate copula—was both a symbol and tool of a new work discipline.
It reminded all of the fact that time was the new deity and that it meant money.
The clock set the standard for when work began and ended. Those failing to
pass underneath it and through the factory gates before it showed 6:00 AM were
locked out; they often were obliged to enter via the pay office to be subject to a
reprimand and fine.[1]

Another key to industrialization was the factory. As many historians
have stressed, it was more the centralization of work rather than mechanization
itself that allowed employers to dictate the length and intensity of the workday.
Weavers, for example, were forced to work in a mill where they lost the ability,
which they had enjoyed in their own cottage workrooms or family farms, to
control the pace or methods of work. Work regulations and factory designs
along the lines of Jeremy Bentham's ideal prison, the Panopticon, were intended
to assure a regular and constant attention to the job. Strategically-placed
overseers capable of watching every worker were combined with a system of
posted rules and fines for the slightest "falling off" of work. By 1760,
timesheets, timekeepers, and fines for tardiness had appeared in the Crowley
Iron Works of Britain. Josiah Wedgwood's pottery works at Eururia had
established a primitive-time card system to monitor punctuality. Even small-
family New England mills in the 1810s "demanded that during working hours
operatives display the traits of punctuality, temperance, industriousness,
steadiness, and obedience to mill authorities." These efforts to instill work
discipline in the factory were similar to the new schools and penitentiaries,
poorhouses, and insane asylums that appeared in the first half of the 19th
century in the Anglo-American world. They all promised to correct social ills
and to create new people "reclaimed, civilized, Christianized," through routinized work.[2]

Southern Pennsylvanian textile factory rules as late as 1846 shared this
spirit:

> No person employed in the manufacturing departments can be
> permitted to leave their work without permission from their
> overseer... No talking can be permitted among the hands in any of

the working departments, except on subjects relating to their
work.... No spirituous liquors, smoking or any kind of amusements,
will be allowed in the workshops or yards.[3]

Finally, the new machines, themselves, forced the worker to submit to
longer hours and increased intensity of work. First, a small number of power
machines invented between the 1760s and the 1780s (spinning throstles and
mules, carding machines, and looms, e.g.) were harnessed both to James Watt's
steam engine and to the traditional water wheel. Mechanization, of course,
reinforced the tendency of employers to centralize production in a factory.
Spinners and weavers, who continued to labor at their cottage spinning wheels
or hand looms, could no longer compete with the machine. Workers were
obliged to accept the work discipline of the factory. Spinning throstles or mules
may have eliminated the burdens of the peasant women at her spinning wheel,
but they produced new factory jobs that were relentless and monotonous. The
impersonal machine set the pace of work and drove episodes of leisure out of the
job.[4]

The factory sometimes also led to a longer work week in the early 19th
century. Especially in the newly mechanized textile industry, hours of work
extended to 12 or 14 hours per day for six or even seven days per week.[5] In
1844, a French observer in Lancashire (England) commented:

> The operative is a slave, obliged to adapt his movements to those
> of the machine to which he is attached; advancing when it advances
> and retiring when it retires, struggling with it in velocity, and no
> more able than it to rest. Experienced officers declare that a soldier
> cannot remain more than six or eight hours under arms without
> inconvenience. How then must it be for a spinner, who must not
> only keep standing every day, but must walk to and fro, going from
> one machine to the other, for a period of thirteen to fourteen hours,
> and where the attention as well as the muscles are incessantly in
> exercise.[6]

Mill owners had many economic incentives to extend the work week:
They were obliged to meet bitter competition, which constantly drove them to
cut costs, and they had to quickly recover the costs of machinery that rapidly
became obsolete. Finally, they sought to take advantage of new gas lighting by
working their machinery and "hands" into the evening hours. Moreover, factory
workers lacked the means of challenging these innovations. Unlike some skilled
artisans, they were seldom organized; the majority were women and children
who were hired both for their presumed docility and adaptability to the "light"
work, for example, of piecing broken threads on mechanical looms. In 1836,
85 percent of workers employed in a Massachusetts textile company were
women and 80 percent of these were between 15 and 30 years old. In the same
period, English textile mills employed far more children.[7]

Yet it was not only the factory worker who experienced a longer and more intense workday in the early 19th century. Craftworkers in cities like London, New York, and Philadelphia experienced significant loss of autonomy in such industries as tailoring, woodworking, shoemaking, and many other traditional crafts that saw little mechanization before 1850. Nevertheless, they experienced a dramatic change in work. Skilled journeymen increasingly found it difficult to "graduate" to the status of master; instead, many remained throughout their work lives as merely wage-earners laboring in ever increasingly large and impersonal work rooms. For example, by 1835 in New York City, half of the journeymen were aged thirty or more and the majority were married with no hope of leaving wage-earning status. Efficiency-minded managers broke jobs into more productive but less complex and often less satisfying tasks. Individual payment by the piece (number of articles produced) increasingly was used to encourage more steady and rapid output.[8]

Yet perhaps the most onerous working conditions were experienced by the garret or even cottage worker caught in the net of the "sweating" system. Competition among merchants and consumer demand for inexpensive articles of clothing created the "slop" shop. Slop merchants farmed out cloth or other raw materials at low prices to "sweaters" (often craftsmen themselves) who competed bitterly against each other. Sweaters, in turn, contracted out the materials to poor seamstresses, woodworkers, and other artisans at very low prices. The result, declared English journalist Henry Mayhew, was that "underpay makes overwork." By the 1830s, 43 percent of New York craft workers labored under these conditions. Hand weavers in London in 1849, who competed against the mechanical loom, complained that hours had risen one-third since 1824. Moreover, periodic slack seasons obliged slop clothing workers to toil from 5:00 AM to 9:00 PM for six months per year simply in order to pay debts accumulated during periods of unemployment.[9]

During the 19th century, many proud skilled workers clung to the idea that they were "independent" artisans who freely contracted with a supplier of raw materials to make cabinets or shoes on their own time. Still, employers were increasingly able to impose their vision of labor as a commodity—a human machine who sold his or her time to the manufacturer.[10]

These changes in work had a great impact upon leisure. Factory managers were not only able to intensify work, but they could purge play from work. Mill owners in Lowell, Massachusetts, required their largely single female workforce to live in dormitories, which they regulated with a paternal hand. All employees were required to attend church and to meet a 10:00 PM curfew. In the 1830s, the Lawrence Company warned: "every kind of ardent spirit (except proscribed by a regular Physician) will be banished from the limits of the corporation."[11] Employers, increasingly dependent on a regular daily labor supply, came to treat St. Monday as mere absenteeism and punished it as such. This leisure tradition had disappeared from all but the most tradition-bound trades by mid-century in Britain.[12]

Perhaps the most obvious effect of early industrialization on leisure was its impact on children's play. Of course, children in the old cottage industries or on the farm were often horrendously overworked. Labor began at seven or eight years of age and work hours often were as long as those for adults. Yet the physical and psychological impact of the factory was often worse. Long hours were not redeemed by periodic bouts of play or distraction, as was common in cottage trades, and the work was repetitive and tended to distort physical development. Factory children were commonly beaten to keep them awake during their long working hours; child coal haulers toiled in narrow shafts of mines; and little boys assisted chimney sweeps, cleaning the tiny passages that only a child could enter. Many observers to Samuel Slater's Fall River Mills or to the spinning factories of Lancashire noted the stunted moral and educational development of children deprived of not only schooling but even of parental supervision. And, of course, children had little time to play.[13]

From practically the beginning of the factory system, reformers took interest in the fate of mill children, reflecting not merely the deterioration of children's working conditions, but also the growing sensitivity to the developmental affects of constant labor upon the immature. Reformers realized that child's play was a physical and social necessity and that the factory Moloch was devouring time for this essential purpose.

Industrialization, the Home, and Sex Roles

Surely one of the greatest effects of industrialization was the split of domestic from economic time. The French observer, Léon Faucher, noted in 1844: "The factory has invaded the family hearth. To enlarge this circle, hitherto too contracted, it has commenced by breaking it. Life in the future, both for the employer and for the employed, will have two phases—the domestic hearth and society."

When the factory system removed the machine and the worker from the cottage's common room, both the time and space of the laborer became radically disjointed. As one investigation in 1833 noted, the British factory worker's discontent was not merely due to wages but also to "the separation of families, breaking up of households, the disruption of all those ties which link man's heart to the better portion of his nature, – viz his instincts and social affections..."[14]

The workers' day became segmented into hours of work and hours of leisure, each conducted in different, often distant places. The family unit that had traditionally labored together now worked for different employers or in different places in the same mill. Although a father often attempted to keep his working children together (for example, as his helpers if he was a "mule spinner"), this was often impossible. Sometimes factory managers prohibited it.[15]

The impact of this dispersal of the family was complex (and will be developed in subsequent chapters). Still, an outline here is important:

1. It meant that work and leisure would increasingly be experienced as radical opposites, rather than as complementary, even indistinguishable activities. Work was something the factory operative (or clerk) went to. It consumed a period of time in which his or her freedom was relinquished, and work was an instrument for deferred pleasure "after hours." Gradually, people expected less intrinsic satisfaction from work and, instead, sought increased compensation for it and more time free from it.

2. This division localized leisure outside of the work environment. By removing wage-work from the home, it made the domestic shelter the "haven from a heartless world" of increasingly impersonal labor and economic competition. Thus a cult of "domestic pleasures" emerged, deliberately privatized in the home and defined over against the world of business and labor.[16]

3. The segmentation of work and leisure tended to separate, if not polarize, the generations. Fathers, for example, had less control over their children's vocational training (especially in the working classes) and probably less influence over their offspring's social development. The father's guidance of, or even play with, children was probably less common in the era of the early factory than when the family worked together in their nine-foot cottages.[17]

4. Perhaps most subtle, the industrial system separated female from male experiences. While men increasingly became distant "outside" breadwinners, women gradually lost contact with the world of business and labor. The working-class girl might well take a job in a mill (or more often as a servant in the new households of the industrial well-to-do). However, she would retire from employment once she married and had children. Only in low-wage trades was this not common. The reason for this was simple. Because wage work and family life ceased to be conducted in the same place (i.e. the household), women were no longer able to combine economic and family functions. As a result, they had to segment their lives into periods of work before marriage and periods of housewifery afterwards. This necessity, of course, was reinforced by the Victorian ideology of the "women's sphere," which placed all the domestic burden upon the female. Still, lack of birth control and personal services for the working classes made any other solution impractical.

Women increasingly had very different work and leisure experiences from men. For females, work outside the home was a temporary station between childhood and marriage. Interest in improving their wages and working conditions was often slight, even though women were underpaid and overworked compared to men. Moreover, after marriage, women retained many of the same attitudes toward time and work that had characterized the traditional artisan: housewives were often "task conscious"—organizing their day in accordance with the immediate demands of children, cleaning, and cooking. They often interspersed these tasks with episodes of semi-leisure activity, conversation and decorative crafts, for example. Depending on the availability of help from children or servants, a woman's day was relatively "porous," even if usually long and often lonely.

By contrast, the male became "time-conscious" in the factory or office. His day was organized by the clock and was more or less routinized. For him, the coming of "quitting time," separated the compulsion of work from the freedom of leisure. And, of course, most husbands expected to have homes that were "castles"—places exclusively for relaxation and the opposite of the submissive or competitive roles often imposed on them at work. "Home" and "after hours" meant leisure.[18] Women's historians have noted that the "two spheres" dividing male and female became a dominant idea only in the early industrial era.[19]

As an English woman remembered her late 19th-century childhood, "in all our working-class neighborhood, I never knew one mother who went out to work. However, poor, they 'cut their coat according to their cloth' as my mother was fond of saying. In other words, what they couldn't have they did without." Fathers, comments English historian John Burnett, "dutifully brought home their wage-packets on Saturday afternoon [but] were not expected to share in the routine housework: they might mend shoes, repair household articles, dig their allotment [garden] and, perhaps, play with the children, but they expected their meal to be on the table, the fire to be burning brightly and their best suit ready for the weekend."[20]

Finally, if men adopted more "modern" views of work, women developed innovative approaches to leisure. While the male sought to increase productivity or income on the job, the women in the home attempted to reduce the toil of domestic tasks of cleaning and child-rearing. This is one important reason why the number of children women bore decreased nearly one-half in 19th century America (and somewhat less in Britain). Increasingly, wives and mothers shifted time from onerous domestic work to "organizing" leisure in the family. Women became the focal point for new domestic leisure built around "togetherness" and gentility rather than the traditional and often rough community pleasures of peasant society. Working-class mothers were sometimes the allies of reforming elites who often tried to play wives against the traditional leisure of their husbands.[21]

For the early 19th century, the picture that we have just painted is an idealization only. Economic limitations imposed on the working-class family prevented it from becoming a reality. Indeed, the "breakdown" of the working family seldom resulted from conflicts between men and women over their increasingly different views of work and leisure (although this occurred). Rather, the problem was in the inability of the laboring poor fully to adopt this model of the "two spheres"- for women were often obliged to work outside the home and men's income was often insufficient to do without women's wage work.

Even radicals like Friedrick Engels saw in the factory a threat to female-orchestrated domestic felicity: "When women work in factories, the most important result is the dissolution of family ties." Opponents of child labor were particularly concerned about female youth. One British reformer noted in

1844 that the twelve-hour day began for the girl at 13 years of age, "the tenderest period of female life." The survival of civilization required that this practice be abandoned.[22] By contrast, few 19th-century reformers (outside the powerless ranks of the factory operatives) were interested in liberating time for male leisure. It went almost without saying that such freedom would be "wasted" in traditional recreational activities. The "two spheres" appeared first in the middle class; and then as incomes rose, it trickled down into the working-classes (Chapter 9).[23]

Industrialization and Community

Industrialization affected leisure by transforming work and family. It also had a profound impact on the broader social life of the community. Social historians have often claimed that industrialization led to the breakdown of village life and the deterioration of traditional leisure. The outflow of rural people to the factory towns depopulated rural areas and concentrated workers into urban slums. The masses, uprooted from the parish churches and village alehouses, were then deprived of the focal points of their past leisure culture.[24] This picture, as we shall presently note, is exaggerated. Still, new urban environments seldom had the green space or public facilities necessary for maintaining sporting customs or even regular socializing. As the cities expanded, open spaces were gobbled up by developers. What was left, of course, was the street and the pub.

As important, perhaps, was the withdrawal of elites from the patronage of popular leisure. Robert Malcolmson and others have noted how the English gentry after about 1780 abandoned support for traditional sports. The Puritan's fear of idleness had spread to the broader English elite and was combined with a fervent desire to increase labor discipline and productivity.[25]

In the 1810s, the British Society for the Supression of Vice pressed local magistrates to prosecute drunks, cock throwers, bear baiters, Sabbath breakers, and even nude sea bathers. The London Common Council drove the St. Bartholomew Fair out of business in 1854 by harrassing organizers with rent hikes and legal restrictions. Throughout Britain in the 1840s, new professionalized police forces drove the young playing pitch-and-toss from the streets and even exterminated the ancient sport of pigeon-flying. Rural traditions in 1800 of up to 13 days of games, dancing, and drinking at Whitsunside were reduced to a single Bank Holiday by the 1870s.[26]

To a degree, this response was part of a growing revulsion against the violence of traditional culture. Note, for example, the founding of the Society for the Prevention of Cruelty to Animals in Britain in 1824. Yet often there was also a clear class bias in these campaigns. While magistrates repressed cock fighting, they and their gentlemen friends were taking up fox hunting. As one commentator wrote in 1809:

A man of ten thousand a year may worry a fox as much as he
please, may encourage the breed of a mischievous animal on
purpose to worry it; and a poor labourer is carried before a magis-
trate for paying sixpence to see an exhibition of courage between a
dog and a bear! Any cruelty may be practised to gorge the stomachs
of the rich; none to enliven the holidays of the poor.[27]

The English elite was increasingly concerned with the rights of private property;
they fenced in lands and pathways which had been essential for the playing of
popular games and for access to the countryside. The well-to-do had surely
become more exclusive and insistent on physical distance from the "commoner
sort."[28]

    In the American frontier boom-town of Rochester, New York, in the
1820s, there was a similar breakdown of paternalism. Increasingly, employers
ceased to provide lodgings in the shop for their laborers and clerks. The owning
classes moved into new, exclusive neighborhoods and, in so doing, lost direct
influence over their employees' leisure hours. In the U.S. as well as Europe,
leisure time became increasingly class-stratified.[29]

Some Consequences and Mollifying Factors

Perhaps the most obvious effect of the factory was the simple reduction of time
available for leisure. Time is always the most scarce resource, for it is involun-
tarily consumed but never accumulated. The only thing that we can do about
time is to reallocate it. But the industrialists' drive for efficiency did not liberate
time from work even though it may have produced "labor-saving" machinery.
Instead, the new factories often lengthened the traditional workday, at least in
the early nineteenth century; twelve or more hours per day were not unusual.

    Yet this was hardly a unvarying trend. For example, as late as 1851,
even in industrial Britain, workers in non mechanized industries outnumbered
mechanized trades by three to one. The 10-hour workday was not increased
during the century in most construction and metal trades, despite employer
efforts in the 1830s to raise it. Amazingly, only where women and children
worked did employers impose more than an effective three-day week upon
Birmingham and Black Country workers in the mid-19th century! The real
lengthening of the workday in 19th-century Britain took place mostly among
workers in mechanized textile mills and other trades competing against the
machines and overcrowding.[30]

    In rural America, at the Harper's Ferry Armory in western Virginia,
two generations of efforts by Yankee managers failed to eradicate absenteeism
for hunting and fishing in the first half of the 19th century. In the 1830s,
Philadelphia's artisans continued to pass around the communal jug in the late-
afternoon "treating time." The same was true of the "Puritan" New England
factory, where one study found an absenteeism rate of 15 percent in 1830.[31]

Despite the 19th-century trend toward an unvarying and more intense work year, laborers were often able to defend traditional leisure institutions and customs. Many dock workers preferred a seasonal work year, alternating long and arduous workdays with long periods of what the workers called "playing." This custom survived despite the efforts of reformers. As late as 1914, young machinists at a Glasgow Scotland engine works "never started work after holidays on the appointed day.... At some places they used to assemble at the gate and throw a brick in the air: if the brick stayed up they started work, but if it came down again they went for a drink."[32] The pace of mechanization was far slower than is painted in the textbook picture of the Industrial Revolution, and the resistance of especially skilled male workers to the imposition of clock-discipline is often underestimated. Perhaps the "Puritan" psychologist, Sigmund Freud, is correct when he wrote that "human beings manifest an inborn tendency to negligence, irregularity, and untrustworthiness in their work and have to be laboriously trained to imitate the example of their celestial models."[33] The low output of offices on Friday afternoons and the well-known gaps in the workdays of professors and students is evidence of the continued success of the lucky and resourceful to evade the standards of the time and motion ethic.

Still, critiques of the early factory almost unanimously complained that industrialization stimulated degrading forms of leisure. The frequenting of the brightly-lite "gin mill" after work, where wages were quickly drowned in strong drink, is a common image. The association of the breakdown of social controls in the industrial cities with the rise in sexual promiscuity was equally strong. Implicit, and often explicit, in these analyses is the view that the disintegration of family, especially of paternal authority and responsibility, is to blame for debauchery.

Drinking, which we noted was central to traditional peasant leisure, may have, in fact, changed in the industrial context. Consumption probably increased, as did the number of dispensers of drink in both America and Britain. In the 1820s, in England, drink retailers were roughly equal in number to food dispensers. In 1831, the per capita consumption of spirits was 1.11 gallons (compared to .22 in 1931); each Englishman drank 21.6 gallons of beer (dropping to 13.3 gallons one hundred years later). In the late 1820s, American men were drinking, on average, half a pint of hard liquor per day. Long days of unemployment brought on by trade depressions were often filled by drinking. And, in many trades, laborers waited in taverns to be called to work by hiring agents. Drink was also an obvious escape from the dead-end of the monotonous factory job and the loneliness of the city. It was, said Friedrich Engels, the "quickest way out of Manchester." In America, "solo-drinking" seems to have increased as did alcohol dependency in the disruptive decades of the 1820s and 1830s.[34]

Charles Dickens's *Sketches by Boz* contrasts the slum with the gin palace and gives us insight into the appeal of the bar:

> The filthy and miserable appearance of this part of London can
> hardly be imagined.... Wretched houses with broken windows
> patched with rags and paper; every room let out to a different
> family and in many instances to two or even three; a bird-fancier
> in the first floor, three families on the second, starvation in the attics,
> Irishmen in the passages.... filth everywhere—a gutter before the
> houses and a drain behind them.... Men and women, in every variety
> of scanty and dirty apparel, lounging, scolding, drinking, smoking,
> squabbling, fighting and swearing.
>
> You turn the corner. What a change! All is light and brilliancy. The
> hum of many voices issues from that splendid gin-shop which forms
> the commencement of the two streets opposite, and the gay building
> with the fantastically ornamented parapet, the illuminated clock, the
> plate-glass windows surrounded by stucco rosettes, and its profusion
> of gas-lights in richly gilt burners, is perfectly dazzling when cont-
> rasted with the darkness and dirt we have just left.[35]

The gin-palace offered a gaudy elegance, the opposite of the home lives of working people.

Besides intoxicants, industrialization also produced an epidemic of extramarital sex. Illegitimacy rates in Europe increased up to tenfold between 1750 and 1850. The social pressures of the traditional village and the careful supervision of masters and relatives, which had been a powerful impediment to youthful sexuality, apparently had broken down in the new industrial towns.[36]

However, there are a number of alternative ways of understanding this increase in alcohol consumption and sexual activity. The pub may be under-stood as the one true institution of the working man (seldom of women). The pub or tavern was, for many, the only place available for socializing, and the publican or bar owner often replaced the church and gentry in patronizing traditional sports (e.g. bull baiting) or serving as the impresario of musical entertainment. In the 1830s, the English publican often hired professional singers and other acts to attract customers from the unregulated beershops. As Léon Faucher describes how the Manchester gin palace had emerged in the 1840s:

> By degrees, the dim lights have been replaced by the dazzling gas;
> the doors have been enlarged; the pot-house has become a gin-shop;
> and the gin-shop a species of palace. The games hitherto carried on
> in these places not being sufficient, the proprietors have added music,

dancing, and exhibitions, as additional attractions to a dissolute people. ... The swelling of the organ, and the sounds of the violin and the piano, resound in their large saloons. One of these houses.... collects in this manner, one thousand persons, every evening, until eleven, PM.

The bar provided not only the space for drinking but the club atmosphere essential for free discussion of political and cultural issues. Trade unions, choral societies, sports clubs, and other working-class institutions had only the pub to shelter them.[37]

Even the data on alcohol consumption can be read in optimistic ways. Industrialization reinforced the traditional view that liquor was a safe replacement for unhealthful and even absent water supplies in the growing cities. Intoxicants were one of the few ways of disposing of grains and fruits in both countries in this era before modern food preservation; thus, farmers and the drink interests were often together powerful lobbyists against temperance. Before 1830, American frontier farmers relied on the local distiller to buy surplus corn and rye. Finally, British historian Brian Harrison argues that the campaign of the 1820s and 1830s against "drunkenness is as much an indication that the ancient inseparability of work and recreation had become inconvenient [to employers] as that drunkenness had itself become more prevalent."[38]

Moreover, Edward Shorter argues that increased signs of "promiscuity" should not be read as a social (or leisure) problem. Rather, increased illegitimacy indicates merely increased sexuality and even the emergence of romantic or individualistic love. Youths, Shorter claims, were no longer willing to forego physical expressions of affection for the sake of economic prudence or parental wish. This argument is debated: others claim that increased illegitimacy is an index of declining social controls, which had formerly pushed male courtiers into marrying pregnant lovers.[39]

Less controversial is the view that these trends in alcohol use and sexuality were not unmitigated examples of the breakdown of family. Indeed, despite these signs of atomized leisure, family solidarities survived the decline of the domestic economy. In the Lancashire town of Preston, social historian Michael Anderson has shown that families—far from breaking under the strain of urban and industrial life—actually were strengthened. Family members relied on each other for material and psychological assistance. Herbert Gutman shows the same phenomenon for black families in slavery and in the urban environment of the late-19th century. And Tamara Haraven makes a similar point for New Hampshire textile families.[40] These economic alliances were solidified in family leisure; early industrialization produced Sunday evening family get-togethers and family reunions during annual summer "wakes weeks." If industrialization broke up the extended family, the railroad made possible its reconstitution during holidays.

Finally, the withdrawal of patronage from traditional leisure has been blamed for the decline of communal sport and festival customs. The American historian, Mary Ryan, finds a linkage between the growth of cities in the 1840s and the decline of voluntary associations. Old community ties were fragmented by class stratification, and the impersonal character of urban life undermined fraternal groups such as fire departments.[41] Numerous historians have noted a similar decline of mechanics and other societies of skilled artisans as well as traditional festivals during the disruption of early industrialization.[42]

However, the tenacity of community and traditional leisure must be stressed. Despite years of pressure to eliminate the unruly mass football game at Derby England, players were able to overcome official harassment until 1847. Many workers from Derby found in this annual event an opportunity to assert a right to a traditional holiday, a reunion of old friends, and casual competition. The same tenacity was shown toward the celebration of the Stamford Bull Run. The authorities required 20 metropolitan police and 43 dragoons, in addition to 90 local constables, to prevent a Bull Run in 1839. And, in any case, important sections of the British political elite were wary of abandoning traditional sports and leisure.[43] Traditional fairs and circuses were, in fact, revived by the railroads and trams. The new freedom of distance allowed urban workers to flood traditional village wakes or to attend formerly remote races (Chapter 9).[44]

Portents of Change

The industrialization of the early 19th century was not merely a story of loss of traditional leisure and resistance to it. This new economic world helped to produce changes in the meanings of work and leisure. These changes may be divided into three broad areas:

1. Even if industrialization intensified and, to a degree, lengthened the work year, it also spurred movements for new allocations of time. As a result, the day, week, year, and life would be rearranged to carve out new blocks of time for leisure in the evening, weekend, summer vacation, childhood, and old age.

2. The breakdown of community leisure traditions may have deprived workers of their past recreational outlets and sparked class-cultural conflict; yet industrialization also helped to create new leisure attitudes and values. Not only the owning classes and religious groups advocated a more "rational," individualistic, and humane leisure culture, but large sections of the working classes and secularists shared this perspective. New ideas about recreation became the foundation of the modern leisure ideals of physical fitness, adult education, and cultural enrichment. The next three chapters will explore these three trends.

3. If the separation of work and home weakened the bonds of the family, it also tended to liberate the domestic sphere for leisure. The home became the focus of family-based recreations centered around the child and often organized by the mother. New attitudes toward the leisure of youth also resulted.

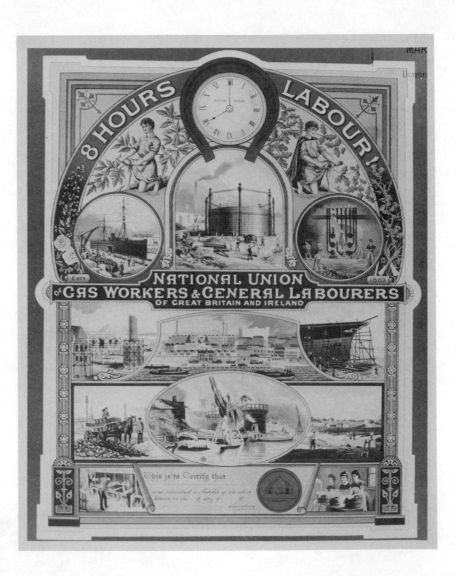

6

The Quest for Leisure: 1820-1900

In the long run, industrialization brought the reduction of worktime. The hours per year committed to work have declined in the industrial West in a range from 3,000-3,600 to 1,800-2,000 from 1840 to the present. Simultaneously, the work life of the average individual has also decreased sharply at both ends—as the age of entry into the full-time workforce has risen from about 10 to 20 and retirement has become a common experience. Of course, not all of this time liberated from work went to additional hours of leisure; still, this gradual reallocation of time has made possible a dramatic change in the quantity and quality of free time.

This redistribution of time has been accompanied by a drastic "repackaging" of leisure hours. Industrialization drove play from labor and eliminated the seasonal ebbs in the flow of work so characteristic of artisanal and agricultural life; it also made possible new forms of leisure time, including the typically modern notions of free evenings, the weekend, paid summer vacations, as well as a lengthy childhood and retirement.[1]

Why and how this occurred over the last one hundred and fifty years is more complex than it might first appear. This reallocation of time was not simply a byproduct of mechanization—a tetter-totter effect of rising productivity and declining working hours. In fact, as new technology increased output, that gain was more likely to be absorbed in higher profits or increased consumption than in freedom from work. Labor-saving devices did not often mean less work but more goods and investment. An increase in hours for leisure was sporadic. In a trade-off between money and time, money usually won. Indeed, as we say, time became money, signaling a defeat of the preindustrial "leisure ethic" that had so often frustrated merchants in the 17th and 18th centuries.

The reallocation of time was discontinuous. It occurred in brief and often sharp changes, usually only after years of political and intellectual ferment. This quest for leisure had two faces. First, it was a complex accommodation to a new industrial understanding of time. Second, it was a challenge to the social and cultural implications of the 19th-century gospel of work.

A Revolution in Thinking About Time

"All society," says the French thinker Jacques Attali, "is constructed around a sense of time." Temporality is both a matter of technology and politics: changes in the means of measuring time has a decisive affect on how we organize society. Moreover, whoever controls the use and significance of other people's time has power over them. These two factors came together in the advent of the modern clock and the industrialist.[2]

It is a commonplace that the cadence of preindustrial societies was often set by the agricultural cycle and was marked by feasts and fasts organized by the clergy. The dominant attitude toward time was the notion of recurrence—the eternal repetition of nature—and the desire to merge past and present. This attitude sharply contrasts with the rhythm of industrial society, where work and society are synchronized and paced by the immutable regularity of the clock in service to business and industry. The driving compulsion in the modern world is mechanical regularity and the anticipation of the future in the present. Society no longer seeks to suppress time; rather, the object is to "gain" and "save" it.[3]

Technologically, the modern clock, with its capacity to measure minutes and (later) seconds, allowed a new intensification of the tempo of life. As a result, time has lost its religious meaning. Rather, in the eighteenth century, time became a measure of work and wealth. The ancient measure of time, the calendar, allowed for the play of irregular labor. Not so with the clock, which became an economic weapon to eliminate the gaps in the traditional day of work and assured a continuity and uniformity of output.

Politically, clock time become a tool of industrialists to regulate the minute flow of production. The clock, in part, allowed the employer to impose the work ethic upon the masses. From the 18th century British industrialist Josiah Wedgewood, with his fixed factory hours, to the early 20th century American engineer Frederick Taylor, with his stop watch, management capitalized on the power of the clock to regularize and intensify the pace of work.

As a result, traditional pleasures were purged from work and the pride of skill was diminished. More and more, a day's work meant merely the selling of time rather than a "way of life." Employers placed a monetary value on the hour and sought to increase its economic output; laborers responded in kind: they demanded overtime pay and a cap on the length of the "normal" workday. Thus they hoped to gain economically from their increased productivity, to make a job last longer, and often to share work among a larger group of wage-earners. Workers became aware that time was a scarcity to be protected and increased in value. They, too, realized that time was money.[4]

But industrialization had a more profound impact on thinking about time. Workers and employers not only adjusted to the new economic realities of worktime, they attempted to recapture leisure hours lost during industrialization and to "repackage" it. There were several alternative plans for rearranging leisure time. For example, as you may remember, Benjamin Franklin's strategy was to defer leisure to a later period in life—as early retirement. Other successful and well-to-do people concentrated leisure in lengthy holidays. In the 19th-century, this tradition spread from the independently wealthy to the hard-working business and professional classes.[5]

In contrast, the strategy of workers in the reallocation of time was more short-term. Their goal was to liberate hours from daily toil and to free a day or two from labor each week. Because the wage-earner lacked the opportunity to forego income for an extended period, he or she was unable to imitate the merchant, lawyer, and politician on the August vacation. With insufficient resources to "save" time (in reality, income), the worker sought to "spend" free time in frequent, regular, and necessarily short doses. Saint Monday was to the wage-earner of the mid-19th century, says British artisan Thomas Wright, what the vacation was to the businessman. Part of the middle-class resentment of the worker's inconstancy and apparent lack of "time thrift" may simply reflect contrasting ideas about distributing life time.[6]

By the end of the 19th-century, these different time strategies had largely merged. The goal increasingly became that of uniform durations of work, compressed into as few hours as necessary to maintain production and income. Leisure time was radically segmented from work and packaged into predictable frames of time. Leisure was distributed into long blocks of free hours extended over the day, week, year, and life span. This new approach to time contrasted with the traditional pattern of irregularity and the intertwining of work and leisure.[7]

This change of strategy was, in part, an accommodation to the exigencies of industrial capitalism. Workers had surely adapted to the reality of the segmentation of life introduced by the separation of work and home. They recognized the necessity of synchronizing interpersonal activities in the complex organizations that characterize industrial society. After all, the compression of work into an 8:00 AM to 5:00 PM schedule, five days a week, is one of the most rational ways of solving these problems. This changing view of distributing time may also simply reflect a growing instrumental attitude toward work as a mere economic means to practically the only remaining arena of personal freedom: leisure.[8]

This time strategy may also reflect the trickle down of the middle-class ideal to the masses. "Saving time"—forbearance of leisure until it could be coupled with income—was gradually embraced by all classes. Workers discovered the advantages of saving enough to purchase vacations sufficiently long to allow time away from the industrial environment. They also came to see the virtue of withholding children from work; and they even realized the value of time after retirement before ill-health reduced the use of "free time."

The repackaging of leisure time was not without conflict, however. First, the differences of time strategies between classes was surprisingly persistent. In particular, the ten-hour and eventually eight-hour movements captured the imagination of workers long before vacations, retirement, or even an extended childhood. These latter doses of leisure were far more popular with the elite.[9]

More important, the quest for leisure of workers in the 19th century challenged the status quo and its gospel of work. Shorter working hours represented a concrete demand for liberty, a demand for not only freedom from the fatigue and boredom of industrial work, but from the increasingly authoritarian environment of the modern factory or office. For example, shop and office workers from the 1840s sought to limit the right of employers to their time. Retail clerks strove to end the "living in" system, wherein the employee had lodgings at the shop and was often expected to be on call at all hours; they attempted to create a clear separation between the masters' time and space and their own.[10]

In many subtle ways, common people understood "free time" as a concrete expression of personal liberty. In an increasingly democratic age, the opportunity of leisure was seen as a right of citizenship. In the 1830s, reformers frequently compared long factory hours with New World slavery. In the 1860s, the American short-hours movement equated reduced working hours with the emancipation of Black slaves. And the American slogan, "Eight Hours for What We Will," perfectly expressed the quest for a common right to autonomous time.[11]

Finally, the wage-earner's embrace of the segmentation of time reflects a positive quest for family life. The ideal became not merely shorter workdays but the sharing of blocks of domestic leisure time. In effect, the objective was to reclaim family time lost when work and home were separated in industrialization. Nineteenth- and twentieth-century wage earners repeatedly resisted multiple shift work, sex and age-based variations in working hours, and even staggered vacations. There goal was simultaneous leisure time for working family members. With increases in income in the 19th century, people began to demand that working hours accommodate social as well as economic needs.[12]

Movements for Shorter Working Time: A Brief History

The above analysis has been rather abstract. Some of these points, however, can be illustrated by a concise overview of the movements for the reduction of worktime in American and Britain. Both 19th-century America and Britain were "liberal" or laissez-faire societies, reluctant, on principle, to regulate the interior life of business. The factory, like the cottage workroom, was viewed as private space, to be free from government intervention. The contract signed between worker and employee was likewise to be unconstrained. To regulate this relationship would deny the freedom to work. To be sure, this philosophy of government often coincided with business interests. Still, even when some employers called for reduced worktime, legislators and judges ruled for laissez faire. Thus, despite evidence that the new factories and their workday of thirteen or fourteen hours was detrimental to the health of workers, legislation was slow to reduce worktime. When hour laws were passed in the United States, they appeared in piecemeal fashion at the state level and were frequently reversed by the courts. And in Britain, such changes in worktime came very slowly and were formally limited to children and women.

Perhaps the earliest short-hour movement was the Manchester Cotton Spinners' Association. It was organized in 1818 by the English worker John Doherty. While it failed in its efforts to gain a legal ten-hour day, the movement was revived in 1831. Craft journeymen in Philadelphia and Boston in the 1820s also began appealing to the state to expand their leisure; and, in the early 1830s, women textile workers around Lowell, Massachusetts, orchestrated a ten-hour movement. The depression of 1837 stilled these struggles but, again in the mid-1840s, short-time committees sprang up in the industrial regions of both countries.[13]

The question of what motivated these movements is complex and controversial. One obvious goal was to reduce fatigue insofar as employers repeatedly increased the workload of operatives. Another was to spread work among the laboring community as mechanization and (especially in England) rapid population growth combined to create a surplus of workers.[14]

Beyond these economic goals were views that reflected changing attitudes toward leisure. The women workers of Lowell, Massachusetts, sought a ten-hour day in order to cultivate their own education and "improvement." Indeed, the religious piety that had swept New England in the 1830s served to instill not only a work ethic, but also a belief in the necessity of time for moral improvement. One short-hours activist wrote, "as a society we want to improve our moral condition—we want to increase the boundary of our knowledge and understanding—we want to have sufficient opportunity each day to perform the duties enjoined on us by our Maker and by mankind."[15]

Family life was especially an important issue in Lancashire, where mothers, fathers, and children all worked in the mills. As an English leader of the short-time movement said in 1833, free time would teach both sexes to be "good fathers and mothers, good husbands and wives." Short-hour activists linked free time to the rights of "free born Englishmen" and to the American ideology of "Republicanism." John Doherty asked "Is the personal liberty, or the actual imprisonment, of a very large portion of the king's subjects, *a mere matter of private business*."[16] Doherty certainly did not think so. He believed that free time was essential for removing "slavery in every form" in that it provided the means essential for self-education and participation in public life. The New England-based journal, *The Mechanic*, argued for the "necessity of promoting that independence, intelligence and virtue of the laboring classes which will enable them to wield the powers with which they are vested, with wisdom...."[17]

The idea that all citizens had an equal right to personal liberty was well expressed in the American anthem of the eight-hours movement published in 1866:

> We mean to make things over,
>   We are tired of toil for naught.
> With but bare enough to live upon.
>   And never an hour for thought;
> We want to feel the sunshine,
>   And we want to smell the flowers.
> We are sure that God has will'd it.
>   And we mean to have eight hours.
> We're summoning our forces
>   From the shipyard, shop, and mill:
> Eight hours for work, eight hours for rest,
> Eight hours for what we will![18]

Yet what were the results of these movements? In the 19th century, their victories were few and were channeled through the perspective of middle-class reformers and politicians. The British led the way: legislation in 1819 demanded a 12-hour daily maximum for children in cotton textile factories; in 1833, it was reduced to eight (with provisions for education); and in 1847, the working hours of women and children in textile mills were restricted to ten. Gradually, protection was extended to a variety of trades. While they excluded men, the close relationship between men's work and that of minors often led to reduced hours for adult males.

In America, the results were even more meager. While children under 12 were prohibited from working in Massachusetts as early as 1842, this law was slowly adopted by other states. Following the granting of a ten-hour day to federal government employees in 1840, skilled male workers were able to win a ten-hour day in the 1850s. Yet, only after thirty years of agitation, were women factory operatives able in New England to win meaningful legislation in the 1870s.[19]

Two factors about this halting movement to liberate personal time should be noted. First, legislators focused their attention on the factory rather than on labor in general. Second, they applied restrictions first to children and then to women, leaving men outside formal legislation, reflecting in part, the fact that some men working outside the factory were sufficiently organized to prevent an extension of traditional workdays beyond ten hours. The restriction, of course, directly affected the textile factories, where women and children predominated. In any case, legislators believed that the time of women and children should be protected from economic competition, whereas that of men should not.

From the late 18th century, there were signs of increased public interest in the welfare of the young, which was a direct consequence of the breakdown of the domestic economy or home-based work. While children of the poor had always worked, they had traditionally done so under the direct supervision of parents or a surrogate in a household. The factory often eliminated this tutelage and reformers sought to replace these natural protecters with a benevolent government.[20]

When legislators found that English parents were no longer in control of their children, they passed a law restricting the working hours of the young in 1819. The same argument was used by Richard Oastler in 1831, when he declared that children were "compelled to work as long as the necessity of [their] needy parents may require or the cold-blooded avarice of your worse-than-barbarian masters may demand."[21] Witnesses before an 1832 Parliamentary investigation complained of the "over-exertion and long confinement" of children in the factory and the need for the "improvement of their minds, the preservation of their morals and the maintenance of their health." Rough discipline and immoral environments reminded observers of "brothels." This led to an 1833 act restricting child labor to eight hours.[22]

The public in both countries was increasingly aware that children needed formal education (e.g., as provided in the 1833 law in England). The American educator, Horace Mann, supported hour laws for children. But the young also needed play. Some enlightened British employers like Robert Owen and Robert Peel provided playgrounds in the 1820s and a number of Manchester mill owners did the same by the 1840s.[23]

However, working-class parents, themselves, were often slow to embrace the idea that their offspring should enjoy a work-free youth. Children often earned half of the family income. Workers generally believed that child labor was a necessary form of discipline and training. Fathers sought to maintain authority over the training of their offspring by finding them jobs near them. Sociologist Niel Smelser has argued that early industrial families clung to the traditional ideal of the domestic economy, where the whole family worked together, and sought to transport it into the factory. Therefore, they favored the same workday for their children as for themselves. Thus, many families opposed the English eight-hour law for children only, and often attempted to evade it. In contrast, the middle classes adopted a new time strategy by withdrawing their offspring from the workforce; parents tolerated and even encouraged a lengthy childhood of education and play.[24]

Middle-class reformers accepted free time for women more slowly, however. By the 1840s, the idea of shorter working hours for females was widely embraced as a means of reversing an assumed decline of the family. Because of overwork, factory girls failed to receive proper domestic training; they were unprepared, reformers argued, to become mothers and anchors of social stability in the home. The Massachusetts House justified a ten-hour day for women on the grounds that "it was for the protection of the health of a large class of women of the State, and for the advancement of education among the children of our manufacturing communities." Even Friedrick Engels (a socialist but no less middle-class) believed that women working outside the home in factories frustrated male roles and thus "unsexed" the man and took "from the women all womanliness."[25]

These reformers advocated a new, far sharper, sexual division of labor: males as essentially breadwinners and females as domestic workers and organizers of family leisure. During the 1820s and 1830s, this ideal was coming to dominate middle-class families. Reformers were simply advocating it also for laborers.

If workers were slow to adopt the middle-class view of the child, the cult of female domesticity won widespread support. For example, the West Riding Short Time Committee in 1841 called for a ten-hour workday for women. The objective was to see the "gradual withdrawal of all women from the factories," for the "home, its cares and its employments, is woman's true sphere."[26] To be sure, male factory workers may have been advancing their own leisure interests "behind women's petticoats," as it was often said. Protective legislation for the "dependent" female (like the child) did not violate the "sacred" idea of the free labor contract (for women were legally incapable of making a legal contract). More important, such gender-based ideas had wide support during the Victorian era; the notion of a natural woman's "sphere" that had to be protected from economic pressures was widely accepted by conservatives and liberals alike. It was also embraced by working-class men; many hoped that shorter hours for women would lead to the discharge of women workers. Laboring men may have been able to realize this dream of having a housewife later than the middle-class, but they probably clung to it with more tenacity in the 20th century than did the more economically advantaged.[27]

Reformers did not, however, show this same openness to increased time free from work for adult males. Part of this was doctrinal: men were "free agents," whose liberty would be abridged if the state regulated their worktime (or wages). Lurking behind such articles of laissez faire faith was suspicion that male workers would "waste" additional leisure hours. Their presumed moral inadequacies were not consequences of the drudgery of overwork or the lack of time to cultivate family or refined leisure values. Such a view would have justified increased free time. Rather, their sins derived from the degrading culture from which the working classes sprung. More free time, the argument went, would only extend the period of immoral influence.

For example, Boston building contractors opposed a ten-hour day in the 1820s by claiming that "we consider idleness as the most deadly bane to usefulness and honorable living....[W]here there is no necessity, there is no exertion....We fear and dread the consequences of such a measure upon the morals and well being of society." And, another employer confirmed that viewpoint by saying that shorter days would open "a wide door for idleness and vice."[28]

Elites feared that adult males would use free time for political or trade-union agitation. Englishman George Bull, a Tory supporter of shorter hours for children, opposed its extension to men for that would be "too Republican" (i.e. democratic). Such men may have found palatable the "liberation" of children from work (if that would provide time away from immorality at work and for the inculcation of middle-class values in school and organized play). Even free time for women was a virtue, for no one expected them to be diverted from their many domestic duties to muddle in politics. Not so for the working-class male. Shorter worktime meant cultural autonomy, which undermined the political order.[29]

Finally, doctrinal laissez-faire ideas undermined the rationales for reducing the worktime of women and children. British economists argued against any regulation of the hours of children and, even more so, of women. In 1835, Alexandre Ure, in a famous passage in his *Philosophy of Manufacturers,* asserted that children took "pleasure in the light play of their muscles" in their work as piecers in textile factories. And Nassau Senior (1847) claimed that "the extraordinary lightness of the labour, if labour it can be called" made long hours for children perfectly acceptable. Despite the ideology of protecting "motherhood," economists warned again and again that shorter hours for women— essential to production—would destroy profit and give overwhelming advantage to foreign competition.[30] Similar views were held across the Atlantic. The Massachusetts legislature rejected a ten-hour law for women in 1846, claiming that, if it were passed, the state "could not compete with sister States, much less with foreign countries."[31]

In Britain, a political crisis of the late 1840s was necessary to establish the principle of a ten-hour day in industrial work. A massive petition for universal manhood suffrage (Chartism) in 1847 and the revolution on the continent in the Spring of 1848 comprised the backdrop for the concession of shorter worktime. Universal white male suffrage brought unskilled males more political power in the USA. Still, the fact that Americans faced no parallel political crisis in the late 1840s may help explain the slower evolution of hours legislation in the USA.[32]

Following the mid-century crisis, there gradually emerged a broad consensus in Europe that child and female workers should be protected from overwork. By the end of the 1850s, British textile employers generally conceded that sub-teenage children should not be allowed to labor in factories;

despite dire predictions, they recognized that industry could flourish with a ten-hour day. From 1860 to 1878, the British ten-hours act was gradually extended to most branches of manufacturing; yet, these laws never reduced worktime below the standards of skilled workers.[33] In America, following the Civil War, Short Time Committees sprang up in many industrial towns. In Massachusetts, these movements led by 1867 to a ten-hour law for children which was extended, in 1874, to women.[34]

In the late 1880s, there appeared another upsurge in labor activism in an extraordinary confluence of international movements for increased leisure. Between 1884 and 1891, a wave of agitation for the eight-hour day swept western European and American labor. It pointedly rejected the paternalism of earlier legislation, demanding a shorter workday as a right for all, regardless of age, sex, or working conditions. In America, the eight-hour movement peaked in a march of 20,000 through Chicago on May Day in 1886. It was discredited in the eyes of many by the famous "Haymarket Massacre" three days later in the same city when at a rally, a policeman (and others) were killed by a bomb. Still, when the American Federation of Labor called for national eight-hour demonstrations on May 1, 1890, admiring European labor representatives at the Second Socialist International joined with a similar appeal in Europe. Petitions were made for general eight-hour laws throughout the industrial world.[35]

The economic and social causes of this upsurge are complex. Despite diminutions of worktime at mid-century, continuing industrialization had not produced a corresponding decline of the workday. Instead, despite increases in real wages, sharp trade swings produced repeated bouts with unemployment in the 1880s. Many workers sought hour reductions in order to increase job security and wages.[36] Most important, workers viewed a uniform hour maximum, regardless of age or sex or even of the intensity or danger of work, as an extension of the rights of citizenship. In Britain, hour demands followed quickly on the extension of male suffrage in the 1880s. Sidney Webb, a moderate socialist reformer, declared in 1890 that the eight-hour day would be the "inevitable result of an age of democracy."[37]

The power of the eight-hour message was in its dream of increased and more predictable opportunities for leisure. The development of recreational opportunities in the 1870s and 1880s (Chapter 9) may explain a new interest in this reallocation of time from work. An eight-hour day, for example, to British painters and dockers meant a more regular work year, insofar as jobs would be stretched out over longer busy seasons. An eight-hour day would "equalize things a little" claimed an English miner in the 1890s. It would end alternating cycles of overwork and unemployment; instead, shorter working hours would create predictable blocks of leisure time and link income and free time.[38]

Workers also sought a more compressed workday. For example, British coal miners demanded improved machinery to reduce time wasted in the pit. Others insisted on the end to early-morning work. Many Victorians had pity for the textile worker of Lancashire, who was obliged to be awakened by a "knocker-up," who rapped on the bedroom windows of workers' lodgings with his long pole and attached umbrella wire. Many a laborer had to dress in a fireless room, trudge off to work to a cold and dark factory to make a 6:00 AM bell, and to work until 8:00 AM before having breakfast. Workers deeply resented this custom both because management often did not arrive until 9:00 AM and because so little work was done. Many Victorian workers sought a single-break system (beginning work *after* breakfast at 8:00 AM). Not only was it more "natural" but it allowed workers to stay up later and still be rested in the morning. As one supporter argued, the eight-hour day would assure the "full utilization of [workers'] evenings." After-work hours were necessary for the "satisfactory training of their families" and in order that workers would no longer be "strangers to the pleasures of home and domestic comforts."[39]

Another source of interest in increased free time came from commuters to cities. Increasingly in the second half of the 19th century, workers moved to more spacious and wholesome housing in suburbs usually far from work. Shorter hours were necessary to compensate for the increased time taken to journey to work and to make more extensive use of domestic leisure opportunities. The quest for reduced working hours can be seen as the only practical means of recovering the "bits" of play time lost in industrialization in "blocks" of family/leisure time. As historian G. Stedman Jones notes, with suburbanization, working-class men abandoned the pub of their workmates for the neighborhood bar, which they increasingly visited with their wives. Long evenings began to count more than long workbreaks.[40]

Finally, by the 1890s, some workers no longer felt the need to justify their leisure on family or moral grounds. The American slogan "Eight Hours for What We Will" expressed this attitude clearly. Leisure was a right that required no rationale. Listen to T. Steel from the Tyneside General Labour Union, who refused to apologize for the leisure activities of his workmates after they finished a 4:00 AM to 12:00 AM shift: "They please themselves; they have got their time to themselves....If there is a dog fight on or some other attraction, they will go out to that in the afternoon....I may say that dog fights are very nice things."[41]

Nevertheless, this agitation for an eight-hour day produced scanty results. The eight-hour demonstrations on May 1, 1890, quickly subsided into annual May Day rituals. And, while American activists in the 1890s were able to win an eight-hour day for women workers in Illinois, the courts struck it down.[42] Successful legislation had to wait until after World War I in Europe and to more piecemeal hour reductions in the USA (Chapter 11).

Franklin and Carlyle's homages to work stirred many a Victorian heart, but so did Dickens's cautionary tale of Ebenezer Scrooge, the workaholic businessman. Henry David Thoreau and his back-to-nature sojourn at Walden Pond in suburban Boston reveals doubts about the time-as-money ethic. The view that excessive time devoted to work was "unnatural" and "unhealthy" was expressed first by physicians against long working hours for children. But, by the end of the century, similar arguments were being used regarding adults, even men. Reformers recognized the physiological and psychological need for increased time from work. This concern with recreation as an antidote to the rigors of overwork became more intense in the 19th century. It seems to have paralleled the growing pressure and alienation of work, and it increased as salaried labor became, for many, a permanent fate and not a step to master or farmer status.[43]

Movements for shorter worktime are central for an understanding of the history of leisure. Without a reduction of the hours of work, obviously there could be no increase in leisure. Yet, despite dramatic increases in productivity, increased leisure lagged behind the material benefits of industrial society. Powerful political and economic forces frustrated the traditional desire to work less and to enjoy life as long as possible. Movements for shorter hours also represented an adaptation to industrial life—an abandonment of the "porous" and seasonal workday of the traditional domestic economy. In its place, short hours meant a more regular, predictable, and compressed workday, which freed relatively long blocks of time for autonomous family and leisure activity. These movements also expressed a protest against the workaholic society of early Victorian England and America. The content of this new, more positive, attitude toward recreation is our next topic.

THE DRUNKARDS PROGRESS.

FROM THE FIRST GLASS TO THE GRAVE.

STEP 1.
A glass with a Friend.

STEP 2.
A glass to keep the cold out.

STEP 3.
A glass too much.

STEP 4.
Drunk and riotous.

STEP 5.
The summit attained. Jolly companions. A confirmed drunkard.

STEP 6.
Poverty and Disease.

STEP 7.
Forsaken by Friends.

STEP 8.
Desperation and crime.

STEP 9.
Death by suicide.

7

Rational Recreation and the Victorian City: 1830-1900

Industrialization produced the modern city and urbanization created a leisure crisis in the 19th Century. Both the English and Americans were slow to extend leisure in proportion with economic growth. For employers and the upwardly mobile employee, "idleness" was a threat to industrial development and social stability. In Dickens's *Coketown*, "you saw nothing... but what was severely workful." And Alexis de Tocqueville noted in 1835 Americans "care much more for success than for fame." But many, including Dickens, also recognized that leisure time was the only arena for the "re-creation" of the physical and psychological capacity to work.[1] Recreation also had broader cultural implications. By the 1830s, reformers recognized that work and economic time had deprived members of society of the means of expressing the noneconomic values of religion, family, and self-development. For some elites, leisure was necessary for the preservation of the value of the traditional rural community. At the same time, these reformers held that leisure was perhaps the best place to inculcate the personal values essential for a growing commercial economy: self-control, familialism, and "respectability."

They advocated new forms of community and paternalism, perhaps even of social control. The idea was to build bridges to the "dangerous classes" of the new cities and to remake them in the image of the middle class. Yet, their concern with making recreation "rational" meant more than imposing the values of the elites on the masses. Many craftsmen, miners, and cotton spinners, both evangelical and secular, also embraced a rational leisure style. It was more constrained, individualistic, and "improving" than the pleasures of the English village or American frontier. Some of these wage earners were upwardly mobile, aspirants to foreman or self-employed status, who often embraced the personal religion of evangelical Protestantism. Others were militant members of trade unions and hostile to the paternalism of the well-to-do. Both workers and the elite were anxious over the social and economic disruptions of the 1830s and 1840s; they witnessed the certainties of the old family economy give way to a more complex, impersonal urban industrialism.

While a few nostalgically called for a return to the days of rural Merrie England or Thomas Jefferson's agrarian republic, the dominant trend was broadly forward-looking. New leisure forms would help to create a new type of personality in both the middle and laboring classes, more capable of adjusting to the new, expanding world of competition, urban life, and bureaucracy. Leisure reformers were not entirely successful in transmitting their values down the social ladder (or up it, in the case of the aristocracy), yet they helped to solidify a recreational style and ideology that still permeates modern youth and sports institutions.

These reforms were mostly urban. In many ways, the English created the modern urban and industrial landscape. By 1851, England was already half urban and, by 1911, 80 percent lived in towns or cities. Along with this precocious urbanism came the ideas of "rational recreation." Somewhat later the Americans followed these trends when, with urban explosion and the peculiar problems attending mass immigration, the United States also become a center of rational recreation.

This chapter will concentrate on the reform of the leisure of men because public urban recreation was largely masculine and because reformers were concerned about the uncontrolled leisure of men. The role of women in this process of "improvement" and changes in children's play will be treated in Chapter 8.

Restrictive Trends

At the heart of much reform of leisure in the early 19th century was fear of the "dangerous classes" of the urban working poor. Middle-class anxiety toward the disrespectful street behavior of the poor in the rookeries of London or the famous slum of Five Points in New York were similar to the views of many suburbanites to inner-city minorities in mid-20th century America or England. As an English reformer, Joseph Kay, put it, the poor "live precisely like brutes, to gratify...the appetites of their uncultivated bodies, and then die, to go they have never thought, cared, or wondered whither.... They eat, drink, breed, work and die; and... the richer and more intelligent classes are obliged to guard them with police."[2] Social disorder in American cities was, if anything, more threatening: between 1834 and 1844 there were more than 200 gang wars in New York City, involving such gangs as the Dead Rabbits and Bowery Boys. Rivalries between Protestants and Catholics in Philadelphia produced armed conflicts in 1844; and throughout the 1840s and 1850s, Saint Louis was continually disrupted by fist fights between rival voluntary fire companies.[3]

While Victorian employers on both sides of the Atlantic were gaining control over the work habits of their employees in the factory, after hours, and especially on Sundays, they were losing influence. Between 1810 and 1850, fairs and race days meant not only the appearance of pickpockets, prostitutes, and rowdy behavior, but even the prospect of insurrection. The English Beer Act of 1830 had allowed the proliferation of dens of humble ale sellers. The Victorian elite feared that, with higher incomes and increased leisure, the masses would be unworthy of their new freedom.[4]

Some of the business class felt at least partially responsible; in England especially, they had participated in the withdrawal of land and money from traditional leisure and sports. In 1834, Edwin Chadwick reported to Parliament how "the extensive and indiscriminate enclosure of commons which were play-grounds, ...drive the labouring classes to the public-house." The new and old rich almost alone benefitted from the construction of art galleries, concert halls, and lending libraries.[5]

Still the first and most common response was not to patronize working-class leisure but to restrict and to moralize it. The early 19th century witnessed a Puritanical reaction to the geniality of 18th-century leisure culture. Many conservatives in both countries believed that the democratic "excesses" of the American and French Revolutions had reduced the docility of the masses. When the vote was extended in America to the poorer males in the 1820s, elites feared that politicians would look the other way when confronted with the threats of drink, gambling, and prostitution. And the city was the core of the problem. American historian Paul Boyer summarizes the mood:

> The bawdy servant girl was transformed into the painted prostitute soliciting on the street. The village tavern became the beer cellar in the slum; the neighborly wager on the horse race or a cockfight, the organized gambling of the city. The unruly child and the discontented farm youth quarreling with his father became the multiplied thousands of street arabs and young urban newcomers who seemed to have broken free of all familial control.[6]

The American Alien and Sedition Acts (1798) and the British Anti-Combination Act (1800), which were designed to control political or trade union disruptions, were paralleled by efforts to monitor leisure. Religious activists spearheaded this movement. As the English historian Brian Harrison noted: "Nineteenth-century Christians deplored that recreational complex of behaviour which included gambling, adultery, drinking, cruel sports, and Sabbath breaking and blasphemy—all of which took place together at the race-course, the drinking place, the theatre, the feast and fair."[7]

From about 1800, British and American evangelicals organized campaigns to "Christianize" leisure.[8] The most important expressions of this movement were Sabbatarianism and the Sunday School. The Lord's Day was not simply to be a day of rest for all. In fact, English Sabbatarians sometimes revealed their social biases by tolerating work on Sunday for servants of the rich. More important, Sabbatarians sought to purge Sunday of amusement for the sake of unalloyed worship. English Sabbatarians pressed enforcement of a 1675 law prohibiting most Sunday commerce and industry, and placed pressure on post offices, coach, canal, and rail companies to suspend operations on the Sabbath. English Sabbatarians attacked Sunday newspapers and theater. In 1854, they managed to outlaw public drinking on Sunday afternoons until 3:00 PM. This action provoked the famous Hyde Park demonstrations of June 1855. Up to 150,000 workmen barricaded nervous wealthy promenaders in the park and shouted at them, "Go to Church!"[9] Soon thereafter pubs were reopened most of Sunday afternoon. Still, English Sabbatarians won a prohibition against brass bands in the parks on Sundays, prevented the issuance of some music hall licenses in the 1880s, and managed to block the Sunday opening of the British Museum and National Gallery until 1896.

Despite the fact that Sunday was the only day in the week available for workers' amusement, the rigorous Christian beleived that the Sabbath should be spent in Church and in religious study, and that those not sharing this ideal should not be allowed to flaunt their impiety in public. The Various Lord's Day committees were composed mostly of rather inflexible (and perhaps insecure) members of the influential commercial and gentry families; they saw respect of God's law as a barrier against general subversion of authority. In America, efforts at the national level to prohibit Sunday mails and to impose federal Sabbatarian laws produced general hostility from the government of President Andrew Jackson in 1828. Still New England's "Blue Laws" were extended in this period.[10]

Similar forces were behind the Sunday School. With roots in England in the 1780s, it spread to America in the 1820s. By 1830, 350,000 children attended Sunday Schools affiliated with the American Sunday School Union. In England, thousands were enrolled in the Sunday Schools of Midland towns, which were staffed by hundreds of volunteers.[11] Far more than merely a vehicle for religious training, the Sunday School instilled habits of punctuality, deference, self-control, and temperance. It was part of what the New England minister, Lyman Beecher, called a "disciplined moral militia"—the urban substitute for the informal social control of the village. In England until mid-century, working people learned to read and write in Sunday schools.[12]

English and American employers often required employee attendance. Unruly students were turned away from the class circle or placed in stocks. In America, after 1850 the Sunday school gradually became an adjunct of the middle-class church as children of the poor ceased to come. In England, students often willingly came and most of the teachers, if not the sponsors, were from the working classes.

Few students became regular church-goers but, as a result of this training, the Bible and *Pilgrim's Progress* became prominent fixtures of most English working-class homes. While some cynics like the social investigator, Charles Booth, argued that Sunday Schools were primarily an opportunity for parents to gain a little bedroom privacy on Sundays, they provided a wide array of leisure functions. They distributed youth magazines, offered musical training, and stimulated that unique English affection for the oratorio. Some offered social services and most provided an annual cycle of teas and Saturday afternoon excursions. The Sunday school became the home of many amateur football and cricket teams in 19th-century English mill and mining towns. It even became a center for political party agitation from the 1860s after the suffrage was extended to skilled labor.[13] However broad the functions of the Sunday School became with time, it was designed to give a religious content to the leisure of the masses in an era when the village parish church was in rapid decline.

Perhaps even more typical of a manipulative, or even coercive, approach to leisure was temperance or teetotalism.[14] These movements against alcohol, like Sabbatarianism, were mostly inspired by conservative religious forces. Temperance activists often saw abstinence as a complete solution to all society's ills. The temperance movement was a reaction to a perceived epidemic of alcoholism, which swept the Anglo-American world in the 1820s. In Britain, temperance advocates at first favored only voluntary abstinence from distilled spirits; in fact, they approved of loosening beer sales (in 1830) as a means of shifting popular taste from gin to the less malignant malt beverage. Their strongholds were within the dissenting churches and among the middle classes and Liberal party voters—although there were important Chartists and later trade unionists who supported this moderate approach. By 1835, frustrated by the failure of voluntarism, a faction of the British temperance movement group embraced voluntary teetotalism or complete abstinence; still others favored legal prohibition of drink. Teetotalers often came from the ranks of the wage-earner and some were reforming alcoholics. They saw the drunkard not as a weak person lacking the will to be a moderate imbiber, but as a victim who was paralyzed by alcohol. This addict must be liberated totally from the threat of drink and, if possible, be surrounded by a nurturing and separate teetotal culture.

While in Britain, prohibitionism was always politically marginal, in the USA, by the 1830s, socially powerful forces lent support to outlawing alcohol. New England ministers and their businessmen parishioners claimed that the sins of drink were especially prevalent among "the lowest classes [who] yield themselves up to the misrule of sordid appetite."[15] By the 1840s, aided by the religious enthusiasm that had recently swept America, prohibition had gained a prominent position in the Whig Party. Temperance employers eliminated the daily drams that had long been a part of workman's wages in trades like construction. By the 1850s, Prohibitionists had succeeded in restricting alcohol use in 13 states and territories.

Temperance advocates, like Sunday School promoters, were not always from the elite. American groups like the Washingtonians (and the female Martha Washingtonians) had chapters among craftsmen and clerks of New York

City, as did Methodist teetotalers among the miners of Cornwall. They took the pledge to abandon all intoxicating beverages and championed "nature's drink," cold water. Some teetotalers alienated traditional churchmen with their rejection of wine at communion. Total abstinence, not just moderation, was the only alternative to the life of the drunkard. They sometimes aggressively confronted boozers in an effort to convert them; they particularly appealed to young people. In the Cornish town in Redruth in 1838, English teetotalers held a "field day:"

> Following a sermon in the market place, the members marched
> behind a band through the streets with flags, ribbons and banners
> flying. They returned to the market place where about 300 took tea
> before leaving once again behind the band for the Methodist chapel
> where at a large meeting many new members were joined.[16]

By the 1840s, in the USA, Independence Day became the occasion for a contest of leisure cultures: July 4 had developed in the early 19th-century into a day of unrestrained communal drinking. In an act of deliberate confrontation, the Washingtonians held cold-water celebrations and young women vowed to shun suitors who drank.[17] Temperance groups, especially in New England, were dominated by women. For them, the saloon leisure of men was a threat to the economic and social security of the family. "To relieve the distressed mother and helpless children is our aim," claimed one American prohibitionist.[18]

Temperance was an alternative culture within working-class society. It often painfully separated teetotalers from neighbor and workmate who viewed them as "unfriendly" or even "undemocratic." Non-drinkers had to be shielded by an umbrella of alternative clubs, music halls, coffee houses, and reading rooms, in addition to churches, from the pervasive alcohol culture that surrounded them.

Temperance supporters, and especially prohibitionists, provoked powerful opposition. Their enemies were not only distillery and brewery interests, but the broad drinking public. In England, the Conservative Party sometimes rallied working-class support in opposition to teetotalism. In America, the ethnically-mixed Democratic Party (who attracted the Irish and other non-Puritanical peoples) became the party of "noncoercion." Some of the tone of the opposition to temperance can be seen in the following complaint of a man from Rochester, New York, in 1832:

> Who are the most temperate men of modern times? Those who
> quaff the juice of the grape with their friends, with the greatest good
> nature, after the manner of the ancient patriarchs, without any malice
> in their hearts, or the cold-water, pale-faced money-making men,
> who make the necessities of their neighbors their opportunity for
> grinding the face of the poor?[19]

In America, temperance forces reached a high-water mark in the early 1850s, but courts and legislators soon repealed or watered down many prohibition laws. The temperance movement was revived only after the founding of the Women's Christian Temperance Union in 1874 and the Anti-Saloon League in 1895, which won a brief victory in the Prohibition Amendment to the American Constitution (1919-1933). While consumption of hard liquor had decreased by half in between 1850 and 1900, saloon beer drinking rose from 2.7 at mid-century to 29.53 gallons per capita by 1911-1915. By 1900, there was one beer hall for every 50 men in American urban working-class districts.[20]

The emotional intensity of Prohibition can be summarized in this 1914 statement from the Anti-Saloon League:

> The vices of the cities have been the undoing of past empires and civilizations. There is no greater menace to democratic institutions than the great segregation of an element which gathers its ideas of patriotism and citizenship from the low grog shop... Already some of our cities are well-nigh submerged with this unpatriotic element, which is manipulated by the still baser element engaged in the un-American drink traffic and by the kind of politician the saloon creates... If our Republic is to be saved the liquor traffic must be destroyed.[21]

In fact, much of the support for prohibition came from the small-town native American, whose image of the city was that of a beer-soaked Sodom doomed by God to perdition.

In Britain, teetotalism never had such legislative success; however, the more moderate aims of restricting pub hours did have an impact. For example, the 1872 Licensing Act forced pubs to close at 10:00 or 11:00 (depending on location). This law reduced the drunken rowdiness of the early morning hours. Public drinking decreased significantly during the century. The number of persons per pub increased steadily from the 1830s (161 in 1831, to 316 by 1901 and 668 by 1961). The drinking of hard liquor was partially replaced by beer and, thanks in part to the temperance influence of middle-class schools, the affluent largely abandoned public drinking to the working classes. In both countries, alcohol consumption gradually declined in its role as the principal lubricant of leisure.[22]

A final restrictionist approach to reforming city pleasures was the campaign against prostitution. "Social purity" movements in America were an off shoot of the revivalist activism of the 1820s. In New York, for example, brothels were picketed, and the names of patrons published. In 1848, women's purity groups presented the New York legislature with a petition to ban "seducation." In the wake of the gold rush in the 1850s, California vigilante mobs drove out the inmates of red-light districts and even hanged persistent brothel owners.[23] Still, the campaign against prostitution had to wait until the 1880s when many American cities began to drive brothels from riverside and downtown districts. In the 1870s and 1880s, Anthony Comstock organized anti-vice committees and attacked not only prostitution but contraceptives (which officials banned from the mails as "obscene literature"). The infamous red-light districts of the Barbary Coast of San Francisco, Storyville in New Orleans, and the Levee of Chicago became objects of legal harassment in the 1900s. In 1910, the Mann Act made it a federal offense to transport women across state line for "immoral purposes." The horrors of the "white slave trade," the coercion of young women into prostitution, was widely publicized in the 1900s. During World War I, red-light districts in America were cleaned out, and urban renewal often removed most traces of them.[24] While the anti-prostitution movement was rooted in health and social reform, it also reflected a persistent American modesty. For example, the Chicago Vice Commission in the 1900s went so far as to recommended the removal of park benches from "deep shadows" and to advocate "well-lighted" movie houses to discourage young couples from sex play.[25]

In England, campaigns (dominated by women) managed to outlaw whore houses in 1885 with the justification that they spread disease and threatened the health of the middle-class home (via the husbands). A the same time, the private sale of sex was tolerated.[26]

Improving Time

Concern over leisure also took less rigid or authoritarian forms. Some reformers sought not to suppress or simply to moralize popular leisure but to transform it. The idea was, as British historian Hugh Cunningham argues, to replace "public, improvised and inconclusive" play with "regular and privatised" recreation. For example, instead of the anarchy and saturnalia of the bull run, recreation reformers at Stanford in the 1830s favored the race track, which confined sport to a defined area and offered commercial spinoffs. Replacing the day-long mass "football" contest in Derby was the new game of soccer with its well-defined playing field and referees to police action. The gangs of American city streets were to be transformed into supervised participants on municipal playgrounds. This stress on order has led many historians to refer to this movement as "rational recreation."[27]

Yet this movement stressed not only order but "improvement." It shared with religious revivalism a belief that the individual could be converted from a life of sin to a new moral personality with a new sense of community. The close connection between the revivalism of the American, Charles Finney, and cultural reform has often been noted. The same could be said for the English Christian Socialists and other evangelicals.[28] Moreover, elites were often torn between coercive reform and what the American historian Paul Boyer calls "positive environmentalism"—the attempt not to suppress drink or impose a strait jacket of religious conformity on the populace but to substitute the "coarser element of the environment" with wholesome recreational things.[29] After witnessing Chartist demonstrations, Manchester banker Benjamin Heywood called not for more police but for new urban recreation centers. The idea was to create a "community of enjoyment" in order to develop "reciprocal feelings" between the classes. The problem was to restore social harmony—to "bring the individuals of different classes into actual personal contact."[30]

A few English employers attempted to resurrect the old traditions by patronizing rural games. The more common response was to accept the city and to create new recreational settings. The emphasis was often on collective leadership rather than the traditional personal approach of noblesse oblige; and the objective was not simply to provide a new community-controlled leisure but to transform the individual—in a kind of semireligious conversion experience. The ideal environment was a "conventicle of respectability"—alternative sites to the "degrading" working-class recreations of pub, cockpit, and street. This counter-culture was not simply invented by the middle class to be imposed on the common man, but rather reflected (as we shall see in the next chapter) middle-class experience. Through a common intellectual fount of Puritan religion and the Enlightenment, working-class as well as middle-class reformers embraced an ethic of self-control, individualism, and respectability.[31]

The means to achieve these ends were varied and sometimes subtle. The didactic methods of the British mechanics' institutes were early experiments in "improvement." Great time and expense were spent on constructing the imposing buildings for these institutes which were designed to contrast with the pub and music hall. These efforts culminated in the adult education movement of the late 19th-century. The program of lecturers in economics and science, however, seldom appealed to even steady artisans. As Cooke Taylor stressed, "The lectures of the schoolroom will be utterly ineffective when they are counteracted by the practical lessons of the playground." The institutes frequently became centers not of craftsmen but of young clerks seeking cultural enrichment and business connections.[32]

The obvious limits of this approach led other reformers to promote social clubs. From the 1850s in Britain, Henry Solly's Working Men's Social Clubs sought to combine education with entertainment and "unrestrained social intercourse." These clubs, located in most English towns and cities, provided rooms for reading as well as regulated drinking, opportunities for cards and other games, and space for a vast array of musical, sports, and other evening and Saturday-afternoon leisure activity for adult men. Social superiors, argued the Christian Socialists and others who supported this approach, could freely mix with the lower classes in these clubs to the mutual benefit of both.[33] Another "conventicle of respectibility" was the Young Men's Christian Association.

Established in London in 1844, the YMCA targeted young male clerks, whom the organization's directors feared were tempted by saloon and cigar-store life of the city.

Americans adapted much of this approach. For example, in 1851, two young Americans brought back the idea of the YMCA from London to Boston and New York. Unlike the moral reform activists of the 1830s and 1840s, the leaders of the "Y" were not ministers but merchants and bankers. Their objective was to create a substitute 'home' for single lonely men—the new entrants into the commercial world of the city. Attempts to propagate middle-class respectability by founding "slum outposts" or "Y" facilities for transients in railway stations failed. Primarily directed to the young "respectable" clerk, the early "Y"s concentrated on providing shelter, reading rooms, and uplifting lectures. Only later would the YMCA transform into a center of physical fitness. The Odd Fellows served a similar group with cozy lodges that provided a surrogate home for salesmen, students, and other lonely men of the middle class. Domesticity was the model.[34]

Much rational recreation was sponsored by enlightened employers for their workers. In the 1830s, Samuel Gregg, of Manchester, provided his child employees with playgrounds, and for well-behaved youth, he offered Sunday afternoon teas. If their parents lacked the respectable formal parlour, these children could, at least, be "improved" by contact with this domestic leisure culture. Factory employers in Northern England sponsored Christmas parties and supported company choral societies and brass bands in the hope of fostering a communal feeling among workers. Thousands descended regularly on London's Crystal Palace for mammoth choral contests. Thomas Cook, in 1841, organized the first railroad excursion for 2,000 Leicester children to travel to Derby to avoid the temptations of revelry on race day. Excursions to the fresh air and natural settings of the English country-side became a favorite medicine for the disease of urban demoralization.[35]

American historians have noted a similar patronage in employer sponsorship of cultural activities of young women workers at the Lowell mills in the 1820s. In the 1870s, members of small-town churches opened their homes to slum-dwelling children during summer vacations and, with the help of New York City merchants, organized a "Fresh Air Fund."[36]

Still, a lot of this improving leisure was organized by workers themselves. Indeed, prominent English radicals like William Lovett embraced rational recreation as a means of preparing workers for political leadership. By the 1880s, Workingmen's Clubs became independent of their elite sponsors. The same was true much earlier of American voluntarist institutions like Fire Departments—(although these were often far from "improving"). Other institutions like choral societies or brass bands were often part of mutual aid societies, ethnic fraternal organizations, or other working-class organizations.[37]

Rational recreation also meant new urban services like libraries, museums, and especially parks. In England, the movement for the public library to replace costly subscription libraries emerged in 1845. An act in 1850 paved the way for tax-supported free libraries. Although libraries were far less expensive than parks (because of urban land values), few local municipalities jumped at this opportunity to raise their taxes. Public libraries usually depended upon philanthropy rather than public support.[38]

In America, the campaign for public libraries followed a similar course. Surely a dominant influence from the late 1890s were the hundreds of Neo-Roman buildings that housed the Carnegie Public Libraries. The steel baron, Andrew Carnegie, explained his philanthropy: "How a man spends his time at work may be taken for granted but how he spends his hours of recreation is really the key to his progress in all the virtues." This civilizing mission was extended to libraries located in factories, YMCA buildings, and even churches.[39]

The park and playground movements, however, were probably the most important manifestations of rational recreation. As early as 1833, the British parliament appointed a committee to investigate the lack of public walkways. In 1836, the government prohibited the privatizations of common lands near large towns. The objective was to assure that some "open places reserved for the amusement (under due regulations to preserve order) of the humbler classes, would assist to wean them from low and debasing pleasure."[40]

Despite encouragement from London, the earliest English parks were promoted by regional philanthropists (e.g., Preston Moor in 1833 and Joseph Strutt's Arboretum in Derby in 1840). Perhaps the most important event was the creation of Peel Park in Manchester in 1846, which led to many imitations. London's Victoria and Battersea Parks came at midcentury. Management of these parks fit what should now seem a familiar pattern. They were designed to exclude all games and sports; only walking was allowed along pathways, which featured a careful display of nature. This experience was supposed to stimulate a wholesome love of nature and to raise the strollers to new heights of sobriety and familial respectability. Robert Slaney, a key park advocate from the 1830s in England, found in parks the possibility of creating "pardonable vanity" among the poor:

> A man walking out with his family among his neighbors of different ranks, will naturally be desirous to be properly clothed, and that his wife should be also; but this desire, duly directed and controlled, is found by experience to be of the most powerful effect in promoting civilization and exciting industry.[41]

To be sure, Sabbatarian opposition to the playing of brass bands in parks or the opening of museums on Sundays frustrated rational recreationists. Still, groups like the (British) National Sunday League (1855) challenged this restrictive approach, arguing that such wholesome recreations on the Sabbath were the only alternative to the pub. By the end of the century, the rational recreationists largely prevailed.[42]

The American parks movement followed a similar paths. Americans visitors to European capitals were impressed with the majestic scale of royal parks and found the urban blight emerging from their unplanned cities to be shameful. Cholera epidemics in 1832 convinced Americans of the need for open spaces. In the 1840s, American park advocates saw in green space an equivalent of rural life in the city. Frederick Olmsted, the landscape architect who largely designed New York's Central Park in the 1850s, wanted parks that were large enough "to completely shut out the city." These green spaces could inspire urban man to new standards of "courtesy, self-control, and temperance." Meandering walkways, natural vistas, and landscaping would create this morally uplifting feeling for nature in the heart of the mechanical city.[43]

However, large downtown showcase parks were most often used by the middle class in the business districts; some provided golf courses and tennis courts used by the well-to-do. From the 1890s, however, social reformers advocated smaller neighborhood parks to make green space accessible to the poor in their own neighborhoods. In New York, Mulberry Bend Park was created by the clearance of the infamous Five Points District. Beginning with Kansas City in 1893, most American cities installed Park Commissions and networks of parks. Mayor Josiah Quincy of Boston (1895-1899) supported gymnasia, swimming pools, playgrounds, and free concerts in the poorer sections of the city as a means of combatting juvenile delinquency (Chapter 8). Park Commissioners also believed it their duty to reform leisure time as well as space. The city of Pittsburgh, for example, organized Fourth of July celebrations at Schenley Park, complete with vaudeville acts and fireworks, but banned liquor, the traditional lubricant of the mid-summer holiday.[44]

Finally, mass cultural centers became the hallmark of the rational recreation movement. The Crystal Palace, near London, that huge structure built for the Exhibition of 1851, was long after used for cultural events. Americans followed with the construction of White City at the Chicago World's Fair in 1893. In the 1890s, numerous American cities built cultural complexes to house art and natural-history museums. The Carnegie Institute of Pittsburgh (1895) was just one attempt of the urban rich to create a higher leisure tone in the industrial cities of England and America.[45]

After mid-century, the rational recreation idea had influences far beyond its own organizational initiatives. For example, through licensing pressures, British reformers encouraged the growth of the music hall with its family-oriented entertainment. The music hall largely replaced the rough intimacy of the small, all-male singing saloons and supper rooms of the early 19th century, which had been noted for their scandalous songs and patter. By contrast, the music hall created a far more formal setting with a large, more passive audience facing the professional performer. Purged were the more bawdy or political songs, and managers paid for police surveillance of the crowd to assure respectability.[46] These trends (along with regulated sport, which will be considered in Chapter 10) contributed to cultural uniformity and reduced the disorder associated with both rural popular leisure and the "degrading" pleasures of the new industrial cities.

Impact of Rational Recreation: An Assessment

What was the impact of these efforts at instilling the values of domesticity, self-control, and respectability in the working classes? As early as 1844, Léon Faucher noted, "There is no need now, (as there was twelve years ago) to engage an extra police force to keep the public roads clear, and pickpockets at a distance, while the inhabitants go to and from divine service."[47]

By the end of the century, the British gin palace had disappeared, children had been excluded from bars, and disorderly urban fairs had been abolished. In place of the English carnivals and wakes were four regular bank holidays instituted in 1871.[48] Thomas Wright observed that "steady-going" unmarried artisans spent their Saturday afternoons playing in brass bands or attending sporting events in the 1860s. Married men often engaged in home-improvement projects, digging in their small garden plots or tending their pigeons or rabbits. Some went to the reading rooms of the local workingman's club. Saturday night was often reserved for the family at the music hall. Sunday morning was for the Sunday suit and a trip to the barber's shop, fol-lowed by a midday meal with the family, and late-afternoon tea, often shared with relatives and other guests. At least some elements of the middle-class domestic leisure style had penetrated into the laboring classes.[49]

It is doubtful whether workers' leisure became more respectable in pre-cisely the ways endorsed by reformists patrons. Historians Stedman Jones and Peter Bailey have criticized those who have taken too seriously the influence of leisure reformers. To the worker, they argue, the idea of being respectable meant wearing a Sunday suit, not attending church. It meant saving for a carefree holiday, not accumulating for retirement. The wage-earning couple may have devoted more leisure time to home improvement. Some even invested in parlour pianos for Sunday evening family get-togethers. Yet surely more typical was the replacement of cock fighting with pigeon racing, of bull baiting with race-track betting, of gin with beer. The railroad brought not only the excursionist to the London's Crystal Palace exhibition but also funnelled the masses to the Oldham Wakes and to race tracks. Only in the 1870s did alcohol consumption reach its peak in the century.[50] The Saturday half-holiday was not a time for family activities, but rather for male get-togethers at football matches or baseball games. And sporting newspapers, rather than political or cultural magazines, dominated male-working class reading.[51]

Even those who participated in the improving activities sponsored by elites had many motives. Some sought contacts necessary for upward mobility, and others access to the less edifying recreations that were used to lure the people into the educational setting. And in the 1880s, British laborers usually had gained control over the Working Men's Clubs, as they had of other philanthropic organizations. The social classes may have met, but no new understanding, far less camaraderie, resulted. Finally, those poor to whom the rational recreationists appealed were primarily the already "respectable poor," those families who sought escape or shelter from the rough working class culture that surrounded them.[52]

Underneath this, of course, was the survival of traditional attitudes toward leisure, reinforced in some ways by commercialization and politics. Music halls and other seemingly improving recreations retained a great deal of the old leisure. Music halls survived by their drink trade and their songs were often in the saturnalia tradition. They mocked the pompous and kill-joy teetotaler. Humor focused on in-laws and the disappointments of marriage. Tory politicians often lent support to the conviviality of working-class leisure, opposing Sabbatarian legislation and favoring laissez-faire attitudes toward race courses and pubs. This position helped them, in many cases, to solidify a political base in working-class portions of the Midlands. Their belief that little could change—either people's manners or economic conditions—was not far off from the views of many workers. Ethnic neighborhood bars generally withstood the regulatory and moral pressures of "improving" elites in America.[53]

More important to the limited impact of rational recreation was the reluctance of the advantaged to participate in leisure reform. Just as few "ladies bountiful" volunteered to teach Sunday Schools, only 24 libraries were built in England during the first 16 years of the Libraries Act of 1850.[54] This reluctance was not merely a matter of parsimony nor a doctrinaire faith in the free market; businessmen realized that more cost-effective means of reducing social disorder were improved police or urban renewal rather than public recreation. More systematic policing of cities largely cleared the streets of youth gangs and the Victorian underworld. By the 1880s, thanks to urban renewal, the jerrybuilt rookeries of East London, which had frightened the middle-classes, were demolished. They were replaced by far less threatening stands of commercial buildings and rows of brick tenements. Model dwelling companies, with their new caretakers, assured greater order and cleanliness. And finally, the National Sunday Leagues and other promoters of wholesome amusements had to compete continuously with the Sabbatarian for middle-class support.

At the root of the failures of rational recreation was the intractable character of social cleavage. Leisure reformers battered at the high walls that divided Britons and Americans by class and ethnicity. But leisure, after all, reflected the social divisions of society as a whole. In Britain, for example, proprietors of seaside resorts deliberately segregated classes (for the sake of "social tone"). In the 19th century, many seaside towns, including Brighton and even Blackpool, gained snob appeal by discouraging "day trippers," the poor who could not afford a week or more of holiday. In America, Coney Island was divided into different amusement parks catering to various social levels, and Atlantic City appealed to the middle class who sought "symbolic mobility" in the imitations of the aristocratic spa. The boardwalk crowds, "whirlwind vaudeville," and dance halls contradicted the quest for respectability; but the "sentimental poetry, etchings, and prose which bubbled about the sea, and the untrodden shore...conveyed a sense of order and quietude which in fact did not exist." Rich Americans from the northeast retracted to Newport, Rhode Island, and others kept to themselves at Sarasota Springs, New York, or by 1894 "discovered" Palm Beach, Florida.[55]

Despite the fact that the music hall (and American vaudeville theaters) were more orderly than the singing saloons, the middle-class family still avoided them because of their working-class clientele and the presence of prostitutes in the galleries. And the well-to-do in the 1870s in both countries developed socially exclusive sports of tennis, golf, and cycling, which only increased the distance between the classes. Like their social inferiors, middle-class families increasingly were uprooted by urbanization; they, too, moved to suburbs and lost their tight-knit neighborhoods. In response, they formed their own clubs. Some joined "volunteer corps" (or militia in America)—ostensibly for reserve military training but really for social and recreational reasons.[56]

As Peter Bailey writes, the middle classes stood ready to defend the line of their own gentility with a judicious mixture of discrimination and neglect, and the reformers found themselves pulling against the stream. The latter were proposing to alleviate social tensions through the fraternal association of all classes in leisure at a time when the middle classes were acutely concerned to reinforce, not reduce, social distance.[57] One of the things people bought when they consumed leisure was social status (Chapter 9).

However, it would be wrong to dismiss the efforts of recreational reformers and to argue that popular leisure culture and class division defeated them. First, we should remember that the exclusivity of a leisure class, the anarchy of popular recreation, and the organizational drive of reformers all coexisted before and after the Victorian period. Second, if most wage earners did not replace their traditional pleasures with rational recreation, many added elements of the reformers' ideal to their leisure repertory. The result was in part a more privatized, more sedate, and more universal recreational culture. For some individuals, rational recreation may have helped to create a personality suitable to the competitive upwardly mobile society of the Victorian city.

Finally, rational recreation was expressed in more subtle and probably more influential forms than the public (and largely male) leisure discussed in this chapter. The Victorian home, with its full-time housewife, became the site of a new leisure of domesticity. Organized in part by women, it helped to produce not only a privatized leisure, but shaped in many ways the play of children. This domestic leisure will be our next topic.

THE CHRISTMAS TREE.

8

Gender and Generation in 19th-Century Leisure

"Happiness," wrote an English Quaker in 1838,

> Does not consist in booths and garlands, drums and horns, or in
> capering round a Maypole. Happiness is a fire-side thing. It is a
> thing of grave and earnest tone; and the deeper and truer it is, the
> more it is removed from the riot of mere merriment.[1]

One of the most popular songs of the late Victorian English-speaking world was
"Home Sweet Home." In the 19th century, the family shelter was idealized in
the novel, endlessly promoted in magazines, and even encouraged in the occasional housing project of well-meaning reformers. Nonwork time was focused
on the home. Under the special leadership of women, leisure was to provide not
merely diversion but moral training and sustenance for the young and men.

Origins of Home-Centered Leisure

In the 19th century, the home became the specialized place of recreation.
Industrialization and the commercial office had driven work and business from
most residences. Apprentices no longer needed to be sheltered in the master's
house, nor were employers willing to do so. Except in some retail shops where
long hours made this separation of work and leisure impossible, the home was
increasingly a retreat from the market, not its center. It became a haven for a
small circle of family members, opened on special events to a few friends and
distant relatives. In the domestic space, new family traditions were created.
And, to some extent, older community traditions were forgotten. As in many
things, the middle-class rather than the rich or the masses were to dominate this
domestication of leisure.[2]

    The shock troops of "fire-side" happiness were mostly women in the
rather distinct and new role of homemaker. Industrialization meant the removal
of affluent married women at least from the workforce, and changes in the
household and childrearing work of wives cleared the way for female leadership
in the creating a new domestic leisure.

Middle-class women succeeded in shifting some of the arduous labor of cleaning, cooking, and childcare to servants. For example, in Britain, the number of domestics had increased from about 100,000 in 1801 to 2 million by 1881. Still, probably no more than 11 percent of homes in relatively well-to-do London had servants in the 1890s. Servants enabled the privileged—but by no means aristocratic—homemaker to redirect her time and energy to the esthetics of Home Sweet Home.[3]

The 19th century also saw a dramatic reduction in the number of children that mothers bore. In America, white mothers in 1800 gave birth to an average of 7.04 children. That number was reduced by 1851 to 5.42 and, by 1900, to merely 3.56. The British pattern was roughly similar. Middle-class child-bearing strategies changed for a complex of reasons. The drift from the farm meant, of course, less need for children as laborers. Increased educational standards, required in a commercial world, meant that children cost more to raise and only later, if at all, did they contribute to the family's income. Thus, middle-class parents had an economic incentive to reduce family size (mostly through sexual abstinence or coitus interruptus). This decline occurred later in the lower classes. It remained respectable, even necessary, for poorer parents to realize a return on their investment in a child in the earnings of teenage off-spring. The diminution of the middle-class family, of course, meant more time for mothers to devote to the now smaller brood. Child-rearing could be less harsh, more permissive, and more infused with play. Moreover, the mother's career became more concentrated in a relatively short period of child-bearing, reducing the span of married life when child rearing dominated women's concerns. The result was time available for women's personal leisure and in organizing it for the wider family.

Because the husband's life became more specialized as a bread-winner, wives probably saw less of their husbands than they did in the old domestic economy. More important, married women were able to develop an autonomous culture built around domestic management and child rearing. Unlike the more disciplined work that was emerging in the 19th century office or factory, women's labor was still interspersed with leisure.

Finally, reformers recognized that mothers could play a pivotal role in refining the recreational lives of husbands and children. Temperance advocates frequently contrasted the hearth and saloon and saw the angel in the parlour as their principal ally against drink and public rowdiness. The so-called "cult of domesticity," for which the Victorian era is famous, can be understood as a coalition of clergy, educators, advice manual writers, and married women who attempted to privatize life in leisure.[4]

Domestic Leisure and Women

The middle-class Victorian home was both a refuge from the unsettling change that surrounded it and a center for a more refined leisure style. This double function is most clearly identifiable in the new organization of domestic space. As early as the 1790s, merchant families withdrew from the townhouses of London to create more spacious, but also more socially segregated neighbor-hoods, free from both the rowdy poor and self-indulgent aristocrat. Evangelical families built weekend villas on large private lots in a picturesque village setting around a common at Clapham. In the "library," which opened out onto the rear garden, the family gathered for singing, playing the piano, and serious conversa-tion. It was the "Evangelical substitute for all the plays, balls, visits, and coffee houses of London." Here, children were safe from the influence of the street and genteel family life could flourish.[5]

On a less grade scale, the upper middle class of Manchester, New York, and Chicago retreated in the 19th century to their rustic suburbs. Unlike the rich of Paris and other European cities, who built a leisure style around the restau-rant, theater, and gallery from bases in luxurious apartments along tree-lined boulevards, the Anglo-American rich gradually abandoned the inner city to the poor and to business.

By the 1870s, the affluent American family fled the row house in the crowded city streets for the detached suburban home with its surrounding yard built along winding lanes. Mid-19th-century model suburbs like New Jersey's Llewellyn Park and Chicago's Riverside set the pace. Wealthy districts in Westchester County, New York, and Chestnut Hill near Philadelphia radiated from train stations, protected in their isolation by open country. They were supplied with elite amenities like Chestnut Hill's country club located adjacent to the Episcopal Church and a luxurious hotel.[6]

The ideal was a setting that was pastoral but not wild. The home should be set back but visible from the street. "The lawn, as a totally unproduc-tive expanse, succinctly communicated the leisurely nature of the home. The home was to be a place of relaxation, recreation, and reflection."[7] The park-like landscaping in the front both displayed taste and provided privacy. The back and side lawns, accessible to porch and veranda, offered ideal settings for informal games and sports for all ages. In the more congested setting of England, walls, wrought-iron gates, and well-designed gardens served similar functions. The suburb was not divorced from the city, however. Because of their railroad access, these suburbs were tied closely to the city, not only for the business of males, but for the leisure and pleasure shopping of women.[8]

The Victorian suburban home, totally bereft of economic purpose, was transformed into a multipurpose leisure center. This, of course, was only to follow the model of the "great halls" of the aristocracy, which since the late 17th century had been refurbished to privatize and specialize domestic space.

Victorian homes were designed to reflect a clear separation between the formal and private, male and female, adult and child. Often replacing the simple layout of two rooms to a floor was the formal parlor and family sitting room on one side of the entry and a dining room and kitchen on the other. The entry way was also broadened by the creation of a hall for the receiving of guests. It was there that calling cards were deposited on ornate hallstands, essential furniture in the affluent Victorian home. Additional wealth allowed for still more differentiation.[9]

Rooms were decorated to reflect the gender of their space: the male's library walls, with dark oak and leather chairs, and the lady's upstairs boudoir, with chintz and delicate colors. An upstairs nursery for the children allowed room for play away from parents. Housework was separated from diversion (aided by back stairways to hide servants); guests could be entertained in specialized space apart from the privacy of family. Even in the 18th century, wealthy American and British homes featured the parlor as the "best room," dramatically situated in a wing protruding in the front of the house and featuring the best family furnitur; it was reserved for visits from clergy, weddings, funerals, and formal teas. The back sitting room was less formal, often containing a piano or parlor organ.[10]

A well-appointed parlor was thought to have a positive influence on the character of those who entered it. In it were displays of female accomplishment in handicrafts and the site for "uplifting" parlor games. Mother's standards of speech and manners were to be strictly observed by all who entered. "Here husband and children do not corrupt, here household cares do not break through."[11] This room was the site for the custom of "paying calls" in the "walking city" of the early 19th century; yet it separated the outside world from the privacy of the back rooms. The middle-class nursery allowed for not only the withdrawal of the very young from the leisure of parents but created an environment that could be devoted especially to children's needs including toys and play.[12]

Victorians looked upon the home as a sacred space, a private sanctuary, where the rites of passage and of "right relations" were to be carried out. Unlike the church (especially in America) which was fragmented into warring denominations, the home provided a harmonious "spiritual" space—where the "three great mysteries" of "Birth, of growth, of death" were given meaning. Home decoration had not merely an aesthetic worth but provided a morally-uplifting environment. House designs, which were widely published in books and even women's magazines in the 19th century, show how central the woman's role in organizing domestic/leisure space was. As Colleen McDannel writes, homes "expressed the character of the family and they shaped that character."[13]

Even the respectable working class devoted a large share of scarce living space to dining room and parlor, often never used except for the formal visit of guests. Francis Couvares finds, in his study of Pittsburgh culture in the late 19th century, a preoccupation of the upper working class with domesticity. In the 1870s, Pittsburgh's *People's Monthly*, published articles calling for more home ownership. "We hold that no man occupies a truly independent position, nor can he or his family enjoy life until he owns his own home..." Labor support for temperance was often related to this desire to secure a stable home life. And, union balls and outings deliberately promoted familialism as a replacement for the trade-union meeting in the saloon. The development of savings and loans after 1860 contributed to the spread of home ownership in America and the electric street car after 1890 sparked the suburbanization of the artisan and clerk (Chapter 12). English working-class walls were covered with paper strips emblazoned with mottos attesting to domestic joys: "*East, west, home's best; Bless our home; God is master of this house.*" Music hall repertory was full of sentimental songs about home sweet home. Even the factory worker of Lancashire, for example, was famous for his privacy. The wife would carefully wash and clean with pumice stone the white and yellow steps of their modest row houses. But often none but close relatives ever entered the front door; even old drinking chums and workmates were excluded.[14]

The familial trend was evident also in a reorganization of holidays. The idea of the family Christmas with yule log, tree, songs, and the exchange of gifts in England on "boxing day" (December 26) was part of this Victorian stress on family recreation.[15]   Americans, who in the early 19th century, had celebrated July 4th with the bacchanalian abandon of a village mardi gras, were to turn to family picnics by the 1850s. And later in the 20th century, the American Thanksgiving became a tradition of family reunion. Public walkways in parks were designed for family strolls. The same was true of the vacation—no longer just a lark for the aristocratic youth or the taking of the cure for the besotted middle-aged gentleman; rather, from the 1840s, tour organizers like Thomas Cook deliberately appealed to family groups.[16]

A barrage of new magazines reinforced familialism. Made possible by high-speed printing and cheaper paper and by the general increase in literacy, English and American publishers flooded the market with family-oriented periodicals. For example, the *London Journal* (1845-1912) and the *Family Herald* (1842-1939) reached about 750,000 homes by the 1850s. Such magazines included a mixture of serialized adventure and romance—often read to families gathered in the parlor. Domestic tranquility was frequently the happy ending of romantic stories. Other items were character-building stories of a famous man, as well as household hints, riddles, and puzzles. These magazines taught the families of aspiring clerical and skilled workers "proper" etiquette and dress. Matrimonial advertisements offered an alternative to the tawdry courtship provided in dance halls and pubs.[17]

Married women were believed to be the ideal organizers of familial recreation. As the American Victorian Mary Dodge wrote, women were "divinely designed" for a "state of repose, ease, leisure."[18] Both industrialization and the ideology of the woman's sphere encouraged the married women to focus on family leisure. As A.J. Graves wrote in *Women in America* (1841):

> If man's duties lie abroad, woman's duties are within the quiet seclusion of home. If his greatness and power are most strikingly exhibited in associated action upon associated masses, her true greatness and her highest efficiently consist in individual efforts upon individual beings. In this age of excitement, it is especially incumbent upon woman to exert her utmost influence, to maintain unimpaired the sacredness and the power of the family institution.[19]

Only "fireside happiness" assured the male's sanity: "Should [the husband] meet dark clouds and storms abroad, yet sunshine and peace await him at home."[20] Mothers were to provide the moral ballast to counter the harm of peer pressure and to reinforce habits of restraint and temperance among the boys.[21]

Nineteenth-century female education, of course, prepared women for these roles. It offered training in the domestic crafts. Although no longer of much economic value, Victorian middle-class girls were still taught the arts of hand sewing, crochet, and lace-work. Such tasks occupied women in an era when busyness was valued for its own sake; these handicrafts were decorative or were given to the poor. Education in private girls "dame" schools stressed husband-catching skills: coiffure, fashion, singing, and piano-playing for decorous courtship recitals in parental parlors. This education designed for leisure was a great cause for complaint by the feminist Mary Wollstonecraft; it also displeased the conservative Mother of home economics, the American Catherine Beecher. Still, Beecher advocated an education for women that stressed domestic improvements—practical but decorous comforts for the American home.

Private constraint against public excess was the guiding principle. Yet domesticity meant more than avoidance. It encompassed also a panoply of family activities—board games, reading of fiction, piano-playing and singing, and lawn games like croquet. Domesticity probably contributed to a considerable softening of family life and the development of deep emotional attachments between adult women and between mothers and their children. Carol Smith-Rosenberg describes "that endless trooping of women to each others' home for social purposes... Rural women developed a pattern of more extended visits that lasted weeks and sometimes months, at times even dislodging husbands from their beds and bedrooms so that dear friends might spend every hour of every day together." Married women with children sometimes arranged summer holidays to meet childhood friends at spas or even to share country homes. Leonore Davidoff describes an even more elaborate social "season" that women of affluence organized in Victorian Britain. And women's rites of passage, especially the birth of the first child, were often shared by all female family members and old friends. The ritual of "paying calls" was often an elaborate ritual involving leaving calling cards "with the right-hand top corner turned down," A daughter's "coming out" was signified by her obtaining her own cards.[22]

Through periodicals like the American *Ladies Magazine* and the *Godey's Lady's Book,* these values were propagated in essays and fiction surrounded by fashion plates, dress and crochet patterns, recipes, and model cottages.[23] The English Victorian housewife had the advice manuals of Sarah Strickney Ellis to turn to (*The Mothers of England* and *The Daughters of England,* e.g.).[24]

But the Victorian housewife had duties beyond family and home. Especially in America, she was to play an active part in Protestant church life— not only in the fund-raising efforts or charity but also in evangelical work. Women were to be missionaries of familial culture. For example, middle-class wives in New York "adopted" poor families and offered advice to wives on domestic management and "higher" cultural standards. The Englishwoman, Octavia Hill, and the American, Josephine Shaw, in the 1860s and 1870s, set the standard of voluntary charity in the cities. Their "friendly visitors" encouraged working-class wives to withdraw from the labor force and to lead their families to temperance and gentle manners. The settlement house movement (founded first in England and imported to the U.S. in 1886) was similar. It consisted of young volunteers (mostly women) who took up residence in poor (in America, immigrant) neighborhoods. They attempted to recreate a model household of orderly, culturally refined, and restrained life, which, they hoped, the poor would imitate.[25]

Play and the New Childrearing

At the heart of this domestic ideal was a new attitude toward childrearing and children's play. Family historians have long stressed the impact of the Enlightenment on the treatment of children. John Locke's view of man (1690) as a pure product of the environment without any innate propensity toward evil fundamentally undermined the view that children were little devils or animals who had to be broken. The notion that children reflected their surroundings made parents increasingly sensitive to the protection of children from harmful influences. The 18th century views of Jean-Jacques Rousseau that small children were innocents whose naive simplicity was a virtue and whose spontaneity should be guarded by an education that encouraged individual expression had an even deeper impact. Accordingly, children were increasingly seen as unique, not as miniature adults; they should be allowed a long childhood spent with those in their own age group.

This was a revolutionary change. The earlier view—concretely displayed in a child prodigy like Mozart—was that the young should be introduced to adult life as soon as possible. Instead, the affluent Victorian parents gradually withdrew their children not only from the experience of early work but from adult society. Precocity was now harmful. As Rousseau put it, " Nature wants children to be children before they are men. If we deliberately pervert this order, we shall get premature fruits which are neither ripe nor well-flavoured, and which soon decay." Similarly, Bronson Alcott, a New England moralist wrote: "Play is the appointed dispensation of childhood."[26]

It was women's duty to provide a proper childlike environment for the young person. As Catherine Beecher put the problem in 1847: "The success of democratic institutions, as is conceded by all, depends upon the intellectual and moral character of the mass of the people. The formation of the moral and intellectual character of the young is committed mainly to the female hand. "The mother was to select the games and activities appropriate for the child's age. The *Mother's Magazine* repeatedly warned women to guard their children from the "contamination of the streets."[27]

Mothers attempted to shape the playtime of children to inculcate skill and moral values. Children were not only to be protected from the rough games and talk of adults but were to be isolated from older children who might introduce them to bad habits. Thus, schools gradually eliminated the one-room schoolhouse, which mixed students of all ages. The same separation took place in children's literature: separate magazines for children, adolescents, and young adults all appeared in the 19th century.[28]

In the early part of the 19th century, children's games and toys were increasingly in demand. New manufacturing techniques allowed for the inexpensive production of dolls. By 1850, dolls portrayed not only adults but babies and children—a change that reflected a recognition of the child's separate imaginative world. Factory production of dolls, developed first in Germany, led to their mass distribution. Toys took on a new purpose. In the home, bereft of productive tasks and sometimes even baby siblings, toys became a means of simulating adult roles. The American *Monthly Mother's Magazine* in the 1830s advocated "hammers and hatchets" for boys and "dressing dolls" and "mimicry of housekeeping" for girls.[29]

Advice manuals insisted that young children learn checkers, for this game "calls forth the resources of the mind in the most gentle, as well as the most successful manner." In America, games like "Pilgrim's Progress" and "The Mansion of Happiness" were sold to instill Protestant moral themes. In the latter game, children advanced a piece on a board by way of squares marked with character traits (Piety and Honesty, for example) moving toward the goal of "Happiness." Landing, however, on "Passion" meant that you lost a turn.

Children's books also often had an educational message. Stories discouraged cruelty to animals; authors presumed that this would reduce the chance that the child would become a violent adult. This approach corresponded with changing child-rearing methods that stressed parental example, encouragement, and the cultivation of the child's conscience rather than strict rules, mere deference, and punishment. Kindly and obedient children were sometimes rewarded with a toy whistle with the inscription, ""For a Good Child.""[30]

Finally, the attempt to moralize children's play gradually gave way to a greater openness to the imagination and free activity. An American physician in 1868 could write:

> [Children] should be allowed to run, leap, hallor [sic] and be happy
> in the open air just as instinct teaches them in common with the
> young throughout the animal kingdom... Then let them feel that
> during play hours they are unrestrained and unwatched and...they
> will be stronger and more happy and, in consequence, wiser and
> better.[31]

The ideal of self-discipline, which had sometimes defined the early Victorian successful man, gave way to a new ideal of instincts and spontaneity, which could be fostered only in play. And, if the 19th-century adult felt uneasy about such pleasures, he could enjoy them through the children. The old custom of carting young children on mother's social visits and attending adult pleasures like hunting was abandoned. At the same time, middle-class homes provided increasing space for nurseries and playrooms.

Children's literature in the 19th century, in particular reveals, this trend. By midcentury, the piety of the early Victorian period had given way to literature that stressed secular virtues, like thrift and kindness. And the fairy tales of Hans Christian Andersen from the late 1840s began to supplant the moralistic tales of Puritan writers. Still later, celebration of the spontaneity of youth appeared in Mark Twain's *Huckleberry Finn* and Thomas Aldrich's *The Story of a Bad Boy*.[32] The amusements and literary fantasies that had traditionally been enjoyed by adults were increasingly shifted to children. Thus, medieval tales of adventure and romance like *Robin Hood* and *St. George* became the preserve of children, and hoop and ball games, which had been traditional enjoyed by all ages, were increasingly seen as "childish."[33]

New attitudes toward play were largely restricted to the middle classes. Working-class childhood in the 19th century frequently ended by age nine. Most children, especially in rural areas, enjoyed relatively unorganized play with few toys, books, or other manufactured or commercial amusements. Cans were used for "footballs;" hopscotch was played on the street. Despite the short life of a child's play, children have been extraordinarily conservative, preserving with little change traditional games and songs for generations. The young played hiding and chasing games like Fox and Hounds and Sheep Come Home. They also imitated adult rituals in play-acting weddings and "Indians and Squaws."[34]

Leisure and Youth: Dilemmas of Industrial Society

The Victorian ideal was domestic recreation focused on the mother and child.
Yet, there were constant threats to this fire-side ideal. Principal among them
was the problem of teenage youth. Those years between dependence upon one's
first family and the creation of the second family had perhaps always been a
time of ambiguity. Yet this age—which in the 20th century was endowed with
the somewhat pejorative label, adolescence—posed particular problems for
Victorians. The women's influence over the child hardly extended beyond the
age of 10. Older children, especially sons, were ideally the father's responsibility. But in both the households of the laborer and middle-class, fathers had de-
creasing roles to play. As early as the 1830s, reformers had identified a youth
problem and that problem focused on play.

Industrialization reduced the number of middle-class lads who worked
with their fathers (or masters). Increasingly, the transition between childhood
and "manhood" was controlled by professional educators. Many aspiring
parents recognized that their sons would have to be educated for new commercial occupations in skills that their parents were incapable of teaching. Intent
upon preparing their offspring for appropriate positions in adult life, middle-
class parents wanted not only formal education but the formation of "character."
This elusive term had an array of meanings, including competitiveness and a
cooperative spirit, steadfastness to principle but also group loyalty. The school,
then, had to be transformed into a "character factory" and had to be broadened to
include the reformation of youth recreation.[35]

The problem was somewhat different for youth in the laboring classes.
Those teenage children, whose economic opportunities or aspirations were
limited in adulthood, found that their liberty expanded during this period of their
lives. Industrialization meant that they were less frequently supervised by
parents at work. Rather, these youth were hired for a wage by an unrelated
employer with few paternalistic concerns. They increasingly were cut off from
the constraints (as well as opportunities) of the apprenticeship system when the
need for the traditional artisan declined. "Father and son can seldom work
together" complained a Briton in 1907.[36]

The typical working-class youth was increasingly employed in odd-
jobs or factories. Social mobility was surely limited and wages often were low,
but the youth frequently had his own pay envelope. Parents, who had traditionally expected their children to work along side them for the good of the family
economy, continued to expect their teenagers to contribute to the household
wage pool; yet youths found ways of negotiating a share of their wages for
pocket money. And even working daughters were sometimes able to parlay
their economic power into exemption from some household duties. The result
was money and time for leisure.

Moreover, working-class youths left school far earlier than did their middle-class counterparts.[37] As a British observer wrote, "leaving school is his emancipation. His mother anticipates and grants his demands...In short, wage-earning boys and girls assume economic and social independence and responsibility earlier than youths who remain on dependent on their parents."[38]

This youthful autonomy was, of course, only relative. Parents were able to coax obedience out of their teenagers by many means, both subtle and crude. Mothers were especially skilled in tugging on the emotional leading strings that they had spun during childhood to instill the loyalty of their older offspring. Moreover, because the working-class family was slower to reduce family size, the leisure of the first children was often sacrificed for the sake of the feeding of the younger ones. And, of course, parents knew, often from their own bitter experience, the price of a carefree youth. They were strict with their daughters and monitored their contact with suitors for fear of the shame and economic catastrophe of premature pregnancy. While boys were less controlled (and perhaps less controllable), the mark of a "respectable" working class family was its ability to control the teenager's leisure. Referring to England in the 1900s, Robert Roberts writes,

> 'Put that book down!' a mother would command her child, even in his free time, 'and do something useful.' Teenagers, especially girls, were kept on a very tight rein. Fathers fixed the number of evenings on which they could go out and required to know precisely where and with whom they had spent their leisure... Control could go on in some families for years after daughters had come of age.[39]

Parents believed that their offspring should compensate them for years of upkeep as children. Shotgun marriages of daughters were understood as robbery by aggrieved parents.

Still, 19th-century working-class youth had both freedom from direct parental supervision during working hours and money in their pockets, creating a powerful combination for an autonomous leisure culture among the young of the laboring classes. This culture was not necessarily more rebellious or disorderly than it had been before the 19th century, but it surely was more detached from custom and parental control. The upshot was a "youth problem" which was often identified with juvenile crime. Yet, more fundamentally, the free time of youth was less delinquent than it was generational and open to change and manipulation. Reformers naturally sought to shape it even if they fought an uphill battle against the commercial venturers of saloons, dance halls, cheap theaters, (and later) film exhibitioners, and amusement parks.

Youth had perhaps always been a period of psychological stress, rebellion, experimentation, and disorder. Liberated from direct dependence on parents, yet still free from family obligations, male youth throughout the ages had been able to perpetuate distinct leisure cultures, as was evident, for example, in the Middle Ages among apprentices or school boys.[40]

Yet the 19th century brought a new face to this ageless phenomenon. Whereas youth leisure had previously been largely bound to tradition in the ritualized celebrations of the trade or of the charivari and festival, the newly urbanized youth of the 19th century were largely cut adrift from time-honored codes of behavior. And, while playful traditions often had a broader utilitarian purpose, for example the enforcement of community sexual standards in the charivari or courtship procedures in the festival, the free time of the youth of the industrial city was less clearly functional. Leisure was increasingly expressive and influenced by commercial amusements. The tradition-fixed rules of the charivari were replaced by the youth social club, the gang, and the life of the street; St. John's Eve folk dance by the weekend dance-hall; and the spring fair by the amusement park.[41]

These changes were as frightening to working-class parents as they were to middle-class moralists. Urban youths were frequently employed as errand boys and casual laborers, which gave them much freedom on the streets. In mid-century New York City, many children earned income and freedom by huckstering or street vending of snacks and household supplies. While a truancy law in 1853 was designed to banish school-age children from the street, neither the authorities nor their parents were able to eliminate this threat to public order.[42] The street was the playground of children in every city, an unsupervised space that parents often unwillingly allowed their offspring to enter. In America, the anxiety of the immigrant parent was compounded by fears of the Americanization of their teenage children through leisure activities that they did not understand or control. Cramped tenements meant that parents were obliged to tolerate the late evening street play of their older children. By 1850, youth formed a street-corner society built around "social clubs" or gangs in most American and British cities. As in the 20th century, these young people defended their "territory" against outside clubs and drifted into petty vandalism and theft (Chapter 7).

Gangs like the Hooligans of London and the Ikes of Manchester were distinctive for their bell-bottom trousers and heavy buckled belts. Their girl friends often wore clogs, shawls and skirts with vertical stripes. They were beyond the control of parents and policemen hardly contained them. When bored, they engaged in bloody battles with neighboring blocks of 40 or so youths with belt and clog. More innocently, when English street youths graduated from school, they spent their evenings playing "pitch and toss" (a form of gambling) while one member watched for police. Leisure was at the core of generational conflict and of moralist's fear of working-class independence and precocity.[43]

The problem was predominately male. Although Victorian-era American girls might have "climbed trees, fell into rain barrels, fished in the horse troughs," by the age of 13 or 15, the girl's life of play had ended.

Until marriage it was her fate to be mother's helper. One turn-of-the-century English woman remembers: "From six onwards I used to scrub and clean the potatoes and...do all the washing-up. I started from six o'clock onwards doing the cooking. There was no nonsense in those days. You had to learn these rough jobs and get on with them."[44] Still, for the working-class male, the teenage years were a period of play, a brief time when lifetime friends would be made and habits of leisure established.

How different it was for the middle-class youth! Business and professional parents expected their offspring to prepare for an individualistic, rationalistic, and competitive business world. Youth from wealthier families obviously were more dependent upon parental aid than were the working poor. Parents or relatives were often the ticket to entry into the right schools or lawyer's or merchant's offices. Middle-class parents were also able to isolate their youths from the grog shop culture of the young errant boy or mechanics' helper. Moreover, unlike the working parent, the rich found a surrogate for the father in the youth association and school.

In the American northeast in the 1840s, there was a proliferation of middle-class teenage clubs devoted to temperance, debating, and even publishing "boy's newspapers." These imitations of adult social associations were possible because parents were able to withhold their offspring from the workforce into late teenage. Native-born boys in one New York town at midcentury were nearly twice as likely as immigrants to be still outside the workforce in their late teens.[45]

The middle-class ideal was to isolate the boy in school until age 16 or 17. The English "public school" (really a private boarding school) was the incubator of not only elite education but also of new forms of leisure. In the 1830s, Thomas Arnold's Rugby School and others reformed the traditional aristocratic boarding school. Before reform, student disorder (where the older scholars terrorized the younger and both participated in periodic riots) had been combined with harsh discipline and rote learning meted out by schoolmasters. In an effort both to instill discipline and to build "character," headmasters integrated sport fully into the English public-school curriculum. The traditionally rough and chaotic rural game of football was taken over by the elite schools and converted into a very different sport. Individual skill with the feet, teamwork, and regulated contact replaced the free-for-all of the traditional Shrove Tuesday village match (Chapter 10).

In Britain, sport served in the transition from childhood to adulthood by separating male youths from the increasingly "effeminate" domestic world. Boys were expected to be toughened up, to fight fair but not shed tears. Boy play was to be the opposite of female domesticity. A spartan model was cultivated by pseudo-military training. Rifle clubs, drilling, and uniforms permeated the free time of the mid-Victorian middle-class boy. The threat of precocious sexuality was displaced by vigorous activity. This same sports mentality trickled down into the working classes through football teams sponsored by former public-school men (Chapter 10).

In America, sports played a somewhat different role. Although the English school had its American admirers, athletics came late to the state-supported public schools. The initiative was taken by private organizations such as the YMCA. By 1870, the American "Y" had lost much of its early stress on moral refinement. It had become a sports and physical fitness center for the urban middle class. Under Luther Gulick's influence in the 1890s, the "Y" developed a philosophy of manliness based less on mere moral rectitude than on physical conditioning and team sports.[46]

Recurrent anxiety about national security (especially in England) stirred concern with fitness. The Crimean War of 1854-1856 sparked the formation of the Voluntary Force, a citizen's militia that trained for potential military service. Later, the boys' brigades were formed (1883), which were organized to instill parade-ground discipline in working-class boys. Many Englishmen were shocked by the number of British recruits in the Boer War (1899-1902) who failed their physical examinations. Britain was producing physical misfits. National "efficiency" required not only the discipline of military training in the schools and brigades but team sports and athletic training.[47]

While athleticism and even militarism increasingly dominated leisure reform, character building was not neglected. If I may extend this chapter slightly beyond the 14th century, the Boy Scouts are a good example of both trends. Founded officially in 1908 by the English general and hero of the Boer War, Robert Baden-Powell, the scouting movement quickly passed to America under the leadership of Ernest Thompson Seton in 1910. Baden-Powell attempted to create a "character factory." Through organized recreation the virtues of patriotism, chivalry, woodcraft (nature study), and self-sacrifice were to be instilled. The scouts promised both the adventure that ran through youth literature of the period and the discipline of merit badges and rank. Baden-Powell and Thompson-Seton, however, opposed military drills for scouts (favored by the British boys' brigades, e.g.). Troops were organized mostly for the middle classes and were designed to fill the vacuum in the 12-18 year group in which the discipline of home, school, and work were weak and declining. In America, the scouts filled a need for recreation, which schools only began to provide in the 1920s.[48]

The early boy scouts were to provide an antidote to effeminacy and social "deterioration." The scouts took the boy from the "excessive" influence of women: "The REAL Boy Scout is not a 'sissy.' [He] adores his mother [but] is not hitched to [her] apron strings." Fathers holding white-collar jobs feared that men were getting soft and that the "natural" distinction between the sexes was being blurred. They sought to restore their own and their son's "masculinity" by becoming scout masters.[49]

The scout movement also provided an alternative to street play: Scouts were "no longer loafing in billiard parlors or among boys that tend to exercise a harmful influence over them." Historian David MacLeon finds that the scouts targeted middle-class boys in an attempt to isolate them from the precocious independence and immorality of urban poor boys. Other accounts stress that the scouts also focused on those working-class families who strove for "respectability" and were eager to break from the rougher elements in their neighborhoods.[50]

Given the threats posed by the free time of working-class youth to the social order, it is not surprising that middle-class reformers targeted this section of urban society for reform. From the 1880s, groups like the Boys' Brigades in England and the Boy's Clubs in both countries sought a working-class clientele. Both tended to stress discipline and authority far more than did the more middle-class boy scouts.[51]

Less authoritarian, if perhaps equally paternalistic, was the American playground movement. Beginning modestly, when the public schools of Boston in 1885 provided sandboxes for poor children, it expanded in the late 90s with neighborhood parks in immigrant areas of Chicago and other American cities. It culminated in the influential Playground Association (founded in 1906, which later become the National Recreation Association) led by Luther Gulick and Joseph Lee. By 1915, 430 American municipalities had park programs and thousands more followed. Other cities attached the playground to the school system for more efficient use and lower costs. Settlement houses like Hull House in Chicago in 1894 built playgrounds complete with a sand pile, swings, and building blocks, as well as a building for indoor baseball.

The concept of the playground movement was quite simple: alternatives to the street and degrading commercial leisure must be provided by the government in safe, regulated fun. Not only should cities build neighborhood playgrounds, as opposed to downtown "promenade parks," but they should offer programs. Henry Curtis, another leader of the Playground Association, advocated that cities take over dance halls and "sooner or later...also take over the moving picture."[52] According to the philosophy of the playground movement, games and play areas should be age-graded and sex-differentiated. This would prevent the older from corrupting the younger child (creating the damage of premature maturity) and allow play to train the sexes for their "appropriate" roles. The Playground Association encouraged the training of playground workers. By 1918, about 50 teacher's colleges offered recreation courses and even the University of California provided summer classes in parks and recreation subjects.[53]

This movement was influenced by the prevailing fear of the social disorder of immigrant life and the belief that commercial leisure was contributing to delinquency. As Curtis noted, "It is not the play but the idleness of the street that is morally dangerous. It is then that the children watch the drunken people, listen to the leader of the gang, hear the shady story, smoke cigarettes..."[54] The recreation movement reflected a positive assessment of the need of youth for playful expression. As the Playground Association stated:

> Delinquency is reduced by providing a wholesome outlet for youthful energy. Industrial efficiency is increased by giving individuals a play life which will develop greater resourcefulness and adaptability. Good citizenship is promoted by forming habits of co-operation in play.... Democracy rests on the most firm basis when a community has formed the habit of playing together.[55]

The so-called recapitulation theory of American psychologist G. Stanley Hall (ca. 1900) was immensely influential among recreation reformers. It held that each child relived in his own development the evolution of humanity. Teenage gang behavior was little more than the re-experience of man's savage stage. The objective of the play movement was not to suppress this stage—for children were essentially immune to rational persuasion—but to guide the youth through it. Indeed, morality and muscularity or physical action were united in the child. This stage of life should not be skipped but rather channeled into organized activity under the firm, but understanding, hand of the scout master, coach, or youth worker.[56] Joseph Lee put the matter similarly. The "play instinct," the love of adventure, tribalism, and physical activity, was the source of the creative impulse essential in adult life. The famous Settlement House activist, Jane Addams, stressed that the petty vandalism of slum youth was the inevitable expression of the "instinct" for "adventure" which should be redirected in organized play.[57]

The youth camp movement, which was popular on both sides of the Atlantic, shared these goals. The pioneer in camping perhaps was the St. Andrew's Home and Club for Working Boys in London (1866), which took its charges on weekends up the Thames for camping trips. Americans also promoted the idea of liberation from the degradation of the city in the *New York Tribune*'s Fresh Air Fund (1877). Both the Boys' Brigades and Boy Scouts organized camping excursions early in the century. The American, Ernest Thompson Seton, who (in addition to the scouts) founded the Woodcraft League in 1902, rejected the military and patriotic trappings of the brigades for the pure romance of sleeping in tents, tramping, and songs around the fire. The moral objective was still apparent. Its purpose, he argued, was:

> To give pioneers a well-organized communal life, to provide them with opportunities for healthy outdoor activity; to train them in self-reliance and communal responsibility; and to counterbalance the monotony of factory and school life and the complexity of an industrial civilization with a life that is simpler, freer, and more spontaneous.

The permanent summer camp for youth was unique in America. By 1929 there were 7,000 such camps, which reached a million children. The scouts and YMCA were especially prominent in providing children contact with nature as well as a sheltered moral environment. "Roughing it," was low priority.[58]

These reformers were, however, relatively indifferent to organizing the leisure of girls. Not only were there few efforts to organize girls' clubs or to introduce physical fitness into girls' education in the 19th century, but the female equivalents of the Boy Scouts were rather afterthoughts. When a group of girls in khaki shirts appeared at the first official rally of the Boy Scouts at the Crystal Palace in 1909, Baden-Powell enlisted his sister to organize a separate organization to prevent the corruption of the "manliness" of the scouts. They were called Girl Guides; Agnes Baden-Powell's goal was definitely "feminine:" "you do not want to make tomboys of refined girls, yet you want to attract, and thus raise, the slum girl from the gutter. The main object is to give them all the ability to be better mothers and Guides to the next generation." Activities stressed the "womanly arts" of sewing, decoration, and cooking. By 1912, however, hikes and other outdoor activities were added to help the girls become more resourceful and self-reliant. Whereas boys were trained to be loyal and competitive, the girls were supposed to learn domestic skills and to inculcate attitudes of harmony and "happiness."[59]

Limits of Reform:
Youth and the Power of Commercial Leisure

The cult of "fireside happiness" went far to redefine traditional leisure in the industrial era. Built around the home and the homemaking mother, it showed a fresh side of the reforming spirit so powerfully expressed in rational recreation. Rather restrictive attitudes toward play and its use in moral training gradually gave way to greater tolerance of the child's pleasures. This attitude reflects the loosening of the work ethic among adults as prosperity and mechanization reduced the necessity of being "severely workful." Yet anxiety that the adolescent was losing the values of rural life and work discipline and was drifting away from the influence of parent and adult authorities led to a serious effort to reestablish adult control. Increased sophistication in child rearing, perhaps, led to more indirect methods. However the objects of the various youth recreational movements remained character building and social control.

Those sports developed in the British and American schools in the 19th century, of course, remain at the core of the leisure calender of many American and British males today, a point we will explore further in Chapter 10. The scouts became a mass movement and, with summer camps, introduced millions to the pleasures of hiking, camping, and general outdoor activities. Doubtles, these movements sustained loyalty and patriotism (ideals that inspired men to go "over the top" in the trenches of World War I). The early Victorian presumption scouts became a mass movement and, with summer camps, introduced millions to the pleasures of hiking, camping, and general outdoor activities. Doubtles, these movements sustained loyalty and patriotism (ideals that inspired men to go "over the top" in the trenches of World War I). The early Victorian presumption that moral uplift, if adapted by the working class, would end not only poverty but also but social division was equally applied to the later ideal of public-school athleticism and to nature study.[60]

Yet we still must ask how successful were these efforts. Historian Dom Cavallo doubts that more than 10-20 percent of immigrant youth visited urban playgrounds in the period between 1900 and 1920. And increasingly from the 1920s, play programs were integrated into the schools and recess.[61] As we have seen before, high-minded reformers often found their innovations turned to new purposes by their working-class clients. To take just the most obvious examples, the amateur ideal of public-school football in Britain was turned into a professional sport because of the successful infiltration of the northern industrial worker;[62] and the playground movement, which hoped to break down ethnic identities in America, found that the group loyalties of the street were simply transferred to the playing field and field houses.

Most important, the informal, often rough, but autonomous life of the street survived the reformers. Especially in the neighborhoods of the poor, the Playground Association, boy's clubs, and scouts could not penetrate. Finally, the commercial entertainments of the city were hardly replaced by the reformers' clubs. Indeed, as we shall see in the next chapter, they grew with technology. They offered unalloyed fun, often recreating those traditional pleasures that had long attracted people of all ages. The attempt to break down the difference in the generations was hardly successful; indeed, leisure increasingly became a site for conflict between parent and child.

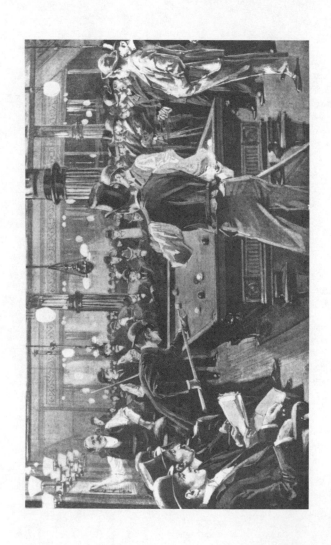

9

Leisure for the Masses:
The Commercialization of Entertainment
in the 19th Century

So far we have concentrated on traditional and reforming leisure. Now we must consider more fully a third, and perhaps the most significant, expression of society's quest for play, commercial entertainment. The business of providing pleasure is surely one of the oldest occupations. What goes by the name of traditional leisure in the seasonal and religious festivals of 17th-century Europe or even colonial and frontier America often centered on the Punch and Judy show or traveling menagerie.

Still, industrialization in the 19th century produced new types of leisure industry. First, the creation of new wealth and technology gave birth to a taste for novelty. The pleasures of the aristocratic spa trickled down to the family fun of the popular resort reached by the railroad. The tradition-bound jugglers and pantomime artists were gradually displaced by the new and more thrilling technological wonder of the amusement park.

Second, leisure was transformed by a new sense of time, pleasure by the hour, weekend, and summer holiday, not the traditional festival or irregular leisure moments of preindustrial society. The institution of the Saturday half-holiday, for example, created a time slot ideal for the emergence of English football and baseball as popular spectator sports. In England, the 1871 Bank Holidays Act not only added Easter Monday, Boxing Day (the day after Christmas), and Whit Monday to the legal holiday calender of Christmas and Good Friday, but created a new secular summer holiday on the first Monday in August. The gradual emergence of vacation with pay also allowed the democratization of tourism.

Third capitalist business practices—especially profit maximization, based not on a luxury market but on a mass market with unfettered competition—had a revolutionary impact on leisure services; they created a mass entertainment industry centralized in the hands of relatively few triumphant corporations of national and even international influence.

Many commentators have lamented the coming of mass leisure, just as they have found wanting the era of consumerism in general. It is easy to argue that the entertainment industry has eclipsed traditional popular leisure and subverted the ideals of the play movement and other forms of rational recreation. Critics find in consumer leisure the manipulation of the capitalist-impresario who has created a passive, if easily sated, crowd of pleasure-seekers, deprived of playing any active role in history or even personal development. Pleasure entrepreneurs have created a modern version of "bread and circuses." Traditionalists lament the passing of the old folklore in the modern culture of rootless ignorance of the past; communities formed and refreshed in traditional play have been supplanted by a "lonely crowd" ever seeking new thrills in the glitzy world of superficial fads and the rise and fall of "stars."

These characterizations may ring true; the reader should decide. But we should keep in mind that this commercialization often had origins that were both traditional and reformist. Historically, people's tastes in fun have remained extraordinarily conservative even when repackaged in modern forms, and many have insisted that their pleasures somehow be "improving." Moreover, if such leisure tended toward national and even international uniformity, it also produced a vast variety of alternatives; it had meanings and uses that were not always passive and depersonalizing. Most important perhaps, whatever we think of the entertainment industry in all of its manifestations, a study of its historical origins is helpful for understanding why it generally has triumphed over traditional popular and rational recreation.

This chapter will be the first installment in an exploration of the problem of the history of mass-market leisure. It will cover the nineteenth century through World War I and will lay the foundation for an understanding of the twentieth-century entertainment industry.

Industrialization and Mass Leisure

Leisure did not become a business in the 19th century, but the industrial economy made entertainment a more thorough and different sort of business. Viewed first from the demand side, the key was the growth in personal income and later its fairly wide distribution. The first classes to enjoy and lead the commercialization of leisure were, of course, aristocratic and landed elites. Possessing both income and a culture that valued pleasure more than productivity, the aristocratic residents of London and plantations of the American South created such characteristically modern leisure forms as tourism, urban entertainment districts, and a taste for various fads and fashion (Chapter 4).

By the mid-century, this leisure style penetrated the hard-working and newly rich middle class, who were breaking away from the strictures against pleasure seeking. In both America and Britain, they aped the old landed elite seeking, in part, validation of their new-found status. The children of Puritan workaholic businessmen of the midcentury had embraced "The Gospel of Relaxation" by the 1850s.[1] The upper middle class joined the aristocracy and royalty in the fashionable "season" at Brighton and other resorts; they modeled their new homes on a similar domestic opulence and elegant dining. American industrialists gathered at the track of Sarasota Springs and the shore at Newport to see and be seen.

The desire for leisure trickled down to skilled and commercial workers, who began to define their status as much by the quality of leisure as by the character of their work. Their early demand for vacations with pay and willingness to make sacrifices for middle-class domestic luxuries is evidence of this trend. The gradual increase in real wages of working people after about 1860 also democratized access to purchased leisure, partly as a function of "Engel's Curve," which describes the tendency of the proportion of family budgets required for necessities to decrease with rising income. The increased share of the pay packet available for pleasure was spent in many ways. For example, in England, the consumption of tea (and sugar) spread broadly to the working classes between 1850 and 1900 (increasing three fold in annual consumption). From the 1860s, the tea shops, which were often first opened by temperance activists, gradually were transformed into commercial chains. Increased opportunity to purchase excursion tickets or admission to music halls reduced the reliance of many working-class people upon alcohol for pleasure. Even beer consumption in Britain dropped from 34 gallons per head in 1875 to 27 gallons by 1914. Other less healthful pleasures like smoking increased by 300 percent in the second half of the century in Britain, especially with the replacement of the pipe with the cigarette after the 1860s.[2]

The revolution in transportation and communications resulted both in new leisure opportunities and in a homogenization of its experience. From the 1830s, the railroad began to conquer time and space. It made distant travel assessable to the middle class and, with the gradual reduction in prices, to time-starved workers. Escape from the city became possible. The steam tram (or streetcar), developed first in America, was brought to England in 1860 by George F. Train, and improved in the mid-1880s with electrification. This vastly eased the movement of workers around the now-sprawling conurbations of London, New York, and many other cities. The tram freed them from exclusive reliance on the neighborhood pub or ethnic fraternal society for leisure and opened their lives to the football or baseball game, the amusement park, and the dance-hall and theater district. The streetcar dominated urban travel until it was replaced by the bus and car in the 1920s.[3]

At the same time, the railroad led to the decline of smaller local fairs. Rural people increasingly traveled to regional urban centers for larger and more diverse entertainment. The train also made it possible for larger, more commercialized amusements to spread costs over a wider market. The traditional troupe of actors or animal acts were able to extend their circuit; but competition for audiences also intensified. Their reliance on agents, impresarios, and owners of chains of music halls naturally increased. Audiences enjoyed more diverse and probably superior entertainment, but local traditions began to die out. Cheaper communications via the steam press and newspaper allowed for rapid and mass dissemination of leisure reading and reinforced the trend toward uniformity.

Perhaps the most complex trend was the influence of capitalist business methods. Most fundamentally, the supply of entertainment reflected the common denominator—the market. Often, a leisure business began by offering a locality a traditional entertainment like a menagerie. Then, with success, it expanded its program to accommodate a wider market. This process took many forms: for example, popular amusements such as the circus were reformed to appeal to a middle-class audience of "rational recreationists." By contrast, an originally uplifting leisure activity like the railroad excursion or holiday camp was shorn of its moralizing lectures and austerity to appeal to a wider, more popular market on a strictly commercial basis.

Competition and cost-cutting pressures also transformed the entertainment industry. Vertical and horizontal integration, well known to historians of the corporation, were equally common to the pleasure industry. From the 1820s British breweries acquired pubs in order to guarantee retail markets, and chains of music halls reduced overhead costs. Important also was the development of advertising from the "ballyhoo" of the carnival "spieler" to the elaborate publicity stunts of P.T. Barnum.[4]

The leisure industry was among the first to adopt new technological and business practices such as the installation of the first British electric street-cars in the resort of Blackpool and the rapid diffusion of new building techniques to the Ferris Wheel. Impresarios were often pure entrepreneurs—quick to find and serve a market, sensitive to the fickle amusement seeker, and eager to beat the less-responsive competitor with a new gimmick or new way of cutting costs. Investors in established leisure industries, such as music halls or vaudeville, were the first to feature films in their houses and to abandon the old entertainment when the market warranted it. Even leisure organizations that began as nonprofit were forced to adopt modern business practices in order to provide the range of services demanded by their patrons. This happened to organizers of railroad excursions (for example, Thomas Cook) and to holiday camps.

During the 19th century, leisure industries entered an international market. By the 1860s, organized railroad tours from England to Paris had become possible. And by the end of the century, Americans traveled on fast steamers and trains to London and even to Paris for several weeks of shopping and theater-going. Improved transatlantic communications created an increasingly common Anglo-American leisure world—with exchanges of popular music-hall artists as well as circus and carnival acts. Fads like roller skating and cycling swept both countries almost simultaneously. The birth of the modern electrified amusement park in the late 1890s was scarcely different on either side of the ocean and the movie industry, when it blossomed after 1896, was closely integrated. If America came to dominate the English-speaking leisure industry by World War I, this dominance only paralleled her economic ascendance in other fields. This "cultural imperialism" was the result of economic dynamics driven by the sheer size of the American market and corporation and the unfettered business civilization that prevailed in the United States. Increasing cultural uniformity and ever-quickening adaptation to technological and market change was the inevitable result of this process. Leisure was torn from its traditional roots in community and history.

The lives of two pioneers of mass-market leisure, the American P. T. Barnum and the Englishman Thomas Cook, may help to illustrate these points. P.T. Barnum was a impresario of amusement in the growing city of New York in the mid-19th century. In his "Museum," he appealed both to the tradition of the rural fair in his display of curiosities and to the quest for respectability in lectures on new scientific invention and wax works of Biblical characters. He tapped the American longing both for culture and for voyeurism in his anatomically-correct statue of Venus. He was an extraordinary promoter. In 1850, Barnum organized a nine-month tour of the "Swedish Nightingale," Jenny Lynd. Through advance publicity and promotional products (Lynd cigars and coats, e.g.), he created a veritable "Lyndomania" that would have made the ad managers behind George Lucas' "Star Wars" films proud. Thomas Cook was a young wood turner and secretary of the South Midland Temperance Association when he decided to organize a railroad excursion from Leicester to a temperance demonstration in Loughborough in the summer of 1841. Unlike the standard third-class ticket, he offered a bargain at one shilling per round trip. Soon he arranged these trips commercially. Cook rented a special train, assumed all the risk, and sold tickets at substantial reductions, making a profit on the volume and low overhead. Gradually his business turned to international tourism.[5]

These leisure impresarios may have encouraged the homogenization of leisure, but age, class, and cultural differences prevailed to assure a diversity of leisure markets. Middle-class reformers persisted in opposing profitable entertainment industries—even if the source of their own wealth was in commercial profit. Higher-class pleasure seekers balked at the invasion of the excursionist or rowdy crowd on a limited budget. And the resort towns, hotels, concert halls, and other businesses dependent upon their trade did their utmost to assure their exclusivity. Most importantly different groups responded to the allure of commercial pleasure in different ways. Perhaps most enthusiastic were youth who found in mass entertainment an escape from parental control and tradition and who were drawn to a setting often deliberately designed for romance and youthful sociability.

Daily and Weekend Entertainments

Mass leisure in the 19th century was snatched in those moments free from work and bought with the odd nickels and pence left from the weekly pay packet. Although literacy was an imperfect skill for many before the 1870s when universal elementary education expanded considerably, the demand for accessible pleasure reading was great throughout the century. The cheap popular press was facilitated by technology (steam press and mechanized bookbinding in the 1840s) and by public policy (e.g., the abolition of taxes on newspapers in England in 1855 and 1861).

In England, popular weekly newspapers by midcentury offered an odd mix of democratic politics and sensational crime news. Especially popular from midcentury were the Sunday papers or weeklies (especially *Lloyd's Weekly Newspaper* and the *News of the World*) read by workers on Saturday afternoon after dinner or at the barber's on Sundays. *Chamber's Journal* (1832) and George Newnes's *Tit-Bits* (1881) offered a compendium of facts to artisans eager to supplement their sporadic education. As Alfred Harmsworth, publisher of *Answers* (1888) put it: "We are a sort of Universal Information provider. Anyone who reads our paper for a year will be able to converse on many subjects on which he was entirely ignorant. He will have a good stock of anecdotes and jokes and will indeed be a pleasant companion."[6]

The taste for fiction was nearly inexhaustible in England as women and men consumed huge quantities of "chapbooks." These were:

> Paper-covered booklets...embellished with a crude and highly coloured woodcut as a frontispiece. The contents were either lurid, violent, and morbid, or sentimental and spicey. The 'last dying words and confessions' of culprits hung at York, lives of infamous highwaymen and murders, and garbled versions of traditional stories of the Seven Champions of Christendom or Friar Bacon and Dr. Faustus."

Chapbooks represented the remnants of traditional peasant culture that survived until midcentury in urban England. By 1850 they were replaced by the "penny dreadfuls" of Edward Lloyd's *Weekly Miscellany of Romance and General Interest* and George Reynolds's *Miscellany,* which dealt in mysteries and scandals in court and high society. The western made a cult figure out of Kit Carson in America, and Europeans who never traveled to America wrote hundreds of westerns with formula stories of cowboys and Indians.[7]

From the 1830s, William Milder offered cheap reprints of classics by Burns, Byron, and Milton. Harriet Beecher Stowe's *Uncle Tom's Cabin* swept not only America but Britain in the 1850s. In 1848, George Routledge started the Railway Library in London offering, over the next 50 years, 1300 titles, mostly cheap reprints of Jane Austen and other contemporary novelists. The market for books, however, remained socially upscale. Even in the early 20th century, the poor in England seldom owned any books except perhaps *Old Moore's Almanack;* and fathers sometimes prohibited book reading as a snare of bad habits and laziness.[8]

What attracted the masses was, of course, the popular newspaper. Although many "respectable Englishmen" feared that the removal of the newspaper stamp in 1855 would open the gates to a flood of lurid dailies, most newspapers retained the dullness of *The Times*. Only with the appearance of the *Evening News* (1881) the *Star* (1888) and especially the *Daily Mail* (1896), was the English tabloid press born. In many ways, it was an imitation of the American "yellow press" with its chauvinism mixed with gossip, sports, and crime news.[9]

Soon English publishers discovered the specialty youth and women's market. The respectable *Family Herald* had a circulation of 125,000 by 1849 and offered romantic short stories. We have already encountered the rise of the women's magazine. But pulp fiction for boys, (ancestors of the 20th-century comic book) spread from the 1860s. Edwin Brett led a troupe of popular authors that offered up stories of highwaymen, pirates, and crime to British youth. They were sold in penny weekly installments of eight pages of text illustrated with lurid drawings. Although magazines like *The Boys of England* were full of crude youthful heroics, the Religious Tract Society felt obliged in 1879 to counter them with *The Boy's Own Paper*, which included hobbyist, sport, and nature features. Alfred Harmsworth, the newspaper publisher, branched out into half-penny boy's weeklies featuring "daring deeds set against an imperial back-cloth." His weeklies, *The Gem* (1907) and *The Magnet* (1908), made heros of public-school boys among slum dwellers.[10] The girl's literary market was somewhat late to develop, perhaps because, unlike their brothers, girls were burdened with housework and lacked pocket money.[11]

The growth of American popular literature was, if anything, even more rapid. If in 1825 there were no more than 100 magazines in the United States, by 1850, there were about 600; the country witnessed the publication of about 5,000 during that generation. In addition to cheap miscellanies from the 1820s like the *Casket: Flowers of Literature, Wit and Sentiment* and knowledge magazines like *The Magazine of Useful and Entertaining Knowledge* (1831), a vast specialized press emerged in *Godey's Lady's Book* and its many imitators. An adolescent and working-class press had much in common with its English counterparts. The production of cheap adventure and romantic "dime novels" was a veritable industry. By 1886, *The New York Tribune's* sports page revolutionized newspapers. William Randolph Hearst did the same in his string of papers a decade later.[12]

In both countries, the demand for indoor music and "variety" was also insatiable.[13] The variety show had its roots in the informal and often disreputable singing saloons or "free and easies," where drink mixed with singing and rough male fellowship. Successful publicans or tavern keepers, like Charles Morton of London in 1851, expanded the entertainment part of the business. Still, the admission fee was not for the show but for a drink voucher. In the 1850s, the interior of Morton's Canterbury Hall (London) sat 1,500 and was well lighted with chandeliers. Thomas Wright, a "Journey Man Engineer" from London, noted that the music hall was a:

> Popular place of Saturday night resort with working men, as at them they can combine the drinking of the Saturday night glass and the smoking of the Saturday night pipe, with the seeing and hearing of a variety of entertainments, ranging from magnificent ballets and marvelous scenic illusions to inferior tumbling, and from well-given operatic selections to the most idiotic of the so-called comic songs of the Jolly Dogs Class.[14]

By the 1860s, American entrepreneurs like the New Yorker, Tony Pastor, found that a more respectable audience, including women and family, could be enticed to his "Opera House" on the Bowery by a program of well-known (and publicized) singers, comedians, and animal and acrobatic acts. Sentimental songs about motherhood and rural nostalgia predominated, though the old raucous tradition survived in the double meanings in comedy and the American affection for sharpshooters. In American vaudeville, impresarios at first were willing to hire semi-amateurs who (depending on audience reception) could be signed for lengthy tours or "given the hook." Popular demand for a variety of acts and the development of fast rail and steamboat lines allowed the spread of a number of entertainment circuits so Jenny Lynd would be widely seen in 19th-century America and Britain. Gradually, music halls replaced tables with stalls and eliminated drinking in the hall. Typical was the London Pavilion and other halls built in the new Piccadilly Circus in the 1870s. New regulations, like those imposed by the London County Council in 1889, forced music halls to eliminate offensive gags and songs. By the 1890s, theater owners like B. F. Keith removed the saloon from his New York establishment and successfully controlled his own booking agency complete with a hierarchy of stars. English syndicates bought or built chains of "Empires," "Palaces," and "Hippodromes," "resplendent in red plush, gilt adorned with the bottomy plaster cherubs and busty nymphs, which today epitomize the glories of the late Victorian and Edwardian Music Hall."[15] The historian, Peter Bailey, describes the process:

> As the simple platform of the singing saloons was gradually superseded by the full theatrical apparatus of a stage and proscenium arch, the big halls were encouraged to introduce greater show and theatricality into their programmes—lavish tableaux of famous battle scenes, hundred-strong corps de ballet, troupes of Can-Can dancers from Paris and Blondin cooking omelettes on the high wire.

By the 1890s star singers made phonograph records and Dan Leno, the British comedian, even published a weekly *Comic Journal*.[16]

The public amusements offered to the young were as important. Penny or "gaff" theatres in London flourished between 1830 and 1880. They attracted apprentices, unskilled porters, and office boys, in the odd hour when they could get away from work, with melodramas concerning the latest murder or the execution of the infamous criminal. Because of British laws that controlled popular theater by outlawing dialogue, gaff theatre relied on pantomime, explanatory placards (anticipating silent films), singing, and dancing. Also popular were tight-rope walkers, magicians, and demonstrations of Galvanism (use of electric current to shock a volunteer from the audience).[17] Later in the century, youth in Chicago attended five-cents theaters, which projected slides to tell popular stories of murder and revenge.[18]

A similar crowd was drawn to the dime museums in New York City with their sideshow-like exhibitions of freaks (the dwarf Tom Thumb, a Bearded Lady), panoramas or huge paintings depicting well-known dramatic events, and wax works depicting famous and infamous biblical and historical figures. Incidental to this appeal to the fantastic were moral messages that warned of the terrors of intemperance or the price of crime. Barnum mixed the fake (such as the supposed black nurse of George Washington) with the real (a gallery of giants and dwarfs). His Museum in New York also included the traditional tight-rope walkers, pantomimes, and tumblers. An English equivalent in the 1840s was the Bianchi's Waxworks of Liverpool and the Egyptian Hall in Piccadilly, which offered sights of two-headed cows and other freaks. Museums and plebian theatres might also offer "cut-throat dramas," which stressed action, special effects (e.g., railroad collisions) and "women in unmentionables."[19]

By the turn of the century, the dance hall was sweeping American and English towns. By 1910, there were at least 500 public dance halls in New York and many saloons offered floors for dancing. One hundred dance academies provided classes to about 100,000 students a year. They attracted especially the young and, to allure males, they offered women cut-price entry. What most impressed observers was the charged sexual atmosphere. "Tough dancing," with origins in San Francisco brothels, was widely popular from 1905. Couples, dancing the "lovers' two-step," "turkey trot," and "bunny hug," "stand very close together, the girl with her hands around the man's neck, the man with both his arms around the girl or on her hips; their cheeks are pressed close together; their bodies touch each other."[20] This behavior, of course, shocked the Victorian and at least suggests the sexual activism of the 1960s. The flashy dance hall dress of working-class females had striking parallels with the fashion of prostitutes. And the "treating" system, made necessary by the lower wages paid young working women, gave males sexual leverage over females. Some became "charity girls" who traded sexual favors for "treats" of drinks, jewelry, and clothes. Still, these young women often were skilled at coaxing men with money into contributing to their costly pleasures without compromise.[21]

New technology in the 1880s and 1890s changed the form but not always the content of such catch-as-catch-can pleasures. Mechanical games and gramophones, offered in penny arcades, hotel lobbies, and amusement parks, were often little different from the pleasures of the museum or penny theater. The peep show or Kenitoscope, introduced by Thomas Edison in 1894, offered the viewer a short show of acrobatics, mock executions, or a lady taking a bath. The emergence of the projected film in 1896 was first just another act in the music hall or vaudeville, not much different from the decades-old arts of pantomime, shadowgraph, puppetry, and magic lanternry. It featured the curiosity of movement, water splashing on a beach or an oncoming train. Some early films offered an improvement on the realism of the panorama, with moving pictures of royalty or other famous people or crude news programs with footage, for example, from the Boar War. The American nickelodeons (specialized movie house first appearing in Pittsburgh in 1905) and English penny cinema offered short programs of 5 to 10-minute films in the back of cigar stores or abandoned shops. Within two years, there were perhaps 10,000 of them in America alone. Often much cheaper than Vaudeville, they attracted the less affluent with action films like the famous *Great Train Robbery*. In America, many appeared in immigrant working class districts where the silent film could be appreciated by non-English-speaking men on their way to or from work. Others appeared along commercial streets or near public transportation, seeking to attract not only single men but also women on shopping trips.

There was no clearer case of the commercialization of leisure than the early development of the film. In its first decade, American producers and distributors were locked in bitter competition. Like the steel and automobile industries of the time, the movie industry sought economic relief in the merger of the largest companies (headed by Thomas Edison and the Biograph Company). They formed the Motion Picture Patent Association and shared rights to film technology in an attempt to create a vertical monopoly, controlling the industry from film stock to projection. A number of independent producers and distributors survived, however, to lead the industry into a new type of entertainment.

In its first decade, the cinema, like the penny gaff or dime museum, was associated with the poor and working classes. Yet again, exhibitors attempted to widen the market. As early as 1907, independent film producers and movie-house owners sought to transform the experience of film by making it more "respectable." They provided, for example, half-price tickets for women and built movie palaces that were plush auditoriums complete with orchestras and uniformed ushers to maintain order. The picture palace drove the nickelodeons and penny cinemas out of business by 1910.

Independents also offered status-conscious audiences "feature-length" films showing, for example, Sarah Bernhardt in the play *Queen Elizabeth* in 1913. Cinema was to be more like the legitimate theater and exhibitors often charged near theater prices for a seat. In 1912, New York businessman Adophe

Zukor organized the Famous Players Film Company (later part of Paramount) to produce feature-length screen plays, like the *Count of Monte Cristo*. In order to attract audiences, independent filmmakers publicized the leading actors, creating the *star*—something Biograph had steadfastly refused to do. The Motion Picture Patents Company was finally declared illegal in 1918, but it had long slipped from prominence because of its unwillingness to adapt to the broadening demand for respectable films. A very similar process occurred in England. By 1914 there were 14 Picturedromes in Birmingham, England, with a capacity of almost 33,000.[22] The film industry became a sort of melange of popular curiosity with roots in the carnival and burlesque and the high-mindedness of the Victorian theater (Chapter 12).

Despite the importance of commercialized public pleasures, the home remained an important focus of leisure and merchants knew it. From mid-century, piano and sheet music trickled down to the artisan class. By 1910, Britons owned two million pianos and supported 47,000 piano teachers. The cult of domesticity, which so pervaded Victorian society on both sides of the Atlantic, was commercialized in the "restoration" of Christmas. A long list of industries were practically created by the mid-19th century celebration of Christmas, including greeting cards and Christmas trees (and decorations). The new custom of showering children with manufactured toys was a commercial boom. By the 1890s, the British had imported Santa Claus from the United States where, since the 1870s, the bearded man had been enthroned in department stores as a inducement to sales.[23] The late Victorian suburb used its lawns to play croquet and its front and backyard gardens to cultivate the hobby of gardening.[24] There emerged a vast market for domestic-centered leisure goods from the camera (advanced in 1888 with the marketing of the Kodak) and phonograph to the table settings for the increasingly more elegant dinner parties of the middle class.[25] Even the respectable worker's Sunday featured an elaborate midday meal.[26]

The Commercial Festival and Tourism

Mass-market leisure offered daily and weekly doses of fun for a routinized world of industrial society; yet the traditional saturnalia of the seasonal fair and festival did not disappear. Rather, these carnivals were transformed by new business methods and technology. For example, ancient fairs like that of St. Giles near Oxford witnessed a tremendous growth in the 19th century. Vendors offered an increased variety of exotic foods and souvenirs, and entertainment and rail services brought throngs in from the countryside.[27] The one-wagon menagerie of colonial America with its "Lyon of Barbary," polar bear, or elephant, and the English circus of Philip Astley with its equestrian acts, gradually gave way to the zoological exhibition and the three-ring circus.[28] This process was the product of steam transportation and the merger. The small family circuses of America, for example, which emerged in the early 19th century from small towns in New York and New England, gradually gave way to the extravagant boat circuses that plied their trade on the Ohio and Mississippi Rivers. In the 1850s, the Floating Palace, a sumptuously decorated barge pulled by steam boats, seated 1,800 and offered a standard circus ring. By the 1860s, the wagon menagerie began to be replaced by the railroad circus, which could make transcontinental tours. P.T. Barnum lent his name, made famous by his "Museum" in New York City, to a circus train in 1872. It toured 16 states with its 61 cars. Its official name reveals the scope of its offerings (or claims): "P.T. Barnum's Great Traveling World's Fair Consisting of Museum, Menagerie, Caravan, Hippodrome, Gallery of Statuary and Fine Arts, Polytechnic Institute, Zoological Garden, and 100,000 Curiosities, Combined with Dan Castello's, Sig. Sebastian's and Mr. D'Atelie's Grand Triple Equestrian and Hippodromatic Exposition." Barnum's show merged with its major competitor, Cooper and Bailey, in 1881.[29]

The circus, often suspect to respectable crowds, adopted the language of learning. For example, the English horseman John Ricketts, on a tour in New England in 1795, lent dignity and an aura of culture to his act of tumbling, tightrope walking, and clowning by referring to recent Egyptian expeditions and giving his acts imaginative and "edifying" names like the Egyptian Pyramids or Roman Monuments. The carnival or fun fair was likewise made respectable and expanded in the 19th century.[30]

Perhaps the most dramatic change in the fair occurred in the 1893 Columbia Exposition in Chicago. Its "Midway," a colorful amusement sideshow, stole the crowds from the White City, a Neo-Renaissance complex of educational exhibits. Almost 21.5 million visited the Exposition and most favored the Midway, with its chaotic display of "mosques and pagodas, Viennese streets and Turkish bazaars, South Sea island huts, Irish and German castles, and Indian tepees." The exotica of the four corners of the world were offered to visitors arriving by streetcar. Advertising stressed the educational: foreigners on display "bring their manners, customs, dress, religions, legends, amusements, that we might know them the better." Yet what attracted the throngs was "Little Egypt" dancing the hootchy-kootchy. Dominating the Midway was the Ferris Wheel, a steam-powered disc some 264 feet high that took 20 minutes for one revolution and cost the hefty price of 50 cents a ticket for 2,160 passengers. The Ferris Wheel was quickly imitated in amusement parks from San Francisco to Vienna. The extravagance of pseudo-oriental and Venetian themes were widely copied in amusement centers like Coney Island, Blackpool, England, and San Francisco's "The Chutes." At the same period, electric-powered rides like the switchback (or rollercoaster) and loop the loop attracted the young thrill-seeker.[31]

The amusement park was often located in a seaside or lake setting accessible by train or streetcar from the city. Coney Island was a mere eight miles from Manhattan, and Blackpool was within a short train ride from a number of English mill towns. The amusement parks provided a magical setting free from the watchful eyes of parents and neighbors. It offered the opportunity for audience and entertainment to merge. Coney Island is a good example. As early as the 1820s, this island south of Brooklyn, New York, had been the location of both an exclusive resort area (Manhattan Beach) and, from the 1860s, a haven for gamblers and swindlers (Norton's Point, on the opposite end of the Island). By the 1890s dance halls and vaudeville, as well as sideshows and penny arcades, attracted a diverse crowd to Central Beach. George Tilyou, among others, attempted to create a more respectable but also popular image at the central beach of the Island. Tilyou's Steeplechase Park (1897), followed by Luna Park (1903), and Dreamworld (1904) offered self-contained amusement centers designed to reassure the respectable but also to offer excitement at five or ten cents a ride. The quest for greater legitimacy led the organizers of Dreamworld to feature "The Creation" and "The End of the Earth" to graphically remind visitors of their Bible lessons. Significantly, Dreamworld was the first park to fail. The picture postcard, just then legalized, became part of the ritual of the visit and a great form of publicity. Coney Island allowed people to subtly break moral codes. The "Barrel of Fun" threw young men and women together; air jets lifted women's skirts; and post cards offered slightly risque themes. Rides were often reminiscent of the new urban elevated trains or electric minecars; but rides like the "Flip-Flap" parodied them with its 25-foot vertical loop.[32] As the historian John Kasson notes:

> Coney Island located its festivity not in time as a special moment
> on the calendar but in space as a special place on the map. By
> creating its own version of carnival, Coney Island tested and trans-
> formed accustomed social roles and values. It attracted people
> because of the way in which it mocked the established social order.
> Coney Island in effect declared a moral holiday for all who entered
> its gates. Against the values of thrift, sobriety, industry, and ambition,
> it encouraged extravagance, gaiety, abandon, revelry. Coney
> Island signaled the rise of a new mass culture no longer deferential
> to genteel tastes and values, which demanded a democratic resort of
> its own. It served as a Feast of Fools of an urban-industrial society.[33]

The episodic escape to the amusement park did not satisfy the crowd's taste for novelty. By the end of the century, guided tours of unfamiliar places attracted millions. Yet again, the rich set the pace and, as the masses joined them, conflicts inevitably emerged. In England, the resort and tourism began as aristocratic diversions. The seaside resorts of Brighton, Blackpool, Torquay, and Scarborough attracted the leisure class for lengthy fall and winter seasons. The rich were attracted as much to the assembly hall, where masters of ceremonies organized formal balls and arranged social introductions, as they were

drawn to the health-giving sea. Brighton's early success was due to the patronage of the Prince of Wales, who first arrived in 1783 and graced it with
subsequent royal visits, culminating in the building of the Royal Pavilion. In the
1820s, the promenade on the chain pier, the theater, and the Oriental baths were
very fashionable even if the royal family gradually lost interest.[34] As an
American described the Brighton "season":

> The modes of getting rid of time, which seemed to be the great end
> and object of all, were various. Some lounged into reading-rooms;
> some sat down deliberately in shops, to make the most of the little
> business they were blessed with..... In the afternoon all repaired, by
> common consent, to walk, ride, or drive along the ramparts by the
> seaside.[35]

The early-19th century resort in America was not much different. As
early as 1825, a booklet, "The Fashionable Tour," identified the passion for
travel among the new rich of the American East. Added to the colonial resort
of Newport was the spa and racing center at Saratoga Springs, New York. Not
only were urban merchants attracted to these resorts, but so were southern
planters, at least until sectional conflicts by midcentury caused southern status
seekers to find an alternative pecking order in southern resorts like White
Sulphur Springs. Besides the snob appeal of just being there and the allure of
the race track, Saratoga Springs provided a courting yard for debutantes and
eligible bachelors. "The gentlemen whiled away long hours in smoke-filled bar-
rooms over their gin slings, sangarees, sherry cobblers, and wine juleps. The
ladies were relegated to the piazza, or possibly allowed an afternoon carriage
drive." Inland along the Mississippi River, the steam boat provided a similar
lethargic leisure, spiced by the risk of playing with the thousands of professional
gamblers at the card table.[36]

Following the laying of rail track, such seaside resorts became accessible to the less affluent, eager for diversion from the cares of trade but unable
or unwilling to devote weeks to leisure. The promised benefit of sea air "ozone"
on the sooty lungs of the city-dweller, attracted thousands to the ocean coast.

The threat to upper-class exclusivity by the 1860s produced a variety
of responses. Some English resorts like Southport and Eastbourne retained their
elite status, owing to the control of the beach by two families who keep out
panderers to the masses. In resorts like Blackpool and Margate, land holding
was fragmented and was thus open to a diverse market. They were abandoned
by the classes for new watering holes in Scotland, Ireland and the Continent.
Some resorts found that differing "seasons" suited various social strata. And in
some resorts, developers assured that portions of the shore were reserved for
elite clientele for whom they provided expensive hotels and furnished

apartments.[37] Despite reformers' interest in the wholesome recreation of the popular excursion, middle-class opinion was often more negative, as seen in the following description of day-trippers from London to Hastings in 1857:

> [They] swarm upon the beach, wandering listlessly about with apparently no other aim than to get a mouthful of fresh air. You may see them in groups of three or four: the husband—a pale, over-wrought man, dressed in black frock-coat, figured waistcoat and bright blue tie—carried the baby; the wife, equally pale and thin, decked out in her best, labours after with a basket of 'prog' [food]. And then there is generally another child... wandering aimlessly behind. She must bear the burden until church-time is over; and the public houses will be open and a quart of porter in the pewter will be forthcoming and the family will dine *alfresco* on the beach.[38]

Resort town governments attempted to regulate the access of rough trade or gypsy beach vendors and to build family-oriented entertainment centers. The scale of enterprise grew with the size of the entertainment. The pier played a major role in this process. Originally merely a facility for docking steamships full of excursionists, the pier gradually became the site of the family promenade and inevitably a market of food, drink, and entertainment. Ever sensitive to the pleasure-seeker's quest for novelty, Blackpool made "progress" its motto and rapidly introduced the latest technological wonders. The Blackpool Tower was built in 1894, a publicity symbol and multipurpose entertainment center designed on the model of the Eiffel Tower. Blackpool introduced electric lighting for its famous Illuminations in the fall and was among the first towns in Britain to have a cinema.[39]

Another development was mass tourism. Educational and pleasure traveling, of course, had been a part of aristocratic life since Elizabethan times. The tutored tour of Italy and France was *de rigueur* for the English gentleman. And, of course, the annual migration between city and countryside was part of the aristocratic cycle of "seasons." Still, poor and crime-ridden roads impeded English tourism except along well-worn paths to Bath or Brighton, and these trips took two or three days each way by coach. By 1815, steamboats were available for rides on the Clyde and Thames river. Only in the 1840s did this ritual broaden with the railway excursion.

As we have seen with Thomas Cook, the popular English excursion began as the paternalism of the "improving" business class. Soon it became a commercial venture offering guided tours to busy middle-class and clerical workers who had neither the time nor knowledge to plan educational trips. From 1844, the British government encouraged railway companies to provide cheap third-class tickets, although only in the 1870s did the rails seriously exploit this mass market. Still, from the 1840s, companies provided excursion rates for weekends and bank holidays. The London Exhibition of 1851 at the Crystal Palace attracted six million, many through excursion trains, and it continued for years to be a center for shows and exhibitions. By 1867, Cook was organizing tours to Paris (for an international exhibition) as well as to the Holy Land; and by the 1880s, Britons of means began to visit Switzerland in the winter (for skiing). Even the British factory worker was taking long weekend holidays aided by savings clubs from the 1870s.[40]

In America also, the railroad revolutionized tourism. The late-19th century resort was also an extension of the railroad. This was true of eastern seaside spots like Atlantic City (a product of a line from Philadelphia in 1852); even the western American National Park was an outgrowth of the railroad. From 1872, tourists entered Yellowstone Park by train and many stayed at the "Old Faithful," a private railroad hotel near the famous geyser. The train created an enforced community of fellow travelers, although railcars, separated by class and purpose, limited unwanted social contact. Linked by ownership to the railroads were large hotels located near train stations. Featuring large formal lobbies (often decorated in pseudo-Renaissance or Oriental themes) and numerous personal services, these hotels were designed for the middle-aged and affluent traveler.[41]

Meanings and Significance of Mass Leisure

Since the early 19th-century, writers have found mass entertainment wanting. Instead of the simplicity of nature, commercial leisure was said to feature shallow showy amusement, mere opportunities to separate customers from their money. Commercial amusements allowed the masses to abandon self-control and the intellect and to surrender to fleeting passion.[42] From Simon Patten to Herbert Marcuse, many critics have claimed that mass leisure only lashes the worker more firmly to the wheel of labor in order to earn the means of further satisfying his craving. Commercial pleasure was the best form of social control.[43] The crowd created by the purveyors of spectator sports, others have argued, only defused social solidarity and created artificial interregional conflicts. The music hall often encouraged crude chauvinism with its jingoistic songs and perpetuated racism with its "nigger minstrels." Professionalization of sport (as we shall see in Chapter 10) led to the downfall of amateur traditions of the early Football Association and baseball. In sum, commercial leisure may be said to have destroyed traditional popular and rational recreation, which became victims of the profit motive and the quest for the lowest common denominator.

There are, however, alternative interpretations of commercialization. For example, we have found that, in many instances, mass leisure was a democratizing of aristocratic play traditions. Merchandisers like Thomas Cook made travel available to the middle-classes in forms fitting their lack of time and experience. Even the imitation exotica of the amusement park afforded the masses a substitute for the adventure of foreign travel. It is not accidental that many impresarios of fun were democrats and were opposed by snobbish elites.[44]

Mass-market leisure was far more than commercial manipulation. Despite the cynicism of pleasure entrepreneurs like P.T. Barnum, the "masses" had their own leisure agenda when they visited seaside resorts and amusement parks. Blackpool attracted not merely an awed crowd passively lured into a variety of purchased thrills and entertainments. The resort was used by Lancashire families for reunions and the meeting of friends and neighbors.[45] Coney Island provided more than the cheap thrills of electric technology. It offered an opportunity for youthful expression, public affection, the Americanization of immigrant children, a carnivalique release from the conformity and restraint of late Victorian society, and just plain fun. Even penny dreadfuls were a manifestation of working-class aspirations, even if expressed often in vicious and escapist contexts.

Commercial leisure was not always a sharp break from traditional popular or rational leisure. Barnum blended aspects of all three forms of leisure in his museums, musical shows, and circus. The simple desire to seek as wide as market as possible assured an appeal to the reform-minded respectable family. It also meant satisfaction of a lingering affection for traditional anarchism of popular leisure. Blackpool retained its donkey rides and gypsy fortune tellers along with its piers, music halls, and orderly pleasure parks. Even the technological wonder of the Illuminations, with their electric tableaux of exotic images, was a modern adaptation of the colored lanterns of the gardens of 18th-century Vauxhall. Remember, too, the traditional content of the early movies, a more lifelike but no less conservative entertainment than appeared in the penny gaffs and dime museums. Often, leisure entrepreneurs simply borrowed common elements from traditional entertainment and rational recreation and packaged them in profitable businesses.[46] These facts may explain the ultimate dominance of commercial play over the best hopes of the leaders of rational recreation. Entrepreneurs responded quickly to consumer wants even when these desires were sometimes torn from their community roots or their uplifting origins.

This complex relationship between commercial, reforming, and traditional leisure can be further explored in a brief analysis of the emergence of organized sport in the industrializing societies of England and America in the nineteenth century.

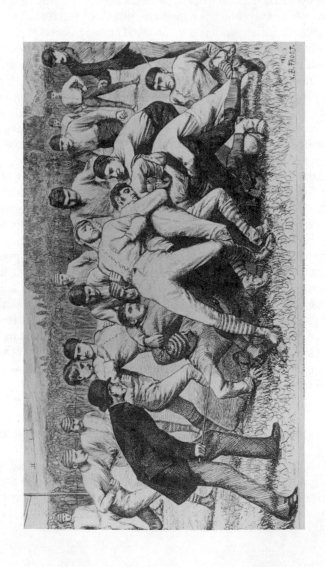

10

Participants and Spectators:
Modernization of Sport as Leisure

The transformation of modern sport in many ways sums up the complexity of industrial-era leisure. In the ways that competitive physical games changed, we see all the elements of the history of leisure: Rural, often chaotic, games rooted in custom and community combined with status-affirming contests of the elite to epitomize traditional forms of play. The regulated activities of the gymnast and school-boy ball game of the 19th century were common forms of rational recreation. Finally, the professionalization of soccer and baseball and the mass appeal of spectator sports in the late 19th century fully expressed the commercialization of much of public leisure in that period.

Preindustrial Sport: A Review

As we saw in Chapter 3, physical contests between men and animals were integral to play in rural society. Local variations of ball, club, and target games predominated in most preindustrial societies. Major modern ball games (like soccer, rugby, American football, cricket, baseball, and rounders) can be traced in a general way from this mixture of traditional ball games. Only in the 19th century would these games deviate sharply from one another, specializing in kicking or throwing and batting.[1] The undifferentiated character of these games was reflected, also, in mass football contests in rural England. Lacking clear boundaries, restrictions on illegal tactics, referees, and even a clear distinction between players and spectators, these rough, sometimes brutal contests were hardly distinguishable from riots. Sporting "champions" were no more than the local butcher or plough boy whose prowess was seldom recognized beyond the parish or county. Traditional sport was also closely associated with gambling. Athletic contests before 1850 were deeply rooted in agrarian society. Foot races, often involving extra feats of physical strength and endurance, such as runners pushing carts or carrying heavy stones, displayed talents germane to an agrarian society. To be sure, there are numerous examples of competitive spectator sports long before industrialization. But the games of ancient Greece and even more of Rome were a part of urban life and escape from its tedium and responsibilities that, until the 19th century, few had known.[2]

Traditional plebian recreations, of course, were thwarted by elites. English Kings, like Edward II in 1365, outlawed ball games, bowling, and hurling because they competed with work and were associated (often justly) with crowd disorder. And, as we have seen (Chapter 4), clerical and reform-minded Puritans attacked sport as a threat to Sunday worship and work. Elites, however, participated in socially exclusive sports such as hunting and the mock war of tournaments. For relatively affluent merchant and tradesmen, there was archery, which kings supported as essential for military preparedness until the 17th century. While King Henry VIII forbade laborers from playing games (except at Christmas and in the presence of the master), he tacitly allowed it for the propertied, and Queen Elizabeth enjoyed bearbaiting while her 17th-century successors were fond of skittles and golf.[3]

Following the defeat of the Puritans and the restoration of the monarchy in 1660, well-to-do Englishmen tolerated and even encouraged popular sports. The Whig oligarchy in London accepted the rough play of the masses (probably more than on the European continent) as a worthwhile price for a weak king and army; the landed gentry (mostly Tories) actually patronized village sport.[4]

For the rich, sport was a way to display privilege and status. Many innovations in aristocratic sport can be traced to the landed elite of England, which emerged from the late 17th century with a great deal of local autonomy and prestige. Not only did they own hunting lands and blooded horses, but they developed a rich culture of sporting clubs. A center of this society was Newmarket, a horse track inaccessible to all but those with carriage and horse, from which the races were usually watched.[5]

A similar search for status may explain the southern American planter's fascination with horse racing at Williamsburg (modeled after Newmarket). Colonists imported hundreds of English thoroughbred horses for racing in the 18th century and imitated the English gentry when they founded Jockey Clubs. Even more illustrative was the "revival" of the chivalric tournament in the 1830s as southern knights, announced by trumpets, jousted with lance and armor in front of admiring ladies.[6] In addition to the extravagant attention the rich lavished on their horses, some also indulged in yachting, an expensive hobby dating from the 17th century and revived in the mid-19th century.[7]

While most of these aristocratic sports were rural in origin, in 17th-century capitals, more "civilized" games like tennis emerged. This sport was developed in France by the urban aristocracy and spread to England in Elizabeth's day. Tennis and cricket (a rural sport taken over by the English gentry in the 18th century) came to be characterized by the genteel notions of "sportsmanship" and courtesy, codes of honor that shaped the modern ideals of amateurism.[8]

The poor and, in the U.S., even slaves participated in aristocratic sporting culture as horse grooms and jockeys. Spontaneous wagers between gentlemen sometimes involved races between their footmen. The rich bet on boxing contests between their laborers in much the same way as they made wagers on horses or cocks. This aristocratic tradition of patronage of boxing champions continued into the modern era.[9]

Of course, sport had long been commercial. Gamblers promoted boxing and wrestling matches for crowds of both rich and poor gamesters. And professional athletes relied not on a share of the "gate" as entertainers did, but as partners with their wealthy sponsors in any prizes that they could win. In fact, the very centrality of gambling encouraged the "rationalization" of sporting contests in boxing and racing. In the 18th century, race courses were standardized and horses were classified by age in an effort to make the gambler's risks more predictable and to reduce fraud. In English boxing, Jack Broughton introduced a primitive set of rules in 1743 to create a more rational setting for gamblers. The mid-1880s saw another major innovation, the Marquess of Queensbury rules, which introduced the three-minute round, a ban on wrestling, a ten-second knockout, and padded gloves.[10]

Despite the fact that gaming introduced regulations into some sports, in 1800, sports were hardly reformed. Among the elite, traditional athletic contests remained exclusive; the wealthy used plebian contestants largely as playing pieces in games that the rich controlled. This attitude would continue during the development of commercial sport in the 19th century and would color the character of the amateur ethic as well. The games of the poor remained chaotic, community affairs, deeply rooted in local custom. These games, however, would be taken up and "purified" by educational and religious reformers in the 19th century to create most modern ballgames.

Nineteenth-Century Transformation

The key to change was in making sport respectable. Activity that the religious middle classes had associated with gambling, drunkenness, and violence gradually gained legitimacy in the 19th century when sport became equated with character building as well as with physical perfection. A new attitude toward the body emerged. It no longer was understood as merely the source of temptation which had to be disciplined by the mind and spirit, as in the notion of the "flesh" in traditional Judeo-Christian thinking. Instead, the body became an extension of moral power concretely expressed in the display of physical courage. By training the body, the new ideology ran, the individual disciplined the will. Morality continued to mean self-restraint, but it also increasingly implied vitality and action in the "real world," values that could be inculcated in sport.[11] Early in the century, Freidrich Ludwig Jahn had popularized "athleticism." This famous Prussian teacher and nationalist founded the Turner or gymnastics movement. By the 1840s, Jahn's exercises on poles, bars, ladders and ropes and competitive gymnastic matches had been introduced to many German schools. But, despite encouragement of American disciples in Boston as early as 1826, few schools built gymnasia until much later. England similarly did not embrace the Turner system. German immigrants brought gymnastics with them when they entered American cities in large numbers after 1848. But the movement was ethnically isolated and suffered decline with the assimilation of the second generation. The Caladonian Games, imported by Scottish immigrants to the American northeastern seaboard in 1853, promoted track and field events. From about 1869, the American YMCA began to build gymnasia as well as libraries.[12]

In the Anglo-American world, however, it was not these individual sports that dominated the transformation of middle-class attitudes toward physical games, but the team games. And these group sports emerged not in the athletic club but in elite schools.

Between 1840 and 1860, the doctrine of "muscular Christianity" in the English Public (private boarding) school laid the foundation for a new attitude toward sports in the upper and middle classes. Sports-conscious headmasters of Harrow, Uppingham, and Loretto (more than the famous Thomas Arnold of Rugby school) promoted the ideology of the "healthy mind in a healthy body." From about 1845, these educators outlawed disorderly unsupervised games and blood sports (like the hunting and and killing of frogs), which were ruining the reputations of the schools. Headmasters replaced these rough games with both a far more disciplined educational environment and enthusiastic support for organized sport. By the 1860s, physical games were the core of the curriculum. For H.H. Almond at Loretto School, education was to inculcate, "First— Character. Second—Physique. Third—Intelligence. Fourth—Manners. Fifth— Information." This anti-intellectualism, which condemned the anemic scholar and glorified the "perpetual school boy," dominated the English Public School. In the late 19th century, school boys at Eton devoted from 5 to 7 hours a day to cricket compared to only 4 to 6 hours to study.[13]

But sports were also to promote morality: "Cricket is a game which reflects the character—a game of correct habits, of patient and well-considered practice." In fact, school-boy sports appeared to have largely replaced drinking and disorder. According to the "muscular Christian" writer, Charles Kingsley, the physically fit were less apt to be tempted by indecent thoughts; only on the playing field could the child learn courage, fair play and teamwork. This type of thinking was as influential in America where headmaster, S.R. Caltrop, could write in 1858: "I cannot tell how much physical weakness, how much moral evil we have batted and bowled, and shinnied away from our door; but I do know that we have batted and bowled away indolence and listlessness, and doing nothing, which I believe is the Devil's greatest engine."[14]

Groton, the college preparatory school founded on the British model by the Anglophile New Englander, Endicott Peabody, in 1884, stressed sports, as did its many imitators among the northeastern American boarding schools.[15]

More important, however, was that the American colleges and universities also embraced the muscular Christian idea and endorsed athletics as part of the extracurriculum. The American patrician Henry Cabot Lodge went so far as to claim in 1896 that college sports actually inculcated the skills of competition and accountability that were at the root of business success. President Theodore Roosevelt found in the "strenuous" life an antidote to the moral degeneration of modern prosperity and materialism. The threat of self-indulgence and even derangement could be averted only by the self-sacrifice of disciplined, competitive sports.[16]

The growing popularity of sport had still other implications. In the 1870s, in a peculiar adaptation of Darwin's theory of evolution, sport became a means of displaying the "fitness" of the individual to prevail. Athletic prowess also was believed to reveal the superiority of the privileged classes, and the right of the imperial nation to "survive" or, more accurately, to dominate the future "evolution" of the world.

Popular songs and romantic adventure stories published in boys' magazines glorified sports and nationalism:

> The playing fields of England
> All up and down the land,
> Where English boys play English games,
> How bright and fair they stand!
> There each one plays for side, not self,
> And strength and skills employs
> On the playing-fields of England,
> The Pride of English Boys.[17]

Loyalty, engendered at public school and college, was to carry into adult life in the company, regiment, or government office. The English Public Schools used games to help forge a new elite around the new industrial and older landed classes.[17] The association of sport with the propertied and educated affected the emergence of the amateur sporting ideal. To be an amateur meant more than not playing for pay and fair play; it required separation from the plebian element. In fact, the amateur philosophy emerged, in part, as a reaction to the flooding of the working classes into the games that the elite had refined.

The emerging cult of health and amateur sport also appeared outside of the school. The urban Amateur Athletic Movement emerged in both countries after 1860 for the sedentary businessman of the city. Athletic Clubs, united in England in 1880 (and America in 1888) into amateur athletic associations, strove to maintain the elite character of gymnastic and field-and-track sports. Some clubs openly excluded the "mechanic, artisan, or labourer," even though others hired workmen athletes in the heat of competition. Athletic clubs provided a setting for indoor exercise but also were used for business and social contacts. The American country club, originating in 1882 near Boston, provided similar opportunities. Designed first for cricket and tennis and later for golf, these clubs were exclusive and imitated similar British sports groups (e.g., Wimbledon's All-England Croquet and Lawn-Tennis Club); they allowed "old boys" from elite colleges to continue to play the games they learned in their youth. The amateur-gentleman, of course, was also at the heart of the ideas of Pierre De Coubertin, who founded the modern Olympic Games in the 1890s.[18]

Amateur athleticism guided also the YMCA. It was at the Springfield Massachusetts "Y" that James Naismith invented basketball in 1891. Basketball was designed to provide exercise and competition without the threat of injury common in other ball games. The key was the raised goal or basket, which obliged the player to throw the ball softly in an arc in order to succeed. Its "civilized" character conformed to the amateur ideal.[19]

Those men of the middle classes who sought refuge from the sedentary and competitive environment of urban business were sometimes attracted to hiking and camping. These sports swept Europe and America from the 1870s. A romantic quest for the simplicity and purity of nature combined with a striving for fresh air, physical vigor, and self-reliance. The mountain, which prior to the 19th century had been the object of superstitious fear of evil creatures, became to thousands of "alpinists" a pinnacle to be conquered and a site of invigorating purity. In America, the camping movement was directed primarily toward children. From the late 1870s, clergymen, seeking a wholesome alternative to the dirty, hot streets for slum children, organized primitive camps. Other leaders were headmasters of private schools seeking for their students a retreat for nature study and moral training during the summer recess. Camping gradually became an integral part of the scouting and church summer programs in the urbanized northeast. In Britain, similar efforts of clergymen to offer parishioners wholesome summer outdoor recreation led to the holiday camp movement of the 20th century. These camps catered to adults and, later, to families.[20]

The athletic cult of the late 19th century, however, was usually militantly male. It reaffirmed the doctrine of the vulnerable female, treating her as constitutionally unsuited for vigorous physical activity, and the male's God-given right to chivalric dominance (as well as to a lifetime indulgence in his boyish games). To be sure, in the 1860s, middle-class women were given croquet and in the 1870s, an unstrenuous form of lawn tennis. So central, however, was sport to late Victorian leisure that women could not be totally excluded from the cult of athleticism. They entered it in a gradual process. First, women were offered exercise, promoted as early as 1832 by the founder of American Home Economics, Catherine Beecher, as an antidote to the physical dangers of sedentary life. Then, individual sport became respectable (for example, in such progressive American women's colleges as Vassar in 1875) but only in sex-segregated games. A similar pattern appeared in the girls' public schools in England.[21]

Despite the elite (male) origins of 19th-century sports, reformers had a "civilizing" mission. In effect, they rationalized the rough, traditional games of the masses and then returned them to the people.[22] In this process too, schools played a major role; unwittingly, they contributed to the emergence of the mass spectator sports of the 20th century. Most generally, this change involved the creation of national rules codified by elite bodies like the (English) Football Association (1863) or the American Bowling Congress (1895). These organizations replaced the muddle of contradictory regulations that customarily governed play in the village or school and made possible contests at the national and even international level. This phenomenon paralleled the nationalization of many other aspects of life in the second half of the 19th century.[23]

Game rules were freed from custom and made subject to the logic of innovation. Like other leisure products, sports became more efficient (especially fast-paced), intelligible, and safe. Rule changes in soccer and American football encouraged individual skill and teamship rather than mass play and the violence that it engendered. Athletes also were encouraged to specialize and train to assure maximization of natural ability in order to meet the increasingly more keen competition. This too paralleled trends in business. Part of this rationalizing process was the emergence of records, which was facilitated especially by the technology of time-keeping when the second hand appeared in the 1860s. The keeping of team and individuals records in cricket and baseball came to resemble modern business accounting. Sport, in effect, underwent a "civilizing process," which parallels a similar decline in personal violence and rise of emotional restraint in many other areas of modern life.[24]

Late 19th-century sport reflected the "improving" values of the middle classes, as well as the stress upon individual competition and nationalism that dominated these social strata. Sport gained support from the reforming middle class because games expressed a new attitude toward the body and promised to discipline the young and blend the upper class with the new industrial classes. Through the amateur ethic, sports gained legitimacy by stressing sport for sport's sake (rather than winning), self-restraint in both victory and defeat, and "fair play" or voluntary acceptance of the rules and chivalrous attitude toward rivals. So powerful were these values that they eventually transformed the games of those lower down the economic and social scale, even if the affluent amateur had misgivings about their "democratization."[25]

The transformation of sport went beyond the conscious values of the reforming middle class. Participation in athletic play was shaped also by complex technological and economic factors. Most basically, modern sport reflected the new urban environment, its restricted space, and even the time constraints of industrial work. The mile-long stretches of land used in medieval football and the hunting forests of the aristocracy largely disappeared with increased population and economic activity. Not only were playing grounds given uniform boundaries, but space-concentrated games like tennis or

Ping-Pong emerged. Time-consuming games like cricket (suitable, perhaps, for the rural cycle of work and festival) declined in favor of far briefer games like football and baseball, which could be integrated into the lives of industrial workers. Invention also bred a number of new physical recreations: among them, the development of the roller skate in 1863, which led a craze among the affluent in the 1870s and 1880s in Australia, Europe, and America. Roller skating rinks offered not only exercise but an arena for courtship and socializing. This was a sport that lacked masculine traditions and thus was open to women. The same was true of the safety bicycle (1887), which replaced various bone-shaking high-wheel cycles. Although expensive (over 100 dollars in the 1890s), the bicycle attracted thousands of middle-class men and women. New business techniques assured the rapid spread of sports fads like tennis and croquet in the 1870s and 1880s to the urban middle class.[26]

The "nationalization of sport" was also a creation of nation-wide networks of railroad and mass communications. Baseball and soccer thrived only after the completion of interregional railroad lines. The prominence of English commerce in world trade explains the globalization of English football in the generation before World War I.

Technology and economic growth contributed also to the rise of the spectator. The city's concentration of people and the advent of rail and streetcar travel made possible the modern sports stadium. Spectators subtly changed from a throng of gamblers to the partisan crowd. Sports wagers hardly disappeared, but rather were increasingly shifted to the football pools and off-site pari-mutuel betting. These activities were too complex and distant from the contest to spark the excitement that fan loyalty engendered. Arguably, it was in the 1880s that the modern spectator emerged. Although only 2,000 watched the English Soccer Cup Finals in 1872, by 1885 the crowd had reached 10,000. It increased to nearly 101,000 by 1901 and to at least 200,000 at the Wembley Cup Final in 1923. Moreover, once the prize or wager declined as a source of financial support for the game, the "gate" became more important. Only in the 1870s did the enclosed stadium with the turnstile (1871) for paying customers become the norm. Admission charges not only made sport a profitable business but it helped to screen access and preserve a sought-after "social tone" of respectability. The crowds not only grew but their character changed as fans identified with the celebrity player and developed passionate loyalties to teams. The fact that early ball clubs were rooted in neighborhoods or colleges made this identification with the team possible.[27]

Another product of industrialization, the mass newspaper, also encouraged "fan" consciousness. Sports journalism created and sustained daily sports mindedness. From 1792, with the English *Sporting Magazine*, sports journalism grew; by the end of the 19th century, there were already 25 sports papers published in London alone. Americans quickly followed in 1819 with the *American Farmer,* which promoted horse racing. Mass-appeal papers like

the *New York Clipper* (1853) and the weekly *Police Gazette* in the 1870s also
featured sports journalism. Still, it was only in the last quarter of the 19th
century that the sports page became an institution.[28]

Finally, the general bureaucratization of modern life perhaps indirectly
encouraged the development of spectator sports. Industrial society placed a
premium on orderly, predictable behavior; yet it also stimulated competitive and
even aggressive impulses. Together, these pressures may have encouraged the
shift (or sublimation) of "excitement" from everyday life to the playing field or
viewing stands, providing relief from accumulated tensions.[29]

So far, we have considered three strands of modern sports: a) their
traditional roots, b) the middle-class sources of their 19th-century reformation,
and c) the impact of technology on sports and the creation of the modern
spectator. These trends, however, did not converge into a uniform product.
Rather, modern sport revealed complex patterns of 19th-century society, patterns
that were products of differing mixtures of reform and tradition and even of contrasting responses to technological change. Sports both democratized and
excluded. Not only the professional athlete (and the spectator) but also the
affluent amateur embodied sports values. Let us try to understand some of these
complexities, first by briefly exploring the origins of several modern British
sports and then by comparing and contrasting these games with those of their
American cousins.

In the 1830s and 1840s, the English Public School modernized the
rough, rural game of football. The rules that shaped the modern game were
taken beyond the gates of such schools when "old boys," or alumni, continued to
play at the university and in urban clubs. Footballers from different Public
Schools found it necessary to codify common regulations; the result was the
Cambridge rules of 1848 and eventually a national code which, in 1863,
became "Association" (or in its shortened form, soccer) football. Not only did
the rules encourage individual ball play (specializing in kicking rather than
handling the ball), but in the 1870s officials began to police play (in 1878
armed with a whistle). In 1891, the penalty kick was introduced to control
illegal and unsportsmanlike behavior. The game of rural youths had become the
sport of gentlemen.

Soon, however, modern football returned to its popular roots. Clergy
with Public-School upbringing and imbued with the philosophy of muscular
Christianity taught football to parish boys on Saturday afternoons. Other
working-class children learned the game in YMCAs, boys' clubs, or schools.
Soccer was easily learned with its simple rules and was widely popular because
of its premium on agility rather than on brute strength or unusual size. Industrialists, businessmen, or churches organized teams as a wholesome recreational
outlet for their young charges. The St. Domingo's Vale New Connection
Methodist Sunday School founded a football club that later became Everton, the
winner of the Cup Final in 1893. Other early famous teams like Aston Villa and

the Wolverhampton Wanderers began in churches; the Blackburn Rovers and Leicester City started in grammar schools. Employees of the Lancashire and Yorkshire Railway and Thames Iron Works formed Newton Heath (later Manchester United) and West Ham United.[30]

The professional player gradually emerged from these local teams. The laborer often required financial support to pay for the time lost from work and for long-distances travel to matches. Competitive pressures encouraged play for pay. Local teams bid for the talents of the country's best footballers, especially those from Scotland.

In the 1880s, the amateur elite protested when clubs seeking an edge hired professionals (often clandestinely). The F.A. Cup Final assured that the inherent conflict between the professional and amateur clubs would come to a head because it pitted the best teams in the nation against one another. In 1883, the working-class Blackburn Olympics triumphed over the Old Etonians in the F.A. Cup Final. This victory ended a decade of Public-School dominance. By 1888, a fully professional league was founded with teams from the industrial North and Midlands. The Football Association, however, remained in amateur-gentlemen's hands, and a separate amateur cup competition was established, thus eliminating direct competition between the gentleman player with his prided amateurism and the working-class professional.

By the 1880s and 1890s, football clubs became limited companies with shareholders and boards of directors. Club sponsors built stadiums that attracted mass fan loyalty. By 1891, games near London attracted about 7,000 on Saturday afternoons; within twenty years the figure was 30,000. The local business elites often owned clubs; their patronage fostered good will from working-class fans. At the same time, football competition encouraged inter-urban rivalry. In the larger cities there were several teams, each providing a sense of community in the otherwise impersonal English city.[31]

Still, the professional player remained a modest hero; he earned wages that were scarcely higher than the skilled artisan. A maximum wage (by 1901) and the "retain and transfer" system eliminated competition between teams for the talents of footballers. And, an incipient trade union movement among players was crushed in 1909. The game perhaps lost its playful character, becoming the display of the specialized skills of working professionals. For the player, the difference between sport and work largely disappeared; his dealings with the club ownership were similar to the relationship between worker and factory owner.[32]

Yet many aspects of traditional sports survived the emergence of the modern spectator and professional. Reformers who condemned the "rabble" participants in village football in the 1830s might have complained fifty years later about similarly unruly crowds on the terraces of the new football stadiums. Football was adapted to working-class leisure styles that had little to do with the ethos of the amateur-gentleman. Soccer players stressed team solidarity and a pragmatic quest for monetary reward for skill. Football crowds displayed noisy partisanship, occasional disrespect for the authority of the referees and club management, and loud festive behavior. Still the "respectable working class" was increasingly drawn into football culture. The turnstile, a policy of segregated seating by ticket prices, security guards, and the practice of fining home clubs that failed to follow rules of order helped to win the support of a family and self-disciplined crowd; even women came out by the end of the century.

If soccer tended to "civilize" traditional football and to overcome social cleavages in English society, rugby had a very different history. About 1841, pupils at Rugby school played a version of football that allowed players to carry the ball and to "hack" (i.e., kick the shins of opponents). Less prestigious schools adopted rugby rather than embraced soccer. These institutions attracted clientele who were less socially secure and perhaps had greater need to prove the "manliness" of their children in a relatively rough sport like rugby. Still, hacking and other expressions of mock war were gradually controlled in a "civilizing" process that paralleled that of soccer.[33]

Like the Football Association, Rugby Football Union emerged from a group of "old boys" clubs in 1871.[34] Rugby, however, was played by a smaller and less influential group and was centered in the south of England. It was not introduced to working classes except in Lancashire and Yorkshire, where socially "open" teams predominated. Professional clubs emerged out of these northern teams in much the same way as they did nationally for soccer. However, southern Rugby clubs were socially exclusive. Perhaps because their members may have been less certain of their social position, they opposed the use of Cup competition to popularize the game. While amateur soccer teams could compromise with the working-class professional club from the industrial north, rugby split in 1895 into an amateur Rugby Union and a professional Rugby League. Rugby remained a relatively insular sport, spreading to the British empire but, unlike soccer, not to most of world.[35]

The social history of cricket reveals still another variation. Cricket was a relatively old game; it was codified in 1787 by the Marylebone Cricket Club and organized around a unique partnership of amateur gentry and lower-status professionals (often hired hands on estates or tradesmen with flexible schedules). For many years, this arrangement produced little social conflict. Gentlemen players were secure in their elite position and professionals knew their place. Lower-status players specialized in bowling (or pitching), a skill long considered a "workaday, at best, guileful craft," while the upper-class amateurs were the batsmen, masters of "the noble, disdainful, at its best, exquisite art."[36]

A century later, incipient professionalization led to County cricket, requiring players to originate from the county teams they played for. Cricket clubs remained organizations of subscribing members and not businesses. Although they, too, relied on admissions charges for expenses, the lack of mass appeal meant that a whole county (larger than the American equivalent) was required to sustain a team). Still, growing social conflict between the professionals and amateurs by the 1890s led to formal segregation between the two groups, not on different teams but in separate dressing rooms, in separate travel arrangements, and even in the fact that the gentleman-amateur's name was posted with his initials before his surname whereas the professional's initials were posted after.

In an interesting contrast, cricket in Australia became a mass spectator sport. Australia led the industrial world in the introduction of the eight-hour day and the Saturday half holiday. Despite its vast frontiers, Australia was largely an urban society. The result was a cricket game that was redesigned to appeal to mass crowds. Australian cricket was more exciting and competitive than the English version and it certainly tolerated fans who were much more boisterous than those who followed English cricket.[37]

Sport and National Divergence:
American Sport in the Light of British Origins

As we have seen, Americans shared much of the British sporting tradition.[38] Immigrants brought traditional British ballgames to the United States and Americans embraced similar complex attitudes toward sports. For Americans, sports could be traditional expression of exclusivity or plebian "anarchy," an agent of moral and social improvement or an entertainment business. Yet Americans profoundly changed British sports—a transformation that reflects important differences between these two societies.

The origins of American baseball is a good place to begin. Much myth surrounds the origins of the "National Game." The legend of its invention in a cowpatch in upstate New York by the civil-war hero, Abner Doubleday, served to associate baseball with rural life and nationalism. In fact, however, the game most likely emerged from English rounders. Its originator probably was a New York City bank clerk, Alexander Cartwright. In 1845, he codified rules (probably derived from a common book on English boys' ball games) for the "Knickerbockers," a club of white-collar employees and tradesmen. By 1858, there was sufficient interest in the game to form the National Association of Base Ball Players, a group whose amateur ethic prohibited play for pay and gambling. By the Civil War, baseball had abandoned the soft ball of rounders (which allowed "soaking" or throwing the ball at the running batter) and adopted the familiar "nine-inning" game.

Why Americans embraced baseball instead of cricket has long interested historians of sport. Cricket was widely played in the northeast, especially among immigrants and Anglophile elites (like members of the Philadelphia Cricket Club). A common view is that Americans preferred the home-grown game, a feeling reinforced by the nationalist upsurge during the Civil War.

Probably more important, baseball (unlike cricket) accommodated both players and crowds by changing rules to shorten, enliven, and balance the game between batter and fielder.[39]

The myth of the democratic roots of baseball did have a ring of truth. Americans, unlike the colonized peoples of India or Australia, had no incentive to adopt cricket, an aristocratic sport of the mother country, in the hope of gaining self-esteem by beating the imperial society at its own game. By contrast, baseball appealed to the native-born and immigrants from places other than England and, unlike cricket, early baseball was completely amateur and lacked the snobbish associations of American cricket. Even the Knickerbockers, who wore respectable brimmed straw hats, were merely white-collar men—not the moneyed elite who embraced cricket in New York City and Philadelphia. By the 1860s, baseball had trickled down to the urban artisan classes. Groups of truckmen, mechanics, and especially voluntary fire departments formed baseball clubs. Rival fire companies (often rooted in ethnic or religious communities) had long indulged in gang-style violence and fighting fires had been a major recreation outlet for young men in pre-Civil-War urban America. Baseball provided an alternative to this violent leisure culture while preserving many aspects of traditional working-class recreations, including group rivalry, gambling, and drinking.[40]

Baseball did not originate in elite schools nor was it disseminated via paternalistic clergy and social workers, as was English football. Rather, its beginnings and growth were more socially fluid. Despite the respectability of the Knickerbockers and the amateurism of the National Association of Base Ball Players, the game had unsavory ties in the generation after the Civil War. Boss William Tweed, the machine politician of Tammany Hall in New York, controlled the "Mutuals," and its successor, the "Giants," were a club owned by a well-known politician with ties to organized crime.[41]

The dynamics of unrestrained competition encouraged professionalization. As early as 1858, New York crowds were willing to pay 50 cents to watch quality baseball games. By 1863, the National Association recognized professional players. In 1869, the Cincinnati Red Stockings, the first completely professional team, proved the disadvantage of the amateur player by defeating all comers in a national tour. The result was the National Association of Professional Base Ball Players (1871), which briefly dominated the commercial game. Players were free to offer their services to the highest bidder and they could take advantage of competition between clubs. Thus, players enjoyed salaries about five times that of the average working man. High player costs and the tendency for the richer clubs to attract the best players weakened the commercial position of "organized baseball." This, plus "hippodroming," the practice of throwing a game for money, diminished public support for baseball in the early 1870s.

In 1876, William Humbert, a Chicago businessman and club owner, and Albert Spalding, once a player and later a famous sports-equipment manufacturer, reorganized the game. They created a cartel, the National League, in an agreement among club owners that prevented clubs from competing in the same urban "markets." These city monopolies were able to build large stadiums, linked to the new streetcar network. This reorganization created a small number of "major" league teams, far fewer than emerged in English football and with roots less deep in working-class communities.

The National League also reduced the players to serf status with the reserve clause of 1879, which obligated a player to work for the club with which he originally signed unless sold, traded, or released. This, of course, gave the employing club a terrific bargaining position in setting the contract; it created financial stability and even profitability for club owners. None of this was very surprising in this age of aggressive big business in America. The baseball "industry," like other anti-labor businesses, spawned a short-lived labor movement. But the Brotherhood of Professional Base Ball Players (1885-1890) failed to get the owners to negotiate with them. In response, in 1890, they founded the Players League. Lacking money and cohesion, this league rapidly disintegrated. The National League and the American League, which was established in 1900, were able to defeat all competition. With the assistance of sentimental probaseball judges, they escaped antimonopoly laws.[42] Major-league baseball became a part of American big business. Minor-league "farm" teams were permanently made secondary (used for apprenticeship and training). This system contrasts with English football, which includes four divisions and the escalator of relegation and promotion for losing and winning teams.

Finally, the National League attempted to make baseball respectable. Spalding outlawed gambling among players and the relatively steep admission price of 50 cents was the rule. Games were played mostly on weekday afternoons, and almost all teams respected Sabbatarian scruples until after 1900 or even 1920. Many clubs offered special "Ladies Days," and other inducements to raise the social tone of the crowd. Night games were played only after 1935, when improved technology and falling attendance (due to the Depression) induced clubs to light the field. Working people lacked both the means and the time to participate equally in early baseball culture.[43]

American crowds were perhaps more passive even in the early days of baseball than were their counterparts on the English football terraces. This, in part, was due to the more socially mixed baseball crowd. It was, perhaps, also due to the greater distance between stadiums which, of course, discouraged conflict between rival fans.[44]

In 1908, an official commission enshrined the myth of Abner Doubleday, giving wholesome rural roots to this urban game. Even then, however, baseball did not shed its disreputable machine and gambling connections. The American League's franchise in New York City (the Yankees) was awarded to a consortium dominated by a gambler and associate of machine politicians. The "Black Socks" scandal around the 1919 World Series could be stilled only by the appointment of James Kenesaw Landis, a well-respected Federal judge, to the post of Commissioner.[45]

Promoters of baseball liked to stress its "democratic" character. Yet, not only did the game tend to exclude the working-class spectator in its early years, but the player's ranks were not open to all. Four years after the emancipation of the slaves, blacks were formally excluded from the National Association of Base Ball Players (1867). Although some teams used blacks until the end of the 1890s, boycott threats from racist fans and clubs drove the last black from white baseball (as well as from other sports) for a half century. The logic of segregation led to the creation of the Negro National League in 1920. While the black clubs were less financially secure than white teams, they produced superior players like Cool Papa Bell, Judy Johnson, and Satchel Paige. Often, however, black owners were obliged to stress the comic antics rather than the skill of the players in order to attract white crowds.[46]

Baseball, like the rest of American society, only gradually accepted recent immigrant groups. Players in the 1880s and 90s were predominantly Anglo-German. Thereafter, owners recruited Irish and Jewish players to attract immigrant crowds. At the turn of the century, Michael "King" Kelly of the Boston Braves drew Irish-American fans. Italian players followed (although the German-American, Babe Ruth, was mislabeled the "Bambino" by adoring Italian-American fans). Black players were admitted to the Major Leagues only in 1947 and then to face racial threats. Social exclusivity was not merely an English phenomenon; in America, it was reflected in ethnic and racial discrimination.[47]

Like baseball, American football has English roots. It sprung, however, not from the American city but from elite colleges and universities. By the 1870s, higher education (rather than the elite boarding school, as in England) was the center of sports innovation. While clergymen and classics professors often dominated the 180 liberal-arts colleges that dotted America at midcentury, students resisted the heavy stress on a fixed curriculum and denial of youthful pleasures. Students not only periodically rioted against what they took to be unreasonable rules, but created their own extracurriculum. These activities included not only debating societies and the social life of fraternities (from the 1880s), but also intramural sports. At first, these contests were between the younger and older "classes," which shared common courses and self-government. "Bloody Monday," in the first week of the fall term in elite eastern colleges, involved spirited "football" or field-hockey matches between first- and second-year classes. These games served as initiation rites and welded loyalty to scholastic class. The first intercollegiate contest took place in 1852 in a crew meet between Harvard and Yale rowers. Similar contests involving baseball and other sports gradually replaced the inter-class rivalries as colleges grew and class loyalties diminished with the diversification of curriculum.[48]

American football emerged out of intercollegiate athletic competition between the prestigious students of Harvard, Yale, and Princeton. Although a soccer-type game had long been played in eastern colleges, a quite different game would dominate the American collegiate Fall term by the 1880s. Harvard students played a variation of rugby (long common in Boston) and refused to join in a league with soccer-playing elite schools to the south. Instead, they met the Canadian McGill University team in 1874, which played English rugby, and quickly adopted this form of football.

Within a decade, this type of football was played at Harvard, Yale, and Princeton. Americans, led by Yale's Walter Camp, soon drastically transformed rugby. Key to the change was the rationalization of the "scrummage" of rugby. The scrummage, which began play, consisted of a tangled mass of players from two opposing teams who struggled to work the ball back to a teammate; in turn, this player could then advance the ball by kicking it, running with it, or passing it back to another player. The American innovation of the scrimmage provided predetermined plays. One team at a time controlled the ball, which was "snapped" back to a player who orchestrated the play forward. In order to assure a more varied game, the advancing team was obliged to move the ball five, and later ten, yards in three attempts or forfeit control. Between 1883 and 1912, the rules were changed still again, reducing the points awarded for kicking the ball (and raising points for running it) over the goal line. These rules encouraged coordinated play and specialized positions that differed from the spontaneity and individualism inherent in rugby. The result, argue the sociologists, Riesman and Denney, was a game whose:

> Choreography would be enjoyed, if not always understood, by non-experts, and its atomistic pattern in time and space would seem natural to audiences accustomed to such patterns in other foci of the national life. The midfield dramatization of line against line, the recurrent starting and stopping of field action around the timed snapping of a ball, the trend to a formalized division of labor between backfield and line, and above all, perhaps, the increasingly precise synchronization of men in motion—these developments...fitted in with other aspects of their industrial folkways.

American football stressed, as did the wider culture, the value of aggressive competition, but within clear rules, in contrast with the perhaps more informal game of English rugby, with its roots in a society where "good form" was more implicit, and had less need of codification.[49]

American football remained, however, injury-prone. The mass tackling that ended plays and the absence of protective equipment guaranteed broken heads and torn knees. Players and alumni boosters may have gloried in the manliness of the game, but by 1905, educators, and even President Theodore

Roosevelt (himself a friend of the "strenuous life"), had called for serious reform or even abolition. The result was a commission called by Walter Camp and still another modification of rules. The most important change was the forward pass, which eventually opened up play by reducing the often brutal concentration of players on the ball carrier. Also important, new rules were designed to make the game more interesting to the spectator.

Football games became the focal points of the recreational calender of the college student. The autumn season often ended with the spectacle of a Thanksgiving Day clash of traditional rivals. At first, students controlled collegiate sport. But with increased competition, as in baseball, the professional coach took over. Hired by the college to enhance its reputation and even financial resources, the coach often sacrificed the amateur ethic for the sake of winning. Some football coaches, like Yale's Walter Camp, attempted to pre-serve the amateur tradition: "It is not courtesy upon a ball field to cheer an error of the opponents. If it is upon your grounds, it is the worst kind of boorishness." More influential, however, were those who stressed competition and winning. In 1891, the fledgling University of Chicago hired Amos Alonzo Stagg to produce a winning football team as a vehicle for advertising the school. With access to a large budget, Stagg recruited and pampered star players. While, in a few colleges, faculty took control of the sports program in order to root out quasi-professionalism, most college sports were dominated by booster alumni. Intercollegiate conferences emerged by the 1890s to regulate competition (e.g., by outlawing players who were not legitimate students). Still, the moralistic cult of athleticism had largely given way to the obsession with winning by the 1890s.[50]

Football fever gradually extended beyond students and alumni. Regional pride (state universities, especially) or ethnic identity (for example, the "Fighting Irish" of Notre Dame University) attracted many to the game. How-ever, at least into the 1920s, football crowds remained primarily middle class. Still, football trickled down into the high schools in the 1920s. More important, the great increase in high-school attendance of the working classes from the 1930s introduced football to the broader rural and urban masses. High school football on Friday nights became a main event for many a small town and city.[51]

Unlike baseball, football remained predominantly an amateur sport. Despite the formation of a professional football league in 1920, only in the 1960s did it emerge to challenge the popularity of baseball. And, when it did, like baseball, professional football was a big business, organized in the major cities, and very different from the English small-town soccer club. Like its collegiate "parent," professional American football was patronized by a more affluent crowd than attended English football. American football was rooted in a different setting, the college, which was less exclusive than the English public school but also more middle class than the working class that patronized the English game.

Twentieth-Century Challenges to Sport

In some ways, sport has been democratized in the 20th century. In the United States, sports slowly were opened to blacks, a change that parallels desegregation in work and politics. After 1810, when the American black slave Tom Molyneux fought the English champion Tom Cribb, blacks were excluded from boxing whites. The hero of the ring in the 1880s, John L. Sullivan, as well as his rivals, "Paddy" Ryan and James Corbett were all Irish. While the brilliant black heavyweight, Jack Johnson, won the boxing championship of 1910, he did not conform to white expectations because of his display of wealth and his marriages to white women, and he was driven out of the game. In the 1930s, white audiences lauded Joe Louis for his "respectful" demeanor and his victories over symbols of fascism (Italian and German challengers). However, he was an exception and played in a sport that had traditionally tolerated the lower-class outsider. Far different was the acceptance of African-Americans in those team sports that had long been dominated by groups who had "arrived" in American society. When Branch Rickey, owner of the Brooklyn Dodgers baseball team, decided to hire the black Jackie Robinson in 1947, he did so over the objection of all other owners.[52]

Another sign of democratization was the improvement of players' rights. Successful attacks on the "reserve clause" and maximum wage agreements, at least in baseball in 1972 and English football in 1961, returned to players economic rights that they had lost in the late 19th century. These changes probably increased the social and economic distance between player and fan insofar as the former increasingly became an entertainment star; but players were partially liberated from their semislave status vis-a-vis the owner.

Opportunities for athletic leisure for women have also increased. Until the 1970s, the ideology of noncompetition and modesty prevailed in the American movement for female physical education. Educators modified basketball for women (requiring play in zones) to encourage participation and reduce unladylike exertion. In the Progressive era, women's physical education was dominated by a reform-minded elite who rejected intercollegiate competition for Play Days—a setting for exercise and play for play's sake.[53] Still, through the Olympics, women like Babe Didrickson and Helen Wills gained attention in individual sports. Only in the 1970s, in the midst of a new of feminism and federal legislation (Title IX of the Education Act of 1972), did American women's sports gain access to funding.[54]

More generally, public access to sports facilities in Britain has expanded greatly, especially since World War II. Quasi-military drills that were introduced by the School Boards in English schools after 1870 were the only form of organized exercise for most urban youths. This activity was only gradually supplemented by playing fields and gymnasia after 1937, when British legislation supported modern physical education and public recreation at the local level. Voluntary associations for cycling, hiking, and camping in Britain grew, especially in the interwar period. The Keep-Fit movement attracted over 120,000 by 1937, but recreational facilities such as swimming pools and multipurpose sports centers which were adapted to the older individual, have grown most since 1960. By the early 1970s, a million Britons belonged to football clubs, over 1.2 million bought fishing licenses each year, and swimming emerged as the most popular participant sport.[55]

In America, schools and voluntary organizations have also greatly expanded sports activity. Important examples of the latter are Little League (1939) and Pop Warner Football (1929). Despite excessive competition sometimes encouraged by parents, these organizations have provided millions of children with organized play. Moreover, during the New Deal government of the 1930s, public works projects provided public access to swimming pools, tennis courts, playing fields, and even low-cost golf courses. As in England, swimming emerged in the 1970s as the most popular leisure sport.[56]

Despite these recent (and often ignored) trends toward mass participation in athletic leisure, sport remains largely a spectator activity. In an age of electronic communications, the character of the spectator has changed significantly. On the one hand, radio and television have greatly broadened audiences: thousands heard the Dempsey-Carpentier fight in 1921 on radio; but the World Cup soccer match of 1982 was seen on television by one third of the world. Television gained large audiences for sports like boxing and snooker, which in England, were well adapted to the small screen. With expert commentary and the instant replay, television has informed the masses on the subtleties of games like American football.[57]

Television, however, also ended the era of collective leisure that had been introduced with the railroad and streetcar. Crowds at British soccer games declined from a peak of 41 million in 1948-1949 to 18.74 million in 1982-1983; and minor-league baseball attendance dropped from 42 million in 1949 to barely 10 million in 1969. Television certainly distorted the pastoral environment and pace of baseball as viewed from the stands. It fostered financial dependency on commercial sponsors and encouraged the superstar system, which makes athletes into entertainers. Even in the relatively less-commercial media in Britain, tobacco and financial companies dominate sports advertising, helping to supplant declining gate revenue and to make up for salary-driven increases in costs. The commercial profit of sports endorsements and sports-related products has exploded in both countries in the 1970s and 1980s. Still, neither the glamorous athlete nor the commercialization of sport is new to the TV age.[58]

The continuing problem of football hooliganism and sports nationalism suggests that spectator sports have hardly displaced collective aggression. A number of investigators suggest that, from the 1950s, a change has occurred in English football crowds. The decline of working-class neighborhoods and withdrawal of the respectable working class from attendance prepared the way for the violence of fans in the stadium, on trains, and in sports bars. The lower English working-class, isolated from the affluence of the relatively satisfied and civilized respectable working class, finds in football a setting for conflicts over turf or territory.[59]

But in America, sport also has become something other than play or entertainment. At the Olympic Games in Los Angeles in 1984, American fans displayed equally boorish behavior in their partisan chanting, "USA, USA!" The mob attacks on football goalposts indicate the same inability of spectator games to diffuse violence; in addition, sporting events have long been the site of racial strife.[60] Sports have not often diffused social problems. Rather, they are a barometer of a society, its values, and its conflicts.

While reformers never succeeded in turning sport into an agent of moralization, sports businessmen have not quite transformed it into a commodity. In the 20th century, sports and other forms of recreation have encouraged debate about the value of mass leisure and the role of public and voluntary action to improve it. This topic will be the subject of our next chapter.

WE DO HOPE EVERYONE WILL USE OUR NEW LEISURE FOR THE RIGHT PURPOSE.

Register 3 July 1933

11

Dilemmas of Leisure and Public Policy:
1900-1940

The first forty years of this century witnessed the most dramatic expansion of leisure in modern history. Both time and resources grew dramatically for recreational activities. According to John Hammond (1933), this was an era of "Common Enjoyment," and soon leisure rather than work would be the core of personal experience.[1] These new opportunities, however, were challenged by the crisis of the Great Depression, and were subverted by both militarism and commercialism. The growth of leisure intensified a fundamental debate in western societies about the utility of leisure and, even more important, the capacity of people to adapt to free time. This literature produced both a profound pessimism about the future of leisure and provided inspiration for advocates of a "democratic" leisure. The debate reveals some of the dilemmas of public leisure policy that continue to the present.

Growth of Leisure Time

In Europe, if not everywhere in America, the eight-hour workday became a norm after World War I, reducing the workweek by six to twelve hours. The paid vacation became a right of most wage earners by the mid-1930s. This trend culminated in the 1930s in movements for 40- or even 30-hour work weeks. These efforts sought to correct the maldistribution of work and leisure in an era of technological change and economic depression. The growth of leisure can be explained by several trends:

a) The mechanization and intensification of work eased employers' fears that shorter worktime necessarily meant reduced profits. Reforming employers found in the 1890s that a workday that began at 6:00 AM, before breakfast, was time wasted. In the assembly line factory of Henry Ford in 1913, more could be produced in eight hours (and with greater labor efficiency) than previously could be done in ten hours. Still, the vast majority of employers resisted any reduction of worktime.

b) The quicker and more tedious pace of work also led to demands from health reformers and unions that fatigue be relieved by reducing worktime. Efficiency science in both America and Europe justified rest and recreation as a physiological necessity. In America in the 1900s, progressivists such as Josephine Goldmark argued that more intense factory and commercial work required shorter hours in order to restore physiological and mental balance. These reformers persuaded state legislatures and courts to embrace ten- or even eight-hour laws, at least for women. British efficiency experts gained a foothold in the Ministry of Labour by 1912 with studies that explained low productivity and absenteeism by the influence of overwork.[2]

c) Perhaps the greatest influence in the reduction of worktime was simply the popular demand for increased personal freedom in leisure. In particular, four years of sacrifice in World War I in Europe created irresistible pressure for an eight-hour work day immediately after peace came in 1918.

From at least the 1910s, organized workers and professional reformers shared a common perspective: technology made reductions in worktime both possible and necessary. Lost work due to hours liberated from labor could inevitably be offset by increased productivity, and shorter hours would stimulate further mechanization. In turn, these improvements would allow a further shift of time to leisure. Reduced worktime would not simply increase the number of jobs; these liberated hours would both lead to the social betterment of laboring families and the expansion of consumer demand.[3] No longer was leisure merely a socially useful privilege to be granted to mothers and children, but a right for all—including adult males. Even New England moralists were beginning to argue that it was not work that defined the human essence but "the free spontaneous activity of play."[4] Reformers believed that the progressive liberation of time from work was a fruit of industrial society that had to be guaranteed by the state.[5]

The popular demand for leisure in the first two decades of the century can be found everywhere. On both sides of the Atlantic, employers complained of increased absenteeism and turnover. Workers apparently were losing their work discipline, preferring a day or two of leisure or even longer vacations instead of increased income. In America, new immigrants from Eastern and Southern Europe sacrificed wages for time with family and attempted to retain the traditional Jewish Sabbath on Saturday despite the official six-day week.[6] Even during the emergency of war, British munitions workers would not abandon their holiday-taking customs; and, despite threats from the authorities, they seldom produced more with overtime because extra-long workdays were followed by absenteeism and tardiness.[7]

The intensification of work, especially during the First World War, surely stimulated a demand for free time. Demand for munitions and labor shortages also improved labor's bargaining position; governments intervened in order to avoid conflict. Quite likely the American government's decision to reduce hours to eight per day in some defense works stimulated European and Latin American interest in the eight-hour standard. During the war years, people throughout the world identified President Wilson not only with a democratic peace but with free time. Also influenced was V. I. Lenin's proclamation of an eight-hour day shortly after his Bolshevik Revolution in November 1917.[8] The "three-eights," the equal division of the day between work, rest, and leisure, had symbolized the aspirations of labor. With unprecedented universality, the eight-hour day became the norm in the aftermath of that war. It spread from the United States and Russia in 1917 to the defeated Central Powers in November 1918 and then on to the British and French Allies in early 1919.[9]

As British Prime Minister David Lloyd George admitted shortly after the Armistice: "It is not a question of whether the men can stand the strain of a longer day, but that the working class is entitled to the same sort of leisure as the middle class." Both British and American workers went on strike and negotiated for the eight-hour day (48-hour week) in 1919. In the U.S., 28 states passed hour legislations in 1919. These movements were part of an international crisis in which labor militancy combined with reformist legislation to produce general reduction of working hours throughout the western world.[10]

Paralleling this quest for daily leisure was a movement for paid holidays. Until 1919, the demand for extended paid leave from work was rare among wage earners. Most working people in America and England enjoyed scattered holidays; fewer were able to take advantage of annual plant shutdowns, which often coincided with traditional festivals like Lancashire Wakes Week. Yet these vacations had little in common with the 20th-century movement for extended summer holidays. They often originated in traditional religious celebrations or communal fairs and sporting events. Seldom did they provide enough time for travel far from work and home environments. Moreover, they were generally uncompensated. For many, an annual shutdown, undertaken in order to refurbish machinery or because of slack sales, was merely a seasonal "lockout." Of course, by the 1910s, civil servants and clerks enjoyed an annual holiday of several weeks. This, however, was a mark of white-collar privilege.[11] After the war, however, about two million British wage earners won paid vacations. More successful were eastern and central Europeans, who gained statutory rights to a vacation. This movement for a legal entitlement to holiday did not catch on in America for reasons that have yet to be explained. In the U.S., the length of vacations was (and remains) part of individual or collective contracts and was generally linked to a period of employment. By contrast, the right of contemporary European employees to five or more weeks of paid holiday is the culmination of the holiday movements of the interwar years.[12]

In Europe, the movement for a shorter work week was hotly contested by management and government after 1920. However, the paid holiday gained widespread political support especially in the 1930s.[13] An annual holiday was often relatively inexpensive for employers. It frequently coincided with seasonal slowdowns in business and it reduced annual worktime by only 40 or 80 hours per worker. By contrast, the demand for a 40-hour week cost about 400 hours. Most importantly, the vacation was understood as a leisure issue, not an economic one like the 40-hour week.[14]

Still, the Depression of the 1930s revived the movement for a shorter working week as a means for more fairly sharing work and leisure. While employers blamed the slump on high labor costs, labor groups and reformers argued that increased productivity in the roaring twenties had not been balanced by either higher wages or a sharing of worktime. The consequence was under-consumption and massive unemployment. The solution for organized labor was to hold wages up and reduce weekly working hours to 40 hours (or even less). The "problem of unemployment, " noted British unions, was "in its essence a problem of undistributed leisure."[15] As the historian Benjamin Hunnicutt notes, the American labor movement had advocated a 40-hour week in 1927 and, at the depth of the Depression, the American Federation of labor supported the introduction of a 30-hour week.[16]

Despite lingering joblessness in Britain, the 40-hour movement met the implacable opposition of business and the conservative government. In Europe, only the French instituted the 40-hour week in the 1930s; and they did so in the midst of massive strikes in 1936. The the threat of economic competition and war forced them to abandon it in 1938. The American New Deal government had abandoned its earlier support for shorter hours by 1936 and, instead, used public works, cheap money, and, by 1940, rearmament, to solve unemployment. A 40-hour rather than 30-hour workweek became the standard in 1938. In this century, any real improvement in a national labor (or leisure) standard has almost always occurred also on the international level. Of course, improvement was impossible in the 1930s when Europe was divided between fascism and de-mocracy.[17]

The shorter workweek posed a number of problems. Employers and policy makers believed that it was an attempt to restrict production, even though advocates argued that productivity should and could increase with shorter hours. The very notion of the distribution of leisure as well as goods increased this sus-picion that short-hour advocates were antiwork. The alternative of government spending to stimulate demand (Keynesianism) had the advantage of not impos-ing on capital the burden of job creation. That policy also promised to preserve the traditional work ethic. As the American sociologists Robert and Helen Lynd observed in their study of "Middletown" in the Depression (1936), "enforced leisure drowned men with its once-coveted abundance, and its taste became sour and brackish. Today, Middletown is emerging from the doldrums of the depression, more than ever in recent years committed to the goodness of work."[18]

However, this did not mean that the movement for leisure had ended by the late 1930s. The 40-hour week was eventually realized in Europe in the 1960s. Moreover, in Europe in the 1930s, if the trend toward additional weekly leisure was temporarily halted, the annual vacation was not. The mid-1930s brought successful legislation entitling wage earners to paid holidays. The British passed a relatively weak holiday law in July 1938, which had the effect of encouraging employers to provide a one-week paid holiday. As a result, the number of wage earners with a paid vacation increased from 1.5 million in 1935 to 7.75 million workers (40 percent of the workforce) by March 1938. In France, in the midst of a national sit-down strike, parliament passed a two-week paid holiday law in June 1936.[19] From the 1930s, the demand in Europe for greater leisure was primarily expressed through a longer vacation.

The Debate Over Leisure

Between 1910 and 1940 many gained increased leisure and had hopes for even more; naturally, it was also a period of serious discussion concerning the utility and future of free time. This debate raised questions about mass leisure and policies toward it that would be appropriate for democratic societies.

Foremost among those who criticized the growth of free time were employers who blamed the leisure gains after 1918 for their economic difficulties and held the line against further erosion of the work ethic. World competition in coal mining led British management to increase the workday from seven to eight hours. This effort was largely responsible for the General Strike and lockout of 1926, which so embittered British labor relations.[20] In America, efforts of Henry Ford to spread his gospel of the five-day/40-hour week in the mid-1920s met with derision from other businessmen. As John Edgerton, president of the National Association of Manufacturers, declared: "it is time for America to awake from its dream that an eternal holiday is a natural fruit of material prosperity ... I am for everything that will make work happier but against everything that will further subordinate its importance ... the emphasis should be put on work—more work and better work, instead of upon leisure."[21]

Underlying these concerns about an eroding work ethic was the fear that reduced worktime would undermine growth. For most businessmen, the objective was not to work less but to create new material needs to stoke the fires of consumption. Of course, Henry Ford suggested that a two-day weekend (based on a 40-hour week) meant increased consumer demand and thus lashed workers ever more firmly to their jobs; however, many businessmen in the 1920s were not convinced that this theory outweighed the more obvious threat that a shorter, 40-hour week posed to production.[22]

Academic economists shared much of this perspective. Many rejected the claim that economic growth inevitably produced a leisure spinoff or that productivity had reached a peak in a "mature economy." Lionel Robbins, for example, argued in 1930 that any linkage between economic growth and leisure time ignored the fact that higher wages made the price of each additional hour of leisure more expensive; more important, the desire for consumer goods increased the tendency of individuals to work longer in order to afford new products. Even more basic was the economist's belief that new technology meant not less demand for worktime but rather new forms of labor. Underlying these arguments was the assumption that no economy could function without a common commitment to work and without meaningful "full-time" work for all. Most economists rejected the utopian vision of a four-hour workday advanced by leisure advocates; instead, they foresaw a consumer economy, stimulated by advertising and the imagination of business, that would require endless quantities of labor.[23]

Others found moral and social reasons to fear mass leisure. The old idea that free time meant dissipation for a working class still unprepared for uplifting leisure survived in the writings of many essayists. The American George Cutten for example, was uncertain that workers were able to benefit from leisure in 1926. While mechanization may have provided an opportunity for creative thinking, he declared, it also was "not conducive to mental strenuosity—and as modern man is finding substitutes for physical labor, he is also looking for substitutes for thought." He concluded that "... if recognized creative work is not supplied in the factory system, and if leisure does not furnish the opportunity for self-expression in creative work, may we not expect an expression of sexual looseness?"[24] The American Richard Edwards shares this fear in his 1910 evaluation of *Popular Amusements:*

> The spontaneity of playful activities, and the originality which creates them are being lulled to sleep by the *habits of being amused* ... Commercial management has been well characterized as tending to sever the individual from the community, to prefer miscellaneous crowds to neighborly groups, to neglect the interest of the child, and to make no provisions aside from moving pictures for the mother of the wage-earning family...In other forms of business, overproduction to the point of "all the market will bear" results in price-cutting, reduction of output, or wider extensions of markets. In the amusement business, overproduction seems to result in a state of glut which drains off in immorality...The lust for profit has picked open the bud. It is no cause for wonder that youth wilts under the process ...[25]

This general perspective was shared by critics of mass production society. For the Englishman Henry Durant, the "machinery of amusement completes the industrial training of turning actors into spectators." The impact of industrialism had been the breakdown of family and community life; this in turn had led to the decline in "spontaneous popular leisure." To the young, "in order to achieve 'a good time,' it is necessary to spend money."[26] In the mid-1920s, many intellectuals held that the mass assembly jobs diminished the capacity of workers to marshall the initiative and imagination required for anything more than passive leisure. The analog to the mechanized factory was the American cinema. Sociologists of work like Georges Friedmann found that mechanization produced more than free time; it shaped the character of leisure. Without meaningful work, leisure became mere escapism; with nerve-wracking labor, the wage-earner sought passive excitement in pleasure. The so-called Frankfurt School, a group of Neo-Marxist German sociologists in the interwar period, developed an even more pessimistic view of what they called the "culture industry." In pursuit of profit, the pleasure industry manufactured a leisure of pseudochoice and illusory freedom.[27]

Leading psychologists and social theorists of the period were perhaps even more pessimistic. Sigmund Freud, for example, was doubtful that civilization could withstand any significant liberation of the play instinct or libido. Instinctual drives had to be repressed or subliminated into constructive activities through work. The pleasure principle, embodied in the play of children, had to be restrained in adult leisure by the reality principle. "Civilized man has exchanged a portion of his happiness for a portion of security." Unbridled pursuit of pleasure will produce chaos. Freud believed it was only through the example and authority of elites (for whom the reality principle was dominant) that the masses (with their relatively unrestrained libidos) could be "induced to perform work and undergo the renunciation on which the existence if civilization depends." The Freudian, S. Ferenczi, identified the problem of "Sunday neurosis," a tendency of the worker to indulge in antisocial behavior on his day off. Mass boredom was at the root of this "death instinct"—an innate avoidance of creative activity and preference for self-destructive behavior. Culture, the Freudians argued, could be preserved only when the nihilistic implications of the "play impulse" were controlled.[28]

The sociologist Max Weber was also pessimistic that leisure (or any other activity) could be freed from the overriding trends of bureaucratization. Creativity, "enchantment," or the restoration of the bonds of community were not possible in a world where economics and politics were increasingly rationalized, Weber claimed.[29]

However, the growth of free time in the early 20th-century produced more optimistic points of view. One largely British school of thought argued that increased leisure would create a more egalitarian culture and even more sympathetic people. John C. Hammond, C.D. Burns, and Bertrand Russell advanced the idea of a progressive democratization of leisure. For Burns, the reduction of worktime had created a "widening of choice of the majority," "a democratic civilization" with a tendency "toward social equality," and a "freer and subtler community between all men." Instead of condemning mass entertainment, Burns argues that "leisure is the time for going beyond what men know of life or can say of it." Travel and experiencing different ways of living could mean greater toleration and openness to change: "The phonograph, moving picture, and radio are bridging the traditional gaps between distinct groups of people." Russell argued that instead of a leisure class, which "produced a few Darwins and many fox hunters, ordinary men and women, having the opportunity of a happy life, will become more kindly and less inclined to view others with suspicion."[30] Ernest Barker argues that, since manual labor "ceases to be an education," it should be limited and replaced by play for personal growth.[31]

The interwar years were replete with books and articles offering advice on the best use of leisure time. These authors were often unsophisticated and even perhaps naive in their faith in the individual's ability to create a personal leisure culture. However, they generally affirmed the need for a public alternative to the prevailing commercial leisure. While the American Henry Overstreet believed that leisure must grow out of satisfying work and new, more humane, environments, he also held that leisure could fulfill needs that work never could. Leisure could provide "the fun of handling materials," the "integrative experiences" of choral singing, the joys of "building the skillful body," the pleasures of "adventuring with thought" and of "being alone," or of wandering by car or foot, of "taking something seriously" as well as "just fooling around." For Overstreet, such a diverse life of leisure would make a "truly civilized" people:

> The older generations have been over-much concerned with the
> tragic business of fighting one another. A new generation, bred to
> the friendliness and good sportsmanship of play, habituated to wider
> horizons of thought and creative imagination, may be more wisely
> equipped to confront the new adventures ahead of us.[32]

Adult educators held a similar viewpoint; they stressed the need for "training for leisure." Education for life rather than merely for work was the only hope for the full development of the individual. In the 1920s and early 1930s, educators were not embarrassed to advocate a liberal-arts education as the best sort of training for leisure. Unlike vocational education, which trained for a job that soon would be obsolete, liberal-arts education prepared the individual for a cultured, self-initiating leisure life—the "real" occupation of the future. Like the Greeks of classical times, the modern person could live the fully free life of leisure. Yet, unlike the Greek elite (described by Aristotle), who depended on the work of the slaves, the modern leisure class would be democratic and freed from work by the machine. Leisure would allow the rediscovery of individualism lost in the new world of mechanical work and boring labor. Play alone could refresh life by restoring the individual's instincts.[33]

Elements of this optimistic analysis were shared even by those fearful that mass commercial entertainment was weakening the "moral fiber" of the nation. The American Richard Edwards advocated "no repression of the instinct of play, but the full and rich development of that instinct through forms of expression which are not dominated by commercialism or tainted by immorality." In response to the threat of "spectatoritis," he offered amateur athletics, while "immoral" dance halls could be regulated and licensed. The Briton Laurence P. Jacks believed that, through the education of the body as well as the mind, people could develop the discipline and initiative necessary to freely develop a creative life of leisure.[34]

Most of this literature reflected the optimism of the 1910s and 1920s, but the Great Depression of the 1930s also stimulated a defense of mass leisure. The general unemployment (or to put it a more revealing way, the unfunded leisure time) of that period sparked a new discussion of free time. In Britain, observations of the jobless did not evoke the images of economic destitution or social degradation common in earlier social investigations. Rather, they revealed the *psychological disability* of workless time. Many studies found that the unemployed were humiliated by unfunded leisure; the jobless felt that free time was a compensation for work and that leisure was meaningless without money and a job.[35]

Adult educators in Britain found that displaced workers grew listless and gradually abandoned pleasures that had been a natural compliment to work life. According to William Boyd, "freedom from toil is a curse." Society needed to make leisure more acceptable and to train workers for adult recreation. F. Zweig noted somewhat later that workers defined themselves not as jobholders but as consumers; thus, their ability to express themselves in "funded time" was critical to their self-esteem. The need for a holiday with pay became obvious.[36] Parallel observations are found in the works of the Americans Mirra Komarovsky and Robert and Helen Lynd.[37]

When "free time" was jobless, spare time took on new meaning. For example, the father's unemployment created the tensions of forced family togetherness. Studies found men who were frustrated by the reversal of parental and spousal roles. Wives and children sometimes became primary breadwinners. These reports stressed that the "unemployed man's wife [has] no holidays" because unemployed husbands failed to do domestic work. While both French and British writers advocated that men assume greater housekeeping roles, an obvious palliative for the wife was the holiday. In fact, British social workers called for volunteers to "adopt" children in order to give wives a chance for a "real change of scenery." It is ironic that the leisure deprivation of married women should be "discovered" in the midst of the Depression.[38]

As important, a more positive attitude toward mass leisure emerged in the 1930s. Notables of the English Left, like G.D.H. Cole, C.R. Attlee, and Harold Laski, organized a National Committee to Provide Holidays for

Unemployed Workers in Distressed Areas; they argued that "industrial refugees ... need to get away from the misery and drabness of their everyday lives."[39] These intellectuals developed a new understanding of the leisure for the majority. Not only was leisure linked to work and its routine, but meaningful leisure also required the security of income and the capacity for self-expression. On closer look, some observers found virtue in what the middle-class outsider might have seen as "degrading" leisure. By the mid-1930s, writers went so far as to defend such traditional "bad boys" of popular leisure as the football pools and the cinema as harmless excitement. Cinema, said Denys Hardy, was a means to "extend and define our sympathies and so control our subtler emotional life..." The American Paul Cressey argued that the taxi dance hall (dime-a-dance) fulfilled a need for a social life for young people, especially the socially handicapped. Adult educators embraced less pedantic models of cultural training through tourism, hobbyism, and other forms of leisure.[40]

Organizing Leisure: Prospects and Problems

These positive approaches to mass leisure have obvious linkages to the traditions of rational recreation of the mid-19th century. The objective of the 20th-century reformers was not to restrict leisure time but to organize it and to channel it into individually uplifting, self-disciplined, and even familial expressions.

The recreation movement in America was perhaps the best example of this approach. Its early leaders—Joseph Lee, Henry Curtis, Clark Hetherington, and Luther Gulick—had founded the Playground Association in 1907 (Chapter 8). They argued for recreation to educate and socialize children. Frustrated by the growth of commercial entertainment, the Playground Association broadened its perspective to include adults. It attacked commercial amusements for encouraging spectator passivity, which denied creativity and the intimate culture of the neighborhood and exploited sex and violence.[41] The American recreation movement was not "prohibitionist," but rather sought to regulate commercial leisure and to use new forms of communication, like film, for educational purposes. Leaders of the National Recreation Association, (successors to the Playground Association) took the short-hours movement seriously and saw it as an opportunity for a development of an alternative leisure culture that would challenge the "gospel of consumption." Their many and varied efforts at supplying playgrounds and recreation programs in American cities should be seen in this light.[42]

Similar views were held by progressive educators and librarians who advocated "education for the worthy use of leisure" and valued liberal arts and library training. On the same track were adult and workers' education leaders who offered courses in fine and liberal arts as well as amateur science, crafts, and home improvement for adult workers in the years between the wars.

These groups recognized that they faced a powerful opponent in commercial entertainment. They generally decried the "unfair" influence of advertising and mass amusements on the individual's free time. Note Jesse Steiner's assessment (1933):

> Business, with its advertising and high pressure salesmanship, can exert powerful stimuli on the responding human organism. How can the appeals made by churches, libraries, concerts, museums and adult education for a goodly share in our growing leisure be made to compete effectively with the appeals of commercialized recreation...[T]he problem of effecting some kind of equality in opportunity and appeal as between the various types of leisure time occupations, both commercial and non-commercial, as between those most vigorously promoted and those without special backing, needs further consideration."[43]

Of course, there was a substantial growth in noncommercial recreation activities in America during the 1920s: the Boy Scouts grew from 250,000 to 800,000 and youth summer camps expanded from their early roots in the Northeast across America in the 1920s. Government policy shifted from mere conservation toward promoting recreational use of federal and state parks. President Coolidge even advocated that cities set aside 10 percent of public land for parks and community centers. Far more impressive were New Deal public works projects, which built a wide array of playgrounds, parks, tennis courts, swimming pools, and public golf courses.[44]

There was similar movement for public recreation in Britain. Department of Education grants to municipalities for adult education expanded dramatically in the 1920s, and largely private efforts at extending playgrounds in cities were impressive. More important, the 1930s culminated a generation of growing interest in affordable holidays and camping. Although the Holiday Fellowship dated from 1913, its greatest growth was in the 1930s. The Youth Hostel Association appeared only in 1929 and the Ramblers Association began in 1932. The British Camping Club grew from 3,000 to 7,000 members between 1927 and 1935. Although these groups were mostly composed of clerical and skilled workers, some attracted manual laborers with their promise of relief from the bleakness of the industrial horizon.[45] Although the influence of the Worker's Travel Association (founded in 1921) was always limited, it and other cooperative agencies promoted the right of workers to a vacation away from home. And, the nonprofit holiday camp long predated the commercial success of Butlin's camps after 1937.[46] Nevertheless, the business-oriented twenties and depression-hamstrung 1930s limited the potential of public leisure.

Totalitarian and Democratic Leisure in the 1930s

Nonprofit recreation was provided not only by adult educators and recreation professionals but, especially in Europe, by ideologies of the right and left. The organized vacation, for example, appealed to political organizers of all stripes. Holiday-with-pay legislation reflected a consensus that modern work required compensatory leisure; industrial life made necessary extended periods of time free from work to "recover" lost values of family and community. In the 1930s, Fascists and Nazis shared with the leftist French Popular Front a common view of organized holidays: patriotism would emerge from touring historical sites and meeting fellow countrymen in different regions and walks of life; popular sports and the return to nature would renew national energies; vacations would give dignity and joy to the worker.

Leisure policy was an animating factor in the struggle for political influence. Most factions recognized that the playground and concert hall were terrains on which the contest for popular opinion could be won or lost. Especially after World War I, when the eight-hour working day became nearly universal, elites of both the left and right realized the political significance of organizing leisure time. The question was who would direct the free time of the masses.

The totalitarian right attempted to create loyalty and consensus to the regime outside of authoritarian structures of the work world. Their goal was to create support for Fascist ideas in organized tours, music festivals, and camping trips. Quite similar nationalistic sports organizations flourished, especially in Germany. In competition with the Fascist right in the 1920s and 1930s were communists and socialists. The left attempted to create alternatives to commercial spectator sports and to the sports press and clubs patronized by employers or the Catholic church. Communists organized sports and cultural groups to "train for struggle." They hoped to create loyalty to trade union and party beyond the workplace and to integrate the workers' family into the movement.[47]

As historian Steven Jones has shown, organized workers' leisure in Britain was built upon earlier efforts of cooperative societies, the trade unions, the Socialist Sunday Schools, and the Clarion cycling movement. During the interwar years, "brass bands, teas, rambles, excursions... and most popular of all, the annual rally..." reinforced loyalty to the Labour party. The Fabian socialist, Beatrice Webb, even organized a Half Circle Club for wives of Labour men and women organizers to help them resist the temptations of "London Society." These groups used the British Workers' Sports Federation to try to win wage earners from commercial spectator sports.[48]

A quite different approach, which had a good deal in common with the National Recreation Association of the United States, was "democratic leisure." It was inspired by the International Labour Office (ILO) in Geneva, and its first Director was Albert Thomas. He insisted that leisure could be no longer structured by either government, business, or even trade unions. Advocates of democratic leisure believed that, not only were workers too individualist to submit to this patronage and its hidden agendas, but only multiclass, community-based leisure organizations could avoid the fragmentation and conflicts of ideological leisure. Thomas was appalled by the attempt of the right to construct blind loyalty through the subversion of "joy;" yet he also opposed leaving leisure to the marketplace and hoped to raise the cultural standard. The idea was an organized freedom, through local, self-initiated agencies composed of organizations representing church, politics, labor, and management. Government was to facilitate, not direct, activities. The ILO repeatedly encouraged mixed-group and international leisure organizations. It stressed alcohol regulation, home economics instruction, improved transportation to reduce commuting time, housing programs, and even more compact workdays as ways of creating more "efficient" and healthy leisure time.[49]

In the late 1930s, especially after the Nazi display of propaganda at the 1936 Berlin Olympic Games, advocates of democratic leisure distinguished themselves from totalitarian leisure. Unlike the Fascist ideal of organized play, which attempted to instill loyalty to the state, these democrats stress volunteerism, local initiative, and individualism. In 1938, the International Commission of Workers' Spare Time met to advance these ideas. The solution to a leisure of "unadorned idleness without recreation" was to train the masses to use their leisure wisely and to provide a wide variety of recreational choices. Delegates were frustrated that the democracies had failed to provide those resources that their Fascist and Soviet counterparts enjoyed; but they were adamant that leisure, like freedom, was to proceed from the individual, not the collectivity.[50]

This perspective prevailed, for example, in the British (and American) adult education movement. Educators found leisure to be the most appropriate outlet for individual expression. Hobbies, E.B. Casle argued, were the best antidote to the "deadening compulsion always to be in a crowd."[51] The same basic idea was expressed by the National Recreation Association in America with its commitment to nonpartisan municipal and state-based recreational programs that stressed diversity and accessibility.[52]

Despite organizational innovation, the movement for democratic leisure remained paternalistic. For example, Albert Thomas admitted that he had no problem saying "what is good leisure." He advocated a "well-directed use of spare time, both physical and moral education" as well as the cultivation of general knowledge. L.P. Jacks and other advocates of adult education in Britain shared this perspective.[53]

The French Popular Front government of 1936-1937 and its minister for sports and leisure, Léo Lagrange, emulated the broad-based model of Albert Thomas. In a number of small ways, Lagrange facilitated voluntarism: he cajoled railway companies into accepting a program of inexpensive tickets for family holiday excursions, he built 653 sports arenas in two years, and introduced physical education in almost half the French schools in hope of encouraging life-long interest in physical culture. Still, the Popular Front opposed "directed leisure." Rather, as Lagrange put it, "we must make available to the masses all kinds of leisure which they may choose for themselves." He advocated autonomous municipal Leisure Clubs, independent of political patronage, which were to express the new "social maturity" of the people.[54]

At the same time, this policy was hardly undirected or market generated. Lagrange reflected the tradition of rational recreation with his stress upon an "equilibrium" between "the health of the body and the health of the spirit ..." Like so many before him, Lagrange emphasized that "specialized work" required the corrective of physical culture and sport. And, like his Nazi counterparts, he stressed the critical role of physical fitness for national renewal.[55]

In Britain, these ideas of democratic leisure were not so well developed; still, there were parallels with the French experience. The Workers' Travel Association provided an array of inexpensive excursions and holidays through nonprofit travel bureaus, summer camps, and holiday savings clubs. A few Labour-controlled towns like Lambeth organized their own summer camps. Trade unionists advocated cruises and even that the government make troop ships available for international cultural exchanges.[56] Proposals for a British Ministry of Sports and Leisure failed in 1937, but laws encouraging the protection of lands for parks and camps passed in 1939. The new Labour government after the Second World War developed an avid interest in leisure policy.[57]

These innovations in public leisure policy met with many, perhaps insuperable, difficulties in the 1930s. First, as we have already noted, the movement for the reduction of worktime was largely defeated. The theory of democratic leisure also met with serious constraints. The key problem was how to organize leisure and yet to guarantee its freedom; how to uplift and yet not to be undemocratic; how to create joy without alienating people by being patronizing. Moreover, the recreation movement seldom was able to compete with commercial leisure. British travel and holiday camp cooperatives lacked the capital, and perhaps managerial skill, to prevail over the commercialized fun of Billy Butlins holiday camps. How many workers would choose the international exchange of workers over the Golden Mile of Blackpool?

The advocates of a democratic leisure recognized these problems even if they lacked the organization, resources, or perhaps imagination to surmount them. Ultimately, the contest was not between totalitarian and democratic leisure but between "organized" and market leisure. And, for many reasons, the latter has all to often won the game.

12

Consumer Leisure and the 20th-Century Suburb

The inexorable power of technology and the market, which had so forcefully recast leisure in the 19th century, played an even greater role in the mass commercial recreation of the 20th. The descendants of the rational recreationists may have been disappointed with how the masses used their free time, but the inheritors of the Victorian music hall took advantage of the growth in discretionary income and reduction of working hours to create profitable leisure industries. Still, the 19th-century cults of family and individual improvement were hardly abandoned; rather, they were adapted to new settings. Indeed, with new technology and mass marketing, they were democratized in the working-class suburb and, in America, in near universal "automobility." Popular leisure culture was also incorporated in the new technologies of film, radio, and television, even though these media furthered the long-term trend away from community and toward privatized uses of free time. Most of these patterns were born or developed in the United States, and American dominance of commercial pleasure became overwhelming by the 1920s. For these reasons, I will focus on the American experience, without, of course, ignoring the British story.

Despite the significant interruptions of war and depression, not only time but also economic resources shifted toward leisure in the first half of this century. Between 1909 and 1929 recreational spending in America rose from 3.2 to 4.7 percent of income—a share that has hardly changed since. American consumption of pleasure was furthered by the installment plan, which financed the purchase of over 60 percent of the cars, radios, and furniture by 1930.[1] Almost across the board, the cost of leisure declined in the 20th century with the shift from the entertainment of the relatively expensive music hall to the cinema and radio. Massive construction of semidetached houses in England and single-family dwellings in the United States broadened access to the Victorian ideal of domesticity.[2]

The 1920s were justly famous for the celebration of pleasure and the erosion of the work ethic. Play had become more permissible as an end in itself. There was a perceptible decline of formality in entertaining and housing.

Women's dress reflected this change when skirts rose over the ankles during World War I, reaching the knee by 1927. The conspicuous consumption that Thorsten Veblen had lambasted in the 1890s in America, and which the rich of Edwardian England celebrated, had become unfashionable in the 1920s. The mistress for the rich male declined but so did the working-class prostitute. The economic status of young women had improved but alternative uses of recreation time also had appeared. Freer attitudes toward romantic or at least noncommercial sex emerged in the 1920s, encouraged in Britain by wartime education in the use of condoms to reduce the risk of venereal disease. In both countries, more recreational attitudes toward sex were revealed in the birth-control campaigns of Margaret Sanger and Marie Stopes to free women from the dread of unwanted pregnancy. Decline of family size between 1900 to 1930 in Britain (from 3.4 children per family to 2.1) and in American (from about 4 to 2.9) freed parents from years of childrearing and opened up new possibilities for leisure. The eight-hour day increased the leisure of working people and daylight saving time (introduced during World War I) made it more pleasurable.[3]

It seems that the industrial democracies were creating classless societies of leisure consumers. As C. Delise Burns claimed in 1932, "You cannot tell a butcher from a bank clerk, at least in his leisure habit."[4] Despite the admonitions of the intelligentsia that quality leisure required education, it was, for most, measured by the bankbook. Still, significant pockets of poverty among the working class of Northern England and among minorities and ethnic groups in the US barred many from the consumer society even during the booms of the 1920s, 1950s, and 1960s. Many more were excluded during the Great Depression and World War II. But merchandisers offered the less affluent their own "Woolworth's culture" of leisure goods, sold at a discount. This leisure may have well been a compensation for the decline of purposiveness in work. Many, too, began to believe that work was but a means of earning the ticket to private pleasure. Work surely had lost its central ethical significance.[5]

Technology and Mass Commercial Leisure

The entertainment of film, radio, and television created both a uniform and privatized 20th-century leisure. The individualized mobility of the car transformed the space of pleasure. New entertainment technology offered an enticing alternative to the social pleasures of the bar, theatre, home, and neighborhood.[6] Quasi-monopolies dominated these industries and created national and even international markets for their products. The result was mass leisure, and with it, a decline of recreation built around church and pub. These technologies produced an entertainment that was enjoyed in silence at the cinema, at home, or in private cars, creating mass conformity but often without social contact.

Clearly, the most popular form of entertainment in the 1920s and 1930s was the film. By 1939 in Britain, (population about 41 million) about 23 million tickets were sold weekly. In the United States as early as 1930, 100 million attended weekly (from a population of 123 million), double the number just five years before, when films were still voiceless. The British Alhambras and Granadas like the American Orpheums and Magistics were more than film exhibition halls, but "Dream Palaces" with Moorish landscapes and mock Buddhas. The working class, "while there...can with reason consider themselves as good as anyone." But the movies were also a popular pastime for all classes and both sexes.[7]

At the same time, the cinema was increasingly concentrated in the hands of a few companies. In its infancy in the 1890s, free-wheeling entrepreneurs dominated the film industry; American companies fought bitterly over patent rights to film technology. By 1908, however, the Motion Picture Patents Company, in an effort to create a monopoly, attempted to control all phases of the industry. Independent producers and exhibitors challenged the patent company; some transferred production from the New York area to Hollywood, not only for the sunshine but also for easy escape to Mexico to avoid legal action on patent infringement. These independent film makers soon prevailed in the market with innovations like the "star system" and feature film (Chapter 9). Out of this group emerged the Big Five (Fox, MGM, Paramount, and, with the advent of the "talkies" in 1926, RKO and Warner Brothers). They dominated not only production but also exhibition of American films. With control over the huge American market, and thus lower fixed production and distribution costs, the Big Five easily prevailed over English and European film makers. Despite legislation to encourage British film makers, English audiences often preferred American movies in the 1930s.

The cinema was certainly a business but it was hardly immune from the sensibilities of moral authorities. Moralists in both countries, concerned about the sexual themes often displayed on the screen, threatened to impose legal restrictions and censorship on the movie industry. In 1909, American filmmakers forestalled government intervention by policing themselves through their own Board of Censorship. Later called the National Board of Review, this body sought to conform to middle-class sensibilities. In 1933, the board created a code that not only prohibited graphic violence and sexual innuendo (as, for example, in the comedies of Jean Harlow and Mae West) but outlawed racial or radical political themes. Conservatives in Britain continued to associate the film with lurid sex and violence, thus prohibiting the viewing of the pictures on Sundays until 1933.[8] As important, Hollywood discovered the profit in the sentimental films of Shirley Temple and Disney cartoons. And, by the mid-1930s, English cinema houses offered children's matinees with wholesome and educational fare.[9]

Historians have stressed the complex impact of the movies upon leisure and cultural values. Films contributed to changing attitudes toward and styles of women. About 1915, the child-like innocence and Victorian moralism of Mary Pickford's "Polyanna" began to give way to films featuring the aggressive sexuality of the "Vamp" of Theda Bara. Even more, the movies set (usually unattainable) standards of fashion and love. Movie magazines like *Motion Picture World* (1911) and *Photoplay* (1912) contributed to this education. English women wore their "'Garbo' coats and waved their hair ala Norma Shearer or Lilian Harvey." In 1935, the American study, *Our Movie Made Children*, complained that stars served as models of faddish experimentation.[10] Despite the strictures of the motion picture code, films sanctioned sex by placing eroticism in an environment of affluence and health rather than poverty and disease; they treated sensuality in marriage as rejuvenating. Cultural historian Jeffrey Richards finds that British film exposed class differences but diffused tensions through the use of humor and stories that ended with the reconciliation of characters representing clashing social groups.[11]

Even more than film, radio was a product of centralized technological development. Shortly after World War I, a few powerful companies like British Marconi, and the American giants of Westinghouse, General Electric, and ATT made wireless military communication into an entertainment industry. Aided by the telephone-line linkages between transmitters, network broadcasting from concert hall and stadia became possible by the mid-1920s. A group of the British radio developers initiated the British Broadcasting Corporation (BBC) in 1922, which soon became a semiautonomous public broadcaster whose monopoly was funded by radio licenses sold through the post office. By contrast, a consortium of American manufacturers formed the Radio Corporation of America (RCA) and subsequently, the National Broadcasting Company (NBC) in 1926. Within a year NBC, with its Blue and Red networks, was competing with the Columbia Broadcasting System, created by independent radio stations.

In both countries, the radio rapidly became an element of mass leisure. In America, there was only one station in 1920, but 600 broadcast programs by 1930; 40 percent of American homes contained a radio despite the price of roughly one hundred dollars. By 1932, Americans devoted about four hours per week to radio listening. In Britain, by 1930, 35 percent of households possessed a radio license and by 1939, 71 percent were licensed.

The BBC helped to create a national taste, even if those purists, who hoped that "BBC English" would be adopted by the masses, were disappointed. BBC radio, led in its formative years by the self-assured John Reith, sought to uplift popular culture with a smattering of educational programs and music. The "Children's Hour," for example, was a mixture of wholesome humor, light classical music, and "a judicious sprinkling of information attractively conveyed." The early BBC respected Sabbatarian sensibilities by restricting Sunday broadcasts to church programs and classical music. In his *Broadcast over Britain*, Reith claimed "that to have exploited so great a scientific invention for the purpose and pursuit of 'entertainment' alone would have been a prostitution of its powers and an insult to the character and intelligence of the people."[12] Nevertheless, the BBC compromised with popular taste. It offered much dance music and music hall favorites.[13] While public opinion on programming was occasionally polled in the 1930s, Reith made decisions mostly on the recommendation of the National Advisory Committee on Education, composed of high-minded individuals like himself. The impact of BBC radio was difficult to determine. It is unclear whether radio hurt the music hall and the amateur performer; but its music programs probably stimulated record sales. Still, it is doubtful whether BBC radio displaced those hobbies that could be enjoyed while listening to the wireless.[14]

By contrast, the American radio network became unabashedly commercial, even though radio officials, and even advertisers, resisted for some years the crude hucksterism that appeared by the mid-1930s. The competitive network system, however, encouraged programmers (often the advertising agencies themselves) to aim entertainment at delivering the largest share of the mass market to sponsors instead of focusing on specialized interests or tastes. Programming developed "a public following comparable to, and in some cases greater than, successful comic strips syndicated in the daily press" noted a government study in 1933. The comparison was apt. Radio produced the peculiar American art of the soap opera (aired in 15-minute segments each weekday afternoon), the situation comedy (beginning with the racial humor of "Amos 'n' Andy," which was played by two white men), the western, the mystery, and the child's adventure program. But NBC also featured classical music concerts. Vaudeville and dance-hall orchestras also gained national audiences through radio. But radio may well have limited the job opportunities of local musicians. By the 1930s, home singing had nearly disappeared and conversation was disrupted by the call of the Lux Hour or the latest episode of Flash Gordon.[15]

Nevertheless, the radio was a perfect accommodation to household activities. It restored the ancient mix of work and pleasure and provided the immobile and lonely with companionship. Although American broadcasting was built on the intermittent listener—15 minute shows—and perhaps led to a reduced attention span, it reached all family members. Radio was an odd combination of popular, commercial, and even improving entertainments.

Television was an extension of radio. It was developed largely by the same companies (NBC and RCA in the United States and the BBC in Britain). The BBC began the first effective television service in 1936. NBC followed soon after at the New York World's Fair. The Depression, and especially World War II, delayed mass purchase of the "box" until after 1945. But TV came soon to dominate popular culture. In 1950, only 9 percent of American homes had it;

four years later, the figure was 55 percent (a percentage that took 37 years for radio to achieve). By 1960, 90 percent of American homes consumed an average of five hours of television per day.

In Britain, the BBC continued its tradition of non commercial broadcasting; and, despite the advent of the commercial ITV in 1955, the role of TV as an advertising medium was limited. In the United States, commercialized TV delivered the mass market to national advertisers. Television was nearly a perfect expression of suburban leisure. It celebrated domesticity in "Sit-Coms" and warned of urban dangers in "Action-Adventure shows" while enticing viewers through commercials to the "miracle miles" of fast foods and shopping malls. By the mid-1950s, American critics argued that television was a good example of "Gresham's Law" in culture: "bad stuff drives out the good, since it is more easily understood and enjoyed." The intelligent and witty Sherlock Holmes gave way to the gun-happy Mike Hammer.[16]

Still others found American television to be an electronic throwback to the 19th-century tradition of popular commercial entertainment: TV revived the "old tabloid yellow press...and carnival sideshows at county fairgrounds, an America of freakishness and sensations treated with solemn import, an America of prurience and violence, nicely coated with sanctimony."[17] Its situation comedies and especially "soap operas," provided a familiar "family" of personalities in a "society that has been in constant transformation through geographic mobility and loss of extended families." The soaps offered a "stand-in for the moral community," where real personal problems (although in mostly middle-class settings) are confronted, affection and advice shared, and family values ultimately affirmed. By 1969, American toy manufacturers used Saturday-morning and after-school cartoon hours for "feature-length advertisements" of licensed characters (like Strawberry Shortcake) sold as toys. While reform groups, concerned about manipulation of children through TV, won some government regulation in the 1970s, these practices returned in the 1980s.[18] Still, despite the frustration of reformers, American television probably tended more to homogenize leisure than to debase it.[19]

Automobility

Probably no consumer product has shaped 20th-century leisure more than the mass-produced automobile. In Britain, a fine railway network and suspicion of self-propelled vehicles on public roads meant a slow embrace of the auto. The early British automobile industry was dominated by luxury cars like the Rolls-Royce and heavy military vehicles rather than mass-produced, light-weight cars. Even though the cost of the small family car in England was halved in the 1920s, a small minority owned automobiles (1 car for 20 people as late as 1939). Only in the 1950s and 1960s would this ratio change.[20] In the interwar years, the auto brought picnicking, camping, and touring to the smart set. But the working-class couple still enjoyed the "mystery tour" on the open-air bus, the "charabanc," which offered a meandering afternoon of pub crawling to be capped by a visit to a "surprise" site. Like the private car, the bus and interurban coach in Britain freed working people from the confines of their immediate neighborhoods and from the fixed routes of the rail.[21]

The manufacture of autos in America also began as a handcrafted luxury. The car in 1900 not only cost several times the working person's annual income, but required as much in yearly maintenance.[22] The innovation of the mass-produced Model-T Ford (1914) offered, according to its creator:

> A motor car for the great multitude. It will be large enough for the family, but small enough for the individual to run and care for....It will be so low in price that no man making a good salary will be unable to own one—and enjoy with his family the blessings of hours of pleasure in God's great open spaces.

By 1927, the United States built 85 percent of the world's cars, and by 1929 there was one car for every five people (about one for every three in California). Ford's innovation included not only a cheap car (costing scarcely $290 in the early 1920s), but the promise of working-class participation in the car culture. Ford's assembly line, introduced in 1914, may have ushered in the era of intense, repetitious, unskilled factory work, but Ford compensated these workers with additional leisure and income (in the unheard-of eight-hour/ five-dollar day). Even factory workers could share in the good life of automobility.[23]

The car revolutionized leisure by liberating the pleasure-seeker from the timetables and routes of the streetcar and train. Time and space was freed for a degree of individuality. By the 1930s, if the auto had often become a necessity for work, the car also was a ticket to pleasure. The parkways (first built in New York in 1911) were designed to be aesthetically pleasing as well as useful. And the Interstate Highway System (begun in 1956) made the vast expanses of America accessible to millions of vacationers who could bypass small towns and metropolitan congestion. Still, improvements reduced both the adventure and esthetic pleasure of driving, increased speed (an average of 125 miles per day's journey in 1916 increased to 400 miles by 1936), limited-access roads, and even uniform traffic signs limited the visual experience of driving. The unplanned commercial strip emerged in the 1920s, and with it the billboard, to clutter well-traveled roads. Solitary travel became a semisomnambulant experience, as the radio stimulated memories and dreams.[24]

The car obviously revolutionized tourism. As noted in Chapter 9, rail travel had tied tourists to schedules and fixed destinations. However, with improvements in roads by the 1920s, the freedom of auto touring attracted thousands of easterners to picturesque New England towns in the summers and to the Florida seashore in winter. Older midwesterners found rest and respite from snow in rented cottages in St. Petersburg, while businessmen sought excitement in night clubs of Miami Beach. The increased mobility of Americans stimulated a variety of tourist experiences from the manufactured historic sites of Williamsburg, Virginia, and Henry Ford's Museum in Dearborn, Michigan, to urban cityscapes, promoted by local Chambers of Commerce. The result may have been, as Daniel Boorstin writes, the "pseudo-event" of tourism. Passive visitors expected an assault on their senses in the prepackaged art of museums or "quaint" if, unhistoric European villages, "restored" to the specifications of the popular imagination. At the same time, the car liberated the average person from an even more unreal "tour" in the mock-orient of the traveling carnival sideshow.[25]

As early as 1908, managers of national parks in the United States began to encourage automobile tourism with improved roads and guidebooks. By 1934, national parks in the West had attracted 34 million visitors (a four-fold increase in the 1920s, alone) who came mostly by car. Auto vacations created a demand for roadside camping. Small-town businessmen hoped to lure tourists to central business districts by providing cheap or free municipal camp grounds nearby. Close quarters guaranteed a cautious familiarity with neighboring auto campers: "You could tell a stranger virtually anything about yourself, except your name." By the end of the 1920s the influx of jobless "hobos" in used cars put an end to this form of small-town friendliness. Soon, "cabin camps" appeared in the west and in Florida, often little more than a semicircle of clapboard cottages set in a grove of trees. Motels sprang up in the 1930s along the new highways. These lodgings catered not only to traveling families but also to couples seeking a few hours of privacy. It was only in 1952, however, that the age of the standardized chain of motor inns appeared with the Holiday Inn that, thanks to the rise of the interstate highways, gradually displaced the small-time motor courts. By the mid-1930s, tourist lodgings had become mobile in the trailer. The mobile home was not only a vacation vehicle but semipermanent shelter for many in the Depression; after the war, the trailer provided housing for the retired in Florida and newlyweds in many small towns, especially in the West. The internal combustion engine also made possible the middle-class lake and mountain vacation, especially in the American West, complete with private cabins and speed boats.[26]

At the same time, airplanes had an immense impact on American tourism. Indeed, in their first commercial use in 1914, "flying boats" transported tourists between Florida and Caribbean resorts. The first transcontinental service (1929) combined air and rail travel in a gruelling 48-hour trip. The plane, a tri-motor "Tin-Goose," covered barely 100 miles per hour and carried only ten passengers. Because of high accident rates (1 in 2,200 passengers was injured), many travelers preferred the train in the 1930s. The popular DC-3 was far more reliable but still only carried fourteen. In 1954, the Boeing Company revolutionized travel with their "707," a plane that could transport 189 at 600 miles per hour. Air travel may have dissolved the barriers of distance and time, but it also eliminated sightseeing in transit and focused attention on the destination. By the 1960s, cheap mass air transportation attracted millions of sun-starved Northern Europeans to Mediterranean resorts and led to the decline of the Victorian English seaside resort.[27]

The car was still more central to everyday leisure. In the 1930s, Coney Island, tied to the streetcar, partially gave way to the cleaner if, still commercial, amusement parks. Playland, at Rye Beach near New York, was approached mostly by car or bus. In 1955, Disneyland was opened along the Santa Monica freeway, accessible by car to the sprawling network of highways that linked suburban Southern California. ABC television (part owners) provided publicity in the Sunday-night program, "Disneyland." Unlike Coney Island (or Blackpool), Disneyland was designed to appeal to the affluent middle class. Thousands of scrubbed, crew-cut, and smiling youths roamed the grounds keeping Disneyland spotless and orderly. Visitors entered the gate onto "Main Street USA," an idealization of a late-Victorian small town. A Plaza led to amusement rides featuring Walt Disney's images of the American frontier, African adventure, cartoon fantasy, and the space-age future. Disney hoped that the crowds would be edified as well as entertained: the old would recall the past, the young would learn the "American spirit" and the adventure of the future, and families would grow closer in their shared experience.[28]

The car culture produced a plethora of new pleasures, some "improving," others not. As early as 1933, the first drive-in movie appeared in New Jersey; by the 1950s, 4,000 of the big screens stretched across suburban fields. They offered cheap films to romancing teenagers and children's fare accompanied with playground equipment. The drive-in restaurant first appeared in Dallas, Texas, in the Royce Hailey's Pig Stand; from the 1940s, these drive-ins (often providing "car-hop" waitresses and "soft ice cream") became haunts of millions of adolescents and their cars; by the 1960s, their disorderly ways drove away families and largely destroyed this colorful institution. The car displaced the downtown business district when parking and congestion problems forced major retailers like Sears to build large stores in suburban districts with large free parking lots. The modern suburban shopping center first appeared in Kansas City's Country Club Plaza in 1923. More than a strip of stores and offices with ample parking, it was a carefully planned commercial "community" complete with a replica of the Giralda Tower of Seville, Spain, and water fountains with expensive landscaping. After 1960, the shopping mall would replace "main street" as not only the retail district of choice but as a place for youths to socialize. Perhaps even more typical was the roadside commercial strip with its gaudy neon signs, which tried to attract fast-moving cars to its bowling alleys, road houses, and fast-food chains.[29]

The American car culture had an ambiguous effect upon Victorian customs, especially domestic leisure. In the 1920s, car ownership forced working families to make choices, replacing other "luxuries" including bathroom fixtures. As it was said, "you can't go to town in a bathtub." In their 1929 study, sociologists Robert and Helen Lynd cite a worker from "Middletown": "We don't spend anything on recreation except for the car. We save every place we can and put the money into the car. It keeps the family together." Yet, for the more affluent "Middletowner," the car had probably the opposite affect: "Our daughters [eighteen and sixteen] don't use our car much because they are always with somebody else in their car when we go out motoring." How different from the social life of the generation before the car:

> In the nineties, we were all much more together.... People brought chairs and cushions out of the house and sat on the lawn evenings. We rolled out a strip of carpet and put cushions on the porch step to take care of the unlimited overflow of neighbors that dropped by. We'd sit out so all evening. The younger couples perhaps would wander off for half an hour to get a soda but come back to join in the informal singing or listen while somebody strummed a mandolin or guitar."[30]

The car transformed not only social life but even domestic space. In the 1920s, the formal parlor and front porch, which had so long served as a buffer between the intimacy of the interior of the home and the public, were eliminated from new houses. They were replaced by a more informal "living room" and the attached garage. So central was the car to the new lifestyle that, even during the Great Depression, the jobless did without necessities to keep their automobility. For the American worker, noted the Lynds in 1937, a car "gives the status which his job increasingly denies, and, more than any other possession or facility to which he has access, it symbolizes living, having a good time, the thing that keeps you working."[31]

Suburban Leisure

The corollary to personalized mobility was the privacy of the individualized dwelling. And, like the car, the suburb was democratized in the 20th-century. Home ownership, facilitated in both countries by building booms after World War I, became, at least, standard for the upper working class. In America, cheap land and inexpensive "balloon" or wood-frame housing made the detached home surrounded with a yard an attainable goal for the working classes. From the 1920s, public-supported housing estates in England freed many from the "back-to-back" lodgings of Victorian slums by offering the relative privacy of the "semidetached" home (a duplex). In the 1930s, in both countries, the spread of low-interest, low-down-payment mortgages made ownership possible for millions. In the United States, the Federal Housing Administration (1934) encouraged the standard 30-year mortgage with a down payment of 10 percent (rather than the traditional 50 or 40 percent).[32] By the end of the 1950s, two-thirds of American families were homeowners (twice the rate in Britain).[33]

The key to the new domesticity was suburbanization, made possible by improved transportation. In both England and America, the suburb was early associated with the rich and their carriages; the middle classes joined them after the appearance of the horse-drawn omnibuses in the 1820s and, a decade later, the steam train. Cheaper and more rapid transportation, which became available for urban workers only when the streetcar appeared in the 1890s, made possible the luxury of separating work and living (leisure) space. In America, the cheap streetcar or trolley extended early beyond built-up areas into open land owned by trolley companies, which hoped to persuade the less affluent to build homes there. This practice helped to create decentralized urban areas from Boston to Los Angeles.[34] Yet it was only the automobile that guaranteed the suburban sprawl of the 20th century. In England, the car, and perhaps more often the bus, freed the suburbanite from the railroad station, allowing the places between to be filled in. Because the suburb was identified with affluence, it became a symbol of upward mobility for aspiring working-class families in both countries.[35]

The suburb was more than a product of technological or economic change. As we saw in Chapter 8, suburban domesticity was a creation of an Anglo-American quest for natural surroundings and freedom from the disorder and decadence of the city. Rather than clustering in enclaves of middle-class respectability in the midst of a cultural urban center (like Paris or Vienna), English, and especially American, elites fled the city. The affluent Victorian suburb, with its "lawn culture," turned inward and cultivated genteel family life. At the same time, 19th-century suburban society was vitally linked (via the railroad) to the cultural amenities of the city.

In the 1920s, the suburb was "democratized" and, with the sprawl made possible by the car and bus, it was gradually divorced from the urban center. Homes in the USA were erected at the rate of 0.85 million a year in the 1920s. Los Angeles opened 3,200 subdivisions to midwestern migrants seeking a promised land of sunshine and bungalow privacy. The car and freeway gradually displaced the streetcar. The city center no longer was a commercial or pleasure hub—for virtually all amenities were widely distributed along the arterial streets.[36]

In the interwar period, the British built some 3.4 million housing units, mostly in relatively spacious suburban estates with their semidetached houses distributed at 8 to 12 per acre. Small private gardens fulfilled the promise of domesticity, but the lack of sufficient pubs, shops, or cinemas in these estates obliged residents to commute (mostly by bus) for services and entertainment.[37]

Decentralized living meant new ideals of domestic and leisure space. Perhaps most characteristic was the English bungalow. This low, broad-roofed structure imported from British India became popular as a vacation home on the southern coast of England in the 1870s. The bungalow offered the London businessman and his family an escape from the city's bustle into a natural and relatively informal setting. Although hardly modest (sometimes including towers and up to 12 bedrooms), the design was adapted to cheap prefabricated iron houses, which dotted beaches near Blackpool and Bournemouth by 1900. Even earlier, in the 1880s, the bungalow was exported to the New England shore as a summer cottage, and in the 1910s and 1920s to California and Florida suburbs.

The American bungalow soon became a practical solution to the middle-class quest for suburban comfort. Plan books and even the *Ladies Home Journal* helped to create a craze for the inexpensive design of these one to one-and-a-half story houses. In contrast to the Victorian house, the bungalow featured an informal living room adjacent to the kitchen, a wrap-around porch, and a low overhanging roof. These themes were designed to enhance a feeling of closeness to nature and to encourage more informal family living. In the 1930s, builders transformed the bungalow into the one-story ranch home spread out on even larger, more private lots.[38]

In the generation after 1945, the American suburb was further democratized. Between 1950 and 1970, largely suburban homes increased the housing stock in the United States by 50 percent, with as many houses added in the 1970s. Gradually, the suburb offered more variety and domestic space. By the mid-1950s, the mass-produced "cape-cod" and "ranch" houses, quickly erected in hundreds of "Levittowns" and "Daley Cities" and satirized in the song "Little Boxes," were replaced. Developers built more spacious bi-level and split-level houses that provided family or "recreation" rooms for domestic leisure.[39]

Mass suburbanization often broke the traditional symbiosis between city and suburb; increasingly, suburbanites both worked and played on the periphery of the city along commercial strips, industrial parks, and shopping malls. This change, critics argue, has reduced not only cultural diversity but has weakened urban cultural centers.[40]

Of course, the suburb was supposed to offer an attractive alternative to the cramped space of the urban town house. Its 19th-century theorists, like Patrick Geddes and Fredrick Olmsted, envisioned a symbiosis between the vitality of the city with its theatres, museums, and restaurants and the natural environment of surrounding "green belt" communities. The suburb was to create a spatial segmentation of work and pleasure, a duality of male industry and female domesticity.[41]

These dreams were only partially realized. In his 1934 study of Westchester County, a wealthy area near New York City, George Lundberg analyzed suburban leisure and what he believed was the future of all America. Lundberg painted a picture of self-indulgent conformity, which would set the tone of many subsequent studies of the suburb. In particular, he noted a life separated by gender. Westchester's 63 golf courses provided males with a time-consuming leisure activity and, in the country club, both business contacts and social status. From the 1910s, middle-class men joined luncheon groups like the Rotary, Lions, or Kiwanis clubs. "[Members] find here," note the Lynds, "some freedom from isolation and competition, even from responsibility, in the sense of solidarity which Rotary bestows."[42]   The more demanding lodge, popular in the late 19th century, with its complex ritual and round of social activities, was on the decline. Businessmen simply lacked the "time."

Lundberg found women in garden clubs (with social as well as horticultural purposes) and the genteel home-like settings of women's clubs. "Service" groups flourished around committee "work," dances, luncheons, and often rather perfunctory philanthropy.[43]   Athletic and more active leisure was more popular for women than in early generations with fads of vigorous dancing, tennis, and golf.[44]

However, these social activities often were more work than leisure. As Lundberg noted: "The round of club meetings, visiting, parties, and 'going places' are no longer ends in themselves, but have become part of the obligatory activities of life. They have become instrumental to ulterior practical ends of various sorts and therefore have lost their essential nature as leisure."[45]

To be sure, the Victorian ideal of self-improvement and association survived and even thrived in the early 20th century suburb. There were, of course, amateur theater and music group; but the center of community leisure was the church. Rather than mere religion (much less traditional community festivals), the suburban church provided the affluent an endless array of individual activities. Committees and special youth organizations met and played in the fellowship halls and Christian education complexes that were built onto the traditional places of worship in the 1920s. Lundberg noted both strong loyalty to church (59 percent of his suburbanites were members) as well as a decline of attachment to religious denomination. Instead of focusing on doctrine, many churches competed with each other to provide leisure activities for members.[46] The postwar suburbanite was perhaps even more devoted to the social leisure of the church (with a record of 63 percent of Americans in the suburbs belonging to a church by the end of the 1950s). The 19th-century ideals of rational recreation were accommodated to the suburban age.[47]

Despite increased free time and a tradition of "self-improvement," few in Lundberg's study spent much time engaged in "improvement." While housewives, who had the most free time, spent 58 minutes per day playing cards and 38 minutes in general "visiting," only 10 percent of any group in the study devoted any time to the fine arts or crafts.[48]   Few middle-class adults read or discussed books in Lynds' Middletown. The old study group, which had been an important part of the late-19th century women's club, seemed to be giving way to the more passive attendance at luncheon lectures.[49]

Private domestic leisure was surely key to the suburban ideal. With the prosperity of the 1920s, the wealthy American family increasingly had play rooms for adults as well as children, furnished with ping-pong or pool tables and often with a bar. The open porches of the 1900s were giving way to the privacy of the glassed-in den and sleeping porch. However, while the home was designed to encourage domestic togetherness, Lundberg found that many middle-class families in the 1920s used the house mostly as a dormitory. Only 16 percent families ate three meals together and a mere 38 percent gathered regularly for one. Automobility and the rigors of commuting defeated the domestic ideal of suburbanism. The teenage couple escaped the front parlor for the privacy of the automobile, movie theatre, or high-school dance.[50]

This trend did not mean, however, the abandonment of domesticity. The suburban homeowner was usually committed to the ideal of home improvement and display. The do-it-yourself movement was largely the creation of the 1920s suburb. Unlike the urban renter, the suburban owner assumed responsibility for maintenance and home improvement. It was also a form of leisure as home-owners competed with neighbors for the most elaborate patio or handsome flowering shrubs. At the same time, the suburb became the democratic equivalent of the life of the landed gentry, where the common man and woman might forget politics and stultifying work in this "last refuge of competence and control;" there, they could "regain a reassuring sense of individual dominion."[51]

The individualism of the suburb had its impact. While socializing across backyard fences may have survived in the American suburb, sidewalk conversation often disappeared with the coming of the car. As Kenneth Jackson describes it: "Residential neighborhoods have become a mass of small, private islands; with the back yard functioning as a wholesome, family-oriented, and reclusive place. There are few places as desolate and lonely as a suburban street on a hot afternoon."[52]

But, the middle-class suburban home was not merely a playroom. Betty Friedan's immensely influential *Feminine Mystique* (1963) stressed that the ranch house was also the work space of the wife. Centered around the open kitchen, the suburban home provided little private space for the wife's relaxation, much less reflection. Isolation and boredom generated the housewife's obsessions with sex and bread baking as well as psychological and physical maladies. Despite advances in home technology, housework continued to absorb as many hours in the 1960s as it did in the 1920s. Homemakers failed to gain more free time not only because domestic servants were increasingly expensive but because of the "inefficiency" of suburban life. Each household required its own cook, laundress, and chauffeur for active children. Unlike the husband, whose worth was measured by his salary, the housewife felt her value as a marriage partner depended upon the *time* she spent at housework. Thus, Friedan emphasizes, "housewifery expands to fill the time available." And even those wives who worked outside the home continued to do a disproportionate share of domestic chores after hours.[53]

These suburban ideals (and realities) surely "trickled-down" to the skilled working classes in both Britain and the United States. The desire to escape from the urban tenements and even the intrusive eyes of neighbors and kin led working-class American ethnics to the cheap "cracker-box" developments of the postwar period. Working-class suburbs in both England and the U.S. became relatively quiet places of contented domesticity in comparison to the old communal and extended family social networks of inner-city tenements. American buyers of those monotonous rows of ranch houses gradually gave them individuality with additions, trim, and landscaping. Because few residents expected to move up the job ladder, they instead concentrated on forming tight-knit neighborhoods organized around familial consumption.[54]

There were obvious differences between affluent and working-class suburbs and everybody certainly did not move to the suburbs. Still, in the generation after 1945, the image prevailed of a virtually classless society where economic and ethnic differences were blended in a "second melting pot" of consumer culture. A lifestyle was, it seemed, a matter of personal choice, not, like the "way of life" of the past, a matter of birth and class.[55]

Age of Consumer Leisure

As early as the 1920s, leisure had become firmly identified with consumption. This equating of free time and spending, of course, had been encouraged by the commercial pleasures of the Coney Islands and Blackpools of the urban working-class of the 1890s (Chapter 9). Mass amusement provided, says historian John Kasson, an antidote to nervewracking and boring work in "a homeopathic remedy of intense, frenetic physical activity without imaginative demands" and "instant pleasure and momentary release from work demands and social prescriptions." It gently mocked "genteel" traditions of morality without challenging the political or economic status quo.[56]

There were other sources of this association of recreation with spending. It was doubtless fostered by the growing American belief in the 1920s that only mass consumption could absorb the increasing capacity of the economic machine to produce. "To keep America growing," wrote an automobile dealer, "we must keep Americans working, and to keep Americans working we must keep them wanting, wanting more than the bare necessities; wanting the luxuries and frills that make life so much more worthwhile, and installment selling makes it easier to keep Americans wanting." Such views became even more prominent in the wake of the Great Depression.[57]

However, the consumer culture also had roots in shifting values of the middle classes. The religious underpinnings of rational recreation were being eroded by 1900. The quest for salvation was being displaced by the desire for social adjustment and self-fulfillment. This glacial but profound change in the modern personality has been attributed to a fundamental shift in Anglo-American society; an entrepreneurial, production-oriented economy that required self-control and thrift gradually gave way to a bureaucratic and consumer economy that demanded cooperative and more spend-free attitudes. The work ethic and an absorbing individualism (corresponding with a faith in personal salvation) was partially replaced by the ideals of "personal magnetism" and "team-playing" on the job and "social adjustment" and "life-affirming" consumption after working hours.[58]

The excitement of consumption may have also helped to overcome a growing feeling of "unreality" and "emptiness." This unpleasant awareness was a by-product of newly acquired comforts of urban life, which were isolated from the reality of physical nature and decision making. Combined with a revolt against the formality and repressive self-control of the Victorian era, this sense of vacuum led to the popular idea of the "Gospel of Relaxation." At least for an elite, the goal by the 1910s was to be both "other-directed" and experientially subjective; it was to seek both peer approval and "self-fulfillment." The quest for intense experience led to an attachment to the "new," even conformist fadism, in a cult of youth over aged sterility. But this longing for fulfillment also produced a nostalgia for the rural and the uncomplex, in the name of natural vitality. By the 1920s, these contradictory desires fed into an immense industry of self-help books and movements, both religious and secular. They offered techniques of self-fulfillment through seeking "more life." It was a philosophy of letting-go, removing inhibitions, of positive-thinking, returning to the innocence and vitality of childhood, and, with Luther Gulick, thinking "strong and happy thoughts."[59]

The Gospel of Relaxation invaded liberal religion, sports, and even advertising. As self-proclaimed "apostles of modernity," advertisers adapted to prevailing cultural attitudes from the 1920s on. Through new consumer goods, they promised to provide both social acceptance and vitality. Advertisers assured women that they were free when they assumed their "right" to smoke Luckie Strike cigarettes along with men; they guaranteed social success for users of Listerine mouthwash which conquered "halitosis." Advertisers became cultural advisers, partially replacing traditional authority figures like parents and pastors; they offered clues into the complex world of adjustment and "happiness." Even the movie star became a model, not by his/her solidity of character but by the star's display (or even commercial endorsement) of "roles, identities, and styles." As an authority on "lifestyles" and trendy consumption, the star offered advice on new leisure choices. As Roland Marchand argues, advertisers in the 1920s and 1930s did not always encourage mindless consumption; rather, they saw themselves as therapists in the "adaptation of consumers to the intensities of a new, complex scale of life" even as they sold Camel cigarettes as a healthful way of soothing frayed nerves and tried to convince people that in free time "you can have it all."[60]

Advertisers attempted to make utilitarian consumption, like the buying of bathroom fixtures, into a personal statement of status and taste. A good example is the merchandizing of cars from the mid-1920s. General Motors and its chairman, Alfred Sloan, developed the annual style change. Cars would allow one to participate in the beauty of classical Greece or to express one's manhood. And, while Henry Ford grumbled that "we are no longer in the automobile but in the millinery business," he soon acquiesced when he abandoned the utilitarian Model-T to the more stylish Model-A in 1927.[61]

This consumption of style and "self-expression" reached its extreme form in the 1950s when Americans indulged in an orgy of mass-buying. This period (which Thomas Hine aptly calls "Populuxe") released a pent-up demand for consumer goods resulting from the depression and the war. Advertisers and the government prepared Americans during the war for this splurge with the message that they were fighting for the "glorious future" of "mass distribution and mass ownership."[62] The 1950s produced the extravagant tailfin on cars, the flying-saucer lamp, the two-tone refrigerator, chip-and-dip, the lounge chair, the aesthetic contradiction of the colonial living room next to the space-age kitchen, and the sheer magic of the push button in thousands of products. This decade "celebrated confidence in the future, the excitement of the present, the sheer joy of having so much."[63] Shopping had never been such a central leisure activity.

Consumption brought not only self-fulfillment but status and a feeling of belonging. This social function of consumers' leisure had been pointed out in Veblen's *Theory of the Leisure Class*. He wrote this book in the 1890s, during a period of extravagant consumption of ultra-rich industrialists. What drove these men was the hope of winning status through the possession of wealth and the display of freedom from work. Leisure, then, was not valued as an opportunity for self-expression or growth so much as a means of demonstrating social status. Wives of businessmen surrounded themselves with servants and luxurious homes, and even wore impractical clothing (like corsets) in order to display their freedom from the herd who had to labor. Such women provided successful hard-working businessmen with "vicarious leisure."[64]

This meaning of leisure time hardly died with the income tax or the decline of aristocratic fortunes in the 20th century. When the automobile became the toy of the American masses in the interwar period, the well-to-do played in private airplanes. When the crowd invaded the golf course in the 1930s in Middletown, the rich took up equestrian sports. The same principle was democratized in the modern suburban obsession of "keeping up with the Joneses;" the display of home furnishings in the ranch house picture window; and the "vicarious consumption" which parents lavished on their children.[65]

This cultural impact of leisure as status-seeking was analyzed in the 1920s by the Lynds:

> In 1890 Middletown appears to have lived on a series of plateaus as
> regards standards of living...; it was a common thing to hear a
> remark that so and so 'is pretty good for people in our circumstances.'
> Today the edges of the plateaus have been shaved off, and every one
> lives on the slope from any point of which desirable things belonging
> to people all the way up to the top are in view.[66]

Some contemporary critics of commercial leisure argue that leisure has become the "self-management of appearance," leaving to a power elite the management of society. As Richard Fox and T.J. Jackson Lears see it: "While the few make decisions about managing society, the many are left to manage their appearance, aided by trained counselors in personal cosmetics. Leadership by experts and pervasive self-absorption have developed symbiotically in American consumer culture."[67] Self-indulgence, driven by the quest for group acceptance, combines with the bureaucratic economy to produce a consumer leisure culture.

By the 1950s, mass (but privatized) leisure built around mass media, automobility, and the suburb seemed to have obliterated most remaining remnants of local, ethnic, or class traditions of play in Anglo-American society. The sheer pervasiveness of this culture led social critics to write of a "one-dimensional" society. To be sure, this consumer culture may have disguised the fact that power was concentrated in few hands and that the real purpose of leisure was often to climb the pecking order. Still, affluence seemed to produce the opposite of traditional class society: the rich and powerful devoted their lives to long workdays, while the masses minimized their hours of toil to enjoy the pleasurable fruits of material progress.

The recessions of the 1970s and 1980s produced a somewhat more sober assessment. Scholars rediscovered that the working classes and ethnic and racial minorities were often bypassed by (or even they resisted) this moderniza-tion of free-time. Moreover, social change in the 1960s and 1970s produced groups that questioned mass suburban leisure. The young especially rejected at least part of familial suburban leisure culture. How these exceptions and challenges to mass leisure emerged is the topic of our next chapter.

13

Working-Class and Youth at Play in the 20th Century

Leisure uniformity was not the inevitable product of 20th century technology and the international entertainment corporation, nor did the car and the suburb destroy all remnants of traditional popular culture. There remained pockets (and even seas) of traditional working-class and ethnic leisure. The domestic ideal of the suburb was also undermined by generational conflict. A youth leisure culture emerged in this century that was poorly controlled or understood by parents and authorities. And, if only briefly, the ideal of suburban privatized consumption was rejected by the children of suburbanites in the late 1960s and early 1970s.

Persistence of Traditional Working-Class Culture

Many working-class cultures survived in the 20th-century, Anglo-American world. Divided by ethnicity and race, as well as region and economic status, these subcultures have been often strikingly different and often in conflict. Yet, relative to the emerging middle-class suburban leisure style, they had much in common. In this section, I will concentrate on the broad English pattern but will review some of the varieties of American working-class leisure culture for comparison.

The "traditional" English working-class neighborhood (really emerging as late as the 1880s) was built around an urban-industrial calendar: the weekly round was predictable. Evenings were spent at home or the pub, and Saturday afternoons were devoted to shopping, gardening, or the football match followed by an evening at the music hall, pub, or cinema. Sundays were dedicated to a bacon-and-eggs breakfast, several tabloid newspapers, and a mid-day dinner. Toward evening a big tea of "tasty food," often with relatives, would be followed by talk around the fireplace and maybe singing in the parlor. Perhaps because of the density of row housing with the ever-present fear of gossip, neighbors and workmates seldom entered each other's homes. "The wife's social life outside of her immediate family is found over the washing-line, at the corner shop, visiting relatives at a moderate distance occasionally, and perhaps now and again going with her husband to his pub or club." Leisure focused on the cramped environs of the flat or semi-detached houses. Richard Hoggart found that working-class leisure before World War II was "of the people" rather than "of the masses," and rooted in neighborhood rather than marketplace.[1]

Studies of American working people well into the "suburban age" reveal a similar pattern of relatively closed domesticity. Blue-collar couples, studied by Mirra Komarovsky in the 1950s, entertained an average of twice a year (outside of the family). Not only did they lack money but the social contacts necessary for more extensive socializing. Few working-class families participated in the sort of clubs that formed the basis of middle-class society. Another sociologist found Italian-American couples met regularly, if informally; but socializing tended to be separated by sex. The peer group was small and frequently life-long.[2]

It is easy to romanticize this domestic leisure. In England, the cramped four-room/two-story house or the tenement apartment of the Depression era often lacked privacy and even amenities like the radio. In the 1930s and beyond, children continued to reign in the streets with their time-honored games of marbles and hoops as well as with pranks like "tip it and run." In America, too, street-corner gangs of teenage boys gathered around the crap game, waged battles with rivals, and just grouped around luncheonettes and candy stores. These gangs often formed friendships that lasted a lifetime. The code of loyalty and sharing among the peer group prevailed over the domesticity and individualism of the middle class. This leisure culture, divorced from school and the wider community, ill prepared American working-class youth for success beyond a local career in crime, petty jobs, or the political machine.[3]

Between the wars, the pub or bar remained the center of male urban working-class leisure in both countries. At the heart of pub culture was the reciprocity of "treating" for drinks. A British study of pub life in the late 1930s likened the Saturday-night pub habit to a church service, a liturgy of group drinking and treating and a litany of verbal exchanges. "The same remarks can be repeated indefinitely in these conversations without any sense of ennui. So long as the subject is right, and everyone has his chance to speak, the purpose of them appears to be served."[4]

Men, who would not think of inviting workmates or neighbors inside their homes, freely gossiped with them in pubs. While respectable women were increasingly appearing in pubs by the 1930s, the age of pub-goers also rose because the young were more attracted to the cinema or dance hall. Drink was more or less incidental to socializing, and actual alcohol consumed had decreased from World War I, even if per capita income spent on drink did not. Still, on Saturday evenings, one witness in the late 1930s counted an average of 3.75 pints consumed per customer in a Lancashire pub; few, however, drank anything stronger than beer. The pub landlord continued to perform the complex role of social mediator, banker, and participant in the nightly round of gossip, drinking, singing of familiar music-hall numbers, and bar games. Pubgoers were not mere customers but members of a community. The pub continued to be a site of the casual sexual encounter, which often culminated in sex performed in the semi-privacy of back alleys, the only recourse to the promiscuous in a world that lacked cars, motels, or private apartments.[5]

The American pattern was somewhat different, owing to the Eighteenth Amendment to the Constitution of 1919, which prohibited alcohol consumption. Although the law was widely violated in speak-easy clubs, in 1933, with repeal, there was a sudden upsurge in public drinking. And, of course, a similar bar culture prevailed in the neighborhood tavern in America. In the Italian-American "Urban Village," studied in the early 1960s by Herbert Gans, customers sometimes played the role of bartender, while the owner played pool or cards. This informality, based on the solidarity of ethnic neighborhoods, had hardly changed since the heyday of the late-19th century saloon.[6]

Beyond the bar was the workingmen's club, which continued to grow between the wars. In the mid-1930s, 102,000 Londoners belonged to 300 clubs. In addition to providing insurance benefits, these clubs provided rooms for moderate drinking (often clubs owned their own breweries), darts, billiards, and sing-songs, and occasionally fund-raising card games. Lodges provided a semiserious aura of ritualized meetings and the "status" of office-holding shared, in time, by most members. English lodges like the Odd Fellows easily made the migration to the United States.[7]

Boxing, patronizing of prostitutes, and other male pastimes were on the decline in the interwar years. But the male-oriented and casual leisure of the mechanical gaming arcade flourished in the cities. The English "fun fairs" included pinball, board games, dodge'ems, and curiosity shows (featuring, in one case, the car of the American gangster, Al Capone). Saturdays at Association Football matches were common diversions that built upon local pride. London, alone, had 11 teams.[8] The old hunting culture, of course, continued to flourish, especially among American men in the annual ritual of deer and fishing seasons. Even urbanization did not destroy this ancient expression of male togetherness and prowess.

These activities were bastions of old-fashioned male informality. The boisterous music hall had become respectable "family" entertainment by the 1890s, preparing the way for the silent viewing of the cinema. Roy Rosenzweig shows how the informal male sociability in the American saloon partially gave way to the orderly couples and families who thronged the movie houses. By the 1910s, movie houses offered the matinee, which allowed housewives a few hours of fantasy interspersed by shopping trips. But English working-class homemakers had little time for leisure outside the their work at home. For them, the radio was a boon in the 1930s. Those women who held jobs outside the home had scarcely two hours of their own per day because of the domestic chores waiting for them at home.[9]

The most notable development in working-class leisure in the 20th century was the growth of off-site gambling. Betting focused not only on horses, but also greyhounds. As English observer H. L. Smith put it (1935): "the place which drunkenness occupied in the category of vices in the minds of moralists during the last century has to-day largely been surrendered to gambling." While a 1903 law in Britain prohibited street betting, bookies freely practiced their trade in and around pubs, as police looked the other way. Gaming gained strength when otherwise unemployed men served bookmakers as runners gathering bets at pubs. In the interwar years, the Littlewood football pools were especially popular; bets were small and the mail-in coupon due the Thursday before the Saturday games, became a weekly ritual for millions. The psychology of the gambler was often observed: "certainly more pleasure is gained in anticipation than is lost in disappointment. The pleasure lasts for some days; but the disappointment is momentary and easily forgotten. Also the fact that many people are excited at the same time about the same event increases the pleasurable excitement of each." Perhaps 80 percent of the working-class families of London engaged in some form of gambling in the interwar years.[10]

Commercial gambling was, of course, widespread in the American urban working classes. For example, in the 1930s, blacks from south Chicago patronized some 500 policy stations (almost as many as churches) which provided an illegal (but protected) lottery for these poor people. And, in the American West, the gambling towns of Las Vegas and Reno served the population centers of southern and northern California. The gambling strip offered a new leisure culture characterized by a new intensity of consumption and activity.[11]

The prevalence of gambling suggests that the traditional quest for excitement in leisure had hardly been "civilized" by the rational recreationists. As Hoggart argued, the English working class of the interwar years had a love for a:

> . . . sprawling, highly-ornamental, rococo extravagance. Oriental themes prevail in designs of cinema houses, sideshows at amusement parks, and in popular magazines. Plastic gewgaws and teapots shaped like country cottages settle very easily with complicated lace-paper d'oyleys, complicated lace half-curtains, crocheted tablerunners, fancy birthday and Christmas cards, coloured wicker shopping baskets, and "fancies" (curiously constructed and coloured little cakes) for tea.

Related to this fascination with the extravagant was the workers' persistent affection for the crowd. In Britain, factory workers, far from avoiding the mob that they knew at work, thought nothing of going by crowded trains to the same packed seaside resorts. Liberated briefly from a life of austerity, everyone spent with abandon. Working-class materialism was a moral necessity in a drab life of stress-filled routine; and tight budgets precluded more "imaginative" holidays. But workers also shared little longing for privacy so valued by the middle-class.[12]

Of course, some categories of "improving" leisure (such as gardening or amateur participation in football and cricket) grew during the interwar period despite persistent complaints of inadequate facilities. But many families had no books other than those given to children for good Sunday-School attendance.[13] Church activities were for many women (and less often for men) a counterculture to male pub or saloon sociability. This pattern can be illustrated among the black urban poor in America. Store-front churches provided nightly friendship as well as emotional outlets in singing and demonstrative religion for many respectable black families. The church was an alternative to the informal card and dancing party, which dominated the leisure hours of many working-class blacks of the 1930s.[14]

Working-class leisure culture often fascinated both American and British intellectuals in the 1930s, who saw in it a survival of a lost innocence and honesty. Listen to this description of a working-class dance hall by a young university-educated Englishman in 1937:

> What strikes me most about this place, its people, is the spontaneous reality and genuineness of everything. All present are working-class people.... To them, this dance is temporary freedom from hard work and worries—"Let's enjoy ourselves to-day for to-morrow we...." No class; no snobbery; no forced laughter—just reality.[15]

Selling Fun to Working People

Still, the allure of commercial leisure challenged this culture long before that watershed of World War II. As noted in Chapter 9, the pleasure industry had been integral to the traditional leisure of workers. The historian G. Stedman Jones suggests that, by the 1890s, commercialized leisure, organized around the "pub, the race-course and the music-hall," had driven out earlier interest in education and politics. After World War I, the cultural landscape surely was leveled when almost all Britons and Americans began to watch the same films and listen to the same recorded music on radio, if even they (especially in Britain) continued to read different newspapers.[16]

It may well be true that workers used this commercial leisure for their own purposes (as they did in the 19th century), creating for example, a distinct social style in pubs owned by chains of brewers. Working-class cinema audiences, dance floors, and football stadium were still different. Even the American "urban villagers" studied by Gans in the early 1960s watched television selectively to confirm their values and to express their skepticism about the outside world.

Still, commercial leisure, not the recreation organized by trade unions or political parties, dominated workers' free time. And, despite the growth of labor theater or documentary, it was the song and humor of Gracie Fields, George Formby, Fanny Brice and Eddie Cantor, not the socialist works of Bertold Brecht or Serge Eisenstein, that the people wanted. Workers had no more sense of the past than the more affluent: their "traditions" were seldom more than two generations old, and they seldom sought to preserve them. Given the willingness of pleasure industries to service profitable popular taste, commercialization inevitably crept into traditional working-class leisure. English working-class migration to the new "housing estates" tended to break up the peer group and the pub culture. The same process occurred in America, accelerated by the advent of mass automobility in the 1920s. Those institutions, which had sometimes integrated work, home, and leisure, gradually succumbed to more commercialized culture. In the United States this process often coincided with the "Americanization" of immigrant working-class communities.[17]

Popular British reading tastes (similar to what we encountered in the discussion of the 19th century) were continuously updated in the magazines that Lord Northcliffe and his successors published: Tidbits of gossip about the famous and notorious were combined with cheesecake in weekly magazines and the tabloids. The entertainment press continued to appeal to separate gender and age groups as new magazines appeared, each with their own form of sensationalism.[18]

The commercial dance hall, which emerged in the 1920s, provided a vital service as a sex market. The dance-hall manager created a "social tone" and, through an often elaborate system of exclusion, assured a homogeneous crowd, prized by patrons. English men, whose ranks had been thinned by war, enjoyed a great advantage. As Robert Roberts describes the English dance hall in the 1920s, "Plenty of working-class girls, in their efforts to 'beat the market', went well beyond the tenets laid down by mothers. Some, we knew dared all and failed; others got their man with a pregnancy.... And the wise boys with their 'self-protectors' went on happily dancing in a city littered with 'common' halls." Paul Cressey's study of the "Taxi dance-hall" in Chicago in the 1920s reveals a complex world of commercial sexual encounter, where men, often from minority ethnic or racial groups, could find a partner at a dime a dance.[19]

The seaside holiday was another leisure provided by the marketplace. By the early 20th century, the seaside holiday was the focal point of the year for many an English working family, prepared for in months of saving and anticipation. In addition to largely perfunctory seabathing, the seaside holiday was a compacted assault on the senses, a candyfloss world of an ersatz exotica of gypsy fortune-tellers and Indian Sharma, of pinball boards and amusement rides featuring Noah's Arc, as well as the opportunity to see George Formby, Gracie Fields, or dance in a sumptuous hall to Reginald Dixon's playing on his "mighty Wulitzer Organ." Austere people spent with abandon and time-card punchers celebrated a week of living without clocks. "Improvers" of the left and right might have preferred that they enjoy a Holiday Fellowship camp, making new friends and communing with nature. But most working people surely favored the mob scene of places like Blackpool; there, all the amusements that the market would bear were provided by the all-powerful Tower Company and the petty stall holder.[20]

While the American "common man" continued to enjoy the Coney-Island-type of amusement park, mass automobility gave their quest for a change of scenery a wider vantage, as we have seen in Chapter 12. The growth of trade unions during the Roosevelt years and World War II, as well as postwar prosperity, democratized the vacation. By 1949, 62 percent of Americans took vacation trips averaging slightly over 10 days.[21]

The Great Depression of the 1930s, of course, interrupted this long trend. The trauma of unemployment (peaking at about 25 percent in America and 22 percent in Britain in 1932) had far more than an economic impact. To be sure, there was "love on the dole." The poor still had access to a "Woolworth culture" of what George Orwell described as "fish-and-chips, art-silk stockings, tinned salmon, cut-price chocolate... the movies, the radio, strong tea, and the football pools." In Britain, clubs for the unemployed were opened by both patronizing elites and labor groups to provide outlets for hobbyists and other "improving" activities. The jobless were able to continue the betting habit (in the inexpensive Littlewood football pool) and cinema (often by attending cheap matinees); but they cut back on drinking mostly to avoid the humiliation of being unable to treat mates.[22] On both sides of the Atlantic, observers noted sharp increases in library usage and, especially in the United States, public works projects made available many parks and sporting facilities.[23]

As we noted in Chapter 11, enforced idleness created less destitution (thanks to public-assistance programs) than a social, indeed psychological, crisis among the unemployed. Not only did unemployment mean a loss of social status and authority in the family for men, but it seemed to undermine their masculinity and caused psychosomatic illness. Work was the anchor in the identity of most wage earners; leisure was both a compensation for and an extension of work. As one British observer noted, "Work is fundamental, there is no leisure without it." Unemployment befell women as often as men; but it led less to idleness than to more domestic work for women because they had to do without "store-bought" goods. Homemakers found their routines disrupted and made more time consuming by the presence of unemployed husbands at home.[24]

Perhaps most important, the Depression reinforced a commitment to the values of work and the things that wages could buy. Instead of a militant class of the jobless, numerous British and American studies found that workers were humiliated by unfunded leisure. E. Wight Baake noted that unemployed English men made a tenacious effort to maintain a leisure schedule structured around the (now absent) work cycle; they tried to stick to the "right sort" of cinema and vacations. And, yet, as the novelist Walter Greenwood noted in his *Love on the Dole*, the unemployed person was "suddenly wakened to the fact that he was a prisoner. The walls of the shops, houses, and places of amusement were his prison walls; lacking money to buy his way into them, the doors were all closed against him."[25]

The notion of fulfillment through consumption grew, if anything, with the experience of the Depression, during which so many were deprived of the feeling of self-worth and freedom that money bought. Advertising, the media, and installment buying had already created a precocious consumerism in America in the 1920s. And the identification of leisure with consumption won many to hard and steady work in disagreeable jobs. By the 1950s and 1960s, millions of working-class Americans could join the middle class in sampling the satisfactions that advertisers had continuously promised during the lean years. As historian Richard Fox summarizes: "[A]ll seemed united by their commitment to acquiring the mass-marketed tokens of 'the American standard of living.'"[26]

Yet again it is surely an exaggeration to speak of a "classless" or "affluent" society. Even in the prosperous 1960s, cultural differences between middle- and working-class leisure persisted despite the relatively high incomes of many industrial workers in both countries. To be sure, in Britain, the growth of automobile ownership produced a change in lifestyle quite similar to that noted in America a generation earlier. The worker with wheels shifted income from drink and other forms of casual recreation to the mobility and status of the private car. The old holiday to the plebian Southend and Blackpool resorts were partially replaced by budget package tours to the sunny beaches of Spain and Greece.

Still, old patterns of sociability survived economic change. Workers remained outside middle-class social organizations and, instead, built a leisure society around the neighborhoods and family. In the 1960s, same-sex socializing or mixed groups organized by the wife rather than the husband were still common. Shift work of blue-collar employees may explain some of this difference, but it was also due to the persistence of a traditional working-class culture.[27]

Youth and Leisure in the Early 20th Century

In 1942, the famous American sociologist, Talcott Parsons, coined the term, "youth culture" to describe what he saw as a juvenile fixation upon consumption and a hedonistic denial of responsibility, an inversion of the adult roles of routinized work and acceptance of family duties. After 1945, social observers increasingly saw youth as a "class" removed from the world of work and adult expectations, "consigned to a self-contained world of juvenile preoccupations."

This thinking merely confirmed a generation of research that had observed the widening chasm between adult and youth culture, the latter often perceived as delinquent.[28] The British C. MacInnes (1961) went further:

> We are in the presence...of an entirely new phenomenon in human history: that youth is rich... In this decade [1950s] we witness the second Children's Crusade, armed with strength and booty, against all "squares," all adult nay sayers. An international movement, be it noted, that blithely penetrates the political curtains draped by senile seniors, as yet unconscious of the rising might of this new classless class.[29]

This anxiety toward youth leisure was hardly new. Concern with the independence of youth had long been a major topic of social commentary (Chapter 7). By 1900, there had emerged distinct territories and styles of youth, for example, dance halls, milk bars, the joys of colorful clothing forbidden at work and in school, and the hero worship of sports and entertainment figures. The autonomy of male youth began at 12 or 14 years of age, when the mother's and schoolmaster's control ceased with employment. Because of overcrowding, older English children were chased out into the street, where they freely played games and traded collections of comics and picture cards of trains and cricketers. Teenage English boys looked forward to the day when they could leave school for the freedom and the pleasure that the full-time wage could bring. Apprenticeships had long been in decline; in any case, many youths preferred the relatively high wage in unskilled jobs to the uncertainties of training. Until reaching the age of 16, English boys hung out in small groups. "[D]eprived of all decent ways of spending their little leisure," says Robert Roberts, "they sought escape from tedium in bloody battles with belt and clog—street against street." Only gradually did these gangs break up as boys discovered girls. Often housework and parental fears of pregnancy kept daughters at home.[30]

In the generation before World War I, American commentators also observed youthful leisure but, because of the American teenagers' greater access to pocket money, it was organized perhaps more often around dance halls, poolrooms, penny arcades, and amusement parks. Yet, like their British counterparts, American critics agreed that these activities undermined the work of school, church, and philanthropic social work. As one moralist in 1915 described Coney Island: "A large number of unescorted young girls and boys stroll about, an easy prey for exploitation.... The carnival spirit of freedom and relaxation frequently degenerates into one of license and gross immorality in the public dancing pavilions and unlighted places." This allure of commercial entertainment was a threat to the influence of parents and their professional surrogates.[31]

In the U.S., alienation between immigrant parents and their American-born offspring also contributed to the problem of a rebellious "Street-Corner Society," which William Whyte (1943) found among second-generation Italian-Americans in the 1930s.[32] For the middle-class youth, the opportunity for "automobility" in the family car added another dimension to the autonomy of teenage boys and couples from the 1920s.[33]

In the interwar years, merchandisers learned how to fully tap the youth leisure market. Among younger children, pleasure makers combined film fantasy with licensing characters for toys. Leading the way was the "Disneyification" of children's fairy tales and the mass-commercialized fads created around Mickey Mouse paraphernalia in the 1930s. Later, in the 1950s, millions of babyboomer boys (including the author) proudly wore their Davey Crocket "coonskin caps."[34]

Armed with pocket money and time, teenagers rapidly adapted to new leisure forms. As we have seen in Chapter 9, the dance hall had been a focal point for the display of fashion and sexuality from the 1980s. Perhaps even more influential was the cinema. Moralists feared that movies harmed the impressionable minds of youth in the 1930s. They believed that films led to copy-cat delinquency or to superficial values. As one teenage American girl observed in the early 1930s:

> The movies have given me some ideas about the freedom we should have....My notion of the freedom I should have... is to go out have a good time, but watch your step.... I believe that "when you are in Rome, do as the Romans do." I used to think just the opposite, but after seeing *Our Dancing Daughters* and *the Wild Party* I began to think this over, and I found out that it is the best way to act.[35]

In part, adults feared youth leisure because it symbolized rapid cultural change; it expressed the inability of parents to control the education of their offspring, which seemed to be dominated by commercial entertainment. Youth slang, dance, and clothing frightened adults not only because they represented rebellion, but because adults did not understand them. Insofar as the content of teenage leisure constantly changed, adults did not see it as similar to their own period of "sowing wild oats." No parent or community could control access to youth culture when media was commercial and international. While the cinema was willing to censor itself (to a degree), the free market's appeal to the novel and exciting prevailed over traditional morality.

Beyond the pervasive influence of commercial leisure was a play culture built around the college and secondary school. In the United States, well-organized extracurricular activities, by the late 19th century, had been accepted by faculty and future employers alike as central to the educational process. In effect, a growing group of affluent American youth enjoyed a moratorium on the responsibilities of adults.[36] The student generation after World War I challenged their elders in new ways. Rejecting the formality of Victorian society (and in some cases, the folly of war), college youth in the 1920s were far more insistent on their "right to self-expression, self-determination, and personal satisfaction," notes Paula Fass. "To traditionalists this smacked of immorality, self-indulgence, and irresponsibility."[37]

Why this quest for fulfillment should appear early in the century has been analyzed in Chapter 12. American college students of the 1920s had grown up with only about half the siblings of their grandparents; with greater opportunities for parental attention, they enjoyed a more "democratic" childhood with less stress on rules and chores and more on "mutual confidence and understanding." This likely encouraged a more spontaneous and experimental youth, even if it did not always prepare them for competitive adult roles. In the 1920s, American college students were less inhibited. They often expected sexual satisfaction in marriage and separated coitus from procreation. They intended to delay and limit pregnancy after marriage. Moreover, this generation of students was bound to be influential: between 1900 and 1930, there was a 300 percent increase in college enrollments and a 650 percent rise in high-school population. By 1930, 20 percent of the college-age population attended an institution of higher education while 60 percent of the high-school-aged population were enrolled in secondary school.[38]

In Britain, school-based leisure culture was far less important than in the United States. In 1926, only 10 percent of elementary school graduates went on to secondary school and only one in a thousand attended a university.[39] Despite the 1944 Education Act, far fewer Britons remained in school through their teenage years than in the United States. Those years that they were in some educational facility were segregated by class, unlike the *relatively* heterogeneous American high school.

In the United States, despite the demands of study and long lists of college regulations, student life was mostly organized around a peer culture. In the interwar years, fraternities and sororities dominated college life. Through the rituals of "rushing" and "hazing" recruits and daily peer supervision of members, these social clubs set standards of style, language, and behavior. They punished individuality and rewarded conformity and the person who "mixed well." In a word, they helped to shape the "other directed" person. One university observer noted, "failure in studies is not as important to college students as failure in social adjustment." And a midwestern student newspaper went so far as to say:

> Who hears of a University as having a reputation for the number of
> hours the students study each day? The youth of America is
> attracted to a university which has a strong football team, a talented
> band; a university which has students who are willing to build up its

activities, to work for it. If a college has a strong faculty, that is good advertisement among the teaching profession but it has little or no weight with the high school graduate. The candidate for college wants to know what the students are doing....

The ritual of pep rallies, football games, and fraternity dances dominated social life. That student newspaper went on to admit that the average student "cannot plead lack of time. He knows that the requirement of two-and-a-half hours of preparation for each class is a joke, and that every day he has from three to seven hours to use absolutely as he chooses."[40] The real work of American collegians was responding to the peer culture, which demanded constant adjustment to fads in dress, speech, music, and dance. While such a recreational culture placed a premium on shallow thought, it taught the useful skill of rapid response to change and social blending in a consumer-oriented society.

Yet this collegiate culture of the 1920s was also innovative. It popularized social drinking (despite prohibition and in anticipation of recreational drug use on the 1960s campus). The student of the 1920s turned the formality of courtship into dating and created codes of behavior for recreational petting. These changes both channeled sexual energies and tested compatibility for future marriage. While perhaps 50 percent of college men and 25 percent of college women in the 1920s had coitus, the real innovation was not premarital intercourse, but a wider, if self-regulated, expression of intimacy in preparation for marriage.[41] Recreational peer culture provided a transition from childhood to adulthood; it offered the student an accepting, but educational, environment for a life of companionate marriage, corporate-business "getting-on," and status-conscious consumption.

The American collegiate lifestyle trickled down into high school. These adolescents imitated the extracurricular activities of their elders even if they lacked the time and freedom to express it fully. Especially after World War I, high school became a powerful setting of peer culture. In the corridors before class, in the cafeteria, and at sporting events, there was ample opportunity for the creation of a deeply imitative culture.

Leisure of a Youth Generation: 1945-1970

In both countries, the impact of commercial youth leisure and extracurricular recreation was felt with particular intensity following World War II. Adult concerns focused on the growing autonomy of the teenager. Youths naturally gained independence when fathers entered the military and mothers took jobs during the war. Access to recreational income increased as American high-school students took part-time jobs (about half of these students did so in the 1950s). In England, in the 1950s, there was perhaps a doubling of teenage discretionary income, at least 75 percent of which was spent on junk food, cigarettes, drinks, records, dances, and magazines.[42] Almost all of this teenage market in England was concentrated in the wage-earning adolescent; the school or university youth generally lacked this autonomy. In England, "between leaving school [at age 16] and going into the army [at 18 years], [working teenagers] could live out a fantasy life, their pockets full of money from a dead-end job."[43] Earlier dating and consequently earlier marriage in the USA began during the war. Adolescents created a premature adult culture with access to cars and spending money. Young males sometimes tweaked the consumer sensibilities of adults by turning their vehicles into "hot rods" and young Hispanics and other minorities in American cities produced a threatening street culture around the flamboyant dress of the zoot suit during World War II.

In the United States, the result was a unique popular culture, nurtured both on the street and in the protected environs of the high school. It was a social construct shaped also by the teenager market for magazines, 45-RPM records and the soda fountain. Youth leisure was not tied to tradition, neither did it admit to the participation of more than one generation; rather, it was driven by fads and an international celebrity system.

At the same time, the American high school was not a classless culture. It was not a social melting pot, as was sometimes suggested in the 1950s. Rather, the high school created (or affirmed) social divisions through a system of testing and tracking students into different programs. Failure in school had a powerful effect upon working-class youths; it often led to withdrawal from sponsored extracurricular activities, antagonism toward authority, and anti-intellectualism. Moreover, during free time, working-class youth retained the traditional "ethic of reciprocity," giving and taking resources among a close-knit group. Few embraced the "ethic of individual responsibility," with its presumption of "getting ahead." And, displays of physical aggression had a legitimacy in home as well as on the street.

As the American sociologist Albert Cohen observed in the 1950s, "the modesty of working-class aspirations is partly a matter of trimming one's sails to the available opportunities and resources and partly a matter of unwillingness to accept the discipline which upward striving entails." The sociologist Robert Hollingshead found in the American high school of the 1950s that far fewer working-class students participated in extracurricular activities (such as dances, sports, and even the scouts) than did the offspring of the middle classes; often this was the result of snubbing by the more affluent. Moreover, differences in access to spending money and expectations regarding college produced the chasm that separated the recreational style of the working-class "greaser" and middle-class "soc" in the early 1960s. These styles were stereotyped, for example, in the film, *American Graffiti*. The working-class youth, alienated from the middle-class extracurricular culture at school, retreated into a male-dominated society built around the hot rod, its upkeep, and its use in the social and sexual rites of cruising main street.[44]

The English version of postwar youth leisure was influenced less by collegiate and high-school society than by neighborhoods. In Britain, the secondary school played a far smaller role, in part because many youth left school at 16 years or earlier and schools were more socially segregated into the state-supported "comprehensives" and the elite schools. New youth leisure was dominated by the working-class entertainment market; middle-class youth were far more restricted in school and university and lacked both the car and spending money of their counterparts in the U.S.

Economic change after World War II broke up many old English neighborhoods with ambiguous consequences for the young. New housing developments weakened old kinship networks and traditional recreational zones. As sociologist Tony Jefferson (1975) noted:

> High-density, high-rise housing [destroyed] the function of the street, the local pub, the corner shop, as articulations of communal space. Instead there was only the privatized space of the family unit, stacked one on top of each other, in total isolation, juxtaposed with the totally public space which surrounded it, and which lacked any of the informal social controls generated by the neighborhood.[45]

This led to a cultural crisis particularly for youth. Cut off from the recreational traditions of their parents, they adopted styles associated with the upwardly mobile consumer culture. For example, the amphetamine-driven and clothes-conscious "mods" of the early 1960s protested the dead-end jobs, which they knew to be their collective fate, through the ritual of consumption. Groups like the Teddy Boys (in the 50s) and later the Skinheads retained the tough macho image associated with the working class. Some protested their loss of territory by attacking immigrants. From the early 1950s, the English media widely publicized youth gang disruptions of dance halls and cinemas and contests between rival groups for "turf." In the "relative freedom of leisure," young wage earners expressed *both* the values associated with survival (for example, macho behavior) and a consumerist release from the discipline of school and work. Youth subcultures came and went, each in turn reacting to the style that preceded it; yet all shared this ambiguous mixture of working-class values and consumerism.[46]

While the street life of the English male youth gained the most attention, the female also developed her own style of leisure. The teeny-bopper culture of adolescent girls gathered in bedrooms surrounded by posters of rock icons and played rock music. Although the teeny-bopper might display herself in the highly demonstrative rock concert, she reaffirmed traditional sex roles in her retreat to same-sex socializing, passive gender roles, and fanaticizing.[47]

In both countries, the most characteristic feature of youth leisure from the mid-1950s was rock music. It was not only commercial and highly transient, but also a folk music. Rock was produced by youth themselves and reflected their lives, thus the popularity of "oldies," which evoked adolescent memories. What predated rock was the Tin-Pan-Alley or Music-Hall tradition of popular song. Such tunes not only remained popular far longer than rock, but were sung by sentimental ballad crooners with cross-generational appeal. While in the U.S., Frank Sinatra, and even Benny Goodman, attracted screaming young women to their concerts before the war, their sophisticated style quickly attracted adults as well.[48]

When rock emerged in 1954, it was a melange of a variety of popular musical styles as different as black American Rhythm and Blues and white Country and Western. Nevertheless, it was essentially a protest against the "lifelessness" of prevailing popular music. The first internationally successful hit, "Rock Around the Clock," was introduced in the film *Blackboard Jungle*, which dealt with the rebellion of urban youth. Elvis Presley, with his gyrating hips, long hair, and tight, outlandish clothes, represented both for adults and for teenagers the vitality and rebelliousness of youth. Rock dance styles also reflected youthful spontaneity by abandoning ballroom steps and substituting dances appropriate for an untrained youth. Some of these dances, as in the case of the Twist, was imitated by adults (1961).

Rock was, of course, closely associated with the mass media. With the advent of television in the early 1950s, radio lost audiences for network programming. Recorded rock music filled this vacuum (and, just as importantly), provided a vehicle for youth-oriented advertising. Disc jockeys, such as Alan Freed and "Wolfman Jack," identified with the youthful listener and were closely associated with the music. They were a radical departure from the authoritative voice of traditional radio announcers. About the same time, the inexpensive 45-RPM record appeared on the market to fit perfectly this new music culture. These records could be rapidly distributed, were inexpensive, and thus were easy for the young to collect; the teenager could play or reject them in an instant. The 33-RPM, long-playing record, which also emerged in the mid-1950s, did not fit this casual listening style because it required a longer commitment to an artist than most youths were willing to give. While originating in the United States, rock, of course, became an international entertainment absorbing the black Calypso and later the Reggae style; and, from 1962, dare we forget, the English sound of the Beatles, Rolling Stones, and Dave Clark Five supplanted the southern American style of early rock.[49]

In the 1950s, adults found it difficult to distinguish youth from delinquent culture, for teenage leisure often shaded toward criminality in street-corner lounging or (in America) in cruising by car and congregating at drive-in restaurants. In particular, adults feared that teenage movies, rock music, and comic books undermined parental authority. In the 1950s both J. Edgar Hoover, the conservative chief of the Federal Bureau of Investigation, and Frederic Wertham, the civil-rights advocate and psychologist, campaigned for the censorship of lurid comic books. While little came of such efforts, film makers responded to criticism that teenage films encouraged delinquency. They precensored story lines to guarantee that fictional lawbreakers were punished in the end. The middle-aged American band leader, Mitch Miller, condemned rock as "musical baby food; it is the worship of mediocrity, brought about by a passion for conformity." The title of the best-selling *The Shook Up Generation: Teen-Age Terror in Slum and Suburb,* by noted writer, Harrison Salisbury, sums up this attitude. At the heart of this anxiety was the fear that working-class values would penetrate (via rock and films) the middle-class teenage culture.[50]

At the same time, enterprising adults saw the potential of the youth entertainment market. In the 1950s, movies had to be tailored to youth because adults stayed at home to watch TV. Advertising moguls, like the American Eugene Gilbert, gushed about the profitability of youth leisure markets. By the end of the 1950s, he wrote popular magazine columns seeking to assuage adult anxieties regarding the crazes of their offspring. Moreover, despite the publicity given to Elvis (The Pelvis) Presley, surveys of youth during the height of his popularity in the late 1950s revealed that only about one-fifth declared him as their favorite singer; a majority preferred the clean-cut, born-again Christian, Pat Boone. A similar point could be made about Tommy Steele and Cliff Richards in Britain.[51]

By 1960, the great fear of teenage leisure had abated when a clearer distinction between youth and delinquent culture emerged. Often this relaxation of anxiety represented merely the discovery that the middle-class and working-class teenager remained in two cultural worlds. When middle-class youth embraced the relatively tame folk song and the "loveable moppets," anxious American parents were relieved. By the mid-70s, longer school attendance and decreased job opportunities reduced the spending money, and thus freedom, of English working-class youth.[52]

The threat of youth leisure had hardly ended, however. It reappeared in the cultural rebellion of the beats in the late 1950s, of hippies from the mid-1960s, and, slightly later, of feminists and the cultural left. At base, all of these movements had in common a rejection of suburban leisure culture and were rooted in the middle classes. Many contemporaries did not see them as transitional rebellion, an age-old response to the moratorium granted to some youth prior to the assumption of adult responsibilities; rather, they found a counterculture, "a definite challenge to the values and norms" of the status quo.[53]

The counterculture of the 1960s was far more individualistic than the gang culture of the working class of the 1950s (and later). Working-class youth focused on a definite space in the traditional social environment, pub, street, or sporting field, and they were constrained by the need to work within the traditional economy. By contrast, middle-class rebels lived in a more diffuse countercultural milieu. They attempted to create alternative institutions (communes, for example), which allowed the children of affluence to "drop out." At least for a time, they rejected family, school, traditional sex roles, and career, all traditional bastions of the status quo.[54]

This dissent emerged first among the beats in their coffee-house enclaves. The wandering existence of the beat hero, Jack Kerouac, and the cult center of San Francisco defined this rebellion from bureaucratic work and conventional family life. It was isolated to a tiny intelligentsia until the 1960s, when the baby boomers hit college campuses in America. Opposition to the Vietnam War and especially to conscription, which had long served to end the freedom of youth, was an important focus of the counterculture. Even though "deferments" protected college students temporarily from the military draft, the possibility of conscription was, for many youths, a gnawing anxiety and sensitized them to the threatened loss of personal freedom. This mood was captured in the popular musical, *Hair*.

Radical youth in the United States were often children of affluent, but liberal parents, who had imparted in them a critical attitude toward suburban culture. So did the satirical *Mad Magazine*, which many read as children. Their parents also encouraged racial tolerance and other liberal ideas, without necessarily acting on these principles. Radical youths felt guilty about their comfort and often rejected affluence as "unauthentic;" they sometimes embraced romantic notions about Black or working-class life. The counterculture rejected the dress codes of high-school for long hair and other unisex styles. Bohemian districts of big cities attracted hippie communities from about 1967, built around the defiant (because illegal) use of marijuana and other mind-altering drugs.[55] In 1970, there may have been 2,000 communes in the United States which attempted to live an alternative to the domesticated, commercial suburban culture of the majority. Many were rural; others involved more informal collective living in urban tenement apartments; some were politically oriented; others quasi-religious, often fueled by drugs.[56]

Countercultural youths enjoyed a freedom from adult economic and family responsibilities that continued into their late 20s or beyond. Perhaps this was only part of a long-term trend of extending the age when careers ended the experimentation and freedom of youth. Kenneth Keniston discovered a generation of the "uncommitted," youthful males insulated from (and fearful of) the professional lives of their fathers and nurtured to value creativity by their mothers. They resisted the male role of provider. Similarly, young women rejected the domesticity of their mothers. But surely also important to the counterculture was the moral opposition to the cultural conformism of the 1950s, as analyzed by David Riesman, Vance Packard, and Herbert Marcuse.[57]

Still, despite efforts of countercultural leaders in the 1960s to avoid commercial manipulation—cooptation as they called it, these rebels were deeply influenced by the suburban commercial culture from which they came. Hippies, far from being a "vanguard of a bloodless cultural revolution" or "fanatically alienated from the parental culture," in fact, expressed the individualistic values of middle-class society. And, if many scorned suburban commodities, most still embraced the goods of their own rock culture. Moreover, the 1960s youth culture perpetuated the class divisions of the adult world. When hippies embraced the "progressive" rock on the LP stereo record, they left the 45-RPM "singles" to the working classes. Seldom was the subordination of the female effectively challenged among the hippies any more than it was among the openly macho working-class subcultures. In any case, the counterculture sparked a reaction from both the adult middle class and working-class youth. This reaction helped to lay a groundwork for the conservatism of the 1970s and 1980s.[58]

In the 20th century, pressures toward a leisure consensus never succeeded in overcoming the fissures of class and generation. A blend of Victorian domesticity and middle-class consumer culture failed to take hold in the ethnic communities and working classes of either country, despite the affluence of the postwar generation and homogenization of car and suburb culture. Still, the autonomy of the bar community and working-class neighborhood was hardly immune to the corrosive impact of powerful media and new leisure technology. A similar pattern fits the history of 20th-century youth culture. It was at once a rebellion against received culture and parental authority and an affirmation of consumerist values of parents. Although for a time, youth gained independence from parental control and economic responsibility, their leisure seldom challenged the status quo or it did so ineffectively. The innovations of the American collegiate in the 1920s probably facilitated adjustment rather than resistance to a new business and family culture. Even the American greasers and English Teddy Boys were rebels without a cause. Still, as shown by the creative, if ephemeral and even self-destructive play of the 60s counterculture, leisure could be a site for social experimentation and dissent.

14

Conclusion:
Looking Forward from the Recent Past

History cannot really be expected to point to the future. Its study can only suggest trends, which are often conflicting, and never is it beyond the realm of human decision to change course. This is true also of the future of leisure; it is not simply an extrapolation from the past or present. In this concluding chapter, I offer, instead, a few trends already evident in the 1960s that suggest future problems and options.

A Harried Leisure Class

One major theme of this book has been that the sheer growth in leisure time has not been the simple by-product of increased productivity. Powerful political, economic, and cultural forces have biased the distribution of the fruits of economic growth toward consumption and investment rather than toward time away from work. We saw this trend in our investigation of the quest for time in the 19th century (Chapter 6) and in the frustrations of leisure advocates in the early 20th century (Chapter 11). In the generation after World War II, the tendency for leisure time to lag behind consumption and economic expansion has, if anything, widened.[1]

From the 1960s, time available for recreation has declined in many families. Since then, the dual-job family has increasingly become the norm. Of course, for many women, entry into the workforce was an opportunity for a meaningful career or, at least, a degree of economic independence. Yet, for others, it was more a response to declining real incomes, especially as housing and (especially in America) health costs rose sharply in the 1970s. The traditional job (mostly held by married men) no longer provided a family wage sufficient to support house, wife, and children. The net effect of the dual-income household was often a drastic reduction of disposable time available per couple. Fewer hours per week for either domestic (and child care) work and for personal activities was one consequence of the two-income family. This entailed a "domestic speedup" as the traditional realm of personal life, family care, and leisure was crammed into shorter periods of the day. The problem of time, even within a 40- or 35-hour work week, was exacerbated by the spatial division of work and home. Time lost to commuting, traditionally an often unpleasant but perhaps bearable sacrifice of male breadwinners, was increasingly the fate of women, too. This situation combined with the experience of shift work, often at different periods for husband and wife, compounded the harried lives of the dual-job family.[2]

Naturally, families adapted to this change by a vast array of shortcuts—eating out far more, a return to catalog shopping, greater tolerance of messy houses, daycare centers for fewer children, and or even rejection of family responsibilities. The so-called traditional gender division of time (really a 19th-century invention), based on the marketplace for men and domesticity for women, has been seriously disrupted. Just what will be the effects of the two-income family and how individuals will adjust to it is, as yet, unclear.

The dual-wage family was not merely an adaptation to economic change. As early as 1898, the feminist Charlotte Perkins Gilman argued that equal participation in public life was essential to free individual development and true mutual love between couples. As long as women were relegated to the status of a domesticated "leisure class," performing inefficiently childcare and housework that best should be assigned to paid specialists, women would always be man's dependent.[3] Gilman's powerful idea was largely ignored until the second half of the century when it was revived by a second wave of feminists. In any case, the position of homemaker as organizer of family leisure, has increasingly become a privilege of the wealthy or a costly option of the culturally conservative.

Yet not only has Gilman's dream of economic equality been imperfectly realized, but the problem of domestic work has been hardly solved. The two-job family has yet to create a new division of work and leisure based on sexual equality. Employed women continue to do the vast majority of housework and childcare, depriving themselves of the afterwork leisure time enjoyed by many men. While public domestic and childcare services may have reduced this burden for some employed women, few would argue that such facilities have replaced the labor of the traditional homemaker. New home-based entertainments, video tapes as well as other electronic media, may well have resolved some of the logistic and time constraints of the harried two-job family, but these changes could hardly be said to satisfy needs for more active exploration of leisure options. Despite the many and often creative maneuvers of families to resolve these problems, they remain and they will probably evoke new public policy and market responses in the future.

Play for the Seniors

If the recent past suggests problems for those obliged to balance work, family, and play, it points also to new leisure opportunities for those beyond such cares. Retirement for the masses is a recent phenomenon. In the 18th and 19th centuries, it was a privilege of the very successful or idle rich. Increased longevity, improved health in late life, and pensions have recently made retirement possible for the majority. In the United States, in the first half of this century, life expectancy from the age of 20 increased by 8.4 years, which partially explains the doubling of the percentage of population over 60 (8.1 percent by 1950). A 60-year-old white female could expect 18.6 more years of life at midcentury (2.8 years longer than white men and 3.5 years more than nonwhite males). The aged in Britain likewise doubled between 1920 and 1970 to over 16 percent of the population.[4]

But changes in public policy explain why these additional years of life were increasingly spent in retirement rather than work. The American Social Security Act of 1935 and the British state pension program which began in 1908 provided (along with private pensions) a minimum income for retirement. From the 1930s, many employers imposed mandatory retirement, which policymakers believed would increase business efficiency, provide jobs for the young, and create a new consumer market in a new leisure class of the elderly. As a result, far fewer held jobs until illness or death.[5]

These trends may have made old age more secure, but they did not answer the question of what the elderly would do with life beyond work, especially when so many of these people had been committed to the work ethic. The solutions offered ranged from calls for only a gradual disengagement from jobs to replacing employment with well-planned and purposive leisure as a "moral equivalent of work." Groups like the American Association of Retired Persons (founded in 1955) propagated the idea of an independent, informed, and leisured retirement. It was not to be a brief period of rest before death but a new life stage of fulfillment and compensation for work, an opportunity for leisure unfettered by geographical or time constraints.[6]

Of course, most of the elderly continued to live in their old neighborhoods and nearby their children; as late as 1950, 45 percent of American widows lived with an adult child. In the 1950s, aged Americans were only half as likely to move as was the younger population. The same pattern applied to Britain, yet a small minority had begun a trend toward migrating to warmer (and sometimes less expensive) regions far from old jobs and family. With no economic responsibilities tying them to the "frostbelt" or city, they were free to pursue a life in a more comfortable climate. Since the 1920s, the elderly had begun a trek to Florida. By 1950, almost 22 percent of the population of St. Petersburg was over 65 years old, about three times the national rate. With the retirement of the veteran of World War II in the 1980s, a uniquely affluent cohort began to change the meaning of old age. This group, which benefitted from often generous pensions, private assets, and improved health care, had the resources to retire even before age 65. Affluent Britons also moved to the southern coasts, hoping to make the annual seaside holiday a permanent way of life.[7]

The appeal of improved climate and freedom from the problems of the industrial environment is self-evident. But the apparent abandonment of family by the elderly was rather harder to explain, given their tradition of domesticity. One answer is the segmentation of generations, a trend evident early in the 20th century as the young, middle-aged, and old peeled off into distinct peer cultures. Moreover, many of the old experienced an "empty nest," as adult children moved far from home and as smaller and delayed families meant the retired had fewer opportunities to play the role of grandparent. In any case, children were far more likely to move away than were their parents. Entitlements (like pensions and even welfare) provided substitutes for the traditional reciprocity between generations. In the U.S., the proportion of the elderly that lived with children declined from 60 percent in 1900 to scarcely 9 percent in 1970. Still, the reality of elder migration was more complex. Many were "snowbirds," seasonal visitors to the trailer parks, apartments, and condos of Florida or the American Southwest, spending warm months near family. And migrants were predominantly the most affluent and healthy of the elderly. More typical were residents in multipurpose geriatric centers near family and old neighborhoods.[8]

Still, a brief look at sunbelt or seaside retirement is worth our trouble for it may be suggestive about the future of leisure. Sun City, Arizona, is a good example of a desire to equate retirement with leisure. Dating from only 1960, this planned suburb in the American Southwestern desert promised maintenance-free housing and a community rich in golf courses, recreation centers, imported entertainment, churches, and shopping malls, with easy access to the boom city of Phoenix. By prohibiting permanent residence to anyone under the age of 50, Sun City people were assured a community of shared values. It was a peer culture, similar to that which many retirees knew when they were young. Municipal restrictions also liberated residents of Sun City from industrial blight and school taxes. Not only did they avoid sharing the responsibilities of urban life (like many suburbanites did), but they evaded the problems of the younger generation. Few residents had difficulty justifying this, for they had already "paid their dues" to society.

One observer rather uncharitably labelled Sun City "a resident Disneyland for old folks." Sun City offered an alternative to a retirement of stagnation; it provided an active life with old friends and people of similar tastes. The developer was especially successful when he advertised Sun City as a resort or vacation community; yet what brought people there was its suburban quality, which offered not only a status house, but a "hometown" feeling. The developer encouraged buyers to refer neighbors or friends back home to join them. The social and even regional homogeneity of residents encouraged a shared vision of active retirement, making aging more satisfying for many.[9] In many ways, then, retirement (at least in this privileged form) was a nearly perfect expression of the modernization of leisure. Play was radically separated from work, shared in a peer culture, and built around a suburban base of wholesome consumption.

An Alternative to Suburbs: Return to the Cities

A very different recent trend is the rejection of suburban familialism. Since the late 1960s, a relatively small affluent group has participated in the restoration of central-city neighborhoods and the refurbishment of their cultural and recreational amenities. This process, somewhat misnamed gentrification, was a product of demographic, economic, and ultimately cultural change. The new urbanites were seldom "returnees" from the suburb. More often, with increased affluence, they moved from modest urban districts to new (or often restored) fashionable districts, where they bought homes and flats and sometimes refurbished them. The entry of the post-war baby boomers in the housing market accelerated this process. So did the trend toward later marriage, double-income households, delayed and reduced arrival of children, and dramatic increases in divorce rates.[10]

The Young Upwardly Mobile Urban Professional (Yuppie) and the Double Income No Kids (Dinks) were surely stereotypes, but rooted in reality. People who fit this profile were naturally less interested in access to quality schools and playgrounds for children (a common advantage of the suburb); they also were willing to trade off living space, backyard patios, and two-car garages for easy access to the urbane night life, high culture, and specialty shopping that was missing from suburbs. Gentrification provided an alternative to the suburbanites' often frustrating effort to balance the demands of work, family, and leisure. Urban residence was a partial adaptation to the time pressures of dual-job households. City living reduced commuting time and provided access to public dining and numerous other services made necessary by the lack of a homemaker.[11]

This was a culturally varied world, comprising not only yuppie districts but also the hippie ghettos that survived into the 1970s in university towns and cities. Yet both groups rejected rigid sex roles and the separation of work and play. The decision not to move to suburbia was the choice of a minority but reflected a significant cultural milieu. Some American children raised with "populux" and educated in the counterculture of the 1960s reacted against the homogeneity of suburban culture. Both men and women rejected the cult of domesticity. If some women resisted (at least for a time) the constraints of children, men also bolted against the limited role of the provider. The avoidance of these traditional roles had been expressed by the lifestyle of the "playboy" in the 1950s as well as by that of the beatnik and later the hippie. Even those urbanites who embraced marriage and eventually parenting sometimes sought an alternative to suburbia. The city, as a center of ethnic and cultural diversity, was treasured by this minority, even if that meant primarily a sanitized ideal of exotic restaurants, specialty stores, and quaint architecture rather than the crime and chaos of the traditional "dangerous classes."[12]

A new urban economy made all of this possible. Clean financial and commercial businesses sometimes replaced "smokestack" industries near city centers. Municipal governments attempted to revitalize selected central city districts in order to attract affluent residents and customers.

However, gentrification can hardly be called the major social trend of the recent past. Not only did the new urbanites not reverse suburbanization in the 1970s, but they inhabited only highly selected neighborhoods: the Washington Square district in New York City, Georgetown in Washington, DC, or Canonbury near London, for example. The homeless and racial minorities, as well as neighborhoods of the older white working class, surely were as important to the social geography of the city of the 1970s and 1980s. Finally, it is not clear whether these gentrified societies will remain unchanged as the young city-dwellers age, have families, and perhaps move to the suburbs.[13]

Still, this group, along with the cosmopolitan suburban affluent, were the principal constituents of the revival of the "pleasure city." In the 1960s, new freeways and improved rapid transit made the city's leisure services accessible to the suburbanite. The industrial city had long been changing into a consumption center. In fact, major metropoles like London and New York City had never been production centers; their principal attractions had been commerce and leisure. In the 1920s, New York offered as many as 32,000 clubs and speakeasies despite prohibition; white tourists and businessmen found excitement in Harlem haunts like the Cotton Club; the skyscraper offered the thrill of the bird's eye vista; and the "Great White" light of nighttime Broadway was an attraction in itself in the 1920s. The same, of course, was true of Piccadilly Circus in London. Museums and historic districts provided tourists with a convenient, if condensed and often artificial, glimpse at art and history.[14]

In the 1960s and 1970s, urban renewal brought neighborhood revival and the building of downtown cultural buildings. Lincoln Center in New York, initiated in 1955 by a consortium of wealthy backers and municipal planners, became, by the mid-1960s, a multipurpose complex for the performing arts, dining, and specialty shopping. It was the first major example of many such cultural renewal efforts in American cities. Public support for the arts grew significantly in this period. The National Endowment for the Arts increased from 2.5 to almost 150 million dollars from 1966 to 1980. Between 1965 and 1975, the number of professional theaters grew from 25 to 101; opera companies increased from 23 to 43; and orchestras expanded from 58 to 103. Paralleling these American trends was the building of London's South Bank complex of cultural facilities.[15]

In both countries, central-city shopping districts were refurbished and, in the cold climates of the American north, indoor downtown malls were constructed. Such revived districts attracted investors to build luxury condominiums and townhouses, often in imitation of 18th- and 19th-century styles. In some ways, these efforts were patterned after the Baroque idea of the walking city with its townhouses, enclosed parks, theaters, coffee houses, and specialty shops. Reformers criticized these urban cultural districts for their tendency to displace poor and elderly residents and for their isolation from and indifference to deteriorating neighborhoods that surrounded them. The high culture of the performing arts and museums remained the preserve of the affluent and well educated. For example, a survey of American audiences in the 1970s suggests that from 41 percent (of museum patrons) to 65 percent (of ballet audiences) were college graduates compared to 14 percent of the general population. And even if there was a trend toward a broadening of audience, high culture remained largely the preserve of an elite, creating a self-perpetuating culture.[16] Still, these facilities provided an alternative to suburban life and attracted tourist income to cities with declining economic bases in industry.

Concluding Remarks

We have come a long way and have covered many topics in this book and, unfortunately have neglected others. This volume has been about societies of leisure and how modern technology, economic organization, and public policy transformed them. We encountered a variety of types of play: traditional (both popular and elite), reforming, and commercial. These complex and diverse orientations toward leisure were sometimes in conflict. But over the course of the 19th and 20th centuries, they often were fused by the market. This history was not simply a specific form of the modernization process, a shaping of leisure by the inexorable trends of industrialization and rationalization. Rather, it was a far more complex history of people and processes.

While traditional forms of leisure had been in decline since the eighteenth century, they survived and reappeared often in unexpected places, in riots at football games, in the pale reflection of pseudo-baroque housing for the rich, and in the glitzy world of the seaside resort. The reformer's quest for a new standard of work and leisure helped both to intensify labor and to create a familial focus to recreation. It informed policymakers in defining "permissible pleasure" and in regulating and sometimes in domesticating popular leisure, creating, in general, a less violent culture. But their efforts to reshape the the people (and the elite) in their own image was never totally successful. Moreover, the reformers' dreams were radically transformed by the commercialization of leisure in the 19th-century city and in the 20th-century suburb. Impresarios of pleasure "improved" popular entertainments to attract the rational recreationists of the middle classes while "popularizing" the domestic culture of

Victorian reformers. The mass demand for free time gradually overcame the prejudice of elites, whose fear of popular leisure was rooted as much in hostility to working-class pastimes as it was in economic considerations.

Yet leisure time did not grow with the economy in the 19th and 20th centuries. Its expansion was episodic, the result of infrequent and hard-fought movements for freedom from work. And, despite the enormous economic gains of the mid-20th century, leisure time actually shrank for many. The efforts of adults to shape the free time of the young met frustration again and again as the young, ever sensitive to social change, created new leisure styles, and the leisure entrepreneur satisfied their quest for autonomy.

What had emerged by the mid-20th-century was a contradictory phenomenon of individualized leisure organized on a mass scale by a pleasure industry. This surely was an achievement of the "hidden persuaders" of capitalism, but this culture was also a product of people's felt needs. It was a rich and contradictory mixture of traditional, reformist, and commercial recreation.   Twentieth-century leisure was a continuously changing blend, the product of economic and technological factors, but also the fruit of individual and social choice.

Notes

Chapter One

1. For analyses of the significance of the decline of work on leisure see, for example, D. Bell, *The Coming of Post-Industrial Society* (New York, 1973); C. Jenkins and B. Sherman, *The Leisure Shock* (Dublin, 1981); A. Gorz, *Farewell to the Working Class* (London, 1982); and A. Toffler, *Previews and Prophesies* (New York, 1984). A critical review of this literature is in K. Kumar, *Prophecy and Progress* (London, 1978).

2. S.B. Linder, *The Harried Leisure Class* (New York, 1978); F. Best, *Flexible Life Scheduling* (New York, 1980).

3. Major proponents of these three positions are S. de Grazia, *Of Time, Work, and Leisure* (New York, 1967); J. Clark and C. Critcher, *The Devil Makes Work: Leisure in Capitalist Britain* (London, 1985); and J. Dumazadier, *Sociology of Leisure* (New York, 1974).

4. See, for example, J.P. Donajgrodski, ed., *Social Control in Nineteenth Century Britain* (London, 1977) as well as numerous sources in Chapter 8.

5. Note, for example, S. Parker, *Leisure and Work* (London, 1983); M. Young and P. Willmott, *The Symmetrical Family* (London, 1975); and M. Kaplan, *Leisure: Theory and Practice* (New York, 1975).

Chapter Two

1. J. Dumazedier, *Sociology of Leisure* (New York, 1984), chap. 1; for quotation, L. Stone, *The Family, Sex and Marriage in England, 1500-1800* (New York, 1979), p. 88.

2. G. Langenfeld, *The Historic Origins of the Eight Hours Day* (Stockholm, 1954), chap. 1; P. Laslett, *The World We Have Lost* (London, 1984), p. 22.

3. T. Harrisson and C. Madge, "A Slight Case of Totemism," in *Britain, A Mass-Observation Study* (London, 1939). For the creation of tradition, see E. Hobsbawm and T. Ranger, *Inventions of Tradition* (Cambridge, 1983).

4. D. Gerhard, *Old Europe: A Study of Continuity, 1000-1800* (New York, 1981), pp. 57-64, especially; F. Braudel, *Capitalism and Material Life, 1400-1800* (New York, 1973), "Introduction."

5. F. Braudel, *The Structures of Everyday Life: The Limits of the Possible* (New York, 1979), pp. 334-384 and 416-435; J. Gimpel, *The Medieval Machine* (New York, 1976), chap. 1 and 7; C. Cipolla, *Before the Industrial Revolution* (New York, 1976), p. 74.

6. Cipolla, *Industrial Revolution*, pp. 120-121 and 198-204.

7. Dumazedier, *Sociology*, p. 34; G. Bouthoul, *La Durée du travail et l 'utilisation des loisir* (Paris, 1924), p. 80; M.A. Bienefeld, *Working Hours in British Industry, An Economic History* (London, 1972), p. 15; H. Hauser, *Ouvriers du temps passé* (Paris, 1927), pp. 78-81.

8. Cipolla, *Industrial Revolution*, p. 66; I. Pinchbeck and M. Hewitt, *Children in English Society,* vol. II (London, 1973), p. 406.

9. Laslett, *World,* chap. 2; Bienefeld, *Working Hours,* p. 19; Dumazedier, *Sociology,* p. 34; Cipolla, *Industrial Revolution,* p. 90.

10. Fascinating details are in A.R. Wright, *British Calendar Customs* (London, 1936-1940), 3 vol.; R. Muchembled, *Popular Culture and Elite Culture in France, 1400-1750* (Baton Rough, 1985), pp. 49-61; and G. Homans, *English Villagers of the Thirteenth Century* (New York, 1960), pp. 353-381.

11. C. Caraccioli, *An Historical Account of Stourbridge* (Cambridge, 1773), pp. 20-21, quotation cited in R. Malcolmson, *Popular Recreations in English Society* (Cambridge, UK, 1973), p. 21; W. Addison, *English Fairs and Markets* (London, 1953), pp. 95-225; E. Shorter, *The Making of the Modern Family* (New York, 1975), pp. 128-137 and 340-352.

12. T.H. Breen, "Horses and Gentlemen: The Cultural Significance of Gambling among the Gentry of Virginia," in E. Pleck and J. Pleck, eds., *The American Man,* (New York, 1980), pp. 77-107; J. Findlay, *A People of Chance: Gambling in American Society from Jamestown to Las Vegas* (New York, 1986), pp. 11-44; A. Cole, "The Tempo of Mercantile Life in Colonial America," *Business History Review* 33 (Fall, 1959): 277-299.

13. A. Franklin, *La Vié privee d' autrefois* 5 (Paris, 1889):125-126.

14. This phenomenon was first and most fully developed in E.A. Furniss, *The Position of Labor in a System of Nationalism* (New York, 1919), pp. 128-134 and 233-235. See also M. Berg, et al., *Manufacture in Town and Country Before the Factory* (New York, 1983), pp. 162-167, especially.

15. Bienefeld, *Working Hours*, pp. 15-19; J. Fourastie, *The Causes of Wealth* (New York, 1960), pp. 171-173; C. K. Dobson, *Masters and Journeymen, A Prehistory of the Industrial Revolution* (London, 1980), pp. 94-95.

16. P. Aries, *Centuries of Childhood* (New York, 1962), chap. 4; J. Strutt, *The Sports and Pastimes of the People of England* (London, 1838), pp. 302-303.

17. E. Le Roy Ladurie, *Montaillou: The Promised Land of Error* (New York, 1979), pp. 251-262; K. Wrightson, "Alehouses, Order and Reformation in Rural England, 1590-1660," in E. Yeo and S. Yeo, eds., *Popular Culture and Class Conflict, 1590-1914* (Brighton, 1981), pp. 1-28; L. Roubin, "Chambrettes de Provence, Un exemple de Club Villageois Mediterranéen," in E. Gargan, ed., *The Wolf and the Lamb: Popular Culture in France* (Saratoga, CA, 1977), pp. 101-109.

18. Shorter, *Family*. pp. 70-71 and 124-126; J. Flandrin, *Families in Former Times* (New York, 1979), pp. 105-110.

19. Braudel, *Capitalism*, pp. 197-212; W.H. Lewis, *The Splendid Century: Life in the France of Louis XIV* (New York, 1957), pp. 37-67; Flandrin, *Family*, pp. 112-140.

20. Quoted by Laslett, *World*, p. 3.

21. D. Roche, "Work, Fellowship and Some Economic Realities in 18th Century France," in S. Kaplan and C. Koepp, eds., *Work in France: Representations, Meaning, Organization, and Practice* (Ithaca, 1986), pp. 54-73.

22. B. Franklin, *Autobiography of Benjamin Franklin and Selections from His Other Writings* (New York, 1932), pp. 49-50.

23. Shorter, *Family*, pp. 126-128; Malcolmson, *Recreations*, pp. 5-36.

24. S. De Grazia, *Of Time, Work, and Leisure* (New York, 1964), pp. 14-16.

25. G.C. Coulton, *Social Life in Britain From the Conquest to the Reformation* (Cambridge, 1956), pp. 387-404; R. Mandrou, *Introduction to Modern France, 1500-1640* (London, 1975), pp. 160-162. Two especially rich sources are T. Wright, *A History of Domestic Manners and Sentiments in England during the Middle Ages* (London, 1862), pp. 175-226 and 306-315 and Strutt, *Sports*, pp. 24-47, 11-149 and 305-338.

26. Braudel, *Structures*, pp. 311-334.

27. B. Castiglione, *The Book of the Courtier* (New York, 1959), pp. 11, 29, 34, 38, 43, 70, 78, 104, 139, 207-211, and 348.

28. W. Baker, *Sports in the Western World* (Totowa, N.J., 1982), pp. 42-57; R. C. Clepham, *The Tournament: Its Periods and Phases* (London, 1919); F. H. Cripps-Day, *The History of the Tournament in England and France* (London, 1918, reprinted in 1980).

29. C. Hill, *Society and Puritanism in Pre-Revolutionary England*, 2nd ed. (New York, 1967), pp. 183-187.

30. Hill, *Puritanism*, pp. 69 and 193; D. Brailsford, *Sport and Society: Elizabeth to Anne* (London, 1969), pp. 101-103; M. Walzer, *The Revolution of the Saints: A Study in the Origins of Radical Politics* (Cambridge, MA, 1965), p. 211.

31. F. Douglass, *The Life of Frederick Douglass* (New American Library edition, New York, 1968), pp. 84-85.

32. This absenteeism in the early part of the week was not all consumed in play nor was it exclusively the privilege of the skilled artisan. For example, miners (especially in coal) seldom worked a full six days in summer. The demand for coal was low during the warm months and working a full week would only lower prices. Then, many miners appeared at the pit only on Tuesdays or even Wednesday. They used their spare time to farm small plots or to tend to chickens or other livestock. Even when the mine owners wanted them to work, miners would give preference to their gardens. D.A. Reid, "The Decline of St. Monday, 1176-1876," *Past and Present* 38 (1967): pp. 56-97; Jeffrey Kaplow, "La Fin de la Saint-Lundi: Etude sur le Paris ouvrier au xixe siécle," *Le Temps libre* 2 (1981): pp. 107-118; E. Hopkins, "Working Hours and Conditions during the Industrial Revolution, A Re-appraisal," *Economic History Review* 25 (February, 1982): pp. 52-57;

33. M. R. Smith, *Harper's Ferry Armory* (Cambridge, MA, 1981), chap. 1.

34. A.R. Wright, *Customs*, vol. 1, pp. 6-23; Shorter, *Family*, pp. 129-135 and 218-226; P. Burke, *Popular Culture in Early Modern Europe* (New York, 1978), pp. 200-204; N. Z. Davis, *Society and Culture in Early Modern France* (New York, 1975), chap. 4.

35. Burke, *Culture*, pp. 178-204; E. L. Ladurie, *Carnival in Romans* (New York, 1979), pp. 305-324.

Chapter Three

1. P. Miller, *The New England Mind: The Seventeenth Century* (Cambridge, MA, 1954), p. 44.

2. J. Calvin, *Institutes of the Christian Religion* vol. I (Philadelphia, 1967), p. 725; W. Penn, *No Cross, No Crown*, quoted in F. Tolles, *Quakers and the Atlantic Culture* (New York, 1960), p. 60.

3. W. Peden, ed., *Testimony Against Profane Customs* (Charlesville, VA, 1953), p. 31. See also M. Weber, *The Protestant Ethic and the Spirit of Capitalism* (New York, 1965).

4. Calvin, *Institutes,* vol. II, p. 1232. See also M. Walzer, *The Revolution of the Saints* (New York, 1968), chap. 1 and 6.

5. Miller, *Mind,* pp. 15-16.

6. D. Brailsford, *Sport and Society: Elizabeth to Anne* (London, 1969), p. 54.

7. Bunyan, *Pilgrim's Progress,* (New York, 1968), pp. 84-85; P.Miller, *The Puritans* (New York, 1938), pp. 410-413; Brailsford, *Sport,* pp. 128-132. See also C. Hill, *Society and Puritanism in Pre-Revolutionary England* (New York, 1967), pp. 180-190.

8. P. Burke, *Popular Culture in Early Modern Europe* (New York, 1978), pp. 207-243. See also R. Muchembled, *Popular Culture and Elite Culture in France, 1400-1750* (Baton Rouge, 1985), pp. 49-61.

9. Hill, *Puritanism,* pp. 124-138.

10. Walzer, *Saints,* pp. 209-211.

11. R. Tawney, *Religion and the Rise of Capitalism* (New York, 1963), pp. 191-192. See also F. Tolles, *Meeting House and Counting House: The Quaker Merchants of Colonial Philadelphia, 1682-1763* (New York, 1947).

12. W. Solberg, *Redeem the Time: The Puritan Sabbath in Early America* (Cambridge, MA, 1977), chap. 2-3; J. Young, *Sixteenth-Century England* (London, 1984), chap. 12.

13. Hill, *Puritanism,* pp. 145-160.

14. T. Shepard, *Theses Sabbaticae: Or, The Doctrine of the Sabbath* (London, 1649), p. 4, cited in Solberg, *Time*, p. 2.

15. Calvin, *Institutes*, pp. 339-340.

16. Hill, *Puritanism*, p. 174.

17. J. Harland, ed., *The Lancashire Lieutenancy under the Tudors and Stuarts*, vol. II (London, 1859), p. 218, cited in Hill, *Puritanism*, p. 184.

18. M. James, *Social Problems and Policy during the Puritan Revolution* (London, 1930), pp. 288-293; Brailsford, *Sport*, pp. 136-146.

19. J. Evelyn, *A Character of England* (London, 1659), cited in Hill, *Puritanism*, p. 216. See also Mass Observation, *Meet Yourself on Sunday* (London, 1947).

20. Hill, *Puritanism*, p. 216. For details of life in the Plymouth colony, see W. Bradford, *Of Plymouth Plantation* (New York, 1948, or other editions of this classic by an early governor).

21. P. Carroll, *Puritanism and the Wilderness* (New York, 1969), pp. 65-87.

22. Miller, *Puritans*, pp. 392-393; F. R. Dulles, *America Learns to Play* (New York, 1940), chap. 1; Solberg, *Time*, pp. 112-114; A. Earle, *Customs and Fashions in Old New England* (London, 1893), chap. 9; G. Myers, *Ye Olden Blue Laws* (New York, 1921).

23. S. Sewell, *Dairy* (New York, 1927), pp. 209 and 255-256; Miller, *Puritans*, pp. 91-93; Earle, *Customs*, chap. 10.

24. R. Baxter, *A Christian Directory* (London, 1678), p. 391, cited in Brailsford, *Sport*, p. 148.

25. Brailsford, *Sport*, pp. 128-135; A. Guttman, *A Whole New Ball Game* (Chapel Hill, NC, 1988), chap. 3.

26. F. de la Rochefoucauld, *La Vie en Angleterre au xviiie siécle* (Paris, 1945, orig. 1784), pp. 79-80, cited in J. Flandrin, *Families in Former Times* (Cambridge, 1979), p. 168. See also L. Stone, *The Family, Sex and Marriage in England, 1500-1800* (New York, 1977), chap. 5 and 8.

27. Brailsford, *Sport*, pp. 101-121; C. Whitefield, ed., *Annalia Dubrensia*, (London, 1962), "Introduction."

28. Hill, *Puritanism*, p. 192.

29. Thomas Morton, "New English Canaan," in P. Force, ed. *Tracts and Other Papers*, (Washington, 1937); W. Bradford, *Of Plymouth Plantation* (New York, 1967), pp. 204-210. See also C. F. Adams, *Three Episodes of Massachusetts History* (New York, 1965), chap. 11-15. For the French case, see R. Isherwood, *Farce and Fantasy: Popular Entertainment in Eighteenth-Century Paris* (Oxford, 1986).

30. R. Porter, *English Society in the Eighteenth Century* (London, 1982), chap. 6; J.H. Plumb, *Commercialization of Leisure in Eighteenth Century England* (Reading, 1973); I. Watt, *The Rise of the Novel* (London, 1957).

31. T. Carlyle, *Past and Present* (London, 1843), p. 239.

32. B. Franklin, *The Autobiography and Selections from His Other Writing* (New York, 1932), pp. 85-89 and 231.

33. Franklin, *Autobiography*, p. 93.

34. D. Landes, *Revolution in Time: Clocks and the Making of the Modern World* (Cambridge, MA, 1983); D. Rodgers, *The Work Ethic in Industrial America, 1850-1920* (Chicago, 1974), chap. 1.

35. D. Hempton, *Methodism and Politics in British Society 1750-1850* (Stanford, 1984), p. 27. See also J. Rule, "Methodism, Popular Beliefs and Village Culture in Cornwall, 1800-50," in R.D. Storch, ed., *Popular Culture and Custom in Nineteenth-Century England* (London, 1982); and E.P. Thompson, "Patrician Society, Plebian Culture," *Journal of Social History* 7 (Winter, 1974): 382-405.

36. B. Caceres, *Loisirs et travail du moyen age á nos jours* (Paris, 1973), pp. 125-151.

37. Rodgers, *Work Ethic*, chap. 1.

Chapter Four

1. K. Thomas, "Work and Leisure in Pre-Industrial Society," *Past and Present* 29 (1964, 98-115); J.M. Golby and A.W. Purdue, *The Civilization of the Crowd: Popular Culture in England, 1750-1900* (London, 1984), pp. 20-24.

2. For general sources on British and American preindustrial leisure, see subsequent notes. For material on slave leisure, note especially E. Genovese, *Roll Jourdan, Roll* (New York, 1974), pp. 566-584.

3. R. Malcolmson, *Popular Recreations in English Society* (Cambridge, UK, 1973), pp. 36-37. See also F. Magoun, *History of Football from the Beginnings to 1871* (Bochum, W. Germany, 1938), for example.

4. W. Hone, *Year Book*, (London, 1832), col. 1525, cited in Malcolmson, *Recreations*, pp. 43-44; C. Cone, *Hounds in the Morning: Selections from the Sporting Magazine, 1792-1836* (Lexington, KY, 1981), pp. 144-164; J. Strutt, *The Sports and Pastimes of the People of England* (London, 1838), pp. 80-84.

5. See, for example, J. Cumming, *Runners and Walkers: A Nineteenth Century Sports Chronicle* (Chicago, 1981).

6. Cited in Cone, *Hounds*, p. 137.

7. Z. von Uffenbach, *Travels of von Uffenbach* (London, 1710), pp. 48-49, cited in Malcolmson, *Recreations*, p. 50. See also A.S. Turberville, ed., *Johnson's England: An Account of the Life and Manners of His Age* (Oxford, 1933), pp. 372-375.

8. H. Misson, *Memoirs and Observations* (London, 1719), pp. 24-27.

9. Strutt, *Sports*, pp. 278-280.

10. J. Findlay, *People of Chance: Gambling in American Society from Jamestown to Las Vegas* (New York, 1986) p. 23; F. R. Dulles, *Americans at Play, A History of Popular Recreation, 1607-1940* (Gloucester, MA, 1963), pp. 34-35; P. Alexander Bruce, *Social Life in Virginia of the Seventeenth Century* (Richmond, VA, 1907), pp. 209-210; J. Carson, *Colonial Virginians at Play* (Williamsburg, VA, 1965), pp. 151-152; C.M. Andrews, *The Colonial Period of American History* (New Haven, 1964), pp. 115-116; E. Morgan, *The Puritan Dilemma* (Boston, 1963), pp. 9-10; M. de Chastellaux, *Travels in North American* (New York, 1827), p. 293.

11. Tuberville, *Johnson's England*, pp. 370-372 and Cone, *Hounds*, pp. 8-9 and 47-48.

12. R. Longrigg, *The English Squire and His Sport* (New York, 1979), pp. 99-178; Cone, *Hounds*, pp. 5-10 and 71-82; N. Cox, *The Gentleman's Recreation* (London, 1973; originally published, 1677), pp. 1-158; R. Carr, *English Fox Hunting: A History* (London, 1976); J. F.C. Harrison, *The Early Victorians 1832-1851* (New York, 1971), pp. 92-100.

13. M. de Rochefoucauld, *A Frenchman in England* (London, 1784), pp. 52-76; Cone, *Hounds*, pp. 7-8 and 71-83.

14. Bruce, *Social Life*, pp. 218-227; Dulles, *Americans*, p. 71 (quotation); M. Chavalier, *Society, Manners, and Politics in the United States* (Boston, 1839), pp. 472-473. See also P. Verney, *Animals in Peril* (Provo, UT, 1979).

15. Bruce, *Social Life*, chap. 17; quotation cited in Findlay, *Chance*, pp. 22-23; J. Dizikes, *Sportsmen and Gamesmen* (Boston, 1981), p. 14; T.H. Breen, "Horses and Gentlemen: The Cultural Significance of Gambling among the Gentry of Virginia," *William and Mary Quarterly* 34 (April, 1977), pp. 239-275; J. Hervey, *Racing and Breeding in America and the Colonies* (London, 1931), pp. 1-11; Carson, *Colonial Virginians*, pp. 108-09.

16. Lewis Mumford, *The City in History* (New York, 1961), pp. 371-377.

17. R. Porter, *English Society in the Eighteenth Century* (London, 1982), pp. 242-250; Turberville, *Johnson's England*, pp. 176-216.

18. Mumford, *City*, pp. 382-387.

19. J. Flandrin, *Families in Former Times* (Cambridge, 1979), pp. 92-111; P. Aries, *Centuries of Childhood* (New York, 1962), pp. 339-410.

20. Turberville, *Johnson's England*, pp. 336-361.

21. Turberville, *Johnson's England*, pp. 176-216.

22. J.A.R. Pimlott, *The Englishman's Holiday, A Social History* (Brighton, 1976, originally published in 1947), pp. 1-36; Porter, *English Society*, pp. 250-252.

23. Porter, *English Society*, chap. 6; J.H. Plumb, *Commercialization of Leisure in Eighteenth Century England* (Reading, 1973); N. McKendrick, J. Brew and J.H. Plumb, *The Birth of a Consumer Society* (Bloomington, IN 1982), pp. 34-99 and 265-285; I. Watt, *The Rise of the Novel* (London, 1957); R. Paulson, *Popular and Polite Art in the Age of Hogarth and Fielding* (London, 1979).

24. Mumford, *City*, chap. 13.

25. Quotation from Dulles, *Americans*, pp. 50-51. See also C. Bridenbaugh, *Cities in the Wilderness* (New York, 1838), pp. 275-280.

26. Bruce, *Social Life*, pp. 228-249; Andrews, *History*, pp. 122-126; Carson, *Colonial Virginians*, pp. 152-164; E. Morgan, *Virginians at Home: Family Life in the Eighteenth Century* (Charlottesville, VA, 1952), pp. 73-94; Dulles, *Americans*, chap. 3.

27. H. E. Smith, *Colonial Days and Ways As Gathered from Family Papers* (New York, 1966), pp. 315-328.

28. Quotation from E. Dick, *The Dixie Frontier: A Social History of the Southern Frontier* (New York, 1948) cited in J. Cary and J. Weinburg, eds., *The Social Fabric* vol. 1 (New York, 1987), p. 120. See also D. Bruce, *And They All Sang Hallelujah: Plain Folk Camp-Meeting Religion, 1800-1845* (Knoxville, 1974), pp. 54-58.

29. S. Margetson, *Leisure and Pleasure in the Eighteenth Century* (London, 1970), pp. 68-70; Tuberville, *Johnson's England*, p. 234; J. Ashton, *History of Gambling in England* (London, 1898), chap. 1; R. Allen, *The Clubs of Augustan London* (Cambridge, MA, 1933), pp. 146-147. See also W. Vamplew, *The Turf* (London, 1976); H.S. Altham, *A History of Cricket* (London, 1962); and E.P. Thompson, *Whigs and Hunters* (London, 1976).

30. Note the handbook on card and board games and the art of detecting cheating in C. Cotton, *The Compleat Gamester* (London, 1674), reprinted in C. H. Hartmann, ed., *Games and Gamesters of the Restoration* (London, 1930); pp. 1-115. See also D. Brailford, *Sport and Society: Elizabeth to Anne* (London, 1969), pp. 210-215 and J.H. Plumb, chap. 1.

31. J. Ezell, *Fortune's Merry Wheel: The Lottery in America* (Cambridge, MA, 1960), pp. 1-29; Carson, *Colonial Virginians*, pp. 70-71.

32. Findlay, *Chance*, pp. 4 and 26-27.

33. I rely especially on the insights of J. Findlay, *Chance*, chap. 1.

34. See, for example, B. Harrison, *Drink and the Victorians* (New York, 1979); C. Andrews, *Colonial Folkways* (New Haven, 1920), pp. 108-112.

35. *Records of the Governor... of Massachusetts Bay*, vol. 63, cited in J. Phillips, *Salem in the Seventeenth Century* (Boston, 1933), p. 244; Dulles, *Americans*, pp. 16-20 and 24-30; Bridenbaugh, *Cities*, pp. 226 and 265-274; C. Bridenbaugh, *Jamestown, 1544-1699* (New York, 1980), pp. 122-123.

36. See W.J. Rorabaugh, *The Alcoholic Republic: An American Tradition* (New York, 1979).

Chapter Five

1. L. Mumford, *Techniques and Civilization* (New York, 1934), pp. 14-17. See also C. Cipolla, *Clocks and Culture: 1300-1700* (London, 1967); D. Landes, *Revolution in Time: Clocks and the Making of the Modern World* (Cambridge, MA, 1983); J. Attali, *Histoire du temps* (Paris, 1982).

2. D. Landes, *Unbound Prometheus* (New York, 1969), pp. 56-59; S. Pollard, "Factory Discipline in the Industrial Revolution," *Economic History Review*, second series, 16 (1963): 256-270; E.P. Thompson, "Time, Work-Discipline, and Industrial Capitalism," *Past and Present* 38 (1967): 56-97; B. Laurie, *Working People of Philadelphia, 1800-1850* (Philadelphia, 1980), pp. 19-21; J. Prude, *The Coming of the Industrial Order: Town and Factory Life in Rural Massachusetts, 1810-1860* (New York, 1983), pp. 112-113.

3. A.F.C. Wallace, *Rockdale: The Growth of an American Village in the Early Industrial Revolution* (New York, 1972), p. 331.

4. For example, see E.P. Thompson, *The Making of the English Working Class* (New York, 1963), pp. 333-340; Wallace, *Rockdale*, pp. 124-185.

5. N. Ware, *The Industrial Worker, 1840-1860: The Reaction of American Industrial Society to the Advance of the Industrial Revolution* (Chicago, 1964), p. 84.

6. L. Faucher, *Manchester in 1844: Its Present Condition and Future Prospects* (London, 1969; first published in 1844), p. 118.

7. T. Dublin, *Women at Work: The Transformation of Work and Community in Lowell, Massachusetts, 1826-1860* (New York, 1979), pp. 25-26; Ware, *Worker*, chap. 5; K. Marx, *Capital*, vol. I (New York, 1967), pp. 197-302. D. Brody, "Time and Work during Early American Industrialism," (unpublished paper for the German-American Symposium, 1984).

8. Classic studies of English artisans in the industrial revolution are J. L. Hammond and B. Hammond, *The Skilled Labourer* (London, 1911); H. Mayhew, *London Labour and the London Poor* (London, 1884), 4 vol., especially vol. 2 and 3. More recent works include Thompson, *Making*, chap. 8; E. Hobsbawm, *Labouring Men* (New York, 1964), chap. 2, 4, 15, and 17 and. R. Price, *Masters, Unions and Men* (New York, 1980), chap.1-3; For America, see Ware, *Worker*, chap. 4. Much fuller analyses of the transformation of American crafts appear in recent works: A. Dawley, *Class and Community: The Industrial Revolution in Lynn* (Cambridge, MA, 1976), pp. 25-72; S. Wilentz, *Chants Democratic: New York City and the Rise of the American*

Working Class, 1788-1850 (New York, 1984), pp. 36-53; P. Faler, *Mechanics and Manufacturers in the Early Industrial Revolution: Lynn, Massachusetts, 1780-1860* (Albany, N.Y., 1981), chap. 2-5; Laurie, *Working People*, pp. 3-33; H. Rock, *Tradesmen of New York City in the Age of Jefferson* (New York, 1979); and S. Ross, *Workers on the Edge: Work, Leisure and Politics in Industrializing Cincinnati* (New York, 1986).

9. E. Yeo and E.P. Thompson, *The Unknown Mayhew* (New York, 1971), pp. 77, 111-112, 123 and 185-194; D. Bythell, *The Sweated Trades: Outwork in Nineteenth-Century Britain* (London, 1978); Thompson, *Making*, chap. 8; Wilentz, *Chants*, pp. 115 and 125-129.

10. C. Behagg, "Controlling the Product: Work, Time, and the Early Industrial Workforce in Britain," in G. Cross, ed., *Worktime and Industrialization, An Industrial History*, (Philadelphia, 1988), pp. 41-58.

11. Dublin, *Women*, p. 78.

12. D.A. Reid, "The Decline of St. Monday, 1776-1876," *Past and Present* 38 (1967): 66-97; E. Hopkins, "Working Hours and Conditions during the Industrial Revolution, A Re-appraisal," *Economic History Review* 25 (February, 1982): 52-67.

13. Ware, *Worker*, chap. 5; Prude, *Industrial Order*, pp. 34-65; I. Pinchbeck and M. Hewitt, *Children in English Society* (London, 1973), vol. II; J. Walvin, *A Child's World: A Social History of English Childhood, 1800-1914* (London, 1982), pp. 61-78; Thompson, *Making*, pp. 331-346.

14. Faucher, *Manchester*, p. 118; P. Gaskell, *The Manufacturing Population of England* (London, 1833), p. 7, cited in Thompson, *Making*, p. 340.

15. Prude, *Industrial Order*, p. 117; N. Smelser, *Social Change in the Industrial Revolution* (Chicago, 1959), pp. 180-212 and 257-286.

16. C. Lasch, *Haven in a Heartless World* (New York, 1977), chap. 1.

17. Among others, Dawley, *Class*, pp. 42-45 stresses this point, although it can easily be romanticized. See also P. Laslett, *The World We Have Lost* (New York, 1982).

18. This topic will be treated more fully in Chapter 6. Basic sources include N. Cott, *The Bonds of Womanhood: "Woman's Sphere" in New England, 1780-1835* (New Haven, 1977), pp. 57-64; E.P. Thompson, "Time, Work-Discipline, and Industrial Capitalism," *Past and Present* 38 (1967): 56-59.

19. Note, for example, Cott, *Womanhood,* chap. 1-3; B. Welter, "The Cult of True Womanhood: 1820-1870," in M. Gordon, ed., *The American Family in Social-Historical Perspective* (New York, 1983), pp. 372-393; M. Ryan, *Cradle of the Middle Class* (New York, 1981), chap. 1 and 2; L. Tilly and J. Scott, *Women, Work, and Family* (New York, 1977), chap. 2 and 3.

20. J. Burnett, *Obscure Destiny* (London, 1982), p. 219.

21. Cott, *Womanhood,* chap. 2-4; P. Branca, *Silent Sisterhood* (New York, 1973); K. K. Sklar, *Catherine Beecher, A Study in American Domesticity* (New York, 1976).

22. F. Engels, *The Condition of the English Working Class* (Stanford, 1968; first published in 1844), pp. 162-163 and "The Ten Hours Bill, The Speech of Lord Ashley, P.M. (May 10, 1844)," in K. Carpenter, ed., *Prelude to Victory* (New York, 1972), p. 17.

23. I deal with this issue fully in my *Quest for Time: The Reduction of Work in Britain and France, 1840-1940* (Berkeley, 1989), chap. 2.

24. Ware, *Worker,* pp. 73-75; Dawley, *Class,* pp. 54-56; Thompson, *Making,* chap. 12.

25. R. Malcolmson, *Popular Recreations in English Society 1700-1850* (Cambridge, 1973), pp. 98-11 and 152-160.

26. A. Howkins, "Taming of Whitsun: The Changing Face of a Nineteenth-Century Rural Holiday," in E. Yeo and S. Yeo, eds., *Popular Culture and Class Conflict 1590-1914: Explorations in the History of Labour and Leisure* (Brighton, 1981), pp. 188-208; P. Bailey, *Leisure and Class in Victorian England: Rational Recreation and the Contest for Control, 1830-1885* (London, 1978), pp. 20-23.

27. S. Smith, *Edinburgh Review* (January, 1809), p. 340, cited in Malcolmson, *Recreations,* p. 153.

28. J.L. Hammond and B. Hammond, *The Age of the Chartists 1832-1854* (London, 1930), chap. 7 and 8; Malcolmson, *Recreations,* pp. 116-118; Thompson, *Making,* pp. 402-403.

29. P. Johnson, *A Shopkeeper's Millenium: Society and Revivals in Rochester, New York 1815-1837* (New York, 1978), pp. 148-54. Prude makes a similar point regarding rural Massachusetts mill towns in the same period, *Industrial Order,* chap. 4.

30. Hopkins, *Working Hours*, pp. 52-67; G.C. Allen, *The Industrial Development of Birmingham and the Black Country, 1860-1927*, 2nd ed. (London, 1966), pp. 166-169 and 314-343; R. Samuel, "'The Workshop of the World,' Steam Power and Hand Technology in Mid-Victorian Britain," *History Workshop* 3 (1977): 49-60.

31. M. R. Smith, *Harpers Ferry Armory* (Boston, 1981), chap. 1; Laurie, *Working People*, pp. 53-56; Prude, *Industrial Order*, pp. 136-137.

32. W.G. Riddell, *Adventures of an Obscure Victorian* (London, 1982), p. 11.

33. S. Freud, *Civilization and Its Discontents* (London, 1946), pp. 55-56, cited in D. Bell, *Work and Its Discontents* (Boston, 1956), p. 3.

34. B. Harrison, *Drink and the Victorians* (Pittsburgh, 1971), chap. 2; W.J. Rorabaugh, *The Alcoholic Republic* (New York, 1979), pp. 11 and 168-174.

35. C. Dickens, *Sketches by Boz* (London, 1926), pp. 168-169.

36. E. Shorter, *The Making of the Modern Family* (New York, 1975), chap. 5.

37. Faucher, *Manchester*, p. 49; Bailey, *Leisure*, pp. 26-31; Harrison, *Drink*, chap. 2.

38. Harrison, *Drink*, pp. 37-40. See also R. Kenna and A. Moroney, *Peoples Palaces* (Edinburgh, 1983).

39. Shorter, *Family*, chap. 2 and 4. L. Tilly and J. Scott, *Women*.

40. M. Anderson, *Family Structure in Nineteenth Century Lancashire* (London, 1971); H. Gutman, *The Black Family in Slavery and Freedom, 1750-1925* (New York, 1976), pp. 185-215, especially. See also T. Hareven, *Family Time and Industrial Time* (New York, 1982), chap.1.

41. M.Ryan, *Cradle*, pp. 105-147.

42. Bailey, *Leisure*, pp. 25-26.

43. H. Cunningham, *Leisure in the Industrial Revolution* (New York, 1980), chap. 2; Malcolmson, *Recreations*, pp. 130-133; A.Delves, "Popular Recreation and Social Conflict in Derby," in Yeo, *Popular Culture*, pp. 89-127; Bailey, *Leisure*, pp. 20-24.

44. R. Poole, "Oldham Wakes;" and M. Judd, "'The Oddest Combination of Town and Country': Popular Culture and the London Fairs, 1800-1860," in J. K. Walton and J. Walvin, eds., *Leisure in Britain in 1790-1939* (Manchester, 1981), pp. 71-98 and 11-30.

Chapter Six

1. For estimates of the impact of industrialization on annual working hours, see F. Best, ed., *The Future of Work* (New York, 1973), p. 88; and J. Fourastie, *Des Loisirs pour quoi faire* (Paris, 1970), p. 35.

2. J. Attali, *Histoire du temps* (Paris, 1982), pp. 11-12.

3. D. Parkes and N. Thrift, *Making Sense of Time* (New York, 1978); G. Gurvitch, *The Spectrum of Social Time* (Dorrecht, 1964), pp. 12-94; M.P. Sorokin and R.K. Merton, "Social Time: A Methodical and Functional Analysis," *American Journal of Sociology* 42 (1937): 615-669.

4. For the classical exposition of these ideas, see W. Moore, *Man, Time, and Society* (New York, 1963), pp. 8-68; and K. Marx, *Capital*, vol. I (New York, 1967), pp. 235-256. For a brilliant modern analysis of work, time, and leisure, see E.P. Thompson, "Time, Work-Discipline, and Industrial Capitalism," *Past and Present* 38 (1967): 56-97.

5. B. Franklin, *Autobiography* (New York, 1932), pp. vii and 93-95; A. Daumard, *Oisiveté et loisirs dans les sociétés occidentales ua xixe siécle* (Amiens, 1983), pp. 9-21.

6. T. Wright, *Some Habits and Customs of the Working Classes* (New York, 1967; first published in 1867), pp. 111-119.

7. This theme is developed in G. Cross, *A Quest for Time: The Reduction of Work in Britain and France, 1840-1940* (Berkeley, 1989), chap. 4.

8. Moore, *Man*, pp. 45-66; N. Samuel, *Le Temps libre: Un Temps social* (Paris, 1984), pp. 9-15; A. Clayer, *Work and Play. Ideas and Experiences of Work and Leisure* (London, 1974), pp. 2, 62 and 93-94.

9. M.A. Bienefeld, *Working Hours in British Industry: An Economic History* (London, 1972), p. 7.

10. Sources and discussion of the problem of retail workers' leisure is in G. Cross and P. Shergold, "'We Think We Are of the Oppressed': Gender, White Collar Work, and Grievances of Late Nineteenth Century Women," *Labor History* 28 (Winter, 1987): 23-53.

11. The classic expression of this idea is in P. Lafargue, *The Right to Be Lazy* (New York, 1910; first published in 1880). For sociological treatments of the relationship between leisure and individualism, see J. Dumazedier, *Sociology of Leisure* (New York, 1974), pp. 39-40; N. Anderson, *Work and Leisure* (London, 1961), p. 62; G. Soule, *Time for Living* (New York, 1955), p. 94.

12. Some sociological sources are L. Hantrias, P.A. Clark, and N. Samuel, "Time-Space Dimensions of Work, Family and Leisure in France and Great Britain," *Leisure Studies* 3 (1984): 301-317; M.Young and P.Willmott, *The Symmetrical Family* (London, 1973); R. and R. Rapoport, *Leisure and the Family Life Cycle* (London, 1975).

13. Basic British sources are E.L. Hutchins and A. Harrison, *A History of Factory Legislation* (London, 1926), pp. 19-38; J. Ward, *The Factory Movement, 1830-1855* (London, 1962), chap. 1. American treatments of this theme are in C. Beyer, *History of Labor Legislation for Women in Three States* (Washington, 1932), pp. 100-109; T. Dublin, *Women at Work: The Transformation of Work and Community in Lowell, Massachusetts, 1826-1860* (New York, 1979), pp. 58-86; N. Ware, *The Industrial Worker, 1840-1860* (New York, 1964), chap. 8 and 10; and K. K. Sklar, "'The Greater Part of the Petitioners Are Female': The Reduction of Women's Working Hours in the Paid Labor Force by Statute, 1840-1917," in G. Cross, ed., *Worktime and Industrialization*, (Philadelphia, 1988), pp. 103-134.

14. M. Berg, *The Machinery Question and the Making of Political Economy, 1815-1848* (New York, 1980), pp. 23-27.

15. *The Artisan* (May 18, 1832) cited in T. Murphy, "Work, Leisure and Moral Reform: The Ten-Hour Movement in New England, 1830-1850," in Cross, *Worktime,* pp. 59-76.

16. *Pioneer* (December 21, 1833). Doherty quotation cited in R. Gray, "Languages of Factory Reform," in P. Joyce, ed., *Historical Meanings of Work* (New York, 1987), pp. 143-179.

17 *The Mechanic* (May 4, 1844) cited in Murphy, "Moral Reform," and S. Weaver, "The Political Ideology of Short Time, 1820-1850," both in Cross, *Worktime,* pp. 77-102.

18. W. Berks, "Linear Notes," *The Hand That Holds the Bread*, (New World Records, NW 267, 1978).

19. Ware, *Worker*, chap. 8 and 10.

20. I. Pinchbeck and M. Hewitt, *Children in English Society*, vol. II (London, 1973), pp. 350-406.

21. K. Carpenter, ed., *Richard Oastler, King of the Factory Children* (New York, 1972), p. 120.

22. S.K. Alfred, *The History of the Factory Movement* (London, 1857) vol. I, chap. 13; quotation from C. Thachrah, *The Effects of the Principal Arts, Trades, and Professions* (London, 1832), p. 41.

23. P. Bailey, *Leisure and Class in Victorian England: Rational Recreation and the Contest for Control, 1830-1885* (London, 1978), pp. 42-45.

24. N. Smelser, *Social Change in the Industrial Revolution* (Chicago, 1959), pp. 180-212 and 257-286. For a critique of Smelser, see C. Calhoun, *The Question of Class Struggle: Social Foundations of Popular Radicalism during the Industrial Revolution* (Chicago, 1982), pp. 191-196.

25. Cited in R. Kingsbury, *Labor Laws and Their Enforcement* (New York, 1911), p. 123; F. Engels, *The Condition of the English Working Class* (Stanford, 1968), pp. 162-165. See also Smelser, *Change*, pp. 180-212.

26. Cited in Hutchinson, *Legislation* pp. 64-66.

27. J. Scott and L. Tilly, *Women, Work, and Family* (New York, 1977), chap. 4-5.

28. Cited in J. Commons, *Documentary History of American Industrial Society* vol. 6 (Cleveland, OH 1910): 70-71 and 79.

29. G. Bull, "To the Friends of the National Regeneration Society," *Crisis and National Co-operative Trades' Union Gazette* 26 (April 1834); cited in Weaver, "Political Ideology," in Cross, *Worktime*, p. 91; R. Price, *Masters, Unions, and Men* (New York, 1980), p. 53.

30. A. Ure, *Philosophy of Manufacturers* (London, 1835), p. 301; N. Senior, *Letters* (London, 1847), pp. 21-23.

31. Cited in Dublin, *Women*, p. 119.

32. See S. Weaver, *John Fielden* (Oxford, 1987), chap. 8; and Alfred, *History* chap. 12-15. Note also Cross, *Quest*, chap. 2.

33. P. Joyce, *Work, Society and Politics* (New Brunswick, NJ, 1980), pp. 58-64; and Berg, *Machinery*, p. 29.

34. D. Montgomery, *Beyond Equality: Labor and the Radical Republicans, 1862-1872* (Urbana, IL, 1981), pp. 243-290.

35. D. Henry, *The History of the Haymarket Affair* (New York, 1936), pp. 198-219; D.R. Roediger and P. Foner, *Our Own Time* (Westport, CT, 1989), chap. 10. Note also M. Dommanget, *Histoire du Premier mai* (Paris, 1953).

36. A.P. Duffy, "New Unionism in Britain, 1889-1890, A Reappraisal," *Economic History Review* 14 (1968): 309-325; A.P. Duffy "The Eight Hours Day Movement in Britain, 1836-1893," *Manchester School of Economics and Social Studies* 36 (1961): 203-222 and 345-363. A good source on American joblessness in the 19th century is A. Keysser, *Out of Work* (New York, 1987).

37. S. Webb, "The Limitation of the Hours of Labour," *Contemporary Review* 56 (December, 1889): 859. See Cross, *Quest*, chap. 3 and Roediger, *Time*, for full bibliography.

38. See, for example, *Royal Commission on Labour*, Report 2, Group A (London, 1892-1894), p. 88.

39. *Royal Commission on Labour*, Report 2, Group B, pp. 427-428.

40. G. S. Jones, *Language of Class* (London, 1983), pp. 205-208 and pp. 218-219. See also S. Meacham, *A Life Apart* (Cambridge, MA, 1977), chap. 4 - 5.

41. *Royal Commission on Labour*, Report 3, Group C, p. 17.

42. See Sklar, *Petitioners,* for details.

43. Space does not allow a full analysis of this topic. See Cross, *Quest*, chap. 4 and 5 for such a treatment.

Chapter Seven

1. C. Dickens, *Hard Times* (New York, 1961), p. 30; A. de Tocqueville, *Democracy in America*, R. D. Heffner, ed., (New York, 1956), p. 260.

2. J. Kay, *The Social Condition and Education of the People of England and Europe*, vol. I (London, 1850), pp. 580-581 cited in R. Storch, "The Problem of Working-Class Leisure," A.P. Donajgrodzki, ed., *Social Control in Nineteenth Century Britain* A.P. Donajgrodzki, ed. (London, 1977), p. 141.

3. P. Boyer, *Urban Masses and Moral Order in America, 1820-1920* (Cambridge, MA, 1978), pp. 68-69; and J. Kett, *Rites of Passage* (New York, 1977) pp. 88-93.

4. H. Cunningham, *Leisure in the Industrial Revolution* (New York, 1980), pp. 80-84; A. Briggs, *The Age of Improvement, 1783-1867* (London, 1959).

5. Select Committee on Drunkenness, *Parliamentary Papers*, vol. VIII (1934), p. 325, cited in J.H. C. Harrison, *The Early Victorians* (London, 1973), pp. 162-173.

6. Boyer, *Masses*, p. 5.

7. B. Harrison, "Religion and Recreation in Nineteenth-century England," *Papers Presented to the Past and Present Conference on Popular Religion* (July 7, 1966), p. 2. See also J. Rule, "Methodism, Popular Beliefs and Village Culture," in R. Storch, ed., *Popular Culture and Custom in Nineteenth-Century England*, (New York, 1982), pp. 48-70.

8. J. Wigley, *The Rise and Fall of the Victorian Sunday* (Manchester, 1980); C. Dickens, *Sunday Under Three Heads* (London, 1836); P. Johnson, *A Shopkeeper's Millennium: Society and Revivals in Rochester, New York, 1815-1837* (New York, 1978), pp. 72-94; B. Wyatt-Brown, "Prelude to Abolitionism: Sabbatarian Politics and the Rise of the Second Party System," *Journal of American History* 63 (September, 1971): 316-341.

9. B. Harrison, "The Sunday Trading Riots of 1855," *Historical Journal* 8 (1965): 219-245; K. Marx, and F. Engels, *On Britain* (Moscow, 1962), p. 435.

10. C. Cole, *The Social Ideas of the Northern Evangelists, 1826-1860* (New York, 1954), pp. 107-108.

11. Good analyses of the Sunday School movement are in Boyer, *Masses*, chap. 3 and T. W. Laqueur, *Religion and Respectability: Sunday Schools and Working Class Culture, 1780-1850* (New Haven, CT, 1976).

12. Still, some extreme Sabbatarians successfully opposed the teaching of writing in the Sunday Schools as unnecessary to understanding the Bible and thus a "secular employment" prohibited by God. Cole, *Ideas*, p. 100; Wigley, *Sunday*, p. 81. A recent study of the American Sunday School is Anne Boyland, *Sunday School: The Formation of an American Institution, 1790-1880* (New Haven, CT, 1989).

13. Boyer, *Masses*, chap. 3; Lacquer, *Religion*, chap. 5; P. Joyce, *Work, Society and Politics: The Culture of the Factory in Later Victorian England* (New Brunswick, NJ, 1980), pp. 246-250; P. Bailey, *Leisure and Class in Victorian England: Rational Recreation and the Contest for Control, 1830-1885* (London, 1978), pp. 45-46; Kett, *Rites*, pp. 117-121.

14. Much of this section is from B. Harrison, *Drink and the Victorians: The Temperance Question in England 1815-1872* (Pittsburgh, 1971); I. R. Tyrrell, *Sobering Up: From Temperance to Prohibition in Antebellum America, 1800-1860* (Westport, CT, 1979); and R. Hampel, *Temperance and Prohibition in Massachusetts 1813-1852* (Ann Arbor, MI, 1982).

15. Daniel Clarke Sanders quotation cited in Tyrrell, *Sobering Up*, p. 41.

16. Rule, *Methodism*, p. 57.

17. S. Wilentz, *Chants Democratic: New York City and the Rise of the American Working Class, 1788-1850* (New York, 1984), pp. 155-157 and 306-314; R. Rosenzweig, *Eight Hours for What We Will: Workers and Leisure in an Industrial City, 1870-1920* (New York, 1983), chap. 6.

18. *New York Crystal Fount* (September 14, 1842), cited in Tyrell, *Sobering Up*, p. 181.

19. *Liberal Advocate* (March 3, 1832), cited in Johnson, *Millenium*, p. 60.

20. J. Kingsdale, "The 'Poor Man's Club': Social Functions of the Urban Working Class Saloon," *American Quarterly* 25 (December, 1973): 472-489.

21. P. Baker, *ASL Yearbook* (1914), p. 16, cited in Boyer, *Masses*, p. 208.

22. Harrison, *Drink*, chap. 15.

23. Boyer, *Masses*, pp. 176-179.

24. See, for example, G. Kneeland, *Commercialized Prostitution in New York City* (New York, 1913).

25. Boyer, *Masses,* pp. 190, 193 and 216-217.

26. J. Walkowitz, *Prostitution and Victorian Society* (New York, 1980); D. Pivar, *Purity Crusade: Sexual Morality and Social Control, 1868-1900* (Westport, CT, 1974).

27. Cunningham, *Leisure,* p. 78.

28. Johnson, *Millenium,* pp. 1-13 and 95-115; M. Ryan, *Cradle of the Middle Class* (New York, 1981), chap. 2 and 3; T. Bender, *Toward an Urban Vision* (Lexington, KY, 1975), chap. 8.

29. Boyer, *Masses,* chap. 15.

30. B. Heywood, *Addresses Delivered at the Manchester Mechanics' Institute* (Manchester, 1843), p. 120, cited in Bailey, *Leisure,* p. 36 and Storch, "Problem," pp. 149-152.

31. J.M. Golby and A.W. Purdue, *The Civilization of the Crowd: Popular Culture in England, 1750-1900* (London, 1984), chap. 2; Storch, "Problem," pp. 148-151.

32. E. Royle, "Mechanics' Institutes and the Working Classes 1840-1860," *Historical Journal* 14 (1971):305-321; for quotation, J.F.C. Harrison, *Learning and Living, 1790-1960* (London, 1961), pp. 73-74.

33. H. Solly, *Working Mens' Social Clubs and Educational Institutes* (New York, 1980; original, 1904), pp. 22-23; W.C. Taylor, *Notes of a Tour in the Manufacturing Districts of Lancashire* (Manchester, 1842), pp. 132-136; R. Price, "The Working Men's Club Movement and Victorian Social Reform Ideology," *Victorian Studies* 16 (1971):117-147; and J. Taylor, *From Self-Help to Glamour: The Working Man's Club 1860-1972* (Oxford, 1972); Bailey, *Leisure,* pp. 92-93 and 106-123.

34. C.H. Hopkins, *History of the YMCA in North America* (New York, 1951), pp. 4-21; Boyer, *Masses,* chap. 7, M. Ryan, *Cradle,* pp. 176-178.

35. L. Faucher, *Manchester in 1844* (London, 1844), pp. 100-104; E.D. Mackerness, *A Social History of English Music* (London, 1964), pp. 130-132.

36. T. Dublin, *Women at Work* (New York, 1979), pp. 123-130; E. Bell, *History of Organized Camping* (Martinsville, IN, 1986), pp. 42-47.

37. Bailey, *Leisure*, pp. 92-120; W. Lovett, *The Life and Struggles of William Lovett* (London, 1876).

38. H. E. Meller, *Leisure and the Changing City, 1870-1914* (London, 1976), chap. 5.

39. F. Couvares, *The Remaking of Pittsburgh* (Albany, NY,1984), pp. 112-114.

40. *Select Committee on Public Walks Report* (London, 1833). cited in Cunningham, *Leisure*, pp. 89-92.

41. *Select Committee on Public Walks* (London, 1834), cited in Bailey, *Leisure*, p. 41; G. F. Chadwick, *The Park and the Town: Public Landscape in the 19th and 20th Century* (London, 1966), pp. 53-66.

42. Harrison, *Drink*, pp. 321-323.

43. F.Olmsted, "Public Parks and the Enlargement of Towns," (Boston, 1870) in S.B. Sutton, ed., *Civilizing American Cities: A Selection of Frederick Law Olmsted's Writings of City Landscapes* (Cambridge, MA, 1971), pp. 80-81; D. Schuyler, *The New Urban Landscape* (Baltimore, 1986), chap. 6-7. See also A. Fein, *Frederick Law Olmsted and the American Environmental Tradition* (New York, 1972). See especially G. Cranz, *The Politics of Park Design, A History of Urban Parks in America*, (Cambridge, MA, 1982)

44. Couvares, *Pittsburgh*, chap. 7.

45. Couvares, *Pittsburgh*, chap. 7.

46. Harrison, *Drink*, chap. 15.

47. Faucher, *Manchester*, p. 34.

48. G. S. Jones, *Languages of Class* (London, 1983), pp. 191-196; H. Jephson, *The Sanitary Evolution of London* (London, 1907).

49. T. Wright, *Some Habits and Customs of the Working Classes by a Journeyman Engineer*, (London, 1867), pp. 184-248. For a treatment of urban working-class culture in the generation before World War I, see S. Meacham, *A Life Apart* (Cambridge, MA, 1977).

50. For example, see S. Alexander, *St. Giles Fair, 1830-1914* (Oxford, 1970); J.M. Ludlow and L. Jones, *Progress of the Working Class 1831-1867* (London, 1973; first published in 1867); Bailey, *Leisure*, chap. 3 and Jones, *Class*, chap. 2.

51. Meller, *City,* pp. 205-213; Jones, *Class,* pp. 202-204.

52. Cunningham, *Leisure,* p. 127.

53. Joyce, *Work,* chap. 8, especially p. 286.

54. T. Kelly, *A History of Public Libraries in Great Britain 1845-1965* (London, 1973), pp. 16-85.

55. H. Perkin, "The 'Social Tone' of Victorian Seaside Resorts in the North West," *Northern History* 11 (1975): 180-194; C. Funnel, *By the Beautiful Sea: The Rise and High Times of that Great American Resort, Atlantic City* (New York, 1975), pp. 132-140; D. Chandler, *Henry Flager: The Astonishing Life and Times of the Visionary Robber Baron who Founded Florida* (New York, 1986), pp. 94-137 and 260-263.

56. H. Cunningham, *The Volunteer Force: A Social and Political History, 1859-1908* (London, 1975), pp. 132-140; Cunningham, *Leisure,* p. 137; Rosenzweig, *Eight Hours,* chap. 4.

57. Bailey, *Leisure,* p. 105.

Chapter Eight

1. W. Howitt, *The Rural Life of England,* vol. II (London, 1938), p. 150, cited in H. Cunningham, *Leisure in the Industrial Revolution* (London, 1978), pp. 85-88.

2. K. Jeffrey, "The Family Utopian Retreat from the City: The Nineteenth Century Contribution," *Soundings* 55 (1972): 21-41; A. Douglas, *The Feminization of American Culture* (New York, 1977), chap. 4.

3. See, for example, P. Branca, *Silent Sisterhood, Middle Class Women in the Victorian Home* (London, 1975), chap. 2, especially.

4. For example, see M. Ryan, *Cradle of the Middle Class: The Family in Oneida Country, New York, 1790-1865* (New York, 1983); and J. Donzelot, *The Policing of Families* (New York, 1979), who stresses the incentive of political conservatives to encourage family stability and female leadership as a bulwark against social unrest.

5. R. Fishman, *Bourgeois Utopias: The Rise and Fall of Suburbia* (New York, 1987), p. 56 and chap. 1-2.

6. K. Jackson, *Crabgrass Frontier,* (New York, 1985), chap. 4.

7. C. McDannel, *The Christian Home in Victorian America* (Bloomington, 1986), p. 28.

8. Fishman, *Utopias,* chap. 5.

9. McDannel, *Home,* p. 26. For more detail, see K. Grier, *Culture and Comfort: People, Parlors, and Upholstery, 1850-1930* (Madison, WI, 1988).

10. C. Shammas, "The Domestic Environment in Early Modern England and America," *Journal of Social History* 14, 1 (Fall 1980): 25; S. McMurry, "City Parlor, Country Sitting Room, *Winter Portfolio* 20, 4 (Winter, 1985): 261-280. For the evolution of rural domesticity, see S. McMurry, *Families and Farm Houses in Nineteenth Century America* (New York, 1988).

11. C. Clark, *The American Family Home, 1800-1960* (Chapel Hill, NC, 1986), chap. 2; "The Passing of the Parlor," *Atlantic Monthly* 91, 547 (May, 1903), p. 713, cited in McMurry, *Parlor,* p. 267. See also Gwendolyn Wright, *Moralism and the Model Home: Domestic Architecture and Cultural Conflict in Chicago, 1880-1913* (Chicago, 1980).

12. S. B. Warner, *Streetcar Suburbs: The Process of Growth in Boston, 1870-1900* (Cambridge, MA, 1962) chap. 11.

13. McDannel, *Home,* pp. 48-49.

14. F. Couvares, *The Remaking of Pittsburgh* (Albany, NY, 1984), pp. 57-59; R. Roberts, *The Classic Slum: Salford Life in the First Quarter of the Century* (Manchester, 1971), p. 35.

15. J. Pimlott, *The Englishman's Christmas* (London, 1974).

16. J. Lowerson and J. Meyerscough, *Time to Spare* (Brighton, 1978).

17. S. Mitchell, "The Forgotten Woman of the Period: Penny Weekly Family Magazines of the 1840s and 1850s," in M. Vicinus, ed., *A Widening Sphere, Changing Roles of Victorian Women* (Bloomington, IN, 1977), pp. 52-71. A full treatment of home-oriented literature for the American woman is in M. Kelley, *Private Woman, Public Stage: Literary Domesticity in Nineteenth-Century America* (Oxford, 1984). See also B. Berg, *The Remembered Gate* (New York, 1979).

18. M. A. Dodge, *Woman's Worth and Worthlessness* (New York, 1872), p. 94, cited in D. Rodgers, *The Work Ethic in Industrial America, 1850-1920* (Chicago, 1974), p. 186.

19. A.J. Graves, *Women in America* (New York, 1841), p. 120.

20. "Women," *Ladies Magazines* 3 (October, 1830), p. 441 and "Essay on Marriage," *Universalist and Ladies' Repository* 2 (April 19, 1034): 371, cited in N. Cott, *Bonds of Womanhood* (New Haven, 1977), pp. 67 and 70.

21. K. K. Sklar, *Catherine Beecher: A Study in American Domesticity* (New York, 1976), pp. 98-99.

22. C. Smith-Rosenberg, "The Female World of Love and Ritual: Relations between Women in Nineteenth-Century America," *Signs: Journal of Women in Culture and Society* 1 (1975): 1-30; C. Smith-Rosenberg, *Disorderly Conduct: Visions of Gender in Victorian America* (New York, 1985); C. Dyhouse, *Girls Growing Up in Late Victorian and Edwardian England* (London, 1981), pp. 25-28. See also, N. Chodorow, *The Reproduction of Mothering: Psychoanalysis and the Sociology of Gender* (Berkeley, 1978). For a superior British source, see L. Davidoff, *The Best Circles* (London, 1973).

23. N. Woloch, *Women and the American Experience* (New York, 1984), chap. 5; H. Green, *The Light of the Home: An Intimate View of Women in Victorian America* (New York, 1983), chap.4.

24. Branca, *Sisterhood*, chap. 1.

25. K. Woodroofe, *From Charity to Social Work in England and the United States* (London, 1962), chap. 1; P. Boyer, *Urban Masses and Moral Order in America* (Cambridge, MA, 1978), chap. 10; A. F. Davis, *Spearheads for Reform: The Social Settlements and the Progressive Movement, 1890-1914* (New York, 1967).

26. J. J. Rousseau, *Emile* and Amos Bronson Alcott, *Observations on the Principles and Methods of Infant Instruction*, cited in S. Cohen, ed., *Education in the United States* (New York, 1974), p. 207. See also B. Finkelstein and K. Vandell, "The Schooling of American Childhood, 1820-1920," in M. Heininger, ed., *A Century of Childhood, 1820-1920* (Rochester, NY, 1985), chap. 3.

27. C. Beecher, *Treatise on the Domestic Economy* (New York, 1847), p. 123; Ryan, *Cradle*, pp. 98-100.

28. J. Kett, *Rites of Passage: Adolescence in America, 1790 to the Present* (New York, 1977), chap. 5; F.J. Darton, *Children's Books in England: Five Centuries of Social Life* (Cambridge, 1958), pp. 298-314.

29. *Monthly Mother's Magazine* (April 1938), p. 30, cited in Ryan, *Cradle*, p. 163.

30. M. von Boehn, *Dolls and Puppets* (Philadelphia, 1932), pp. 156 and 162. M.L. Heininger, "Children, Childhood, and Change in America, 1820-1920," in Heininger, *Childhood*, pp. 6-10.

31. Quoted in Heininger, "Children," p. 16.

32. A. S. MacLeod, *A Moral Tale: Children's Fiction and American Culture, 1820-1860* (Hamden, CN, 1975), pp. 20-24; Rodgers, *Work Ethic*, pp. 108-109 and 133-152.

33. J. Sommerfield, *The Rise and Fall of Childhood* (Beverely Hills, CA, 1982), chap. 13.

34. J. Burnett, *Destiny Obscure: Autobiographies of Childhood, Education, and Family from the 1820s to the 1920s* (London, 1982), pp. 24-47.

35. Some useful sources are B. Wishy, *The Child and the Republic: The Dawn of Modern American Child Nurture* (Philadelphia, 1968); J.R. Gillis, *Youth and History* (New York, 1974); B.K. Greenleaf, *Children Through the Ages: A History of Childhood* (New York, 1979); Kett, *Rites of Passage.* J. Springhall, *Coming of Age: Adolescence in Britain, 1860-1060* (Dublin, 1986); and P. Ariés, *Centuries of Childhood* (New York, 1977).

36. R. Bray, *Boy Labour and Apprenticeship* (London, 1911), p. 118.

37. Among the numerous analyses available, note M. Anderson, *Family Structure in Nineteenth -Century Lancashire* (New York, 1971); T. Hareven, *Family Time and Industrial Time* (New York, 1982); and L. Tilly and J. Scott, *Women, Work, and Family* (New York, 1978).

38. S. F. Jackson, "The New Scholar," in J.J. Findlay, ed., *The Young Wage Earner and the Problem of His Education* (London, 1918), p. 40.

39. R. Roberts, *The Classic Slum*, p. 33.

40. Gillis, *Youth*, chap.1; Ariés, *Childhood*, chap. 4; N. Z. Davis, "The Reasons of Misrule: Youth Groups and Charivaris in Sixteenth Century France," *Past and Present* 50, (February 1971): 41-75.

41. Gillis, *Youth*, pp. 98-100 and 128-130.

42. Springhall, *Coming of Age*, chap. 3; C. Stansell, *City of Women, Sex and Class in New York: 1789-1860* (Urbana, 1984), pp. 205-216.

43. Gillis, *Youth*, pp. 128-130; Springhall, *Age*, chap. 3; R. Roberts, *Slum*, chap. 8; Burnett, *Destiny*, pp. 246-250. A British classic in this anxiety toward working-class leisure is A. Freeman, *Boy Life and Labour* (London, 1914).

44. A. S. MacLeod, "The Caddie Woodlawn Syndrome: American Girlhood in the Nineteenth Century," in Heininger, *Childhood*, chap. 4; quotation from Springhall, *Age*, p. 59.

45. Ryan, *Cradle*, chap. 4.

46. Kett, *Rites of Passage*, chap 5.

47. Springhall, *Age*, chap. 2; J. Springhall, *Youth, Empire and Society: British Youth Movements, 1883 to 1940* (London, 1977). See also G. Searle, *The Quest for National Efficiency: A Study in British Politics and Political Thought, 1899-1914* (Oxford, 1971).

48. M. Rosenthal, *The Character Factory* (New York, 1984), p. 201.

49. See, for example, J.Hantower, "The Boy Scouts and the Validation of Masculinity," in J. Pleck and E. Pleck, eds., *Men in America* (New York, 1977), pp. 287-301.

50. Quotations cited in D. MacLeon, *Building Character in the American Boy: The Boy Scouts, YMCA and Their Forerunners, 1870-1920* (Madison, 1983), pp. 34-50. See also G. Crossick, "The Labour Aristocracy and its Values," *Victorian Studies* 19 (1976), pp. 301-328 and J. Hargreaves, *Sport, Power and Culture* (Cambridge, 1986), pp. 58-79.

51. J. Springfield, *Sure and Steadfast: A History of the Boys' Brigade, 1883 to 1983* (Glasgow, 1983).

52. C. Rainwater, *The Play Movement in the United States* (New York, 1922), pp. 100-105; for quotation, H. Curtis, *The Play Movement and Its Significance* (New York, 1917), pp. 60-65.

53. Curtis, *Play Movement*, pp. 108-109, 30-31 and 56-61; Boyer, *Masses*, pp. 240-248.

54. Curtis, *Play Movement*, pp. 119-123.

55. "The Playground Association of America: Purpose," *Playground* 4 (1910): 73, cited in D. Cavallo, *Muscles and Morals: Organized Playgrounds and Urban Reform, 1880-1920* (Philadelphia, 1981), p. 37.

56. G. S. Hall, *Youth: Its Education, Regimen and Hygiene* (New York, 1906); D. Ross, *G. Stanley Hall, The Psychologist as Prophet* (Chicago, 1972), pp. 279-308; Cavallo, *Muscles*, especially chap. 2.

57. Cited in Rainwater, *Play*, p. 155. See also, Jane Addams, *Youth and the City Streets* (New York, 1972, first published in 1909), chap. 5 and 6.

58. Cited in C. Ward and D. Hardy, *Goodnight Campers!* (London, 1986) pp. 5-8; E. Eells, *History of Organized Camping: The First 100 Years* (Martinsville, IN, 1986), pp. 1-85. See also, Springhall, *Youth*, L. Paul, *The Republic of Children* (London, 1938); MacLeon, *Character*, chap. 13.

59. Cited in R. Kerr, *Story of the Girl Guides 1908-1938* (London, 1976), pp. 25-26.

60. P. Filene, *Him/Her/Self* (Baltimore, 1986); see also his article "In Time of War," in *Men in America* (Englewood Cliffs, NJ, 1980) pp. 321-335.

61. Cavallo, *Muscles*, pp. 46-48.

62. Baden-Powell, in B. Dobbs, *Edwardians at Play*, (London, 1973) p. 31, noted with disgust the growth of spectator sports:

> Football in itself is a grand game for developing a lad physically and also morally, for he learns to play with good temper and unselfishness, to play in his place and 'play the game.' But it is a vicious game when it draws crowds of lads away from playing the game themselves to be merely on-lookers at a few paid performers...Thousands of boys and young men, pale, narrow-chested, hunched-up, miserable specimens, smoking endless cigarettes, numbers of them betting, all of them learning to be hysterical as they groan or cheer in panic unison with their neighbors."

Chapter Nine

1. J. Lowerson and J. Meyerscough, *Time to Spare in Victorian England* (Brighton, 1977), chap. 1 and D. Rodgers, *The Work Ethic in Industrial America* (Chicago, 1974), chap. 4.

2. G. M. Wilson, *Alcohol and the Nation* (London, 1940), p. 14; H. Fraser, *The Coming of the Mass Market, 1850-1914* (London, 1981), pp. 66-71.

3. R. Roberts, *The Classic Slum: Salford Life in the First Quarter of the Century* (Manchester, 1971), pp. 115-116; See also C. Klapper, *The Golden Age of Tramways* (London, 1974); P. S. Bagwell, *The Transport Revolution since 1770* (London, 1974).

4. Fraser, *Market,* chap. 14 develops these themes.

5. See N. Harris, *Humbug: The Art of P.T. Barnum* (Boston, 1973); and W. F. Rae, *The Business of Travel* (London, 1891).

6. *Answers* (February 22, 1888), cited in Fraser, *Market,* p. 73.

7. See H. N. Smith, *Virgin Land: The American West As Symbol and Myth* (Cambridge, MA, 1950).

8. J.F.C. Harrison, *Learning and Living 1790-1960* (London, 1961), chap. 1. See also R. Altick, *The English Common Reader 1790-1848* (London, 1956); L. James, *Print and the People, 1819-1851* (London, 1976); V. Neuberg, *Popular Literature* (London, 1976); A.J. Lee, *The Origins of the Popular Press in England 1855-1914* (London, 1974); and quotation from R. Roberts, *Slum,* p. 133.

9. Note S. Morison, *The English Newspaper* (Cambridge, 1932), pp. 250-270; and G. Boyce, J. Curran, and P. Wingate, *Newspaper History From the Seventeenth Century to the Present Day* (London, 1978), chap. 3 and 13.

10. J. Springhall, *Coming of Age: Adolescence in Britain 1860-1960* (Dublin, 1986), pp. 128-133; R. Roberts, *Slum,* pp. 160-161. See also I. Quigley, *The Heirs of Tom Brown: The English School Story* (Oxford, 1984); K. Carpenter, *Penny Dreadfuls and Comics: English Periodicals for Children from Victorian Times to the Present Day* (London, 1983); and P. Dunae, "Penny Dreadfuls: Late Nineteenth Century Boys' Literature and Crime," *Victorian Studies* 22, 1 (Winter, 1979): 133-150.

11. C. Dyhouse, *Girls Growing Up in Late Victorian and Edwardian England* (London, 1981), chap. 6.

12. J. Tebbel, *The American Magazine: A Compact History* (New York, 1969), chap. 5; M. Denning, *Mechanic Accents: Dime Novels and Working-Class Culture in America* (New York, 1987).

13. American sources include P. Zellers, "The Cradle of Variety: The Concert Saloon," *Educational Theatre Journal* 20 (December, 1968): 578-586; A. McLean, *American Vaudeville as Ritual* (Louisville, Ky., 1965), pp. 65-68; E. Marks, *They All Sang: From Tony Pastor to Rudy Vallee* (New York, 1934), pp. 116-128; J. Laurie, Jr., *Vaudeville: From the Honky-Tonks to the Palace* (New York, 1953), chap. 1 and 3, especially; I. Zeidman, *The American Burlesque Show* (New York, 1967); and K. Peiss, *Cheap Amusements: Working Women and Leisure in Turn-of-the-Century New York* (Philadelphia, 1986), pp. 141-145. For examples of the history of British popular theater and the music hall, see S. Rosenfeld, *The Theatre of the London Fairs in the 18th Century* (Cambridge, 1960); D. F. Cheshire, *Music Hall in Britain* (Rutherford, NJ, 1974), chap. 1-3; and R. Mander and J. Mitchenson, *British Music Hall* (London, 1965), pp. 9-13. See especially, P. Bailey, ed., *Music Hall: The Business of Pleasure* (Milton Keynes, 1986).

14. T. Wright, *Some Habits and Customs of the Working Classes* (New York, 1967; first published in 1867), p. 198.

15. Mander, *Music Hall*, p. 21.

16. P. Bailey, *Leisure and Class in Victorian England*, (London, 1978), p. 151. Note also C.D. Stuart and A.J. Park, *The Variety Stage: A History of the Music Hall from the Earliest Period to the Present Time* (London, 1895).

17. J. Springhall, *Coming of Age*, pp. 120-128.

18. See J. Addams' analysis of this theater in *The Spirit of Youth and the City Streets* (New York, 1909), chap. 4.

19. Harris, *Humbug*, chap. 2; Mander, *Music Hall*, pp. 21-29; F. Couvares, *The Remaking of Pittsburgh: Class and Culture in an Industrial City, 1877-1919* (Albany, NY, 1984), pp. 40-43.

20. L. de Koven Bowen, *Public Dance Halls in Chicago* (Chicago, 1917), p. 5, cited in Peiss, *Amusements*, p. 102. See also Lewis Erenberg, *Steppin' Out: New York Nightlife and the Transformation of American Culture, 1890-1930* (Westport, CT, 1981), chap. 4 and 5.

21. Peiss, *Amusements,* chap. 3 and 4. C. Stansell finds a very similar character to youth leisure in New York in the 1830s and 1840s along the Bowery in *City of Women* (Urbana, IL, 1986), pp. 89-101.

22. Not surprisingly, the history of the early cinema is a veritable industry. Some important British sources are R. Armes, *A Critical History of the British Cinema* (London, 1978), especially pp. 19-22; R. Manvell and R. Low, *History of the British Film,* vol. I (London, 1949), chap. 1; G. Pearson, *Flashback: The Autobiography of a British Film-Maker* (London, 1957); and M. Chanan, *The Dream that Kicks: Prehistory and Early Years of Cinema in Britain* (London, 1981). Key American sources include R. Sklar, *Movie-Made America: A Cultural History of American Movies* (New York, 1976); L. May, *Screening Out the Past: The Birth of Mass Culture and the Motion Picture Industry* (New York, 1980); T. Balio ed., *The American Film Industry* (Madison, WI, 1976), pp. 1-192; G. Kindem, ed., *The American Movie Industry* (Carbondale, IL, 1982), pp. 3-118; A. McClure, ed., *The Movies: An American Idiom* (Rutherford, NJ, 1971), pp. 21-84; L. Jacobs, *The Rise of the American Film: A Critical History* (New York, 1968); and D. J. Czitrom, *Media and the American Mind* (Chapel Hill, NC, 1982), pp. 30-59.

23. J. Phillips and P.K. Phillips, *Victorians at Home and Away* (London, 1978), chap. 2; E.A. Mackerness, *A Social History of English Music* (London, 1964); J.A.R. Pimlott, *The Englishman's Christmas: A Social History* (Brighton, 1978), chap. 6, 8, 9, and 11; A. Miall and P. Miall, *The Victorian Christmas Book* (New York, 1978), pp. 11-68.

24. S. Constantine, "Amateur Gardening and Popular Recreation in the 19th and 20th Centuries," *Journal of Social History* 14(Spring, 1981): 387-406.

25. Lowerson, *Time,* chap. 3 is suggestive on these points, as is C. E. Clark, *The American Family Home, 1800-1960* (Chapel Hill, NC, 1986), chap. 5 and 6. See also F. Bellew, *The Art of Amusing* (London, 1866).

26. Wright, *Habits,* p. 216.

27. S. Alexander, *St Giles Fair, 1830-1914* (London, 1970); H. Cunningham, "The Metropolitan Fairs in the Nineteenth Century, in A.P. Donajgrodzik, ed., *Social Control in Nineteenth Century Britain* (London, 1977), pp. 163-184; M. Judd, "The Oddest Combination of Town and Country: Popular Culture and the London Fairs, 1800-1860," in J.K. Walton and J. Walvin eds., *Leisure in England, 1780-1939* (Manchester, 1983), pp. 11-30.

28. Sources on English circus include T. Frost, *The Old Showman and the Old London Fairs* (London, 1874), chap. 4-11; Rosenfeld, *London Fairs* (Cambridge, 1960); A.H. Saxon, *Enter Foot and Horse: A History of the Hippodrama in England and France* (New Haven, CT, 1968); Joseph Donohue, *Theatre in the Age of Kean* (Oxford, 1975); and E.H. Bostock, *Menageries, Circuses and Theatres* (New York, 1972).

29. Basic sources on the American circus are G. Chindahl, *A History of the Circus* (Caldwell, ID, 1959), p. 94; and E. May *The Circus from Rome to Ringling* (New York, 1932), chap. 8, 14, and 17. A popular treatment of English-speaking circuses is in P. Verney, *Here Comes the Circus* (London, 1978). For a description of another variation of the circus, the Wild West show, see S. Blackstone, *Buckskins, Bullets, and Business: A History of Buffalo Bill's Wild West* (Westport, CT, 1986).

30. Chindahl, *Circus*, chap. 1; Harris, *Humbug*, chap. 2 and 8-10.

31. J. Kasson, *Amusing the Millions* (New York, 1978), pp. 1-26; D. Burg, *Chicago's White City of 1893* (Lexington, KY, 1976), chap. 7 especially; J. McKennon, *A Pictorial History of the American Carnival*, vol. I (Sarasota, FL, 1971), pp. 26-40. An interesting treatment of a regional amusement park at Worcester, Massachusets in the 1870s is in R. Rosenzweig, *Eight Hours for What We Will* (New York, 1983), chap. 7.

32. O. Pilat and J. Ranson, *Sodom by the Sea: An Affectionate History of Coney Island* (Garden City, NY, 1941), chap. 5 and 7; G. Kyriazi, *The Great American Amusement Parks* (Secaucus, NJ, 1976), chap. 2 and 3; Kasson, *Amusing*, p. 29-87; and Peiss, *Amusements*, Chapter 5. See also Charles Kunnell, *By the Beautiful Sea: The Rise and High Times of the Great American Resort, Atlantic City* (New York, 1975).

33. Kasson, *Amusing*, p. 50.

34. J.A.R. Pimlott, *The Englishman's Holiday* (Brighton, 1976), p. 46 and chap. 4; P. Puechler-Muskau, *A Regency Visitor* (New York, 1958), pp. 158-159 and 171.

35. Duchess of Cleveland, *History of Battle Abbey* (London, 1872), pp. 237-238, cited in Lowerson, *Time*, p. 26.

36. F. R. Dulles, *American Learns to Play* (New York, 1940), p. 151. See also M. Chevalier, *Society, Manners and Politics in the United States* (Boston, 1939), pp. 315-316. For details on riverboat gambling, see J. Findlay, *A People of Chance* (New York, 1986), chap. 2.

37. Examples of this vast literature include J. Walvin, *Beside the Seaside* (London, 1978); J. Anderson and E. Swinglehurst, *The Victorian and Edwardian Seaside* (London, 1978); J. Walton, *The Blackpool Landlady* (Manchester, 1978); J. Walton, *The English Seaside Resort: A Social History* (Leiscester, 1983); Lowerson, *Time,* chap. 2; and S. Farrant, "London by the Sea: Resort Development on the South Coast of England, 1880-1939," *Journal of Contemporary History* 22 (January, 1987): 137-162.

38. Cited in A. Delgado, *The Annual Outing and Other Excursions* (London, 1977), p. 30.

39. Pimlott, *Holiday,* chap. 7.

40. J. A.R. Pimlott, *Recreations* (London, 1968), pp. 42-43; P. Bailey, *Leisure,* pp. 80-81.

41. The Victorian Society in America, *Victorian Resorts and Hotels* (New York, 1982); J. Jakle, *The Tourist* (Lincoln, NE, 1985), chap. 3 and 4.

42. See D. Horowitz, *The Morality of Spending* (Baltimore, 1987), chap. 1, for an analysis of the 19th-century origins of these sentiments. Contemporary examples are R. Edwards, *Popular Amusements* (New York, 1915); R. Edwards, *Christianity and Amusement* (New York, 1915); and C. E. Rainwater, *The Play Movement in the United States* (Chicago, 1922), pp. 276-278.

43. S. Patten, *The New Basis of Civilization* (Cambridge, MA, 1968 reprint), pp. 126-137; D. Fox, *The Discovery of Abundance: Simon N. Patten and the Transformation of Social Theory* (Ithaca, NY, 1967); H. Marcuse, *One Dimensional Man* (Boston, MA, 1964); M. Douglas and B. Isherwood, *The World of Goods* (New York, 1979).

44. Rosenzweig, *Eight Hours,* chap. 7, for example.

45. R. Poole, "Oldham Wakes," in Walton, *Leisure,* pp. 92-93.

46. Pueckler-Muskau, *Visitor,* p. 228.

Chapter Ten

1. E. Midwinter, *Fair Game* (London, 1986), pp. 14-16.

2. E. Dunning and K. Sheard, *Barbarians, Gentlemen, and Players* (London, 1979), pp. 25-29; P. Young, *A History of British Football* (London, 1973), pp. 48-58; Midwinter, *Game,* chap. 1; M. Marples, *A History of Football* (London, 1954).

3. For good analysis and bibliography, see A. Guttman, *Sports Spectators* (New York, 1986), chap. 2 and 3. See also T. McLean, *The English at Play in the Middle Ages* (Windsor Forest, England, 1983); and F. H. Cripps-Day, *History of the Tournament in England and France* (London, 1918).

4. This thesis is developed in E.P. Thompson, "Patrician Society Plebian Culture," *Journal of Social History* 7 (Winter, 1974): 382-405; and E.P. Thompson, *Whigs and Hunters* (London, 1976). See also R. Malcolmson, *Popular Recreations in English Society* (London, 1973).

5. W.Vamplew, *The Turf* (London, 1976), pp. 25-30.

6. R. Osterweis, *Romanticism and Nationalism in the Old South* (New Haven, CT, 1949). A. Guttman, *A Whole New Ball Game* (Chapel Hill, NC, 1988), chap. 4; for quotation, J. Lucas and R. Smith, *Saga of American Sport* (Philadelphia, 1978), pp. 98-100.

7. J. Illingsworth, *Twenty Challenges for the America's Cup* (New York, 1969), pp. 11-25, Lucas, *Saga,* chap. 10.

8. See especially, C. Brookes, *English Cricket* (London, 1978); D. Brailsford, "Sporting Days in Eighteenth Century England," *Journal of Sport History* 9 (Winter, 1982); 5-22; and N. Elias and E. Dunning, *The Quest for Excitement* (London, 1986), chap. 3.

9. On the history of English prize fighting, see J. Ford, *Prize fighting* (Newton Abbot, 1971); and J. Reid, *Bucks and Bruisers* (London, 1971). See also Guttman, *Spectators*, pp. 69-77.

10. W. Baker. *Sports in the Western World* (Totowa, NJ, 1982), pp. 92-94 and 172-176. For a recent study of American boxing, see E. Gorn, *The Manly Art: Bare-Knuckle Prize Fighting in America* (Ithaca, NY, 1988). See also A. Lloyd, *The Great Prize Fight* (New York, 1977); and A. Johnston, *Ten—and Out: The Complete Story of the Prize Ring in America* (New York, 1947).

11. D. Mrozek, *Sport and the American Mentality, 1880-1910* (Knoxville, TN, 1983), chap. 1, especially.

12. H. Mann, *Life and Works of Horace Mann*, vol. 3 (Boston, 1865-1868), p. 5, cited in Lucas, *Saga*, p. 93; see also, Lucas, *Saga*, pp. 72-75; G. Redmond, *The Caledonian Games in Nineteenth Century America* (Rutherford, NJ, 1971); and B. Rader, "The Quest for Subcommunities and the Rise of American Sport," in P. Zingg, ed., *The Sporting Image*, (Lanham, MD, 1988), pp. 139-154.

13. S. Baldwin, an English Prime Minister in the interwar years, boasted at a meeting of Old Boy Harrovians:

> Thanks be to heaven, there is in every English boy an unconscious but impregnable resistance to every form of pressure made by any school-master who works him too hard or tries to put too much inside him.... It is to this that Englishmen owe so largely the careful cultivation of their physical growth. They let the body grow, undisturbed by mental storm until they get into their early twenties, and then they go into the world able to graft the sane mind on to the sane body.

J. A. Mangan, *Athleticism in the Victorian and Edwardian Public School* (Cambridge, UK, 1981), p. 55, also pp. 18, 69-70 and 113.

14. S.R. Calthrop, "Lecture on Physical Developments and its Relationship to Mental and Spiritual Development," (August, 1858), cited in P. Levine, "The Promise of Sport in Antebellum America," *Journal of American Culture* 24 (1980): 623-634. See also T. Hughes, *Tom Brown's School Days* (London, 1971); and W. F. Mandel, "Games People Played: Cricket and Football in England and Victoria in the Late 19th Century," *Historical Studies* 15 (1973): 511-535. For an analysis of an American muscular Christian, see J. Lucas, "Thomas Wentworth Higginson—Early Apostle of Health and Fitness," *Journal of Health, Physical Education and Recreation* 42 (February, 1971): 30-33.

15. C. Armstrong, "The Lessons of Sports: Class Socialization in the British and American Boarding Schools," *Sociology of Sport Journal* 1 (1984): 314-331.

16. Mrozek, *Sport*, pp. 32-33 and 44-45.

17. Quoted in Mangan, *Athleticism*, pp. 187 and 201.

18. J. Hargreaves, *Sport, Power, and Culture* (London, 1986), pp. 68-69; Mrozek, *Sport*, pp. 119-126; Lucas, *Saga*, pp. 158-162; Guttman, *Spectators*, pp. 96-97.

19. E. Weber, "Pierre Coubertin and the Introduction of Organized Sport in France," *Journal of Contemporary History* 5 (1970): 3-26. See also R. Mandell, *The First Modern Olympic Games* (Berkeley, 1976); and J. Lucas, *The Modern Olympic Games* (South Brunswick, NJ, 1980); Guttman, *Ball Game,* chap. 6; and N. Isaacs, *All the Moves: A History of College Basketball* (Philadelphia, 1975).

20. E. Eell, *History of Organized Camping: The First 100 Years* (Martinville, IN, 1986); and C. Hardy and D. Ward, *Goodnight Campers! The History of the British Holiday Camp* (London, 1986).

21. See for example, D. Gorham, *The Victorian Girl and the Feminine Ideal* (Bloomington, IN, 1982), chap. 2; M. Bulger, "American Sportswomen in the 19th Century," *Journal of Popular Culture* 16 (1982): 1-16; and C. Dyhouse, *Girls Growing Up in Late Victorian and Edwardian England* (London, 1981), pp. 67-69 and 129-130.

22. The problem of the rationalization of sport is dealt with well by American historians, A. Guttman, *From Ritual to Record: The Nature of Modern Sport* (New York, 1984) and *A Whole New Ball Game* (Chapel Hill, NC, 1988); and R. Mandell, *Sport: A Cultural History* (New York, 1984). A very influential work is H. Eichberg, *Der Weg des Sports in die industrielle Zivilisation* (Baden-Baden, 1973). An important application of these themes is M. Adelman, *A Sporting Time: New York City and the Rise of Modern Athletics, 1820-1870* (New York, 1986). British contributions are also many. Note, particularly, the historically-minded sociology of E. Dunning and his colleagues in works like *The Sociology of Sport* (London, 1971) and *Barbarians,* See also Elias; *Quest,* chap. 7. J. Hargreaves, *Sports, Power and Culture*(London, 1986) has a fine historical section.

23. Midwinter, *Game,* p. 50. For details on the cultural role of the British public school, see D. Newsome, *Godliness and Good Learning* (London, 1961); T.W. Bamford, *The Rise of the Public Schools* (London, 1967); and J. Gathorne-Hardy, *The Public School Phenomenon* (London, 1977).

24. N. Elias, *The Civilizing Process* (London, 1978); and especially insofar as this theory is applied to sport, see his essays (with E. Dunning), *Quest.*

25. Hargreaves, *Sports,* chap. 1, develops an important theory of the social construction of sport in England. Another social interpretation is R. Gruneau, *Class, Sports, and Social Development* (Amherst, MA, 1983).

26. See J. Betts, *America's Sporting Heritage, 1850-1950* (Reading, MA, 1974), pp. 69-85 and 152-156. A good survey is in F. Paxson, "The Rise of Sport," in Zingg, *Image,* pp. 45-67.

27. Vamplew, *Turf*, pp. 18-38, on the shift to grandstands and gate money in English racing. A classic article on the impact of technology on American sport is J. Betts, "The Technological Revolution and the Rise of Sport," in Zingg, *Image*, pp. 171-194. A recent update is P. Shergold, "The Growth of American Spectator Sport: A Technological Perspective," in R. Cashman and M. McKernan, eds., *Sports in History* (Queensland, 1979), pp. 21-42.

28. R. Williams, *The Long Revolution* (London, 1961), chap. 3; Betts, *Heritage*, pp. 53-61; Guttman, *Spectators*, pp. 84-86.

29. Note, especially, Elias, *Quest*, chap. 1.

30. Among the many studies of the origins of professional English football, see T. Mason, *Association Football and English Society* (Brighton, 1980); J. Walvin, *The People's Game* (London, 1975); S. Tischler, *Footballers and Businessmen* (New York, 1981); and S. Wagg, *The Football World: A Contemporary Social History* (Brighton, 1984).

31. In addition to sources cited in note 30, see C.P. Korr, "West Ham United Football Club and the Beginnings of Professional Football in East London, 1895-1914," *Journal of Contemporary History* 13, 2 (1978): 211-232; J. Lowerson, "Sport and Victorian Sunday: The Beginnings of a Middle Class Apostasy," *British Journal of Sports History* 1, 2 (September, 1984): 202-221; and W. Baker, "The Making of a Working-Class Football Culture in Victorian England," *Journal of Social History* 13, 2 (1979): 241-251.

32. G. Stone, "American Sports: Play and Display," in E. Dunning, *Sociology of Sport* (London, 1971), pp. 47-65; B. Rigauer, *Sport und Arbeit* (Frankfurt, 1969).

33. Dunning, *Barbarians*, chap. 4.

34. Dunning, *Barbarians*, is a solid sociological history of Rugby. See also U.A. Titley and R. McWirter, *Centenary History of the Rugby Football Union* (London, 1970).

35. Dunning, *Barbarians*, chap. 7 and 9.

36. Midwinter, *Game*, pp. 78-79.

37. K. Sandiford, "Cricket and Victorian Society," *Journal of Social History* 17 (Winter, 1980): 303-338; C. Brookes, *English Cricket* (London, 1978); for a study of the best-known cricket player in the 19th century, E. Midwinter, *W.G. Grace* (London, 1982). See also Dunning, *Barbarians*, pp. 176-182. On cricket outside England, see R. Cashman, *Ave A Go, Yer Mug* (Sydney, 1984); and C.L.R. James, *Beyond a Boundary* (New York, 1963).

38. Among the many good general histories of sport in America, see B. Rader, *American Sports* (Englewood Cliffs, NJ, 1983); B. Spears and R. Swanson, *A History of Sport and Physical Activity in the United States* (Dubuque, IA, 1978); D. Noverr and L. Ziewacz, *The Games They Played: Sports in American History, 1865-1980* (Chicago, 1983); S. Reiss, *City Games: The Evolution of American Urban Society and the Rise of Sports* (Urbana, IL, 1989); and Lucas, *Saga*. Note also S. Cohen, "More than Fun and Games, A Comparative Study of the Role of Sport in English and American Society at the Turn of the Century," Ph.D. dissertation, Brandeis University, 1980.

39. For the early history of baseball see, H. Peterson, *The Man Who Invented Baseball* (New York, 1971); P. Levine, *A. G. Spalding and the Rise of Baseball* (New York, 1985); H. Seymour, *Baseball: The Early Years* (New York, 1960); and D.Q. Voigt, *American Baseball: From Gentleman's Sport to the Commissioner System* (Norman, Okla., 1966) A good brief account is in W. Baker, *Sports in the Western World* (Totawa, NJ, 1982), chap. 10.

40. A good brief analysis of the rise of baseball (rather than cricket) in 19th century America is I. Tyrrell, "The Emergence of Modern American Baseball c. 1850-80," in Cashman, *Sport in History*, pp. 205-226. A recent thorough treatment is G. Kirch, *The Creation of American Team Sports: Baseball and Cricket, 1838-1972* (Urbana, IL, 1989).

41. S. Riess, *Touching Base: Professional Baseball and American Culture in the Progressive Era* (New York, 1980), pp. 60-72.

42. Guttman, *Game*, pp. 64-66.

43. Seymour, *Baseball,* pp. 90 and 328; Guttman, *Spectators*, pp. 111-115.

44. Guttman, *Spectators*, pp. 121-122.

45. Riess, *Touching Base*, pp. 69-72.

46. The authority on Black baseball is R. Peterson, *Only the Ball Was White* (Englewood Cliffs, NJ, 1971). See also J. Tygiel, *Baseball's Great Experiment* (New York, 1983).

47. On the social and ethnic transformation of baseball, see especially S. Riess, "Professional Baseball as a Source of Social Mobility, 1871-1919," in S. Riess, *The American Sporting Experience*, (West Point, NY, 1984), pp. 291-305.
48. Lucas, *Saga*, chap. 12; especially R. Smith, *Sports and Freedom: The Rise of Big-Time College Athletics* (New York, 1988).

49. D. Riesman and R. Denney, "Football in America: A Study in Cultural Diffusion," in Zingg, *Image*, p. 216, especially.

50. W. Camp, *Walter Camp's Book of College Sports* (New York, 1893), pp. 8-9, in Reiss, *Sporting Experience*, p. 166. See also Mrozek, *Sport*, chap. 3.

51. Betts, *Heritage*, pp. 256-257 and Smith, *Freedom*.

52. Good sources on sport and race are in Riess's *Sporting Experience* and Guttman, *Ball Game*, Chapter 9.

53. R. Smith, "The Rise of Basketball for Women in Colleges," in Riess, *Sporting Experience*, pp. 237-270 and Lucas, *Saga*, chap. 15.

54. E. Gerber, "The Controlled Development of Collegiate Sport for Women, 1923-1936," *Journal of Sport History* 6 (Spring, 1979): 1-28; Lucas, *Saga*, chap. 20; W. Beezley and J. Hobbs, "'Nice Girls Don't Sweat': Women in American Sport," in Zingg, *Image*, pp. 337-352. See also R. Howell, *Her Story in Sport: A Historical Anthology of Women in Sport* (West Point, NY, 1982). For English background, see M. Talbot, *Women and Leisure* (London, 1979).

55. S. Jones, *Workers at Play* (London, 1986), chap. 3 and 4; Hargreaves, *Sports*, pp. 88-93, chap. 8 and 9.

56. On the history of English physical education, see W.D. Smith, *Stretching Their Bodies* (London, 1974); and P. McIntosh, *Physical Education in England Since 1800* (London, 1968). For the American history, see P. Welch and H. Lerch, *History of American Physical Education and Sport* (Springfield, IL, 1981); and Lucas, *Saga*, chap. 23. See also the citations in Guttman, *Ball Game*, chap. 7.

57. See Guttman, *Spectators*, chap. 5 for a good analysis and bibliography on the impact of electronic media on sport.

58. Hargreaves, *Sports*, chap. 6.

59. I cannot do justice to the complexities of the problem of contemporary sports hooliganism. Some good entrees into this complex literature are J. Lever, *Soccer Madness* (Chicago, 1983); J.Williams, E. Dunning, and P. Murphy, *Hooligans Abroad* (London, 1984); E. Dunning, P. Murphy, and J. Williams, *The Roots of Football Hooliganism: An Historical and Sociological Study* (London, 1988), which stresses that football violence has late 19th century origins; I. Taylor, "Soccer Consciousness and Soccer Hooliganism," in S. Cohen, ed., *Images of Deviance* (London, 1971), pp. 134-164; J. Walvin, *Football and the Decline of Britain* (London, 1986); R. Ingam, ed., *"Football Hooliganism: The Wider Context "*(London, 1978).

60. See R.Yeager, *Seasons of Shame* (New York, 1979); Guttman, *Spectators*, chap. 7.

Chapter Eleven

1. J. Hammond, *The Growth of Common Enjoyment* (London, 1933).

2. Some sources are M. Cahil, *Shorter Hours: A Study of the Movement Since the Civil War* (New York, 1922), pp. 118-133; J. Goldmark, *Fatigue and Efficiency* (New York, 1912); A. Rabinbach, "The European Science of Work: The Economy of the Body and the End of the Nineteenth Century," in S. Kaplan and C. Koepp, eds., *Work in France* (Ithaca, NY, 1986), pp. 475-513; and P. S. Florence, *Economics of Fatigue and Unrest* (London, 1924). See also G. Cross, *Quest for Time* (Berkeley, 1989), chap. 5.

3. For the American version of this "productivity theory of shorter hours," see J. T. McKelvey, *AFL Attitudes Toward Production 1900-1921* (Ithaca, NY, 1952), pp. 2-11. I analyze the Western European version of this theme in "The Political Economy of Leisure in Retrospect: Britain, France and the Origins of the Eight-Hour Day," *Leisure Studies* 5 (1986): 69-90.

4. Quoted in D. Rodgers, *The Work Ethic in America* (Chicago, 1978), p. 28. See also B. Hunnicutt, *Work Without End: Abandoning Shorter Hours for the Right to Work* (Philadelphia, 1988), pp. 30-36.

5. For example, Lord Leverhulme's influential *The Six Hour Day* (1918) held that technology increasingly made labor superfluous and that machines, not man, should be slaves to work. When the "dull monotonous grind" of long hours would end, the principal cause of "labor unrest—nervousness"—would be eliminated. Machine-driven efficiency would allow higher wages and, with shorter hours, new markets for consumer goods would be generated. With increased leisure, Leverhulme argued, Britain could build an "improved race," create garden suburbs, and, by extending the school-leaving age, develop an educated citizenry. Lord Leverhulme, *The Six Hour Day* (London, 1918), pp. 5-12 and 28-29.

6. V. Yans-McLaughlin, "Patterns of Work and Family Organization: Buffalo's Italians," *Journal of Interdisciplinary History 2* (Autumn, 1971): 299-314; A. Kessler-Harris "Organizing the Unorganized: Three Jewish Women and Their Incomes," *Labor History* 17 (Winter, 1976): 5-15. See also Hunnicutt, *Work Without End,* chap. 1 and J. Gilbert, *Work Without Salvation: America's Intellectuals and Industrial Alienation, 1880-1910,* (Baltimore, 1977).

7. Summary is provided in Health of Munitions Workers' Committee, "Final Report," *British Parliamentary Papers* (1918), vol. 12, pp. 40-42. Lengthy documentation is offered in Cross, *Quest,* chap. 5.

8. A. Link, *The American Epoch,* (New York, 1963), pp. 210-212. See also D. Roediger and P. Foner, *Our Own Time,* (Westport, CT, 1988) chap. 9. and S. Bauer, "The Road to the Eight Hour Day," *Monthly Labor Review 2* (August, 1919): 41-65.

9. Summaries are in A.A. Evans, "Work and Leisure, 1919-1969," *International Labor Review* 91,1(January, 1969): 45-69 and Bauer, "Road."

10. See Cross, *Quest,* chap. 6 and Roediger, *Our Own Time Time,* chap. 10. Quotation cited in K. Middlemas, *Politics in Industrial Society* (London, 1979), pp. 142-143.

11. J. Pimlott, *The Englishman's Holiday* (London, 1947), chap. 1-3; C. Mills, *Vacations for Industrial Workers* (New York, 1927), p. 149; F. Curtis et al., (Industrial Relations Staff) "Annual Paid Vacations for Workers in Countries Outside of the United States," (New York, December 1925, a copyrighted manuscript in the Trade Union Congress Archive, HD 5106), pp. 4-6; House of Commons, *Minutes of Evidence Taken Before the Committee on Holidays with Pay* (London, 1937), pp. 36-38.

12. Curtis, "Paid Vacations," p. 6; Mills, *Vacations,* p. 307.

13. For analysis of the paid vacation movement see G. Cross, "Vacations for All: The Leisure Question in the Era of the Popular Front," *Journal of Contemporary History 24* (Autumn, 1989): 549-621. For the British account, see S. Jones, *Workers at Play: A Social and Economic History of Leisure 1918-1939,* (London, 1986), pp. 17-20 and 27-33.

14. See Cross, *Quest,* chap.10; and S. Jones, "Trade Unions Movement and Work-Sharing Policies in Interwar Britain," *Industrial Relations Journal,* 16, 1(Winter, 1985): 57-69.

15. Trade Union Congress, *Annual Proceedings* (1933), p. 71.

16. B. Hunnicutt, *Work,* chap. 3 and 5. British sources include M. Steward (New Fabian Research Board), *The 40 Hour Week* (London, 1937), pp. 25-31 especially; *Industrial Welfare* (October, 1934), pp. 42-43; and E. Bevin, *My Plan for 2,000,000 Workless* (London, 1936).

17. For extensive analysis see, G. Cross, "Working in International Discontinuity," in G. Cross, ed., *Worktime and Industrialization* (Philadelphia, 1988), pp. 155-182.

18. R. Lynd and H. Lynd, *Middletown in Transition* (New York, 1937), p. 146.

19. See, for example, J.R. Pimlott, *The Englishman's Holiday* (London, 1948), pp. 215-241.

20. See, for example, C. Forman, *The General Strike, May 1926* (London, 1972); and G. Noel, *The Great Lock Out of 1926* (London, 1976).

21. *Pocket Bulletin* 27 (October 3, 1926), pp. 2-12, cited in B. Hunnicutt, *Work Without End,* p. 40. See also D. Roediger, "The Limits of Corporate Reform: Fordism, Taylorism, and the Working Week in the United States, 1914-1929," in Cross, *Worktime,* pp.135-154.

22. Again, B. Hunnicutt, *Work,* chap. 2 is invaluable.

23. J. Owen, *Price of Leisure* (Rotterdam, 1971), pp. 62-67; L. Robbins, "On the Elasticity of Incomes in Terms of Effort," *Economicia* 10 (June, 1930): 123-129; Hunnicutt, *Work,* chap. 3. The English were slower to develop such thinking; but a similar perspective may be found in J. Hobson, *Rationalization and Unemployment, An Economic Dilemma* (London, 1930), p. 123.

24. G. Cutten, *The Threat of Leisure* (New Haven, 1926), pp. 89 and 99. A similar source is J.P. Sizer, *Commercialization of Leisure* (Boston, 1917).

25. R. Edwards, *Popular Amusements* (New York, 1915), p. 133 and 138-143. A similar point of view is expressed by the British observer, C. Harris, *The Use of Leisure in Bethnal Green* (London, 1927), p. 43.

26. H. Durant, *The Problem of Leisure* (London, 1938), pp. 10-19.

27. See, for example, G. Friedman, *The Anatomy of Work* (Glencoe, IL, 1961); T. Adorno and M. Hornheimer, *Dialectic of Enlightenment* (London, 1979, originally published, 1944); and the later influential work, H. Marcuse, *One-Dimensional Man* (Boston, 1964). For an analysis, see M. Jay, *The Dialectical Imagination* (New York, 1973), chap. 6.

28. S. Freud, *Civilization and its Discontents* (London, 1930), pp. 34, 86-87, 121-122 and 141-142; S. Freud, *The Future of an Illusion*, (London, 1927), p. 7-8, cited in C. Rojek, *Capitalism and Leisure Theory* (London, 1985), p. 80.

29. M. Weber, *Economy and Society*, vol. I (New York, 1968), pp. 148-149 and 223; M. Weber, *From Max Weber* (London, 1970), p. 155. A helpful analysis is in Rojek, *Capitalism*, pp. 61-74.

30. B. Russell, *In Praise of Idleness and Other Essays* (London, 1935), pp. 26-27.

31. Russell, *Idleness*, pp, 16-17; E. Barker, *Uses of Leisure* (London, 1936), p. 6.

32. H.A. Overstreet, *A Guide to Civilized Leisure* (New York, 1934), p. 246. Similar sentiments are found in S. Greenbie's works; for example, *Leisure for Living* (New York, 1940).

33. Typical of this approach are W. Pangburg, "The Worker's Leisure and His Individuality," *American Journal of Sociology* 27 (January, 1922), pp. 433-444; and C. Rainwater, "Socialized Leisure," *Journal of Applied Sociology* 24 (January, 1919), pp. 373-388. See B. Hunnicutt, *Work Without End*, chap. 4.

34. Edwards, *Amusements*, pp. 13 and 143; and L. Jacks, *Ethical Factors of the Present Crisis* (Baltimore, 1934), chap. 4.

35. R. Evans and A. Boyd, *The Use of Leisure in Hull* (Hull, 1935), pp. 6, 18-21 and 47-49; C.N. Greene, *Time to Spare* (London, 1933), pp. 119-133; Pilgrim Trust, *Men Without Work* (London, 1938), pp. 144-160; A.C. Richmond, "The Unwanted Worker and His Time," *The Nineteenth Century and After* 731 (January, 1938): 11-20. See also L.R. Missen, *The Employment of Leisure* (Exeter, 1935), p. 34; and E.Wright Baake, *The Unemployed Man: A Social Study* (London, 1933), chap. 6.

36. W. Boyd, *Challenge of Leisure* (London, 1935), pp. 47-49; W. Greenwood, *Love on the Dole* (London, 1933), pp. 130-131 and 171; F. Zweig, *Labour, Life, and Poverty* (London, 1951), pp. 43-44 and 75-76.

37. M. Komarovsky, *The Unemployed Man and His Family* (New York, 1940); R. Lynd and H. Lynd, *Middletown in Transition* (New York, 1937).

38. W. Boyd, *Challenge*, p. 50; F. Zweig, *Women's Life and Labour* (London, 1952), pp. 141-148.

39. "The National Committee to Provide Holidays for Unemployed Workers in Distressed Areas" (London, 1938), in Trade Union Congress Archive HD 5106, *News Chronicle Survey* (June, 1939), cited in J. Walvin, *Beside the Seaside* (London, 1978), p. 108; on the problems of "family" vacations.

40. J. Hilton, *Why I Go For the Pools* (London, 1935); S.B. Rowntree, *Poverty and Progress* (London, 1941), pp. 370-371; D. Hardy, "The Place of Entertainment in Social Life," *Sociological Review* 26 (October, 1934): 393-406. Note also J. Richards, "The Cinema and the Cinema-going Public in Birmingham in the 1930s," in J. Walvin and J. Walton, eds., *Leisure in Britain* (Manchester, 1983). pp. 31-53.

41. P. Cressey's list of commercial leisure threats include:

> The growth of professional baseball, the building of stadiums seating tens of thousands for university football contests, the emergence of championship prize fights as national events, the mounting number of automobiles which now average almost one to a family, the rapid increase in the number of radios, the replacement of the neighborhood saloon by the 'blind pig' and the speakeasy, the expansion of the motion picture with its twenty thousand theaters, 'Miss America' beauty contests, endurance contests including dance marathons, the construction of magnificent dance palaces in our large cities, the night club, and the road house.
>
> In all of these the center of interest has gravitated from the home and the neighborhood to the outside world, in nearly all of them the effect of participation goes little beyond the stimulation of individual emotion and has little or no function for social integration, and practically all of them are operated on a basis of commercialization.

P. Cressey, *The Taxi-Dance Hall* (Chicago, 1932), p. xiv.

42. See, for example, J. Lee, *Play in Education* (New York, 1921); L. Gulick, *A Philosophy of Play* (New York, 1920); J.B. Nash, *Spectatoritis* (New York, 1932); and H. Braucher, "The Machine Revolution," *Playground* 23 (February, 1931). Useful sketches of recreation leaders in this period are in G. Butler, *Pioneers in Public Recreation* (Minneapolis, 1965). A very good analysis is in B. Hunnicutt, *Work Without End*, chap. 4.

43. R.D. Steiner, "Recreation and Leisure Time Activities," in President's Research Committee on Social Trends, *Recent Social Trends in the United States* vol. 1 (New York, 1933), p. xiii, cited in Hunnicutt, *Work*, p. 139. See also T.R. Adam, *The Worker's Road to Learning* (New York, 1940) on the worker's education movement.

44. J. Steiner, *Americans at Play* (New York, 1933), Chapter 3.

45. E. Brunner, *Holiday Making and the Holiday Trades* (London, 1945), p. 5; J. Lowerson, "Battles for the Countryside" in F. Gloversmith, *Class Culture, and Social Change: A New View of the 1930s* (Brighton, 1980), pp. 251-271; L. Arthur, *Adventures in Holiday Making* (London, 1945); T.W. Price, *The Story of the Workers' Education Association, 1903-1924* (London, 1924).

46. I. Jeffrey, *The British Landscape 1920-1950* (London, 1984), chap. 1; Mass Observation Archive, "Worktown Project," Box 51, September 1937. For an analysis and sources of the holiday camp, see C. Ward and D. Hardy, *Goodnight Campers* (London, 1986).

47. For French examples, see P. Marie, *Pour la sport ouvrier* (Paris, 1934), pp. 1-14 and 24-29, and M. de Vetch, "La Politique culturelle des syndicates ouvriers pendant l'entre-les-deux-guerres," (Thesis Institut francaise d'Utrecht, 1981), pp. 116-121 and 150-188.

48. *Labour Magazine* (October, 1933), p. 45; and (December, 1933), p. 94. See also, S. Jones, "Sport, Politics, and the Labour Movement: The Workers' Sports Federation, 1923-1935," *British Journal of Sports History 2* (1985): 154-178. S. Jones, *Workers,* pp. 142-147.

49. International Association for Workers' Spare Time, *Official Bulletin* 1 (1938): 4-19, 48-49. See also ILO, *International Labour Conference, Report on the Development of Facilities for the Utilization of Workers' Leisure* (Geneva, 1924); and G. Mequet, "Workers' Spare Time," *International Labour Review* 10 (November, 1924): 555.

50. See, for example, A. Sternheim, "Leisure in the Totalitarian State," *Sociological Review* 30, 2(June, 1928): 29-49. A good analysis is in V. de Grazia, "La Politique sociale du loisir: 1900-1940," *Les Cahiers de la recherche architecturale* 15-17 (1985): 24-35. International Association for Workers' Spare Time, *Official Bulletin* 2 (1938): pp. 15 and 35-36. For the fascist equivalent, see International Central Bureau, *Joy and Work: Report of the World Congress for Leisure Time and Recreation, July 1936* (Berlin, 1937).

51. E.B. Castle, *The Coming of Leisure* (London, 1935), p. 35. Other related sources from the adult education movement include W. Boyd. *Challenge* , pp. 1-3; L. Hogben, *Education for an Age of Plenty* (London, 1937), pp. 10-14.

52. See note 42.

53. Speech by A. Thomas in Comite national d'etudes sociales at politiques, *L'Organisation des loisirs ouvriers* (Paris, 1930), pp. 6-7; and L.P. Jacks, *The Education of the Whole Man* (New York, 1931), chap. 5-6.

54. For analysis and bibliography, see Cross, "Vacations."

55. See note 54.

56. E. Brunner, *Holiday*, pp. 3-10. See also Industrial Welfare Society, "Conference on Workers' Holidays" (London, November 30, 1938); and National Saving Holiday Clubs, "Holidays with Pay" (London, 1939) in the Trade Union Congress Archive, HD 5106.

57. G. Lansbury, "Playing Fields Make for Prosperity," *Labour Magazine* (August, 1931), pp. 146-149, and *Labour's Immediate Programme* (London, 1937), p. 6, cited in Jones, *Workers at Play*, p. 135.

Chapter Twelve

1. J. Owen, *Price of Leisure* (Montreal, 1970), pp. 80, 94. For British data on leisure consumption, see D. A. Rowe, *The Measurement of Consumer's Expenditure and Behavior in the U.K., 1920-38*, vol. 2 (Cambridge, 1960).

2. K. Jackson, *Crabgrass Frontier* (New York, 1985), p. 7 and chap. 2.

3. H. L. Smith, *The New Survey of London Life and Labour* vol. 9 (London, 1935): 33. T. Veblen, *Theory of the Leisure Class* (New York, 1899); R.K. Middlemas, *Pursuit of Pleasure* (London, 1958), chap. 9; R. Graves, *The Lost Weekend* (London, 1940); H. Perkin, *Age of the Automobile* (London, 1976), p. 92. See also M. Stopes, *Married Love* (London, 1919).

4. C. Delise Burns, *Leisure in the Modern World* (London, 1932), chap. 1-2.

5. Much sociology in the 1950s and 1960s confirms this. For example, see E. Chinoy, *Automobile Workers and the American Dream* (Garden City, NY, 1955); M. Young and P. Willmott, *Family and Kinship in East London* (London, 1961); and B. Berger, *Working Class Suburb* (Berkeley, 1960).

6. Still, theater seating in London increased in the 1920s despite the nearly 350,000 spaces in cinemas by 1930. Smith, *Survey*, p. 9.

7. D. Atwell, *Cathedrals of the Movies* (London, 1980), p. 130; D. Shaper, *The Picture Palace and Other Buildings for the Movies* (London, 1969); quotation from J. Richards, *The Age of the Dream Palace* (London, 1984), p. 11; H. Powdermaker, *Hollywood, the Dream Factory* (London, 1951).

8. K. McCarthy, "Nickel Vice and Virtue: Movie Censorship in Chicago, 1907-1915," *Journal of Popular Film* 5 (1976): 37-55; R. Fisher, "Film Censorship and Progressive Reform: The National Board of Censorship of Motion Pictures, 1909-1922," *Journal of Popular Film* (1975): 143-156; T. Balio, *The American Film Industry* (Madison, Wis., 1976), pp. 103-118 and 213-228; M. Rosen, *Popcorn Venus* (New York, 1973), chap. 9. British sources include J. Richards, "The Cinema and Cinema-Going in Birmingham in the 1930s," in J. Walton and J. Walvin, eds., *Leisure in Britain, 1780-1939* (Manchester, 1983), pp. 31-53.

9. R. Schickel, *The Disney Version: The Life, Times, Art, and Commerce of Walt Disney* (New York, 1985; first published in 1968). J. Richards, *Palace*, p. 31. See also, J. Richards and D. Sheridan, eds., *Mass-Observation at the Movies* (London, 1987).

10. Smith, *Survey*, p. 46 and H. J. Forman, *Our Movie Made Children* (New York, 1935), p. 164. See also Rosen, *Venus*, especially chap. 3, 4, and 6. For an analysis of the American star as consumption and 'live-style' trend-setter, see L. May, *Screening Out the Past* (New York, 1980), p. 116.

11. L. May, *Past*, p. 213 and E. May, *Great Expectations: Marriage and Divorce in Post-Victorian America* (Chicago, 1980); Richards, *Palace*, chap. 17 and 18.

12. G. Lundberg, et al., *Leisure, a Suburban Study* (New York, 1934), p. 263, C. Kirkpatrick, *Report of Research into the Attitudes and Habits of Radio Listeners* (St. Paul, 1932); J.Reith, *Broadcast over Britain* (London, 1924), p. 17.

13. P. Black, *The Biggest Aspidistra in the World* (London, 1972), pp. 48 and 55-66.

14. A. Briggs, *The Golden Age of the Wireless* (London, 1965), pp. 35 and 40; M. Pegg, *Broadcasting and Society, 1918-1939* (London, 1983), pp. 92-109 and 195-215; S. Frith, "The Pleasure of the Hearth: The Making of BBC Light Entertainment," in F. Jameson, ed., *Formations of Pleasure* (London, 1983), pp. 101-123. See especially, D. LeMahieu, *A Culture for Democracy* (Oxford, 1987), pp. 138-153 and 178-196.

15. The President's Research Committee on Recent Social Trends, *Recent Social Trends* (New York, 1933), pp. 941-943. Still the best account of the history of American radio is E. Barnouw, *The Tower of Babel* (New York, 1966) and *The Golden Web* (New York, 1968). For a recent treatment of the early years of radio advertising, see R. Marchand, *Advertising the American Dream* (Berkeley, 1985), pp. 88-110. See also, S. Douglas, *Inventing Broadcasting, 1899-1922*, (Baltimore, 1988).

16. C. Steinberg, *TV Facts* (New York, 1980), p. 3; R. Meyersohn, "Social Research in Television," and D. MacDonald, "A Theory of Mass Culture," in B. Rosenberg D. White, eds., *Mass Culture* (New York, 1957), pp. 352 and 361.

17. R. Sklar, *Prime-Time American* (New York, 1980), p. 3.

18. R. Rosen, "Soap Operas: Search for Yesterday," and T. Engelhardt, "Children's Television, The Shortcake Strategy," in T. Gitlin, ed., *Watching Television* (New York, 1986), pp. 42-111, especially 46. See also W. Susman, *Culture as History: The Transformation of American Society in the Twentieth Century* (New York, 1984), p. 160.

19. M. Meyer, *About Television* (New York, 1972), pp. 389-391 and R. Marchant, "Visions of Classlessness, Quests for Dominion," in R. Bremner and G. Reichard, eds., *Reshaping America* (Columbus, OH, 1982) pp. 166-167.

20. Perkin, *Automobile*, pp. 35-43, 112 and 138-139.

21. Burns, *Leisure*, chap. 4.

22. F. R. Dulles, *America Learns to Play* (New York, 1940), pp. 308-309.

23. Cited in R. Wik, *Henry Ford and Grassroots America* (Ann Arbor, MI, 1972), p. 233. Of the many works on the impact of the car on America perhaps the most accessible is R. Flink, *The Car Culture* (Cambridge, MA., 1975) and R. Flink, *The Automobile Age* (Cambridge, MA, 1988).

24. Jackson, *Frontier*, pp. 182 and 248-51. For background, see M. Rose, *Interstate: Express Highway Politics, 1941-1956* (Lawrence, KS, 1979) and J. Jakle, *The Tourist* (Lincoln, NE, 1985), chap. 6 and 7.

25. D. Boorstin, *The Image: A Guide to Pseudo-Events in America* (New York, 1972).

26. Jakle, *Tourist*, p. 157 and chap. 7 and 9; W. Belasco, *Americans on the Road: From Autocamp to Motel* (Cambridge, MA, 1979), pp. 111-115.

27. C. Solberg, *Conquest of the Skies: A History of Commercial Aviation in America* (Boston, 1979); and K. Hudson, *Air Travel, A Social History* (Totawa, NJ, 1973).

28. Useful sources are J. Mosley, *Disney's World* (New York, 1985); and M. King, "Disneyland and Walt Disney World: Traditional Values in Futuristic Form," *Journal of Popular Culture* 15 (Summer, 1981): 16-40.

29. Lundberg, *Leisure,* pp. 77-78; Jackson, *Frontier,* chap. 14; D. Lewis, "Sex and the Automobile," in D. Lewis and L. Goldstein, *The Automobile and American Culture* (Ann Arbor, MI, 1983), pp. 12-33; T. Wolfe, *The Kandy-Kolored Tangerine Flake Streamline Baby* (New York, 1963), pp. 8-12; R. Venturi, *Learning from Las Vegas* (Cambridge, MA, 1977); C. McWilliams, *California: The Great Exception* (New York, 1949); W. Kowinski, *The Malling of America* (New York, 1985).

30. R. Lynd and H. Lynd, *Middletown* (New York, 1929), pp. 251-257.

31. F. Kihlstedt, "The Automobile and the American House," in Lewis, *Automobile,* pp. 160-175; and R. Lynd and H. Lynd, *Middletown in Transition* (New York, 1937), 244-246.

32. R. Fishman, *Bourgeois Utopias* (New York, 1987), chap. 6.

33. Jackson, *Frontier,* p. 7 and chap. 2.

34. A comprehensive classic is A. Weber, *Growth of Cities in the Nineteenth Century* (New York, 1899). See also S.B. Warner, *Street Car Suburb: The Process of Growth in Boston, 1870-1900* (Cambridge, MA, 1962); for a broad view, see J. Stilgoe, *Borderland: Origins of the American Suburb 1820-1939* (New Haven, CT, 1988).

35. A summary of English suburbanization is found in D. Thorns, *Suburbia* (London, 1972), pp. 35-61. See also D. A. Rieder, *Suburbanization and the Victorian City* (Leiscester, 1980); and H. J. Dyos, *The Victorian Suburb: A Study of Camberwell* (Liverpool, 1967).

36. Fishman, *Utopias,* chap. 6; Jackson, *Frontier,* pp. 172-187. See H. Preston, *Automobile Age Atlanta* (Athens, GA, 1979) for a view of southern American suburbanization.

37. Perkin, *Automobile,* chap. 6.

38. A. King, *The Bungalow* (London, 1984), chap. 2-4; C. Clark, *The American Family Home, 1800-1960* (Chapel Hill, NC, 1986), chap. 6-7; and C. May, *Western Ranch Houses* (Menlo Park, CA, 1958).

39. For good material on the suburban ranch house culture, see May, *Houses*, pp. 93-122; and E. Eichler and M. Kaplan, *The Community Builders* (Berkeley, 1967). For a critique of postwar American suburbia, see, for example, J. Keats, *The Crack in the Picture Window* (Boston, 1956); W. Whyte, "Suburbia," in his *Organization Man* (New York, 1956). For critiques of this thesis, see S. Donaldson, *The Suburban Myth* (New York, 1969), pp. 2-9 and; Clark, *Home*, pp. 218-230.

40. Fishman, *Utopias*, chap. 7.

41. A. Fein, *Frederick Law Olmsted and the American Environmental Tradition* (New York, 1972); P. Boardman, *The Worlds of Patrick Geddes* (London, 1978).

42. R. Lynd and H. Lynd, *Middletown*, p. 304; President's Research Committee on Social Trends, *Trends*, pp. 936-937.

43. Lundberg, *Leisure*, pp. 59-72 and 142-160.

44. Smith, *Survey*, p. 10 and chap. 3.

45. Lundberg, *Leisure*, p. 82.

46. W. L. Warner and P. Lunt, *The Social Life of a Modern Community: Yankee City Series*, vol. 1 (New Haven, CT, 1941), pp. 301-356; Lundberg, *Leisure*, chap. 7. For postwar analysis of the leisure function of religion in America, note the work of W. Herberg, "The Contemporary Upswing to Religion," in N. Birnbaum and G. Lenser, eds., *Sociology of Religion* (Englelwood Cliffs, NJ, 1969). For British comparisons, see Thorns, *Suburbia*, chap. 8.

47. S. Ahlstrom, *A Religious History of the American People* (New Haven, CT, 1972), p. 950.

48. Lundberg, *Leisure*, pp. 104-106.

49. Lynd, *Middletown*, pp. 228-236 and Lundberg, *Leisure*, pp. 146-148.

50. Lynd, *Middletown*, pp. 95-96, 99 and 134-142; Lundberg, *Leisure*, pp. 175 and 182-183.

51. Marchant, "Visions," p. 168.

52. Jackson, *Frontier,* p. 281.

53. B. Friedman, *The Feminine Mystique* (New York, 1963), chap. 10 and 11;
S. Strasser, *Never Done, A History of American Housework* (New York, 1982);
R. S. Cohen, *More Work for Mother: The Ironies of Household Technology
from the Open Hearth to the Microwave* (New York, 1983).

54. R. Sennett and R. Cobb, *Hidden Injuries of Class* (New York, 1973);
H. Gans, *The Levittowners* (New York, 1967); B. Berger, *Working-Class Suburb*
(Berkeley, 1960); M. Young and P. Willmott, *Family and Class in a London
Suburb* (London, 1967). This domestic pattern of leisure in the working classes
was identified in the 1920s in American studies. See, for example, G. Cutten,
The Threat of Leisure (New Haven, CT, 1926), pp. 67-73.

55. Marchant develops this theme brilliantly in his "Visions of Classlessness,"
pp. 168-70.

56. J. Kasson, *Amusing the Millions* (New York, 1978), pp. 110-112.

57. W. Engard, "The Blessing of Time Sales," *Motor* 49 (April, 1928):122,
cited in Flink, *Car,* p. 147. See also B. Hunnicutt, *Work Without End* (Philadelphia, 1988), chap. 2.

58. This shift is impressionistically investigated in the classic, D. Riesman,
et al., *The Lonely Crowd* (New York, 1950). British studies concerned with the
abandonment of work-centeredness for a leisure or domestic ethic are J.H.
Goldthorpe et al., *The Affluent Work: Industrial Attitudes and Behaviour*
(London, 1968); and F. Zweig, *The Worker in the Affluent Society* (London,
1961). For additional American analysis and citations, see B. Hunnicutt, *Work
Without End,* chap. 2.

59. See Riesman, *Crowd*; D. Meyer, *The Positive Thinkers* (New York, 1980);
P. Rieff, *The Triumph of the Therapeutic* (New York, 1966); and especially T.J.
Jackson Lears, *No Place of Grace: Antimodernism and the Transformation of
American Culture* (New York, 1981).

61. This was more than the merchandiser's manipulation of the vulnerable
social psyche. Part of the attraction of advertising was as a form of leisure. Just
as the 19th century American impresario, P.T. Barnum, provided an entertainment in the "humbug" of his stunts and faked curiosities, people enjoyed being
conned in advertisements and seldom took them *that* seriously. R. Marchand,

Advertising The American Dream: Making Way for Modernity, 1920-1940
(Berkeley, 1985), pp. 1 and 18-22; T. J. J. Lears, "From Salvation to Self
Realization," in R.W. Fox and T.J.J. Lears, eds., *the Culture of Consumption*,
(New York, 1983), pp. 1-38. For an English analysis, see R. Williams, "Adver-
tising the Magic System," in his *Problems in Materialism and Culture* (London,
1980), pp. 170-195.

62. Marchand, *American*, pp. 158-160.

63. J. Blum, *"V" Was for Victory* (New York, 1976), p. 101.

64. T. Hine, *Populuxe* (New York, 1986), p. 4 and chap. 2.

65. T. Veblen, *The Theory of the Leisure Class* (New York, 1922), chap. 3 and
4, especially.

66. D. Riesman, *Thorsten Veblen, A Critical Interpretation* (New York, 1953),
pp. 170-208; Lynd, *Middletown in Transition*, pp. 147-148; V. Packard, *The
Status Seekers* (New York, 1959).

67. Lynd, *Middletown in Transition*, p. 83.

68. R. Fox and T. J. J. Lears, "Introduction," in Fox, *Culture*, p. xii.

Chapter Thirteen

1. See, for example, P. Willmott, *Growing Up in a London Village: Family Life
Between the Wars* (London, 1979); and F. Wilde, *The Clatter of Clogs in the
Early Morning* (London, 1986); for general background on early 20th century
working-class family life. See also G. Orwell, *The Lion and the Unicorn*
(London, 1941), p. 39; R. Hoggart, *The Uses of Literacy* (London, 1957),
chap. 1; and R. Roberts, *The Classic Slum* (London, 1971), pp. 130-132. For
examples of "time budgets" from the late 1930s detailing uses of leisure time in
York, England see B. S. Rowntree, *Poverty and Progress* (London, 1941), pp.
429-445.

2. M. Komarovsky, *Blue-Collar Marriage* (New York, 1962), chap. 14;
H. Gans, *The Urban Villagers* (New York, 1962), chap. 4 especially. Gans's
study is much influenced by the work of the English sociologists, especially M.
Young and P. Willmott, *Family and Kinship in East London* (London, 1957).

3. S. Humphries, *Hooligans or Rebels: An Oral History of Working-Class
Childhood and Youth 1889-1939* (Oxford, 1981), pp. 121-149; T. Willis, *What-
ever Happened to Tom Mix* (London, 1971), pp. 34-48; and W. Whyte, *Street
Corner Society* (Chicago, 1943), pp. 3-51 and 255-277.

4. B.S. Rowntree, *Poverty*, pp. 333-342 and 350-373; Mass Observation, *The Pub and the People* (London, 1943), especially chap. 6 and 7.

5. H. L. Smith, ed., reports that convictions for drunkenness in London dropped from 85 per 1000 in 1913 to 15 by 1932 in *The New Survey of London Life and Labour*, vol. 9 (London, 1935), pp. 30-32 and 70-71. See also, S. Jones, *Workers at Play*, (London, 1986), pp. 77-78; Mass Observation, *Pub*, chap. 2; and B.S. Rowntree, *English Life and Leisure* (London, 1951), chap. 3 and pp. 200-212. Although the social function of drink was emphasized in the Mass Observation study, drinkers reported also the following: "This stuff gives me a good appetite and puts plenty of lead in my pencil." *Pub*, p. 46. For a brief discussion of working-class sociability around the lodge and bar at the turn of the century America, see J. Cumbler, *Working-Class Community in Industrial America* (Westport, CT, 1979), pp. 148-159.

6. R. Lynd and H. Lynd, *Middletown in Transition* (New York, 1937), pp. 275-279; and H. Gans, *Villagers*, chap. 4. An excellent source on American saloon culture before 1920 is R. Rosenzweig, *Eight Hours for What We Will: Workers and Leisure in an Industrial City, 1870-1920* (Cambridge, MA, 1983), chap. 4 and 8. For an update, see the analysis of American midwestern tavern culture in E. E. LeMasters, *Blue Collar Aristocrats* (Madison, WI, 1975).

7. See note 5.

8. Smith, *Survey*, pp. 38-42 and 52-53.

9. F. Zweig, *Women's Life and Labour* (London, 1952), pp. 141-148; Rowntree, *Life*, p. 230; C. Harris, *The Use of Leisure in Bethnal Green* (London, 1926), p. 33; C. Forman, *Industrial Town: Self Portrait of St. Helens in the 1920s* (St. Albans, 1979), p. 128; Rosenzweig, *Eight Hours*, chap. 8.

10. Mass Observation, *Pub*, pp. 262-266; C. D. Burns, *Leisure in the Modern World* (London, 1932), p. 102; Smith, *Survey*, p. 271; B. S. Rowntree, *Poverty*, pp. 399-406; J. Hilton, *Why I Go In for the Pools* (London, 1935). Note especially, Jones, *Workers*, pp. 38-40.

11. Note the classic St. Clair Drake and Horace Cayton, *Black Metropolis 2* (New York, 1962; first published in 1945), pp. 470-494 and J. Findlay, *A People of Chance* (New York, 1986), chap. 4 and 5.

12. Quotation from Hoggart, *Literacy*, pp. 119-120. See also G. Cross, ed., "Worktowners at Blackpool: A Mass-Observation and Popular Leisure in 1930s," (Forthcoming, London, 1990).

13. Note, for example, B. S. Rowntree, *Poverty*, pp. 386-406; and R. Roberts, *The Classic Slum*, p. 135.

14. Drake, *Metropolis*, chap. 21.

15. Quotation from Mass-Observation Archive, Worktown Project, W 42D. Some examples of this genre for Britain include J. B. Priestley, *English Journey* (London, 1934), pp. 263-265 and T. Harrisson and C. Madge, *Britain, A Mass Observation Study* (London, 1939). An interesting analysis of this is in S. Laing, "Presenting Things as They Are: John Sommerfield's *May Day* and Mass-Observation," in F. Gloversmith, ed., *Class, Culture and Social Change. A New View of the 1930s* (Brighton, 1980), pp. 142-160.

16. G.S. Jones, "Working-Class Culture and Working-Class Politics in London, 1870-1900," *Journal of Social History* 7 (1974): 460-508.

17. A. Howkins, "Leisure in the Inter-war Years: An Auto-Critique," in A. Tomlinson ed., *Leisure and Social Control* (Brighton, 1981), pp. 79-81; Gans, *Villagers*, pp. 187-196; Jones, *Workers*, pp. 81-86 and 133-163; Hoggart, *Literacy*, pp. 414-470. For American examples see Cumbler, *Community*, chap. 10-11; and R. Edsforth, *Class Conflict and Cultural Consensus: The Making of a Mass Consumer Society in Flint Michigan* (New Brunswick, NJ, 1987), chap. 2 and 4.

18. Hoggart, *Literacy*, chap. 7 and 8.

19. G. Mungham, "Youth in Pursuit of Itself," in G. Mungham and G. Pearson, eds., *Working Class Youth Culture* (London, 1976) pp. 82-104; R. Roberts, *The Classic Slum*, pp. 223-224.

20. See Cross, *Worktowners;* and for an analysis of postwar Blackpool, see G. Thompson, "The Presentation and Consumption of Leisure: Blackpool as a 'Site' of Pleasure," in A. Tomlinson, ed., *Leisure and Popular Cultural Forms* (Brighton, 1983), pp. 116-148; and T. Bennett, "A Thousand and One Troubles, Blackpool Pleasure Beach," in F. Jameson, ed., *Formations of Pleasure* (London, 1983), pp. 138-155. Note also A. Hern, *The Seaside Holiday* (London, 1967); J. Walvin, *Beside the Seaside* (London, 1978); and J. Walton, *English Seaside Resorts* (Leiscester, 1984).

21. J. Jakle, *The Tourist* (Lincoln, NE, 1985), pp. 50-90.

22. S. Jones, "Work, Leisure and Unemployment in Western Europe Between the Wars," *British Journal of Sports History* 3 (1986): 55-81. R. McKibbon, "Work and Hobbies in Britain, 1880-1930," in J. Winter, ed., *The Working Class in Modern Britain, 1919-1939* (London, 1983); R. Hayburn, "The Voluntary Occupational Centre Movement, 1932-39," *Journal of Contemporary History* 6 (1977): 156-171; and G. Orwell, *Road to Wigan Pier* (London, 1979), p. 77.

23. B. S. Rowntree, *Poverty*, pp. 378-381 and Lynd, *Middletown in Transition*, pp. 252-257.

24. B. S. Rowntree, *Poverty*, pp. 370-371; D. Hardy, "The Place of Entertainment in Social Life," *Sociological Review* 26 (October 1934): 393-406; R. Evans and A. Boyd, *The Use of Leisure in Hull* (Hull, 1935), pp. 6, 18-21 and 47-49.

25. C. N. Greene, *Time to Spare* (London, 1933), pp. 119-133; Pilgrim Trust, *Men Without Work* (London 1938), pp. 144-160; A. C. Richmond, "The Unwanted Worker and His Time," *The Nineteenth Century and After* 731 (January 1938):11-20. See also L. R. Missen, *The Employment of Leisure* (Exeter 1935), p. 34; E. W. Baake, *The Unemployed Man: A Social Study* (London 1933), chap. 6; for quotation, W. Greenwood, *Love on the Dole* (London 1951), pp. 43-44 and 75-76.

26. Lynd, *Middletown in Transition* (London, 1929), pp. 81-83; R. W. Fox, "Epitaph for Middletown," in R.W. Fox and T.J.J. Lears, eds., *Culture of Consumption* (New York, 1983), p. 103.

27. H. Gans, *The Levittowners* (New York, 1967), chap. 9; M. Kamoravsky, *Blue-Collar Marriage* (New York, 1962), pp. 28-32 and 311-329; J. Goldthorpe et al., *The Affluent Work in the Class Structure* (Cambridge, MA, 1969), chap. 4.

28. T. Parsons, *Essays in Sociological Theory* (New York, 1962), pp. 89-103; F. Musgrove, "The Problem of Youth and the Social Structure of Society in England," *Youth and Society* 1 (1969): 38-59. Seminal studies include E. B. Reuter, "The Adolescent World," *American Journal of Sociology* 42 (1936): 414-427; and F.M. Thrasher, *The Gang* (Chicago, 1927). For typical post-World War II approaches, note A.B. Hollingshead, *Elmtown's Youth and Elmtown Revisited* (New York, 1975); J. Colman, *The Adolescent Society* (Glencoe, IL, 1961).

29. C. MacInnes, *England, Half English* (London, 1961), p. 47, cited in Mungham, "Youth," p. 100.

30. For British studies see, for example, A. Paterson, *Across the Bridges: Life by the South London River-side* (London, 1911), chap. 9; and A. Freeman, *Boy Life and Labour: The Manufacture of Inefficiency* (London, 1914), chap. 6-7; and Roberts, *Slum*, p. 123. An excellent commentary is in S. Meacham, *A Life Apart: The English Working Class, 1890-1914* (Cambridge, MA, 1977), chap. 6.

31. See, for example, J. Adams, *The Spirit of Youth and the City Streets* (Chicago, 1909); R. H. Edwards, *Popular Amusements* (New York, 1915), for quotations, pp. 106 and 133; and P. Cressey, *The Taxi-Dance Hall: A Sociological Study in Commercialized Recreation and City Life* (Chicago, 1932).

32. W. Whyte, *Street Corner Society* (Chicago, 1943).

33. Lynd, *Middletown*, chap. 9.

34. R. Schickel, *The Disney Version* (New York, 1968); M. Real, *Mass-Mediated Culture* (Engelwood Cliffs, NJ, 1977), pp. 75-86. An interesting update of this phenomenon is in T. Englehardt, "Children's Television: The Shortcake Strategy," in T. Gitlin, ed., *Watching Television* (New York, 1986), pp. 68-110.

35. See, especially, the output of the Payne Fund on the influence of films upon youth in America. For example, E. Dale, *The Content of Motion Pictures* (New York, 1935); H. J. Forman, *Our Movie Made Children* (New York, 1934), p. 165 for quotation; and H. Blumer, *Movies and Conduct* (New York, 1933).

36. F. Rudolph, *The American College and University: A History* (New York, 1965), pp. 136-155; J. Kett, *Rites of Passage* (New York, 1977), pp. 51-60 and 174-183.

37. P. Fass, *The Damned and the Beautiful, American Youth in the 1920s* (New York, 1977), p. 23. Influential contemporary sources include G. Coe, *What Ails Our Youth* (New York, 1923); F. Dell, *Love in the Machine Age* (New York, 1930); and B. Lindsey and W. Evans, *The Revolt of Modern Youth* (New York, 1924).

38. Fass, *Damned*, chap. 2, p. 134. See also C. Lasch, *Culture of Narcissism* (New York, 1979).

39. D. LeMahieu, *A Culture for Democracy* (New York, 1988), p. 10.

40. *Daily Illini* (September 22, 1921), cited in Fass, *Damned*, pp. 182 and 199.

41. Fass, *Damned*, chap. 6-7.

42. M. Abrams, *The Teenage Consumer* (London, 1959), pp. 10-11.

43. J. Melly, *Owning Up* (London, 1970), pp. 163-164.

44. A. Cohen, *Delinquent Boys: The Culture of the Gang* (Glencoe, IL, 1955), quotation on p. 125; see also R. Havighurst and H. Taba, *Adolescent Character and Personality* (New York, 1949). A typical analysis of the youthful use of cars is R. McFarland and R. Moore, "Youth and the Automobile," in E. Ginzberg, ed., *Values and Ideals of American Youth* (New York, 1961), pp. 169-191. Hollingshead, *Elmtown*, chap. 6 and 8. Cf., J. Coleman, *The Adolescent Society* (Glencoe, IL, 1961); see also R. Sennett and J. Cobb, *The Hidden Injuries of Class* (New York, 1972), 79-98. An interesting recent study of youth culture is in W. Graebner, *Coming of Age in Buffalo,* (Philadelphia, 1989).

45. T. Jefferson, "Cultural Responses of the Teds," in S. Hall and T. Jefferson, eds., *Resistance through Rituals: Youth Subcultures in Post-War Britain* (London, 1975), pp. 81-105.

46. P. Cohen, "Sub-Cultural Conflict and Working Class Community," *Working Papers in Cultural Studies*, 2 (Spring, 1972): 16, cited in Hall, *Resistance*, p. 31. See numerous papers dealing with youth subcultures in Hall, *Resistance*, especially the theoretical essay by J. Clarke, "Style," pp. 175-191. Another good analysis and bibliography is in Mungham *Youth Culture*, especially chap. 1, and G. Murdock and R. McCron, "Youth and Class: The Career of a Confusion." For a critique of this approach to youth leisure, see K. Roberts, *Youth and Leisure* (London, 1983); and D. M. Smith, 'New Movements in the Sociology of Youth: A Critique," *British Journal of Sociology* 32 (1981): 239-251. Note also P. Willmot, *Adolescent Boys* (London, 1969); and J. Springfield, *Coming of Age* (Dublin, 1986), chap. 6.

47. A. McRobbie and J. Garber, "Girls and Subcultures," in Hall and Jefferson, *Resistance*, pp. 209-221.

48. C. Belz, *The Story of Rock* (New York, 1969), chap. 1. Several accessible histories are C. Brown, *The Art of Rock and Roll* (Englewood Cliffs, NJ, 1987); S. Frith, *Sociology of Rock* (London, 1978); H. London, *Closing the Circle: The Culture of The Rock Revolution* (London, 1984).

49. Belz, *Rock*, p. 36 and chap. 2.

50. Cited in J. Gilbert, *The Cycle of Outrage: America's Reaction to the Juvenile Delinquent in the 1950s* (New York, 1986), p. 16. See also F. Wertham, *The Seduction of the Innocent* (Port Washington, NY, 1953).

51. Gilbert, *Cycle*, chap. 12. Note, too, the parallel role of M. Abrams in England with his *The Teenage Consumer* (London, 1959).

52. K. Roberts, "Youth and Leisure," in A. Graefe and S. Parker, eds., *Recreation and Leisure Hnadbook* (State College, PA, 1987), p. 283.

53. R. Flacks, *Youth and Social Change* (Chicago, 1971), p. 17.

54. Hall, *Resistance*, pp. 60-63. See also B. Ehrenreich, *Hearts of Men* (New York, 1983), chap. 5, 8, and 9.

55. For background on the beatniks, see B. Cook, *The Beat Generation* (New York, 1971); and T. Newcomb et al., *Persistence and Change* (New York, 1967). Note also K. Keniston, *The Young Radicals* (New York, 1968); and Flacks, *Youth*, chap. 4. For a synthesis, see T. Kando, *Leisure and Popular Culture in Transition* (St. Louis, MO, 1980).

56. A. Rigby, *Alternative Realities* (London, 1974); K. Melville, *Communes in the Counter Culture* (New York, 1972); T. Wolfe, *Electric Kool-Aid Acid Test* (New York, 1969). A recent scholarly treatment of 1960s radicals in America is W.J. Rorabaugh, *Berkeley at War* (New York, 1989).

57. K. Keniston, *The Uncommitted* (New York, 1962), Ehrenreich, *Hearts*, chap. 5 and 8.

58. T. Roszak, *Where the Wasteland Ends* (New York, 1972), p. 259; T. Roszak, *The Making of a Counter-Culture* (New York, 1971), p. 1; J. Young, "The Hippie Solution: An Essay in the Politics of Leisure" in I. Taylor, *Politics and Deviance* (Harmondsworth, 1973); Murdock, "Youthand Class," pp. 22-24.

Chapter Fourteen

1. For studies of the stability (or increase) of worktime after 1945, see, for example, J. D. Owen, *Working Hours: An Economic Analysis* (Lexington, MA, 1979), chap. 3; J.Kreps, *Lifetime Allocation of Work and Income* (Durham, N.C., 1971); W. Leontief, "The Distribution of Work and Income," *Scientific American* (September, 1982), pp. 100-113; W. Leontief and F. Duchin, *The Future Impact of Automation on Workers* (New York, 1986); and B. Jones, *Sleepers Wake! Technology and the Future of Work* (London, 1982), pp. 200-205.

2. The literature on this subject is large and growing. Several good starting points are R. Rapoport and R. Rapoport, *Dual-Career Families* (Harmondsworth, 1971) and the sequel, *Dual-Career Families Re-examined* (London, 1976). A good anthology of sources is R. N. Rapoport, M. P. Fogarty, and R. Rapaport, *Families in Britain* (London, 1982). A rather pessimistic American assessment is P. Berger, et al., *The Homeless Mind: Modernization and Consciousness* (New York, 1973); and J. Hunt and L. Hunt, "The Dualities of Careers and Families: New Integrations or New Polarizations?" *Social Problems* 29 (June, 1982): 499-510. Historical perspectives are provided in G. Matthews, *Just a Housewife: The Rise and Fall of Domesticity in America* (New York, 1987); S. Strasser, *Never Done* (New York, 1980); and R. Cowan, *More Work for Mother* (New York, 1982). For Britain, see M. Talbot, *Women and Leisure* (London, 1979) and C. Hardyment, *From Mangle to Microwave,* (New York, 1988).

3. C.P. Gilman, *Women and Economics* (New York, 1898).

4. A good survey of American patterns is in H. Sheldon, "The Changing Demographic Profile," in C. Tibbitts, ed., *Handbook of Social Gerontology* (Chicago, 1960), p. 38. For a later British account, see R. Allen-Smith, "The Evolving Geography of the Elderly in England and Wales," in A.M. Warnes, ed., *Geographical Perspectives on the Elderly* (Chichester, England, 1982), pp. 35-52; and C. Victor, *Old Age in Modern Society* (London, 1987), chap. 6.

5. See W. Graebner, *A History of Retirement: The Meaning and Function of an American Institution, 1885-1920* (New Haven, CT, 1980), chap. 1-3, especially.

6. M. Kaplan, "The Uses of Leisure" in Tibbitts, *Handbook*, pp. 407-443; E. Friedmann, R. Havighurst, et al., *The Meaning of Work and Retirement* (Chicago, 1954), pp. 32-39 and 187-194. See also W. A. Achenbaum, *Shades of Gray: Old Age, American Values, and Federal Policies Since 1920* (Boston, 1983), p. 20, chap. 4; and Grabner, *Retirement*, pp. 227-240.

7. Sheldon, "Profile," in Tibbitts, *Handbook*, p. 5; C. Longino, "The Comfortably Retired," *American Demographics* (June, 1988), pp. 24-26; V. Karn, *Retiring to the Seaside* (London, 1977), chap. 9, especially.

8. C. Longino, Jr., "American Retirement Communities and Residential Relocation," in Warnes, *Elderly*, pp. 247-250; M. Hunt et al., *Retirement Communities: An American Original* (New York, 1984), pp. 13-15; S. Golant, "Residential Concentrations of Future Elderly," *Gerontologist* 15 (February, 1975): 16-17. For Western European retirement villages around 1960, see

W. Donahue, ed., "European Experience in Operation and Services," in
E. Burgess, ed., *Retirement Villages* (Ann Arbor, MI, 1961), pp. 103-104. See
also C. Sargent, ed., *Metro Arizona* (Scottsdale, AZ, 1988), pp. 132-136.

9. P. Gober, "The Retirement Community as a Geographical Phenomenon: The
Case of Sun City, Arizona," *Journal of Geography* 84 (September-October,
1985): 190; Sargent, *Metro*, pp. 120-121. I owe much of this material on Sun
City to a draft chapter of a book by J. Findlay on planned communities in the
American West after World War II.

10. Excellent starting points for material on gentrification are J.J. Palen and
B. London, *Gentrification, Displacement, and Neighborhood Revitalization*
(Albany, NY, 1984), especially pp. 2-27; and K. Nelson, *Gentrification and
Distressed Cities* (Madison, WI, 1988). See also S. G. Lipton, "Evidence of
Central City Revival," *Journal of the American Institute of Planners* 45 (April,
1980): 136-147; S. B. Laska and D. Spain. eds., *Back to the City* (New York,
1980); and C. Hamnett and P. Williams, "Social Change in London: A Study in
Gentrification," *Urban Affairs Quarterly* 15 (1980): 469-485.

11. N. Smith and M. LaFaivre, "A Class Analysis of Gentrification," in Palen,
Gentrification, pp. 43-64.

12. I. Allen, "The Ideology of Dense Neighborhood Redevelopment," in Palen,
Gentrification, pp. 27-42. See also C.S. Fischer, "Toward a Subcultural Theory
of Urbanism," *American Journal of Sociology* 80 (1975): 1319-1341.

13. For sources on gentrification in Britain, see P. Williams, "Gentrification in
Britain and Europe," in Palen, *Gentrification*, pp. 205-229; and P. Ambrose, *The
Quiet Revolution* (Brighton, 1974).

14. J. Jakle, *The Tourist* (Lincoln, NE, 1985), pp. 260-262 and 292-296. See
also D. Boorstin, *The Image: A Guide to Pseudo-Events in America* (New York,
1972), pp. 99-102 and 120-121.

15. W. Baumol and W. Bowen, *Performing Arts—The Economic Dilemma*
(New York, 1966), chap. 1, provides an early assessment of audiences. An
update is in J. Kamerman and R. Martorella, eds., *Performers and Performances*
(New York, 1983), section 5.

16. P. Dimaggio and M. Useem, "Cultural Democracy in a Period of Cultural
Expansion: The Social Composition of Arts Audiences in the United States," in
Kamerman, *Performers*, pp. 199-225. See also H. Gans, *Popular Culture and
High Culture: An Analysis and Evaluation of Taste* (New York, 1974), p. 74.

Index

OTHER BOOKS FROM VENTURE PUBLISHING

Acquiring Parks and Recreation Facilities through Mandatory Dedication:
A Comprehensive Guide, by Ronald A. Kaiser and James D. Mertes

Amenity Resource Valuation: Integrating Economics with Other Disciplines,
edited by George L. Peterson, B.L. Driver and Robin Gregory

Behavior Modification in Therapeutic Recreation: An Introductory Manual,
by John Dattilo and William D. Murphy

Beyond the Bake Sale - A Fund Raising Handbook for Public Agencies,
by Bill Moskin

The Community Tourism Industry Imperative - The Necessity, The Opportunities, Its Potential, by Uel Blank

Doing More With Less in the Delivery of Recreation and Park Services:
A Book of Case Studies, by John Crompton

Evaluation of Therapeutic Recreation Through Quality Assurance, by Bob Riley

The Evolution of Leisure: Historical and Philosophical Perspectives,
by Thomas Goodale and Geoffrey Godbey

The Future of Leisure Services: Thriving on Change, by Geoffrey Godbey

Gifts to Share - A Gifts Catalogue How-To Manual for Public Agencies,
by Lori Harder and Bill Moskin

International Directory of Academic Institutions in Leisure, Recreation and
Related Fields, edited by Max D'Amours

Leadership and Administration of Outdoor Pursuits, by Phyllis Ford and James
Blanchard

The Leisure Diagnostic Battery: Users Manual and Sample Forms, by Peter
Witt and Gary Ellis

Leisure Education: A Manual of Activities and Resources, by Norma J. Stumbo
and Steven R. Thompson

Leisure Education: Program Materials for Persons with Developmental Disabilities, by Kenneth F. Joswiak

Leisure in Your Life: An Exploration, Revised Edition, by Geoffrey Godbey

A Leisure of One's Own: A Feminist Perspective on Women's Leisure, by Karla Henderson, M. Deborah Bialeschki, Susan M. Shaw and Valeria J. Freysinger

Outdoor Recreation Management: Theory and Application, by Alan Jubenville, Ben Twight and Robert H. Becker

Park Ranger Handbook, by J.W. Shiner

Planning Parks for People, by John Hultsman, Richard L. Cottrell and Wendy Zales Hultsman

Playing, Living, Learning: A Worldwide Perspective on Children's Opportunities to Play, by Cor Westland and Jane Knight

Private and Commercial Recreation, edited by Arlin Epperson

Recreation and Leisure: An Introductory Handbook, edited by Alan Graefe and Stan Parker

Recreation and Leisure: Issues in an Era of Change, edited by Thomas Goodale and Peter W. Witt

Recreation Economic Decisions: Comparing Benefits and Costs, by Richard G. Walsh

Risk Management in Therapeutic Recreation: A Component of Quality Assurance, by Judy Voelkl

Understanding Leisure and Recreation: Mapping the Past, Charting the Future, edited by Edgar L. Jackson and Thomas L. Burton

Wilderness in America: Personal Perspectives, edited by Daniel L. Dustin

Venture Publishing, Inc
1640 Oxford Circle
State College, PA 16803
814-234-4561